RUMORS OF WA[R]
AND INFERNAL MAC[HINES]

# Liverpool Science Fiction Texts and Studies
*General Editor* DAVID SEED

*Series Advisers:* I.F. Clarke, Edward James, Patrick Parrinder and Brian Stableford

A complete listing of titles in this series can be viewed at
www.liverpool-unipress.co.uk

4. Brian W. Aldiss *The Detached Retina: Aspects of SF and Fantasy*

5. Carol Farley Kessler *Charlotte Perkins Gilman: Her Progress Toward Utopia, with Selected Writings*

6. Patrick Parrinder *Shadows of the Future: H.G. Wells, Science Fiction and Prophecy*

7. I.F. Clarke (ed.) *The Tale of the Next Great War, 1871–1914: Fictions of Future Warfare and of Battles Still-to-come*

8. Joseph Conrad and Ford Madox Ford (Foreword by George Hay, Introduction by David Seed) *The Inheritors*

9. Qingyn Wu *Female Rule in Chinese and English Literary Utopias*

10. John Clute *Look at the Evidence: Essays and Reviews*

11. Roger Luckhurst *'The Angle Between Two Walls': The Fiction of J.G. Ballard*

12. I.F. Clarke (ed.) *The Great War with Germany, 1870–1914: Fictions and Fantasies of the War-to-come*

13. Franz Rottensteiner (ed.) *View from Another Shore: European Science Fiction*

14. Val Gough and Jill Rudd (eds) *A Very Different Story: Studies in the Fiction of Charlotte Perkins Gilman*

15. Gary Westfahl *The Mechanics of Wonder: the Creation of the Idea of Science Fiction*

16. Gwyneth Jones *Deconstructing the Starships: Science, Fiction and Reality*

17. Patrick Parrinder (ed.) *Learning from Other Worlds: Estrangement, Cognition and the Politics of Science Fiction and Utopia*

18. Jeanne Cortiel *Demand My Writing: Joanna Russ, Feminism Science Fiction*

19. Chris Ferns *Narrating Utopia: Ideology, Gender, Form in Utopian Literature*

20. E.J. Smyth (ed.) *Jules Verne: New Directions*

21. Andy Sawyer and David Seed (eds) *Speaking Science Fiction: Dialogues and Interpretations*

22. Inez van der Spek *Alien Plots: Female Subjectivity and the Divine in the Light of James Tiptree's 'A Momentary Taste of Being'*

23. S.T. Joshi *Ramsey Campbell and Modern Horror Fiction*

24. Mike Ashley *The Time Machines: The Story of the Science Fiction Pulp Magazines from the Beginning to 1950*

25. Warren G. Rochelle *Communities of the Heart: The Rhetoric of Myth in the Fiction of Ursula K. Le Guin*

26. S.T. Joshi *A Dreamer and a Visionary: H.P. Lovecraft in His Time*

27. Christopher Palmer *Philip K. Dick: Exhilaration and Terror of the Postmodern*

# RUMORS OF WAR AND INFERNAL MACHINES

Technomilitary Agenda-Setting in American and British Speculative Fiction

CHARLES E. GANNON

LIVERPOOL UNIVERSITY PRESS

First published 2003 by
Liverpool University Press
4 Cambridge Street
Liverpool L69 7ZU

Copyright © 2003 Charles E. Gannon

The right of Charles E. Gannon to be identified as the author of this work has been asserted by him in accordance with the Copyright, Designs and Patents Act, 1988

All rights reserved.
No part of this book may be reproduced, stored in a retrieval system, or transmitted, in any form or by any means, electronic, mechanical, photocopying, recording, or otherwise, without the prior written permission of the publisher.

British Library Cataloguing-in-Publication data
A British Library CIP record is available

ISBN 0-85323-698-4 cased
0-85323-708-5 paper

Typeset by Servis Filmsetting Ltd, Manchester
Printed and bound in the European Union by
Bell and Bain Ltd, Glasgow

This book is a testament to the support and inspiration of the following people: my beloved wife and soul-mate Andrea Trisciuzzi; my dear mother, Cecilia Gannon; my late father John Gannon; and last, but certainly not least, my sons, Connor and Kyle. Most particularly, this book is for the two of you and the safety of your future—since the worlds we imagine will influence the one you inherit.

# Contents

| | | |
|---|---|---|
| *Acknowledgements* | | viii |
| *Introduction* | Assessing Rumors—of War and Infernal Machines | 1 |
| 1 | Armageddon by Gaslight: Victorian Visions of Apocalypse | 8 |
| 2 | Opportunistic Anticipations and Accidental Insights: William Le Queux's Exploitation of Edwardian Invasion Anxieties | 32 |
| 3 | Promoters of the Probable, Prophets of the Possible: Technological Innovation and Edwardian Near-Future War Fiction | 62 |
| 4 | H.G. Wells: The Far-Future War Prophet of Edwardian England | 91 |
| 5 | Hard Numbers, Hard Cases, Hard Decisions: Politics and Future-War Fiction in America | 112 |
| 6 | An Imperfect Future Tense(d): Anticipations of Atomic Annihilation in Post-War American Science Fiction | 128 |
| 7 | Nuclear Fiction and Silo Psychosis: Narratives of Life in the Shadow of a Mushroom Cloud | 146 |
| 8 | Radio Waves, Death Rays, and Transgressive (Sub)Texts: Future-War Fiction in the Wide Black Yonder | 173 |
| 9 | Making Man-Machines of Mass Destruction: Future-War Authors as Seers in an Age of Cyborg Soldiers | 208 |
| 10 | Cultural Casualties as Collateral Damage: The Fragment-ing/-ation Effects of Future-War Fantasies vs. Fictions | 239 |
| *Afterword* | On Conducting a Literary Reconnaissance in Force—and in Earnest | 256 |
| *Notes* | | 259 |
| *Bibliography* | | 287 |
| *Index* | | 292 |

# Acknowledgements

I wish to extend fond thanks to my colleagues Philip Sicker (Fordham University), Ian Clarke (Emeritus Professor, Strathclyde University), and David Seed (Liverpool University). Other invaluable contributions were made by Peter Wright (Edgehill College), Jerry McClellan, and Mark.

I thank the Fulbright Commissions of both the US and the UK for their generous Fellowship to conduct a year of writing and crucial research in the United Kingdom. I also thank Fordham University for years of exceptional support.

I also acknowledge the assistance and use of the following collections: the Liddell Hart Centre for Military Archives at the Library of King's College, London; the British Library; the National Library of Scotland, and the Blackwood Archives in particular; the Sydney Jones Library of Liverpool University, and the Foundation Science Fiction Archive in particular.

## Illustration Credits

Comparison photographs of before/after shelling results at Verdun: Suddeutscher Verlag, Munich

*Starship Troopers* in fatigues pocket: US Naval Institute Photo Archives (Chuck Mussi)

Objective Infantry Combat Weapon (OICW), and Land Warrior: public website, United States Army

Artist's rendering of Boeing Unmanned Aerial Vehicle (UAV): Boeing Aerospace

Artist's rendering of Future Combat System: public website, DARPA

# Introduction: Assessing Rumors—of War and Infernal Machines

This book, which examines how the fundamentally Utopian enterprise of orderly speculation has often produced destructive technologies, is furnished with a title compounded from two phrases culled (respectively) from the discursive archives of peace and war. The first phrase—'rumors of war'—appears in the gospels of Mark and Matthew, part of Christ's warning to the apostles (and, arguably, humankind) that the future path to final peace will be marked by violent trials that will attend 'wars and rumors of wars.' In contrast, the second phrase—'infernal machine'—has much more recent, and much more martial, origins.

While on his way to the Paris Opera on the night of December 24, 1800, Napoleon Bonaparte narrowly escaped an assassin's primitive time-bomb. Napoleon's angry characterization of the device—*'machine infernale'*—was subsequently inscribed not only on the back of a commemorative medal, but upon the linguistic consciousness of the Western world. By the time of the American Civil War, the phrase 'infernal machine' had become a favorite with journalists, who used it to refer to landmines, time-bombs, or other mechanisms that killed without the presence or immediate control of an attacker.[1] However, the semantic components of the phrase are ultimately more pertinent than its history.

The inclusion of the adjective 'infernal' is particularly interesting: not merely a consequence-descriptive word (such as 'deadly'), 'infernal' also suggests hellish origins and a corresponding moral taint. This word choice also reflects Western society's initial and (avowedly) enduring derogation of automated killing devices. Certainly, the 'evils' of such weapons are many: they abet the basest subterfuges of terrorism; they are undeterred by the presence of unintended, innocent victims; and once activated, their attacks cannot be aborted. However, the moral quandaries posed by this species of device are what make it a singularly fitting metasymbol for the other innovative or imaginative weapons that are examined herein and which have come to increasingly dominate military thought, design, and operations, particularly since World War I. Like Napoleon's 'infernal machine,' 'smart' bombs and other weapons of the increasingly automated battlefield, explode—and destroy—notions of personal honor and responsibility just as readily as they kill humans. Inextricably bound within the mechanized massacre of physical bodies is a congruent (if unintended) attack upon the greater body politic: pluralism itself is eviscerated by these weapons' destruction of the sanctity, significance, and effectiveness of the individual.

Yet, even as the semantics of the expression 'infernal machines' resonates the humanitarian purposes of this project, the history of the phrase recalls the prolonged social ambivalence regarding the morality of such weapons. From their very inception, ethical denunciations of them have contended with undeniable claims of military efficacy and political pragmatism. Two centuries after Napoleon decried (but, soon thereafter, used) 'infernal machines', the West has neither conclusively renounced nor accepted them. However, American and European focus upon (and fascination with) these devices—in factual reportage and fictional representations—has grown exponentially.

The title's other epigrammatic phrase—'rumors of war'—certainly underscores the project's primary field of focus: war. However, in this phrase, it is the word 'rumors' that deserves special attention. 'Rumors' is a crucial qualifier, a reminder that the texts under consideration are not 'reports' or repositories of 'facts,' yet neither are they 'fantasies' or 'myths' or 'fairytales.' Rather, because they are works of *orderly* speculative fiction, they are more akin to 'rumors' of the future.

The subgenre of speculative fiction which is most often associated with future wars, and which is the focus of this investigation, is customarily referred to as 'hard' science fiction. Hard science fiction is distinguished from other species of imaginative narrative both in its ends and means: it posits serious challenges to contemporary understandings and expectations by proposing provisional changes in reality that are, to quote theorist/critic Darko Suvin, 'validated by cognitive logic.'[2] In short, hard science fiction is a narrative form of the *gedankenexperiment* or 'thought experiment': where such narratives propose changes in the consensual notions of reality, they must also furnish sound, scientifically responsible hypotheses to explain the alterations. Such fiction, is, therefore, not a fantasy, but a 'rumor' of the future. Like any other rumor, it has its origins in fact: it extrapolates from known history, events, and conditions. Also like a rumor, the degree and type of speculation that the author employs must remain somewhat modest in scope. Without careful restraint upon authorial invention, a 'rumor' degenerates and is labeled as a 'fantasy,' or a 'delusion' or—in the most extreme and pejorative case—a 'lie.' Conversely, when a rumor is particularly responsible—when the author readily admits and volunteers the provisional status of the conclusions adduced—it is redesignated as a 'conjecture:' it becomes, in effect, a socially sanctioned, high-quality 'rumor.' Hard science fiction is the narrative equivalent of such conjecture. It, too, traffics in information that is uncertain and/or unproven, but accrues credibility both by the care with which uncertainties are speculated upon, and by the open declaration of the provisionality of the resulting conclusions. Furthermore, whether its purpose is to inform or entertain, true hard science fiction does not resort to gratuitous terrors or titillations, but holds a reader's interest by postulating outcomes to serious, structured questions or situations.

For the purposes of this project, the most pertinent speculative 'rumors' are not merely conjectures about the future of war in general, but upon the consequences of one or more specific technological innovations or changes. Many future-war texts simply project expected or novel international crises that would precipitate an outbreak of new hostilities. However, although these texts hypothesize *which* war might come next, they do not hypothesize on *how* war itself might change. Narratives that employ the latter form of speculation are not merely offering readers 'rumors of war' but 'rumors of 1) war, and 2) infernal machines:' machines that might hypothetically alter not just the location but the conduct and consequences of future battles. Arguably, these are the most politically relevant—and powerful—future-war fictions, and therefore, those most likely to illustrate how the military (and related political) agendas and actions of modern technophilic superpower states have been influenced by speculative fiction.

This phenomenon of political influence is explored in detail within the domain of post-World War II American literature. However, in order to ensure that the results are not seen solely as artifacts particular to one nation and one epoch, a similar analysis of Victorian and Edwardian British speculative fiction is also conducted. This dual structure is informed and motivated by the observation that, along with international political dominance, various discursive styles and preoccupations were transferred from Britain to the US in the decades immediately preceding and following World War I. Significantly, this discursive transfer, and the relative increase in the political influence of future-war fictions, has paralleled the rise of the true superpower state and its technophilic ideologies.

This trend has been evident since the heyday of the Industrial Age: the profusion of future-war fictions in Victorian England paralleled the British Empire's struggle to convert itself into the first modern superpower. These imaginative Victorian texts were also the direct discursive forebears of American hard science fiction, which in the past fifty years has been increasingly dominated by speculations about advanced military technology. Indeed, the relationship between American hard science fiction and future warfare is often overtly institutionalized. Readers who are tempted to reject the notion that such narratives influence political and military agendas might be surprised to learn just how much detailed official evidence there is in support of this contention. The armed forces have sponsored numerous gatherings of military science fiction authors to work in forward-looking 'think tanks.' Examples include the air force's *Futurist* series of future-war planning conferences (where almost a quarter of the invitees were authors of military science fiction); open admission by defense industry engineers and executives regarding the influence of hard science fiction texts and authors upon research and development initiatives and tactical design considerations; and the heavy overlap between both the discursive and social domains of the military and future-war authorship communities. This list represents only the briefest and most general sampling of the various examples that establish the existence of a constantly growing literary/political symbiosis that has extended from Victorian/Edwardian Britain into post-Cold War America.

******

The decision to seek evidence of significant exchange between speculative narratives and political entities by investigating the domain of future-war fiction is anything but commonplace. However, this critical approach may not be as irregular as it first seems, particularly after explicating its three key methodological praxes: why the analysis is not merely textual, but also historical and political; why and how two different superpowers were selected for study; and why future-war and weaponry fictions have been chosen as the specific subgenre of speculative fiction for examination.

First, any theorist who adopts the somewhat provocative stance of attributing powers of social influence to fictional narratives would do well to survey, and gather evidence, across a broad social spectrum. Furthermore, a great many of this project's most pertinent and corroborative discursive objects were not produced exclusively within either the literary or the political sphere, but at the intersection of the two. Because of this, it is necessary to map these coupled domains by examining both the relevant texts *and* the historical/political environment in which they were created and received. This is hardly a novel or radical approach: Foucault, Spivak, Todorov, Said, Jameson, Williams, Steiner, Kuhn, and countless others have analyzed texts through specifically political lenses and have framed their findings and assertions within historical contexts. This project follows the same methodological and critical tradition.

Second, the decision to examine the fiction of both Britain and America was almost inevitable: such a comparison is the only methodological means of establishing the *general* applicability of the findings. As the adage has it, something that occurs once is chance, but twice suggests a pattern. Therefore, by examining the experiences of two superpower states, it can be shown that future-war fiction's transformative powers are not an artifact peculiar to any *one* such state. The specific shapes, directions, and consequences of its political influence will vary from culture to culture, and from epoch to epoch, but the presence of the influence itself actually inheres in the social and discursive fabric of superpowers *qua* superpowers. By conducting two such investigations, a 'line' can be drawn that links these separate occurrences, and, by projection, would logically run through all such polities. Furthermore, Late Victorian and post-war US linkages between military discourse and speculative fiction constitute a historical dyad that facilitates analysis of important political, cultural, and technological progressions. Late Victorian England was, arguably, the first true superpower state: it possessed and strategically utilized the characteristic technologies of such a state to maintain and expand its hegemony. Its use of rail, steamship, telegraph, wireless communication, and the systematic restructuring of the government to incorporate scientific method (including statistical analysis and a crude, nascent version of war game theory) into its organs of political control and information management all indicate the dawn of superpower praxes in the British Empire—ironically, just as the sun was finally beginning to set on it. However, Edwardian Britain is an 'early stage' example of superpower praxes when compared with the more 'mature' version evinced later by the United States where electronics, telecommunications, computers, scientific method, games theory, and strategic technology development are not late-stage additions to, but integral superstructural elements of, that state's political hegemony and identity.

This technological progression is further complemented by the political and cultural progressions that connect these two polities. It has often been suggested that America's ascendance is simply a recentered continuance and extension of the white Anglophone global dominance initiated by the British Empire. America's deepest political roots are found in post-Renaissance Britain, and—especially for individuals from well outside this cultural tradition (i.e. the overwhelming majority of the world's population)—the change from Union Jack to Stars and Stripes may largely be one of external form, not political substance. Although the manner and means of their political projection may vary, there are obvious and striking similarities in the two nations' languages, legal institutions, value systems, traditions, gender roles, etc. Therefore, to the many still-marginalized peoples whose history is marked by recent colonialist intrusions, the fact that the *lingua franca* form of 'farewell' has changed from

'Cheerio' to 'Have a nice day' may be unimportant, since the underlying cultural consequences remain unchanged.

Finally, why focus this critical project upon fiction that deals with future warfare and weaponry? Bluntly, because it is a singularly sensitive and telling register of the interactions between texts and policy in superpowers. Marshall McLuhan's comment that 'If mechanical technology ... exerted a fragmenting force, psychically and socially, this fact appears nowhere more vividly than in mechanical weaponry' underscores the logic of this genre choice.[3] Nowhere are the disruptive and transformative powers of technology anticipated and illustrated so overtly as in war fiction: the battlefield is frequently the stage upon which new technologies are first unveiled, where their consequences are most keenly felt, and where their application is most dramatically and graphically presented. For instance, it is far easier—and more believable—to figuratively encounter new aircraft technologies (engines, aerodynamics, new materials, weapons, sensors) in a fiction about a new hypersonic interceptor than in a story focused upon a new passenger aircraft. Since the nature of a combat aircraft is to go in harm's way, the basic operation of a military plane naturally puts it in a highly dramatic situation where the pilot's mission experiences (and therefore, the plot points) are a *direct outgrowth* of the new technology. Consequently, there is a direct and natural relationship between 1) the new technologies, 2) the new capabilities of the aircraft, and 3) the new activities it will undertake because of those technologies. Ultimately, these new and changed 'combat missions' are not only enabled by the new technologies, but their execution provides the logical, dramatic scenarios wherein the operation of the new technologies is graphically displayed (often in painstaking detail).

There is a further analytical value to using futuristic military stories as the means of discussing the relationship between practices of cultural reproduction (i.e. narratives) and the praxes of the superpower state: such fiction evinces—in its assumptions, imagery, implied value structures, and even style—a distinct and revealing gender bias. Future-war fiction is, largely, fiction for and about individuals who are gendered as 'men' (regardless of their actual sex). Accordingly, its recurrent themes orbit about a trinary value system with an immense amount of male-socializing gravity. The narrative components of this weighty triad are warfare (traditionally both a male rite of passage and expression of redirected sexual energy), new technology (which reinforces the post-industrial redefinition and refocusing of masculine prowess through mechanical extensions of self), and political drama (in which war, as the ultimate contest between patriarchies, is the ritualized epitome of primal dominance struggles that are brimful of sexual implications, energies, and anxieties). Consequently, this subgenre of speculative fiction reinforces the authority and structure of the superpower state in two separate but complementary ways. First, in being technology-centered, these fictions are ineluctably technophilic, for even if new technology 'fails,' the *idea* of technology as a crucial element of political discourse is reinforced. Second, future-war fiction focuses on traditionally male roles, activities, and interests, thereby showcasing and celebrating the patriarchy that pervades superpower political practices and governmental structures. Even texts of the 'anti-war' variety present sympathetic 'warrior-characters,' such as William Mandella in Joe Haldeman's *The Forever War*[4] and Martin Diaz in Poul Anderson's *Kings Who Die*.[5] In following these characters' lives, the texts inevitably also spend considerable time detailing the tools and techniques that are these future warriors' stock-in-trade. Collectively, these narrative elements strongly imply that both the material and cultural components of soldiering are suffused with 'social salience:'[6] what else would vindicate the invariably central role of these components within such stories?

In conclusion, the diverse array of issues raised by a sustained examination of superpowers' obsessions with (and susceptibilities to) rumors of both war and infernal machines not only dictate the investigative methodologies to be employed, but also establish the project's raison d'être. Although deconstructive (and later) criticism is obliged to maintain a disingenuous awareness of the gamesmanship that inheres in both texts and analytical confrontations with them, it is also true that war, weapon-making, and political manipulation are deadly serious 'games.' This does not mean that an assessment of future-war fiction need be 'deadly' serious in its rhetorical mannerisms. Nor can such a project reasonably presume to provide answers, or even perspectives, that could become the basis of political action. Rather, the merit of critical projects that unashamedly address issues of social gravity—no matter the topic—is that they celebrate the intrinsic and indispensable beliefs of socialized humanity: that discourse is not futile, that investigations may eventually lead to answers, and that the insights gained through both are the fuel-source and inspiration for subsequent journeys of inquiry and hope.

*Chapter 1*

# Armageddon by Gaslight: Victorian Visions of Apocalypse

> We are making the future . . . and hardly any of us troubled to think what future we were making. And here it is!
> 
> H.G. Wells, from *When the Sleeper Wakes*

It has been said that one of speculative fiction's most enduring and significant thematic fixations is the preconstruction of possible histories, whether in the form of prescriptive social blueprints or proscriptive cautionary tales. The pedigree of such narratives is as long as it is mixed. Its origins extend back into the pre-Enlightenment centuries, and since issues of warfare and weaponry are never too far removed from any extended consideration of competing societies and statecraft, it is equally impossible to make any definitive claim as to what constitutes the 'first' future-war narrative.

However, one can say with some certainty that the *genre* of the future-war narrative, both as an identifiable subtype of speculative fiction and as a source of political influence, did not slowly evolve into existence. It arrived with the suddenness—and reverberation—of an exploding bomb.

\*\*\*\*\*\*

In the first week of May 1871, Number 667 of *Blackwood's Edinburgh Magazine* carried an anonymously penned story entitled 'The Battle of Dorking.' This fictitious eyewitness account—told in bitter retrospect—chronicled the invasion and defeat of England by the same efficient Prussian armies that had defeated France in the Franco-Prussian War of the preceding year. The author was, in fact, a distinguished officer in the Royal Engineers, Lieutenant Colonel (later General Sir) George Tomkyns Chesney, who was strongly opposed to the Empire's policy of relying upon volunteer units for Britain's home defense. His story portrayed the failings of such a force in action, and the disastrous consequences that would result if it was entrusted with the safe-keeping of the seat of the Empire: general defeat, loss of all colonies, foreign occupation, and ultimately, the end of national sovereignty.

This portrayal of Britannia beneath the heel of the Hohenzollerns electrified the nation and touched off a brush-fire of heated debate, spirited approvals, and barbed retorts. By the end of the month, this issue of *Blackwood's* had been reprinted six times. Continually escalating interest in the story prompted editor John Blackwood to take the unusual step of publishing 'The Battle of Dorking' as a six-penny pamphlet. Sales once again skyrocketed, increasing by an unprecedented 20,000 copies a week and peaking at a grand total of 110,00 in July.[1]

These sales statistics indicate the duration and intensity of the political furor generated by 'The Battle of Dorking.' Debate over the issues it raised were still on the increase four months after its initial publication: on September 2, Prime Minister Gladstone attempted to quell the growing uproar and anxiety by attacking both the strategic and sensational presumptions of 'Dorking.' In a speech at Whitby, he shared his opinions in pointed and specific terms:

> In *Blackwood's Magazine* there has lately been a famous article, called 'The Battle of Dorking'. I should not mind this 'Battle of Dorking', if we could keep it to ourselves, if we could take care that nobody belonging to any other country should know that such follies could find currency or even favour with portions of the British public; but unfortunately these things go abroad, and they make us ridiculous in the eyes of the whole world. I do not say that the writers of them are not sincere—that is another matter—but I do say that the result of these things is practically the spending of more and more of your money. Be on your guard against alarmism. Depend upon it that there is not this astounding disposition on the part of all mankind to make us the objects of hatred.[2]

What is most remarkable about the Whitby speech is that it is a wholly unintentional, and therefore undeniable, testimonial of both the perceived and actual political power of a piece of 'future-war fiction.' Gladstone indirectly but clearly asserts that four extraordinary political powers reside in Chesney's text: influence upon other nations' opinions of Britain's political climate; determination of external perception of British national character; budgetary effects; and (by strong implication) influence upon foreign perceptions of the military vulnerability of England (thereby increasing the threat of invasion).

Ironically, Gladstone's remarks only expanded the story's peripheries of social influence. Drawing upon Blackwood's correspondence, leading 'Dorking' scholar I. F. Clarke provides an excellent overview of this steady growth:

On 5 September William Blackwood wrote to his uncle and partner, John Blackwood: 'Gladstone's speech is contemptible but it will do "The Dorking" good and introduce it to quite a new class of people. We will soon have to think of a people's edition. I think at 1$d$ or 2$d$.' It was a sign that the times were changing. War had become the concern of all citizens. A short story for the middle-class readers of *Blackwood's Magazine* had caught the attention of a 'new class of people' throughout the world. . . . [T]here were translations of the *Blackwood's* story in Danish, Dutch, French, German, Italian, Portuguese, and Swedish; and there were instant reprints in New Zealand, Canada, and the United States. By the end of 1871 there had been some eighteen British variations and counter-blasts . . . and in final proof of an unprecedented notoriety, there were two music-hall songs on the invasion theme and a fictitious edition of *The Official Despatches and Correspondence relative to the Battle of Dorking, as moved for in the House of Commons, 21st July 1920*.[3]

In many ways, the influence of Chesney and his narrative continued well past the inception of World War I. 'Dorking' was periodically reprinted and frequently imitated for many years. As late as 1940, Nazi Germany found the text's images of England crushed beneath Prussian jackboots to be useful grist for their master-race propaganda mills: 'Dorking' was reissued with the optimistic title *Was England erwartet*! (*What England Fears!*) However, the immediate heyday of the story was diminishing rapidly by the winter of 1871, at which point it became fodder for a brief fad in national humor: any small injury was likely to attract the mock-serious inquiry, 'Weren't you wounded at the Battle of Dorking?' However, Chesney's career certainly did not become a laughing matter: a well-known public figure after 'Dorking,' popular recognition and opinion of him remained high enough to eventually secure the ex-sapper a seat in Parliament's House of Commons.

Despite the rather humorous note on which this brief episode of British invasion hysteria (the first of many) ended, even its whimsical conclusion points to future-war fiction's influence upon, and interconnection with, the political sphere. In the first place, the story was so widely known that it became reliable fodder for some unknown pundit whose glib one-liner about being 'wounded at Dorking' depended upon a reference to a specific piece of fiction that must (if the joke is to work) enjoy immediate, nation-wide recognition. Secondly, the publication of 'Dorking' drew Chesney into a public limelight that ultimately illuminated his way to the benches of Parliament. Consequently, in the case of 'Dorking,' a fiction about the future of a nation became the means whereby the author of that fiction entered into the official process of determining that nation's political future. The domains of fiction and political process had effectively merged.

This close relationship between future-war fiction and both official agendas and personages was to continue unaltered and unabated through to World War I. Over that period of time the increasingly politicized subgenre of future-war fiction bifurcated into two discursive threads, each with distinctive narrative styles and political purposes. The first, and most prevalent, followed Chesney's example: politically motivated, near-future stories in which only international events are imaginary, not the technologies involved in their resolution. These might best be labeled the 'political future-war narratives' since they are invariably cautionary tales that offer learned opinion—and instruction—on the consequences of pursuing one line of national policy over another. The second variety of future-war narrative emerges later, in the 1880s, and it might be reasonably labeled the 'technological future-war narrative.' These tales offered opinion and instruction also; however, their lessons were not in policy but engineering. Usually written with an increased emphasis on verve, action, and description, these narratives proposed to deliver the vicarious experience, thrills, and terrors of actually being in a future war. Whether the domain was land, sea, or air, the authors often emphatically stated that their intent was not, ultimately, to entertain, but to educate people regarding the 'new kind of war' that was rapidly approaching, largely because of the new technologies that would be employed in its conduct. However, whether the innovations were primary 'political' or 'technological,' the authors of Victorian future-war fiction lacked neither credentials nor renown: they were, as Clarke puts it 'eminent Victorians' such as the distinguished General Sir William Francis Butler (*The Invasion of England*), Sir William Laird Clowes, and Alan Hughes Burgoyne (*The Great Naval War in 1887*).[4]

The most noteworthy aspect of this century-end flurry of future-war texts is the implicit assumptions governing both its creators and consumers: that fiction was an effective means of both informing and persuading the majority of the growing reading public of that day. This was particularly true concerning the second, and ultimately dominant, variety of future-war fiction, which presented novel military technologies in action. This branch of the genre can also, in its turn, be split into two relatively distinct species. The earliest texts endeavored to introduce the public to untried (or unfamiliar) extant weapons or to technological innovations that were either in development or imminent. The other, later species of technological future-war tales extrapolated more boldly, proposing and portraying wholly imaginary future weapons and warfare.

The first category might be called 'near-future' technological war fiction, a distant ancestor of the contemporary 'technothriller' subgenre that was supposedly created by the works of Tom Clancy. One of the earliest and most dramatic examples of this subgenre is (then Member of Parliament) Hugh Arnold-Forster's 'In a Conning Tower,' first published in *Murray's Magazine* in 1888, a short story of combat between the ultimate in 'modern' warships.

Arnold-Forster's tale is a first-person narrative, told in retrospect by the commander of HMS *Majestic*. However, the drama of the naval engagement is ultimately secondary to and, arguably, a mere prop for, the explication and detailed examination of the technological wonders and prowess of the new class of battleship to which the *Majestic* belongs. New engines, guns, armor, speed, command and control mechanisms, and crew requirements are translated easily into new tactics and operational imperatives, which, in turn, shape the plot and provide the drama of the story. For the Victorian middle-class readership, whose keen interest in new weapons was matched only by their lack of detailed technological understanding, such a story was a compelling example of what Clarke calls 'commingling entertainment with instruction in exciting tales about "what it will be like"' on the new battlefield, wielding and evading lethal new weapons.[5] It was through influential and authoritative fictions such as these, therefore, that the inhabitants of the West's would-be superpowers began to adapt to and order their visions of a changed military (and, therefore, political) reality.

In addition to the extraordinary information that was relayed through 'near-future' technological narratives, there were also extraordinary profits to be realized by publishing them. Naturally, this capacity for generating tremendous revenue points to political influence of another sort —the kind that shapes editorial decisions based on anticipated financial returns. One individual whose editorial decisions, political agenda, and profit motives found a singularly harmonious confluence in the form of future-war narratives was Alfred Harmsworth (later Lord Northcliffe), owner of *Answers* and later, the *Daily Mail*. Harmsworth's political aims and ambitions certainly did influence the content of the future-war stories he commissioned, particularly those assigned to his most sensationalistic and profitable fabulator, William Le Queux. However, Harmsworth would not have undertaken their publication and promotion had they not also promised huge financial returns. Harmsworth's formula was simple and certified by repeated success: 'war not only created a supply of news but a demand for it. So deep-rooted is the fascination in war and things appertaining to it that . . . a paper has only to be able to put on its placard "A Great Battle" for its sales to mount up.'[6]

If actual wars were wanting, however, imagined ones could always take their place, and the most frequent (and successful) concocter of non-existent conflicts was William Le Queux. Le Queux, unlike his more politically minded predecessors, was willing to dispense with strategic plausibility and journalistic accountability if either stood in the way of generating the levels of drama and lurid imagery that guaranteed maximum readership. Ironically, both he and Harmsworth learned their initial lessons about the appeal and profitability of future-war fiction from one of the most responsible, yet flawed, projections of the period: *The Great War of 189–*. However, even this tale—crafted by a collaborative group of diverse and internationally respected experts—arose primarily from speculation on increased circulation figures, not speculative visions of world wars. The illustrated weekly that commissioned this serial—*Black and White*—had commenced publication less than a year before and its editor was looking for a way to increase sales. He did so by blazing a new trail in the rapidly growing realm of future-war fiction: he retained the services of the esteemed Admiral P. H. Colomb and other well-known military experts and journalists to write as though they were 'reporting' from the fictional front lines of a Continent-consuming conflict. Their projections would not be related as dry theory, or even as a single, rushed fiction, but in the fashion of war reportage, replete with delayed dispatches and lingering uncertainties. To add the finishing touches to this simulation of reality, the editor commissioned artists to design photo-quality illustrations for this model imitation of the 'new journalism' (which was employing pictorial coverage as an integral part of its presentation). The editor's expectation was that this combination of dramatic story, serialization, renowned commentators, and graphic representation would result in dramatically increased circulation numbers for *Black and White*. This expectation is evinced not only by the editor's willingness to invest in expensive writers and supporting illustrations, but also by the clarion-call tenor of his introduction:

> Authorities are agreed that a GREAT WAR must break out in the immediate future, and that this War will be fought under novel and surprising conditions. All facts seem to indicate that the coming conflict will be the bloodiest in history, and must involve the most momentous consequence to the whole world. . . . The Editor . . . has sought the aid of the chief living authorities in international politics, in strategy, and in war . . . Admiral Sir Philip Colomb, Mr. Charles Lowe, Mr. D. Christie Murray, Mr. F. Scudamore and other experts in military campaigns have taken part.[7]

The successful serial was quickly collected into a book and was soon afterward translated into several European languages. In less than two years, a fifth edition had been issued in German, whose readers obviously took the text very seriously: no less a figure than General von Bülow praised the work. Von Bülow unintentionally confirmed the value of weaving expert testimony into a future-war narrative when he asserted (in his introduction to the German edition) that the serial's appeal for both experts and laypersons was not only due to its generally sound premises and predictions, but to the reputations of the persons who were responsible for its creation, particularly Admiral Colomb.

Thus, the key components of financially successful Victorian future-war fiction had been identified and proven in practice: the imaginary war should erupt from an already smoldering (or likely) international crisis or conflict;[8] one or more of the combatants should pose a tangible threat to England's interests (or better still, the British Isles themselves); the latest weapons and technologies should be shown in action; and the story should either be told or endorsed (preferably both) by military experts and/or persons in government posts.

Alfred Harmsworth and William Le Queux obviously took to heart the tutelage offered by *Black and White*'s experience with future-war fiction. Their aptitude for mastering these mercenary lessons is reflected in 'The Great War in England in 1897,' a Le Queux serial that Harmsworth ran in *Answers* during the 1893 war scare.[9] It was then published as a book in 1894 with a preface by the esteemed Lord Roberts, victor of Kandahar. It went into five editions in the first four weeks of publication and received public praise from the Duke of Connaught, Lord Wolseley, and other respected Victorians. Ultimately, it generated solid sales for six years, and in that time, was issued in 16 editions and received front-page coverage in the Paris *Figaro*, the Rome *Opinione*, and the *Secolo* of Milan.[10] The Harmsworth–Le Queux partnership would realize even greater successes in the following years by repeatedly (and profitably) pricking Britain's ever-sensitive 'invasion' nerves in narratives such as *The Poisoned Bullet* and, especially, *The Invasion of 1910*—arguably the most (in)famous and sensationalistic of all Victorian future-war fictions.

Finally, however, this subgenre also attracted narrative efforts that defied polarized categorizations as simple as 'sensationalistic' or 'serious.' More even-handed commentary or, alternately, satires came from Wodehouse, de Maurier, Waugh, Belloc, Saki (H. H. Monro), and Childers, to name only a few. Admittedly, these contributions make up only a very small percentage of the immense mass of future-war texts that were a popular literary staple in Britain from 1871 to 1914. However, their presence indicates that the character of Victorian future-war fiction was neither uniform nor simple: it was comprised of equal measures of sincere prognostication, alarmist propaganda, strategic preposterousness, and journalistic profiteering. However, whatever narrative diamonds or dross may be found in this mixture, there are some identifiable and significant constants that emerge.

One such constant is the often commanding presence that these narratives had in both the popular consciousness and official political discourse of their day. Prime Ministers, Members of Parliament, Field Marshals, international experts, and influential editors all participated in the discussions that were fueled (and often ignited) by such speculations, often responding with their own alternative (or counter-) speculations.

A second constant among the more 'conservative' narratives of this genre is their almost total lack of visionary accuracy regarding military operations. As I. F. Clarke also points out, the authors of these fictions failed to anticipate how the next major war would be fought, envisioning modernized versions of Waterloo rather than the horrors of extended trench warfare. Indeed, one of Clarke's most interesting assertions is that the appeal of these fictions was paradoxically linked to their prognosticative inaccuracy, in that they promoted a 'comfortable accommodation with the arms race . . .' The short campaigns and immediately decisive battles of these fictions not only failed to anticipate, but made unthinkable, the battlefield horrors and staggering casualties that would come to define the actual 'Great War.' Rather, '[t]he seeming modernity of their narratives and the careful precision of the illustrations concealed archaic habits of mind and a romantic attachment to the self-transcending glories of warfare.'[11] Ultimately, these narratives promoted dangerously misguided expectations about the conduct and consequences of 'the next Great War,' and in so doing, encouraged an ingenuous complacency regarding the entire future of warfare. Arguably, it was this complacency that made possible the military myopia that produced the Western Front massacres—and concomitant public shock—of 1914–15.

Ironically, Victorian and Edwardian future-war tales were often much less flawed in their tactical and technological particulars than they were in their overarching strategic and operational visions.[12] This is largely because the authors failed to integrate the many individual tactical-level innovations that they foresaw into a totally reconceived strategic scenario. Therefore, although Clarke's assertions about their failure to foresee the horrors of 1914 could not be more accurate or appropriate, some of the technologies and the tactics portrayed in even the most sensationalistic of these works anticipate innovations that later materialized as reality. Many of these narratives demonstrated bold prognosticative leaps that carried them clear over the trenchlines in 1914 France, and landed them in operational terrain that much more resembles the Polish frontier of September, 1939. The writers of these fictions, unfettered by professional dedication to the military conventions of their day, often made the intuitive jump that the general staffs of World War I could not: that the age of the machine ultimately meant increased mobility, which in turn portended the fluid blitzkrieg and the demise of the fortified bunker. Consequently, Clarke's conclusions regarding the fallacies that were so liberally, earnestly, and innocently disseminated by such narratives pertains primarily to the strategic or 'macroscopic' perspective of future-warfare fictions. However, their 'microscopic' view of specific technological innovations and concomitant tactical consequences were not only less severely flawed, but often provided readers with their first, relatively reliable, illustrations of new military 'realities'—such as the advent of magazine rifles, machine guns, armored fighting vehicles, and new munitions. Consequently, these texts may have failed as political projections, but they nonetheless exerted political influence by facilitating social acculturation to new technologies and to the specific changes those technologies introduce to the concept of 'combat' as experienced and conducted on an individual level. Given the centrality and urgency of issues of war- and peace-making within any nation or culture, such information and acculturation has a distinctly political component.

Ultimately, the Victorians not only 'invented' technologically speculative future-war fiction, but they pursued it along three distinct discursive avenues which suggest an enduring model for a tripartite typology of such narratives. The first category portrays new or untested technologies but no imaginary ones, the second introduces technological innovations which are imminent or belong to the 'near future,' and the third incorporates radical or 'far future' leaps in technology.

******

The overwhelming majority of both Victorian and Edwardian future-war fiction was ultimately interested not in technological, but in political, invention. Fantasies of what might *possibly* happen next in a laboratory were of less concern, and of less immediate importance, than projections of what would *probably* happen next in the council chambers of the great European powers. Of course, the 'probable' events never did become reality in any detailed sense, although some anticipations of how a Great War might begin, and how the tangled alliances of Imperialist Europe would finally shake out, evince some prognosticative merit.

However, one of the first future-war fictions that was informed by military expertise, knowledge of the latest technology, and possibly imminent events was entirely apolitical, insofar as it studiously avoided identifying the nationality of the forces which confronted the servants of Queen and Country. This text was 'In a Conning Tower,' whose author, Hugh Arnold-

Forster, explained in a preface that the story was written so that readers might be given 'a faithful idea of the possible course of an action between two modern ironclads availing themselves of all the weapons of offence and defence which an armoured ship at the present day possesses.'[13] The protagonist—the unnamed captain of the (fictional) HMS *Majestic*—certainly delivers on Arnold-Forster's promise, describing the new capacities of his ship with a minimum of numbers and a maximum of colorful metaphors and similes. These later provide the basis for the visceral, brutally vivid imagery he uses to describe the vessel's combat with a capital ship of a rival power.

However, what may have been of greatest interest to the general reader then and the scholar now is the way in which this text announces the radically increased degree of command-and-control centralization on the war vessels of the period. Indeed, Arnold-Forster illustrates how control over the ominous power of such lethal leviathans had narrowed so as to be necessarily borne upon the shoulders of a single individual—a psychologically punishing burden of responsibility over unprecedented forces of mass destruction:

> Here in this spot is concentrated the whole power of the tremendous machine which we call an ironclad ship. Such power was never . . . concentrated under the direction of man, and all that power, the judgement to direct it, the will to apply it, the knowledge to utilize it, is placed in the hands of one man, and one only.[14]

For a modern reader, the protagonist's extended ruminations upon the isolating responsibility of this power, and the automata which allow him to employ it at a moment's notice, may echo with an eerie premonition of push-button nuclear Apocalypse:

> [T]he captain in his conning tower has but to press the button by his side, and in a moment the . . . great ship . . . will be rushing onwards at a speed over twenty miles an hour. In her turret and in her broadside batteries there is a deep hush of expectation: but there too, waiting to respond to the 'flash of the will that can', lie forces of destruction which appal the imagination.[15]

Arnold-Forster was not speaking of—and certainly never foresaw—a world in which the turn of a key in an ICBM control bunker could initiate Armageddon, but he certainly *was* calling attention to the then-little-appreciated trend toward synergy between automation and weaponry. Indeed, the popularity and influence of his story indicates that the significance of his narrative synthesis of the two was not lost on Victorian readers. First published in *Murray's Magazine* in July 1888, 'Conning

Tower' was swiftly reissued in eight successive pamphlet editions, and was translated into Danish, French, Italian, Spanish, and Swedish. Arnold-Forster was a moderately distinguished Member of Parliament when he wrote the tale, but his consequent celebrity made possible his ascension to a series of higher government posts, including Secretary of the Admiralty from 1900–1903, and Secretary of War from 1903–1905.

The success of the story, and its emergence from the pen of Arnold-Forster, is not without its ironies. Hugh Arnold-Forster was also the nephew of Matthew Arnold, whose anti-machine, anti-automation stances were so forcefully and frequently articulated that history has come to associate him with technophobia. The second, and more profound, irony is that the final dramatic focal point of Arnold-Forster's technologically driven story is the one weapon on the ship which — unbeknownst to both author and audience — had already been consigned to the dustbin of military anachronisms: 'And, last . . . of all, there is . . . the ram, the most terrible, the most fatal of all the engines of maritime warfare.'[16] Ironically, 'Conning Tower' was intended as a narrative tribute to the naval preeminence of the below-water ram, but it was, in fact, this archaic weapon's epitaph: no major engagement had been decided by rams in some years, and they never would be afterward.[17] That so perceptive a naval expert as Arnold-Forster could make such an error in an era of new wire-guided torpedoes and high-velocity guns is a particularly telling example of how older, romantic expectations of warfare were almost impossible to avoid completely — even for foresighted authors of future-war fiction.

However, Arnold-Forster did realize his express purpose of presenting middle-class readers with the changes in naval weaponry and combat that they would experience were they to find themselves 'In a Conning Tower,' and he did so by providing them with both technical and experiential information. In adopting this narratalogical strategy, Arnold-Forster proved that he not only understood then-current naval technology, but his audience's limitations and interests as well: rather than technical diagrams, his text is accompanied by stirring illustrations of the *Majestic* in action. Rather than including quantitative descriptions of new machinery, he depicts its operation during the course of a dramatic combat mission. In place of a dull recitation of specifications, Arnold-Forster's descriptions place readers where they can vicariously feel the bone-jarring recoil of newer, bigger guns, and the horrible, sweaty speed with which decisions must be made and outcomes are reached. This narrative strategy of focusing on the tangible, experiential consequences of new technology, while avoiding any detailed presentation of its technical specifications, was to become a staple in future-war fiction of all types. Over the next thirty years, readers of such narratives would often encounter innovations as diverse as gas warfare, wireless telegraphy, automatic weapons, and self-propelled combat vehicles in exactly this fashion: as dramatic components within stories of a war to come, rather than as objects of technological interest in themselves.

The instructional value of 'Conning Tower' was not, evidently, limited to a lay audience: the story was listed in the 'Naval Bibliography' (compiled by the influential W. Laird Clowes, and approved by the service editors) of *The Naval Annual: 1892*.[18] Written and compiled by 'T. A. Brassey, et al.,' it is interesting to note that one of the authors of this prestigious almanac of naval technology and tactics is none other than Arnold-Forster himself. Also listed in this august reference's Naval Bibliography is Rear-Admiral P. H. Colomb's *Naval Warfare: Its Ruling Principles and Practice Historically Considered*.[19] Of the latter text, bibliographic compiler Clowes says that it is 'the most important English work of the kind that has appeared in recent years. It deals exhaustively with the nature of war, the struggle for the command of the sea, the differentiation of naval force, etc.'[20] What Clowes does not mention is that its eminent and world-respected author was also at the helm of the collaborative writing group that created another highly influential—and trend-setting—piece of future-war fiction: *The Great War of 189–: A Forecast*.[21] Although Arnold-Forster's narrative does receive brief mention in the body-copy of the *Annual*, Colomb is specifically invoked as a leading naval authority, particularly in regards to the dubious future of the ram in combat: 'Students of Admiral Colomb's writings will know what a hair's-breadth separates in a ramming attack the case of ramming your adversary from that of being yourself rammed.'[22] Indeed, Brassey, like most other experts of his time, was keenly aware of just how rapidly the technology and tactics of his day were changing: 'The progress of invention is ceaseless. The best designs of 1892 will in a few years be condemned as obsolete.'[23] Consequently, experts were at least as interested in responsible future-war projections as were the members of the general reading public: in an environment where the useful shelf-life of the most modern warships was measured in years, not decades, naval architects, strategists, and budgetary allocators alike were concerned with the practical necessity of trying to anticipate the emerging trends in the inextricably linked domains of technology and tactics that would determine the construction of new weapons. Hence, the painstaking research and rigorous attention to the laws of 'probability' that informed the writing of *The Great War of 189–* was the key to its success.

The authors approached their text with the studied premeditation of a general staff planning a campaign, but here the objective was to ensure that the readers of their narrative gave it the same credence as they would a journalistic account. No tactic for creating the illusion of verisimilitude was spared. The interplay of contemporary treaties, trade, and politics was charted and followed, giving detail, texture, and immediacy to Europe's domino-effect tumble into 'The Great War.' The narrative was patterned into a collage of reports, editorials, and telegrams that convincingly recreated the hurried, patchwork-quilt characteristics of late-breaking war news. Frequent intrusion of the 'fog of war' supported the verisimilitude of the format: battlefield outcomes were left uncertain; information was often maddeningly incomplete. The accompanying visuals were of the highest quality. And, perhaps most importantly, there was no partisan subtext: *The Great War of 189–* was not a disguised policy pamphlet. It was a sober projection, by internationally recognized experts, on how a 'Great War' might start, might be waged, and might be concluded.[24]

It also became both the guidebook and golden mean for later authors within the future-war subgenre, whether serious or sensationalistic in their style. *The Great War of 189–* taught them all (but Le Queux in particular) that a sense of narrative immediacy and veracity was best imparted by weaving the narrative tapestry from the actual fibers of a reader's reality. Therefore, in The *Great War of 189–*, known generals and politicians went through their expected paces in familiar and appropriate geographic locations. Military units were not fictional, but drawn from current lists. The same held true for the names and fleet dispositions of the ships. No attention to detail was spared, for the inclusion of these details was one of the most effective means of engendering a profound suspension of disbelief in readers. And the degree to which this had been achieved largely determined a reader's enthusiasm and appetite for the next installment of the serial.

It is significant, yet hardly surprising, that this methodical deployment of stylistic strategies for maximizing verisimilitude should first occur within the pages of *Black and White*. One of the first of a new wave of major illustrated weeklies, this periodical set its sights on attracting a decidedly 'high-brow' segment of the middle-class readership.[25] It featured regular reportage on high society, peerage, nobility, and all in a highly literate tone, and always with a decidedly pro-Imperialist slant. For instance, on January 9, 1892, the lead editorial story was of the ascendance of General Sir Frederick Roberts (commander in chief of Her Majesty's forces in India) to the Peerage and House of Lords. This is the same Lord Roberts who was to figure so prominently in the planning and promotion of the 1906 Le Queux–Northcliffe sensation, *The Invasion of 1910*.[26] Only one week earlier (January 2, 1892, No. 48, Volume III), the already much talked-about serial, *The Great War of 1892*, had begun, accompanied by an extensive editorial announcement, and flanked by contributions from well-respected authors, including a piece of short fiction by Arthur Conan Doyle. Only a few issues before, Robert Louis Stevenson's travelogue serial 'Three Cruises' (exclusive to *Black and White*) had come to an end, and, as Colomb's imaginary war raged on, the editor continued to offset it with *belles lettres*. In one issue, Emile Zola stymies an interviewer by declining to comment on the work of Ibsen, explaining '*C'est bien obscur;*' in another number, Henry James' short story 'The Real Thing' sees its first publication alongside a review of his 'The Lesson of the Master.'

This was the literary environment within which *The Great War of 189–* began: not a sensationalistic scandal sheet, but a highly respectable weekly magazine for highly respectable, well-educated readers. As a consequence, the story's narrative style is relatively restrained: there is none of the John Bull jingoism and 'Britannia Uber Alles' rhetoric that would later frequently betray the nationalistic origins of, and marketing influences upon, Le Queux's decidedly populist thrillers. In comparison to its sensationalistic offspring, *The Great War of 189–* is a serious, even somber, piece of fiction, consistent in its adherence to the format of *faux* reportage. In fact, the writers retain their own identities within the narrative reality, presenting themselves as witnesses to the events they report, or as special correspondents on the scene. By writing through their own voices, and (apparently) by affixing their bylines to the sections of the 'reports' that they have written, the authors invite a reader to infer a correspondingly higher degree of reliability in the speculative content of the reports, since the reputations of the individual contributors are now tied to their exact words and extrapolations.

However, for the editor of *Black and White*, authorial credibility was essential primarily because it suggested and supported the central selling point of the story: its prognosticative validity. As the editors pointed out in the preface to the collected book version of the text, the writers, in order to 'forecast the course of events preliminary and incidental to the Great War . . . have striven to derive material for their description of the conflict from the best sources, to conceive the most probable campaigns and acts of policy, and generally to give to their work the verisimilitude and actuality of real warfare.'[27] Indeed, on one occasion when fact dramatically coincided with fiction, the editor spared no ink in pointing this out to his readers and in reemphasizing the importance and appeal of his centerpiece serial:

> It is a striking proof of the accuracy of this forecast that within a few days after the publication of the first installment containing the fictitious account of the attempted assassination of Prince Ferdinand a plot was discovered at Sofia having this end in view. The persons of both the Prince and M. Stambouloff were to be attacked, and it is said

that fifty officers have been arrested. We must ask pardon of Prince Ferdinand for the liberty we have taken with him.[28]

The editors and owners of *Black and White* clearly saw themselves not merely as *reporters* of political events and opinions, but as *shapers* as well. In the collected book version of *The Great War of 189–*, the editors of *Black and White* give further evidence that their aspirations were at least as much advocational as educational; they include two lengthy interviews with Government members who had read and expressed their appreciation of the serial. These two individuals, Sir Charles Tupper, a High Commissioner for the Canadian Commonwealth, and Sir Charles Dilke, a well-known observer and official commentator of the day, were persons unlikely to tarnish their professional credentials by associating themselves with a serial unless they felt that the text itself was meritorious.

Interestingly, the authors were frequently more perspicacious prognosticators of international events than these two experts, particularly concerning how such a war might actually begin. In the text of *The Great War*, the conflict is ignited by the attempted assassination of Bulgarian Prince Ferdinand in the town of Samakoff, 40 miles north of Sofia. This flares into a conflict between various Balkan ethnic groups—including, notably, the Serbs. This, in turn, blossoms into a full-blown international firestorm— all very reminiscent of the commencement of war in 1914, which, of course, was touched off when a Serb nationalist assassinated Archduke Ferdinand in Sarajevo.

However, Sir Charles Dilke is largely dismissive of this conjectured flashpoint: '[I] do not believe that the next great war ... will arise from events in the Balkan Peninsula.... The most probable cause of a war, which I nevertheless think wholly improbable, will be a frontier incident between Germany and France...'[29] Although the latter region was the setting for the most protracted and terrible campaign of World War I, the conflagration on the Western Front was ultimately lit by the murderous spark that Gavrilo Prinçip struck in Sarajevo. Furthermore, the tangled alliances that ensnared the European powers and ensured their collective tumble into all-consuming war largely followed the domino-effect pathways that Colomb et al. propose as leading up to the full-scale hostilities predicted in *The Great War of 189–*. As the authors foresaw, the actual Great War would not commence as a premeditated clash of continental titans, but would begin as a brawl between tiny states that inexorably drew in the greater powers. In accord with their projections, Europe did not leap, but stumbled, into the abyss of the first truly mechanized war.

Dilke's other assessments of the serial range between open admiration and rejection of various predictions. However, his capstone statement is decidedly positive: 'With few exceptions, the consequences flow well and naturally, and in perfect logical sequence from the foundation in facts.'[30] This statement may be honest praise or it may be evidence of one politically influential hand carefully washing the other: it is impossible to determine this with certainty. However, it is clear that the text was accepted as appropriate and authoritative in the discursive domain of Dilke, Tupper, and the other ministers and military officials upon whose approbations it rose to international prominence.

Despite these aspects of superior insight, the strategic elements of *The Great War of 189–* are more remarkable for their prognosticative errors than accuracy. Ironically, no other future-war fiction demonstrates the utter failure of large-scale military projections as dramatically and completely as does *The Great War of 189–*. Paradoxically, this failure stems from the extraordinary care and forethought with which it was constructed. *The Great War* followed all the discernible rules of war, as well as all the projected strategies for Continental conflict. Colomb's imaginary conflict received the accolades it did, in part, because it confirmed the thinking of the major military minds of his era. This was the war that they all expected to fight: it illustrated the German offensive that von Moltke had planned, that Ludendorff would revise, and for which Joffre was preparing his Gallic ripostes. The great political virtue of Colomb's narrative—its expertly informed conservatism—proved to be its crippling prognosticative vice: the future would prove to be more radically different than any of these eminent leaders dared imagine—or admit. Lacking any proleptic anticipations of a grueling and costly stalemate, the 'Great War' is, instead, conceived of as a series of key, short-duration battles at crucial locations.

However, when *The Great War* begins to focus on the narrower, tactical elements of warfare, its predictive accuracy improves somewhat. On the one hand, the number of new technologies that the authors describe, and the immediate consequences they ascribe to them, are often reasonably accurate anticipations of what would materialize 20 years later in the actual 'Great War.' However, these insights are not synthesized into a larger strategic vision, for the authors do not consider how these individually small changes might amplify each other and thereby alter the nature of combat, all the way up to the most overarching, strategic levels of campaign planning, management, and assessment. For instance, the authors were aware of, and wrote authoritatively on, the improvements in artillery, the increased volume of fire and accuracy enabled by new 'magazine' rifles, the use of barbed wire, and even the application of searchlights for night combat. However, they did not foresee how these (and other) new technological variables would lead to the stalemated trenches of the Somme, the protracted struggle over the No-Man's Land between

*Figure 1  Portrayals of how massive fortifications could be 'simply swept away' by heavy artillery featured in Colomb et al.'s* The Great War of 189–. *This projection was conclusively proven during the World War I siege of Verdun (seen here in before and after pictures), where great forts were reduced to rubble-strewn moonscapes.*

them, and the soaring casualty lists generated by both. However, this failure to create a generally accurate overview of the ecology and conduct of 'the next Great War' did not prevent the authors from providing many Victorian readers in numerous countries with their first vicarious 'look' at many of the new, but largely untried, technologies (and terrors) of mechanized warfare—a discursive act with the political power to shape middle-class conceptions of warfare and statecraft.

Depictions of the increased potency of artillery collectively constitute one of the most noteworthy anticipatory aspects of Colomb's work. At Verdun, the German shelling had the following effect: 'The forts are now shapeless heaps of ruin, the cavaliers cut down, and the guns either dismounted or buried under the earth thrown out by the bursting shells.'[31] This is exactly

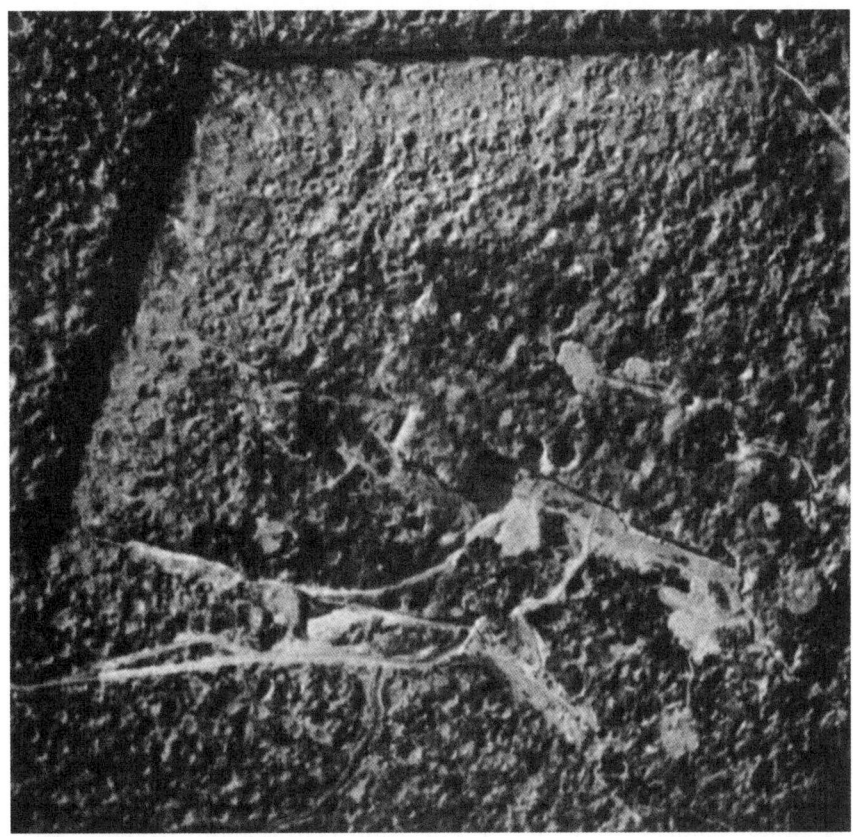

the fate suffered by Verdun in World War I, as shown by a famous set of comparative aerial photographs from before and after the sustained shelling. (See Figure 1: in the latter picture, the outlines of the ramparts are almost completely obliterated, and the entirety of the structure so cratered as to resemble a lunar landscape.) These results were consistent with the effect of the text's cordite shells, 'now first used in war,' which are also rained upon the defenses of Novo Giorgiewsk in such an unremitting deluge that they 'simply swept away the solid defences of the place.'[32] The authors' projection of the effects of saturation bombardments with high-explosive munitions, fired from increased range and with increased accuracy, is not restricted to its physical effects: they foresee the emotional impact upon observers as well, even hardened war correspondents. At the battle (more accurately, 'massacre') of Vaux Champagne, the fictional correspondent writes:

> [N]ow the gunners changed from shrapnel to common shell, with high explosive bursters, and we saw limbs and trunks of men thrown

high in the air above the dust clouds, whilst even the screams of the wounded reached us above the din. It was ghastly beyond the power of description, and I dropped back to look the other way . . .[33]

The authors also demonstrate their awareness of how more subtle differences in technology can completely change the outcome and experience of battle. One such difference is in the German shells, which employ smokeless powder as their propellant: 'It was plain that although the Russian artillery was more advantageously posted, it had the utmost difficulty in finding the range, and even the exact position of our guns, owing to the comparative smokelessness of their discharges.'[34] Prior to the introduction of sound-ranging equipment and tactical air support, the ability to *visually* locate enemy artillery was a prerequisite to interdicting or destroying it with counter-battery fire. In Colomb's day, artillery was still 'queen of the battlefield' (to quote the most prodigious artillery manufacturer of all time, Josef Stalin) and if it did not betray its location by the smoke of its discharges, it was then free to play havoc with an opponent's massed infantry formations. Consequently, the seemingly minor technological innovation of smokeless powder allows the German artillery to operate under a cloak of comparative invisibility; it can shell the Russian forces with impunity, and, not being rushed by the possibility of imminent discovery, may do so with maximum attention to accuracy.

One of the most frequently mentioned pieces of new technology is the 'magazine rifle,' which refers to breech-loading weapons which hold multiple, ready rounds in a compartment (the magazine) that feeds them into the firing chamber. Although the effects of such weapons would be well understood by the time World War I commenced, the full significance of these shoulder arms was not generally recognized in the early 1890s. Accordingly, the authors present their readers with a foretaste of how these rifles—in deadly combination with other new technologies—might alter the battlefield environment. Facing the Germans at Alexandrovo, the Russians decide to attack at night in an attempt to minimize their disadvantage in firepower (they are not equipped with 'magazine rifles'). However, because of reduced visibility, the Russians do not detect the Germans' innovative new anti-personnel barrier: barbed wire. Secure behind this barrier, and entrenched, the Germans use their new magazine rifles to thwart the impending Russian night assault:

> [T]wenty paces in front of us, their onward career was suddenly stopped short by some invisible barrier, which made them crowd upon each other like penned cattle, passive targets for the bullets of our repeating rifles . . . This barrier . . . was composed of fencing wire of several coils, strongly stretched and impaled, which had been run

along all the front of our entrenched lines as an additional measure of defence against the contingency of such an attack, and formed one of the most recent innovations . . . of the Germans . . . but, beyond saying that about 10,000 dead and wounded Russians lay in front of our extended lines, and nearly a third of that number of Germans . . . I will not disgust . . . readers with a realistic description of the ghastliness of the battlefield— the first of its kind, and one which has resulted from an endeavour to neutralise, or at least minimise, the destructive effects of the murderous magazine-rifle.[35]

Colomb and his experts also envision how this new type of rifle will encourage the evolution of guerrilla-like commando tactics: the Germans adopt a practice of infiltration and sniping that presages the standard operating procedures of the Dutch colonists in the Boer War:

[T]he Jager Battalion . . . courting every dip in the ground, had stealthily crept forward for some considerable distance in a hollow beyond our batteries, and lined the edge of a rye-field within about 3000 metres of the Russian guns, opened fire at this very long range . . . [W]e could see the Russian artillerists dropping beside their pieces, a fact which made us realise . . . that if field guns are to hold their ground . . . their range must still be further increased beyond that of the newest type of small bore rifle.[36]

This sniping is not only conducted at ranges that would have been considered impossible only fifteen years earlier, but the troops conducting it are 'invisible,'[37] once again owing to the smokeless propellant of the German cartridges.

These changes in personal weaponry also constitute the basis and impetus for the evolution of new tactics. Individual accuracy has increased and therefore, the need to maneuver infantry in large formations, thereby guaranteeing concentrated firepower, has diminished. The Germans once again seem to be the first to realize that this translates into increased flexibility and mobility, which in turn suggests that combat operations might be thought of in terms of fluid movement, not set-piece slugging matches. Anticipating tactics that would realize their full maturity in the blitzkriegs of World War II, 'reporter' Charles Lowe (who in actuality had served as a correspondent in Berlin) wrote of mass flanking and pincer movements for Victorian readers who were largely ignorant of, and probably unconvinced by, the military advisability of such maneuvers:

I had seen operations of this kind repeatedly carried out at the autumn maneuvers in Germany, but deemed them *Kriegspiel*[38] in the literal sense of the word—and not to be thought of or hazarded in real warfare. Yet here was a vivid proof that the Germans are terribly earnest . . . and that they apply in war what they practise in peace.[39]

Other, newer technologies are portrayed—air bombardment from a (French) dirigible,[40] machine guns, rapid firing 'Krupp' guns[41]—but since these were all still considered 'questionable' weapons in 1892, and were not yet routine issue to the armed forces of any nation, the authors do not explore their possibilities in any great detail, nor do they anticipate how a broad adoption of such technologies might radically change the combat environment. They do emphasize the importance of the telegraph and underscore how, in any action requiring rapid maneuvers, immediate relay of information was of paramount importance. Conversely, belligerents concerned with hampering their enemies are depicted severing rail links and cutting communications lines. The success of such operations is portrayed as being more decisive than superiority in men or matériel, revealing the rapidly emerging importance of battlefield intelligence—the keystone of superpower military practice.

Many of these 'cutting-edge' weapons may seem pedestrian to contemporary readers, but it is worth reemphasizing that many of these devices were still largely unknown to the general public. Similarly, their practical consequences were largely matters of conjecture at the time Colomb and his associates were writing. Consequently, it is significant that they also managed to anticipate some of the larger psychological and experiential alterations that would accompany these unproven technologies. For instance, describing the difficulty of reporting on the battle that he 'witnesses,' one correspondent writes:

> It can scarcely be expected that I . . . should be able to detail the incidents and development of a battle which extended along a line of more than six miles. . . . [In the past] a pretty complete description of a general kind could always be given by one pen . . . but now that science has robbed war of one of its most picturesque appendages (smoke), a modern battle by day is a most bewildering spectacle.[42]

Paradoxically, even though the literal 'fog of war' is diminishing, the figurative import of this phrase—murky, uncertain clashes with half-seen enemies—is emerging as the new dominant character of the battlefield. For the individual soldier, this has profound psychological consequences:

> [T]he German infantry were less disconcerted by these unseen terrors of modern war than were their Russian foes, who are most dour and indomitable devils when they can fight shoulder to shoulder and in the mass, but lose much of their morale . . . when each

man has to mainly rely upon his own intelligence . . . his own initiative, and his own isolated sources of courage. Indeed, we thought we could now and then detect traces of panic among the soldiers of the Czar; in one case . . . we distinctly saw an officer draw his revolver on some of his men who would rather have fled than fallen before a foe whom they could neither see nor feel.[43]

But finally, even at the level of psychology and tactics, Colomb's work is as remarkable for its failures in foresight as it is for its successes. Most notably, it lacks any anticipation of the consequences of the belt-fed machine gun, which already existed and was being issued in limited numbers. This weapon was to render obsolete the traditional cavalry tactics and massed infantry charges that Colomb presents as an integral part of the Franco-German battles in Belgium—battles that are anachronistically reminiscent of Napoleonic conflicts. Indeed, at the great battle of Machault, the 'special correspondent' realizes 'that I was at length about to see a real Napoleonic battle, the blow to pierce the centre or fail.'[44] This late and sudden change in Colomb's prevision of warfare-to-come would hardly warrant special mention, except that it is one of several tell-tale signs that *The Great War of 189–* was, in fact, subjected to some significant editorial restrategization as it ran its original course in *Black and White*. Indeed, there is substantial evidence that Colomb's hand may not have guided it from start to finish.

In the first place, not all of Colomb's sections—presented as letters from the front lines— turn out to be 'from him'. Colomb submits a disclaimer in the February 13 edition—written in keeping with the narrative conceit of having his voice emanate from 'within' the fictional world of the serial —that protests the use of his byline:

> [S]ome confusion has arisen as to the authorship of the letters from the Baltic and North Sea relating to the terrible war now raging. They are not mine. The author is my friend, Sir Rambleton Seaforth, . . . not a naval man, or he would have no doubt been able to give us fuller details, and a more correct view of the situation.[45]

Since none of the subsequent dispatches bear Colomb's byline, there is no way of knowing how much, if at all, he contributed to the serial after this point. However, from the tone of this disclaimer, the promptness with which he submitted it, and his subsequent lack of overt affiliation with the narrative, one can only assume that Colomb wished to change the conditions of his involvement with *The Great War of 189–*. Unfortunately, no extant records shed any additional light on why Colomb felt it necessary to make this appendation to the serial, nor why he disappears as an active contributor. However, Colomb's decision to distance himself from the naval episodes seems connected, in part, to his reservations regarding their professionalism. He specifically indicates that had *he* written them, these sections would have provided 'a more correct view of the situation.' If Colomb's chapters were indeed ghostwritten by another collaborator, or a hack, then such a disclaimer might be his attempt to remove himself from direct accountability, which in turn suggests that, at this juncture, the serial lacked the thorough expert review, and therefore the prognosticative values, claimed by the editor. Colomb's disclaimer also suggests the degree of social exposure and influence he felt this text might have. Furthermore, it implies that he at least suspected (and possibly knew) that his peers—the senior strategists of the Empire—would be reading this narrative with interest.

There is further evidence of editorial redirection in *The Great War of 189–*. After the midpoint of the book, there is only one direct attribution to a correspondent. This contrasts with the original narratological pattern established, in which every entry, letter, and report was connected to the byline of one of the 'correspondents.' Towards the end of the serial, there is also growing inconsistency both in tone and national sympathies. The originally Teutophilic narrative veers decidedly in a new direction when an entry from a Francophilic 'American correspondent,' whose language is incongruently lush and hyperbolic, depicts Germans using tactics and combat procedures that conflict with all earlier portrayals. In the final battle of the war, the one that shatters the Kaiser's offensive in France, the German lines

> moved forward with even more than the precision of a parade; in little squares, but shoulder to shoulder, with all the rigidity of a birthday review. I could even see the officers halting and actually correcting the alignment. Needless to say, these living targets were riddled through and through in the very moment of their pedantic folly. In the rear, too, came lines of men, gallantly moving forward to beat of drum, with that extraordinary, high-stepping pace which excites the ridicule of the Transatlantic visitor in Berlin. How the veterans of our Civil War would have scoffed at this slave-driver's discipline![46]

This scene is not only wildly improbable, but in direct contradiction with the earlier established tactical *modus operandi* of the German infantry. The heretofore mobile, versatile, and above all modern, German army suddenly begins to goose-step to the front in packed masses, prepackaged by their officers into easy-to-hit bunches. This inconsistency is further evidence of the uncertain—and possibly very compromised—editorial pedigree of this narrative. The same effusive American correspondent concludes his description of the final, victorious French advance using rhetoric more appropriate to grand opera than journalism: 'And then, whilst the setting sun, pouring his red rays athwart the opposing hosts and striking radiance from the golden eagles of the tricolours, sank slowly on that awful Aceldama, the French army moved onward to its triumph.'[47]

This peremptory wrap-up may suggest editorial preemption of the series in response to either flagging reader interest or flagging confidence on the part of the editors themselves. The onrushing German armies are defeated in an improbably decisive, single battle, fought with tactics and strategies that Napoleon might have employed. The narrative makes no attempt to explain how the superior technologies and tactics of the Germans were counteracted, nor why they suddenly abandoned these successful innovations in their last and most crucial battle. This rather lackluster conclusion apparently did not diminish Colomb's value to the editors or readers of *Black and White:* only a few weeks after the serial ended, Colomb's 'Future Naval Warfare' (appearing in the June number of the *United Service Magazine*) was reviewed at length by the editor of *Black and White*, and was warmly recommended over a rival article. Nor did *The Great War*'s many weaknesses undercut the appeal or influence of future-war fiction: on the contrary, the narrative suffused the genre with increased respectability, credibility, and, above all, profitability. The tales grew longer, more frequent, and more eagerly sought after. However, the sudden surge of popularity led to decreased quality: the premises became more outlandish, the prose more florid, the sensational elements more lurid. And the high priest of this new breed of future-war fiction was William Le Queux: a master at exploiting, and then expanding, all these excesses.

*Chapter 2*

# Opportunistic Anticipations and Accidental Insights: William Le Queux's Exploitation of Edwardian Invasion Anxieties

William Le Queux's nationalistic and sensationalist excesses marked all of his (often best-selling) future-war fabrications, but *The Invasion of 1910* (1906) stands head and shoulders above the rest, both in terms of sales and melodramatic alarmism. It also defines the high-water mark of the Victorian and Edwardian discursive tendency to alloy hysterical fears of invasion with anticipations of social, political, and military change.

The story behind *The Invasion of 1910* is, in many ways, more interesting—and revealing of the influence of future-war fiction—than is the narrative itself. Le Queux's association with the influential editor and owner of the *Daily Mail*, the paper that serialized *The Invasion of 1910*, dates from the early 1890s, when they began their profitable collaboration in the fabulation of titillating near-future war fictions. In the intervening years, editor-owner Alfred Harmsworth had been as busy amassing a publishing empire as Le Queux had been in cranking out lurid yarns of foreign invasion and despoliation. By 1906, Harmsworth (now Lord Northcliffe) had been owner of the *Daily Mail* for almost ten years, and had also acquired *The Times*. Northcliffe's ambitions were not restricted to the publishing and business spheres; his interest in attaining both political influence and elected office is a matter of record. In 1895, Harmsworth stood as Portsmouth's Unionist candidate for the House of Commons. Harmsworth, however, eschewed basing his electoral efforts solely on the issues: he purchased Portsmouth's very respectable leading paper, the *Evening Mail*, and put William Laird Clowes at its editorial helm. Clowes was the naval correspondent for *The Times* and a renowned and respected historian of the Royal Navy. He was also a crony of a discursive circle responsible for a great deal of military speculation: Clowes had written, along with General Sir William Francis, *The Great Naval War in 1887*, and had also worked on the *Naval Annual: 1892*, compiling the Naval Bibliography, which featured articles by both Colomb and Arnold-Forster. One of Laird Clowes' first duties at Portsmouth's *Evening Mail* was to collaborate with one of Harmsworth's young reporters, Beckles Willson, in concocting a story 'designed to play on local fears and local patriotism' in which 'plot mattered less than authenticity of atmosphere. Readers were to be impressed above all by its scientific authority . . .'[1] The dramatic center of the serial was a Franco-Russian invasion of Portsmouth. Harmsworth's reasoning was that by highlighting the city's outdated and insufficient defenses, the Liberals' responsibility for their deterioration, the town's vulnerability to invasion, and the inevitable loss of work and unspeakable atrocities that would follow, he could terrify the dockworkers into voting Unionist. In order to bring the tale home to the Portsmouth readership, Harmsworth instructed Willson to go around the town and get names (and where practicable, descriptions) of all the prominent citizens, who were then placed as characters within the tragic yarn. Harmsworth's strategies were in the very best style of professional scaremongering, but the dockworkers were unmoved and Harmsworth's dreams of holding an elected office were dashed.

However, this anecdote not only illustrates Northcliffe's political ambition, but also reveals the tactics he employed in pursuit of this objective. His willingness to orchestrate a text specifically designed to influence key voters through vicarious fear and intimidation shows him to be fully committed to acquiring and exerting political influence not merely through texts, but specifically through the medium of fiction. By the time Harmsworth was made Lord Northcliffe, his *Daily Mail* had revolutionized every aspect of Britain's popular journalism and periodicals business. He was also unparalleled in the amount and openness of political influence he exercised through his publications, including persistent clarion calls for greater awareness of, and response to, the 'German threat.' The premises for his international concerns were often dubious, the accompanying rhetoric inflammatory and dramatic, and attention to evidence inconsistent—all sad indicators of his opinion of the intelligence and sophistication of his readers.

However, the saddest part of the story may be that, judging from the unprecedented popularity of Le Queux's most ambitious project—*The Invasion of 1910*—Northcliffe's assessment of his readership was all too accurate. He had been no less astute in perceiving the political and pecuniary opportunities latent in Le Queux's suggestion for an anti-German invasion yarn designed to threaten and thrill *Daily Mail* readers. Northcliffe realized that the time had come to capitalize on the surging tide of Teutophobia that was rising in direct proportion to Germany's increasing commitment to constructing a blue-water fleet. This maritime build-up was seen as a potential colonial challenge, or even as a homeland invasion threat against the British Empire. As if to underscore this, in 1898 the weapon manufacturer Krupp instituted the *Flottenverein* Navy League. After only two years of existence, the League had a membership of 600,000, had sponsored more than 3,000 lectures, and had distributed more than 7 million pamphlets on naval (and consequently, international) policy. As the century turned, so did relations between Britain and Germany—for the worse. Accordingly, the diverse ranks of future-war authors began to turn their prognosticative lenses upon this developing situation: the time had come for an expert assessment of the probable resolution of these rising tensions.

However, the 'eminent experts' (such as Arnold-Forster and Colomb) were not destined to have the greatest impact on this new body of discourse. Rather, that honor fell to the battering-ram blow that was delivered to the national consciousness by chief scaremonger William Le Queux. His *The Invasion of 1910* had its origins in perhaps the most ludicrous of Le Queux's many ceaselessly bubbling alembics of alarmism: his conviction, either real or feigned, that England was literally crawling with German spies.

In his article 'How I Write my Sensational Novels,' Le Queux maintained that, in addition to writing a 'sensational story' in such a way that 'the reader once commencing it cannot lay it down until the last word is reached,' it was also essential for an author of such fictions to have a thorough understanding of the world's many police and intelligence services.[2] Le Queux's own claim to such credentials was extraordinary both in its expansiveness and implied level of intimacy: 'I count among my friends all the chiefs and many of the agents of the secret police of Italy, France, Russia, and Austria.'

The dubious plausibility of such a claim did not deter Le Queux from making assertions and accusations that largely depended upon its veracity. This was certainly the case when Le Queux claimed that he had received (otherwise unsubstantiated) insider information that the Kaiser had created a special 'Spy Bureau,' which was, according to Le Queux's biographer N. St. Barbe Sladen, 'a vast network of German espionage in the United Kingdom.'[3] When Le Queux tried to interest newspapers around Great Britain in articles revealing the existence of this immense 'fifth column,' he received a flurry of rejections that all more or less followed the tenor of the example provided by his biographer:

> The Editor of one of the most powerful newspapers wrote:
> My Dear Le Queux,
> We cannot publish this! Spies exist only in your imagination. We don't want to alarm the public.[4]

But Le Queux did want to alarm the public, and he was determined to gather support for his efforts. He started by contacting 'Field-Marshal Earl

Roberts of Kandahar, who paid great attention to the matter and said that he was also suspicious. Le Queux introduced the late Lord Northcliffe to Lord Roberts and the three individuals discussed the peril for over an hour.'[5] The significance of this introduction cannot be overstated: Roberts was at the time arguably the Empire's most influential military figure; Northcliffe was unquestionably its most powerful press and news publisher. Therefore, even before Le Queux began to spin his yarn, he started spinning a web of interconnected political elites to support it. After the meeting between Roberts and Northcliffe, the web continued to expand: Le Queux contacted and effectively recruited Colonel Lockwood, MP (subsequently Lord Lambourne), Rear-Admiral Prince Louis of Battenberg (later the Marquis of Milford Haven), and Lord Admiral Charles Beresford (who had assisted Northcliffe with his earlier Portsmouth invasion yarn). However, when even this august assembly was unable to compel Parliament to take the 'threat' of German infiltration seriously, Roberts urged Le Queux to 'write a work of fiction, a description of what would happen if a great war came and we were invaded . . .'[6] When Le Queux pointed out his lack of military expertise, Roberts offered to 'prepare the scheme of attack and defence, and give you hints, if you will write the book.'[7] Le Queux agreed and proposed the project to Northcliffe, who gave his trusted scaremonger

> an open commission . . . to write, regardless of expense, a forecast of *The Invasion* for *The Daily Mail*. . . . 'I know your pocket has suffered very much, Quex', this was Northcliffe's invariable nickname for Le Queux, 'write a good stirring forecast. Tell Lord Roberts we will both try and wake up the country to a sense of its peril.'[8]

'A good stirring forecast,' attempting to 'wake up the country' are lofty objectives that can, ultimately, be resolved into the two much more mercenary-sounding motivations that actually gave birth to *The Invasion of 1910*: profit margins and political influence. The German spy scare did not start with Le Queux, but in Parliament itself, and it endured right up until 1910: Le Queux simply took advantage of it, and in so doing, amplified a simmering fear into roiling hysteria. Criticisms of this spy scare were numerous and often quite barbed. Charles Lowe, one of the 'correspondents' of *The Great War of 189–*, declaimed 'the baneful industry' of the spy-obsessed anti-German future-war stories as being not merely irresponsible but dangerous.[9] Much of the other ridicule generated by *The Invasion of 1910* (and its sensationalistic kin) was in response to the strategic implausibilities of the scenario and its lurid prose. However, the narrative's melodramatic military inanities did not arise from a lack of promised advice by military experts, but were the byproducts of editorial fiat.

By all accounts, Le Queux began his 'Invasion' research in earnest. Although warned by some strategists that 'the mass of technical detail was far too great to digest and present in an intelligible manner to the public,'[10] he consulted not only with Field-Marshal Roberts, but with Colonel Cyril Field, RMLI, a Major Matson, and H. W. Wilson (a 'well-known naval expert').[11] Le Queux did not restrict his homework to note-taking and reading; he did field work as well. In his 'Introduction,' Le Queux claims that:

> Before putting pen to paper it was necessary to reconnoitre carefully the whole of England from the Thames to the Tyne. This I did by means of a motor car, travelling 10,000 miles on all kinds of roads, and making a tour extending over four months. Each town, all the points of vantage, military positions, all the available landing-places on the coast, all railway connections, and telephone and telegraph communications, were carefully noted . . . With the assistance of certain well-known military experts, the battlefields were carefully gone over and the positions marked upon the Ordnance map.[12]

Although there is little to verify Le Queux's claims of painstaking research (other than his £3,000 bill for expenses, paid by Northcliffe), his text includes maps and descriptions that went largely unchallenged. Moreover, the text was recommended by a personal letter from Earl Roberts, adapted from his speech before the House of Lords, and reproduced as the novelization's frontispiece.[13] However, as editor and press chronicler Bernard Falk reveals, when Le Queux brought the outline of the invasion plan before Northcliffe,

> the great newspaperman caustically remarked that from a military point of view it might be all right, but from a circulation point of view it was all wrong. 'Bobs' or no 'Bobs',[14] the Germans must pass through towns of size, not keep to remote one-eyed country villages, where there was no possibility of large *Daily Mail* sales. That, thus transformed to suit his argument, the invaders' route became a little zigzag and a bit of a chase round the mulberry bush, and not at all what the astute Von Moltke would have planned, did not unduly strain the credulity of the bulk of the *Daily Mail* readers, nor prevent the serial from being an enormous success. Lord Northcliffe was justified in his objections, and the voluble protests of doddering generals in Pall Mall clubs, 'By Gad, sir! The thing's preposterous', was so much wasted splutter.[15]

Northcliffe's military revisions in place, *The Invasion of 1910* made its first appearance in the *Daily Mail* of March 20, 1906, and concluded on July 4 of that same year. The force of economically-driven popular journalism did not merely displace, but ran roughshod over, reasonable military speculation. In so doing, this brand of journalism revealed itself to be a powerful and overt political force by giving shape—and thereby, credibility—to one vision of the future over others.

This exemplar of Northcliffe's brand of political pressure—advocacy by maximum circulation—had immediate and profound effects. Within 24 hours, the Prime Minister, communicating through Sir Henry Campbell-Bannerman, denounced Le Queux as a scaremonger—even though he had only read advertisements for the story, rather than the story itself. He also declared that such stories were just so much alarmist bombast, 'calculated to inflame public opinion abroad and alarm the more ignorant public at home.'[16] A day later, the Prime Minister responded to Le Queux's request for a more detailed critique in an unusually congenial, even conciliatory, fashion:

> Sir Henry sent Le Queux a note in his own handwriting, by special messenger and marked Strictly Private. In this letter the Prime Minister apologised for the words which he had used. He meant to say 'the more ignorant section of the public at home' and hoped that Le Queux would not, in the exigencies of politics, take any word of his as being personally offensive. He concluded by asking Le Queux to call at Downing Street, when convenient, as he desired to make a full explanation![17]

Since St. Barbe Sladen's recounting of this exchange was never challenged, it is not rash to assume that it is essentially accurate, and that therefore, Le Queux's narrative had an immediate and profound political impact at the very highest level of the Empire's government.

For every critical sneer directed at Le Queux's pot-boiler, there were hundreds of hands extended in warm congratulations and appreciation. The Savage Club, the Devonshire Club, Boodle's, and the Reform Club, all either toasted or fêted him. St. Barbe Sladen lists the laudatory letters received from (among others)

> the Duke of Northumberland, the Duke of Argyll, the Duke of Fife, the Earl of Derby, the Earl of Rosebery, the Earl of Wemyss, Viscount Milner, Viscount Hardinge, Lord Brassey, Lord Tweedmouth, Field-Marshal Sir George White, VC, distinguished generals and members of parliament, many of who became his supporters and personal friends. Shortly afterwards a meeting to consider national defence was convened by the London Chamber of Commerce and the Lord Mayor presided at the Mansion House. Lord Roberts made a vigorous

speech... Lord Brassey proposed a vote of thanks... and afterwards, when Lord Roberts introduced Le Queux to him, he congratulated Le Queux on *The Invasion*.[18]

Le Queux's (and by proxy, Northcliffe's) web of political influence was now so large as to cover and conjoin some of the most powerful Conservatives in the Empire. Much to their hawkish approval, Le Queux had brought Great Britain's 'imminent peril' to the attention of the nation, and had galvanized a great deal of right-wing support for further inquiry into the German 'fifth column' or 'secret army' that was reportedly gathering within England. That this spy-scare was, in fact, an almost laughable example of unwarranted nationalistic and ethnic paranoia run amok is unimportant: what is important is how this incident illustrates the power of a novel—and an author—to coalesce inchoate and nascent fears into a burning political debate with serious domestic and foreign consequences.

Ironically, there is some suggestion that Le Queux's narrative may have been more effective at promoting eventual warfare with Germany than it was at providing a timely, preventive warning against it. Translated into 27 different languages, with global sales amounting to approximately a million copies, Le Queux's portrayal of Britain's Teutophobia left a widespread and enduring impression of the deteriorating state of Anglo-German relations and the lack of trust underlying them. Not surprisingly, Le Queux's text made its strongest foreign impression in Germany, where periodicals began publishing a number of angry responses to *The Invasion of 1910*. Many of them were vengeful portrayals of Prussia's struggles with the forces of a selfish and/or oppressive British Empire. Whether in response to a sneak naval attack—depicted in *Hamburg und Bremen in Gefahr* (1906)—or as a campaign of retribution for international insults and obstructionism—as in *Mit deutschen Waffen uber Paris nach London* (1906)—these fictive return salvoes echoed, and tragically amplified, the rumbles of hostility and distrust that were growing between the two nations.

Attempts to quell this rising tide of acrimony included a meeting of the influential Anglo-German Friendship Committee. The German members were welcomed by King Edward VII to a banquet given by the Lord Mayor of London, where they heard a young Winston Churchill decry 'the attempts of alarmist journalists to set up strife between the nations.' The *Annual Register* described the visit as 'an important step... towards dissipating the fears of an eventual Anglo-German conflict, which was fostered, both in Germany and Great Britain, by a section of the "patriotic press".'[19]

As history has recorded, these efforts at diplomatic rapprochement were futile. The role played by Teutophobic future-war fictions in paving the road to war in 1914 is impossible to estimate, let alone concretely establish. However, there is ample evidence that the political elites of the day—politicians, military officers, businessmen, publishers—assumed (and feared) that these tales exerted considerable influence. Whether or not their assumptions were accurate is immaterial: these same elites inevitably created the textual influence they assumed to exist by believing in it and acting accordingly. In actualizing their own expectations, they exemplified the now aphoristic contention that 'perception *is* reality.'

*****

Le Queux's talents as a wordsmith and self-promoter may have been noteworthy, but he certainly could not claim an equal measure of aptitude in military matters. Le Queux is neither methodical nor professional in his presentation of new military technologies, although various devices did get their popular debut by being featured on the dramatic stage of his narrative. These include wireless communications, motorized infantry and armored cars, extensive use of 'quick-firing' and machine guns, gas attacks, incendiary rounds, and air-burst artillery.

However, even if we ignore the preposterous invasion scheme (since it originated not with Le Queux, but with Northcliffe), we still have plentiful evidence of Le Queux's indifferent abilities as a military writer and prognosticator. For instance, at several points Le Queux uses the phrase 'the rattle of musketry' when referring to the sound of small arms fire. This usage is either perversely anachronistic or indicative of profound military ignorance. The sounds and even the 'pace' of the reports generated by the 'magazine' rifles of the early twentieth century were thoroughly unlike that of either individual or collective musket fire. Furthermore, none of the combatants had been using muskets for some time. By 1906, the German army was already equipped with the five-round, 7.92 millimeter Mauser bolt-action rifle that was to endure as their standard infantry weapon in both World Wars. The British army had adopted the largely analogous Enfield .303 bolt-action rifle. Even among the country folk of England (the narrative's third and most unlikely source of firearms), the majority of the weapons were single- or double-barreled breech-loading shotguns—fowling pieces used for both sport and killing vermin and crop-damaging animals. Consequently, there was no longer any 'musketry' to 'rattle' as Le Queux suggests. Even if he simply meant to evoke a stock expression from an earlier era of romanticized combat writing, he reveals either his absolute ignorance regarding the actual sounds that he is purporting to describe, or his indifference to both technological and experiential accuracy.

Le Queux displays another remarkable failure in military common sense by blaming the government for (among other things) failing to encourage 'the establishment of rifle clubs to teach every young man how to defend his home . . .'[20] Although Le Queux's German invaders would have found a better-armed and firearm-familiarized populace marginally more troublesome, the majority of Le Queux's narrative serves to illustrate the essential helplessness of the amateur marksman before the organized onslaught of a professional army equipped with the latest military technology. This kind of contradiction and gross inconsistency is widespread in the text. For example, early in the story, a daring German naval assault surprises and destroys (or disables) key elements of the British fleet that are lying at anchor in the Firth of Forth. The portrayal of this action begins with a lethal game of hide-and-seek and uncertain identity played between the advance elements of the German task force and the British picket ships. From these first probes, all the way through to the conclusion of the battle, Le Queux never mentions wireless communications: all maritime signals are sent by signal lamps and all land dispatches are relayed by (compromised) telegraph. Because of the poor coordination and exchange between these communication systems, the first reports of the German attack seem inconsistent, and an uncertain Admiralty wastes critical time awaiting a clearer account. However, much later in the text, when the main body of the British fleet is returning to England, Le Queux makes extensive mention of wireless communications.

This profound inconsistency regarding the availability of wireless communications technology is significant for two reasons. First, it suggests that Le Queux did not do as much technical homework as he might have for his first several chapters. In 1906, wireless sets were already available: they had been a decisive (if under-reported) feature of the naval contests of the 1904 Russo-Japanese war, and had been aggressively researched, developed, and adopted by the Royal Navy, which, in 1905, could already boast a thirty-word-per-minute transmission rate. Therefore, wireless sets would have almost certainly been present with the British pickets in Le Queux's hypothetical battle of the Firth of Forth, and their use would have been likely to change the outcome of that action, thereby altering the course of war. By neglecting to account for this technology at such a crucial point in his text, Le Queux unintentionally demonstrates his ignorance of the latest naval technologies and equipment. In doing so, he invalidates his own speculative portrayal of the battle and its consequences.

Second, the later appearance (and even highlighting) of the relatively new innovation of wireless communications suggests that someone pointed out his earlier blunder and that, untroubled by the need for consistency, he simply integrates this new information into his subsequent chapters.[21]

In light of Le Queux's sloppiness, it may seem strange to suggest that many of his depictions of military technology could have been both informative and influential. However, there are two skills with which Le Queux was generously blessed: he was a fast learner and an accomplished descriptive writer of entirely imaginary events. It is, for instance, doubtful that Le Queux ever personally witnessed the effects of an air-bursting artillery shell; indeed, his failure even to mention this relatively new technology in the first part of his narrative suggests that he was unaware such a munition existed. However, about a third of the way through the novel, these shells—and their effects—begin to appear, and later, receive increasingly detailed attention. What is most remarkable about these descriptive passages is how they transform a technological concept—a shell that explodes overhead due to the ignition of a proximity fuse—into an event that a lay reader can understand and vicariously appreciate. The reader is given the visceral, tangible consequences of such a weapon without being tasked to understand the science underlying its operation. By using this rhetorical strategy, Le Queux succeeds at presenting new technologies in three specific areas of military applications: artillery, mobility, and psychology.

The first of these—artillery—offers the most textually concrete evidence of this (probably unintentional) achievement. Although Le Queux never uses the terms 'air-burst' or 'proximity fuse,' it is clear that this is precisely what he is describing through the observations of Mr. Alexander, the mayor of Maldon: '[L]ittle faint puffs and rings of grey smoke were just visible in its vicinity every now and again, sometimes high up in the air, at others among the trees at its base. They were exploding shells . . .'[22] The pattern of these shells—a mixture of high- and low-bursting projectiles—can only reasonably be explained by an anti-personnel barrage utilizing a mixture of ground-burst and air-burst munitions, the latter equipped with proximity fuses set to explode above the ground and rain their shrapnel down upon troops without substantial overhead cover. While this tactic was well enough known in World War I, and became standard operating procedure in World War II, it is the kind of information that, in 1906, Le Queux might not have discovered without actually investigating the finer points of what in his day would have been 'cutting-edge' artillery technology and application.

As the narrative progresses, Le Queux increasingly appreciates the tactical importance (or maybe, simply the narrative shock value) of air-bursting artillery shells. In a much more definitive scene from the middle of the text,

> four dazzling flashes opened in the air overhead, and shrapnel bullets rattled on earth, walls, and roofs, with sound as of handfuls of pebbles thrown on a marble pavement. But the hardness with which they struck was beyond anything in my experience.[23]

This scene also illustrates Le Queux's ability to translate technology into vicarious narrative experience. The sight ('dazzling flashes') and sound ('bullets rattled . . . [like] pebbles thrown on a marble pavement') of his description of air-bursting shells are energetic and accessible to any reader. The phrasing also makes a special claim upon a reader's attention and asks to be committed to long-term memory, since the narrator asserts that the force of the impacts is 'beyond anything in my experience.' This, therefore, represents a new level of lethality to readers, and to the extent that they accept this depiction, it also influences their perception of the sensory realities and personal consequences of modern warfare.

It is tempting to imagine that a military officer familiar with munitions confronted Le Queux not just on his initial failure to portray air-bursting shells, but on his other oversights regarding the many lethal options that were the modern artilleryman's stock-in-trade. Starting shortly after page 100 of the text, Le Queux's acumen regarding artillery seems to undergo a dramatic increase. In addition to an uncharacteristically speculative portrayal of (as yet unproven) gas warfare shells— 'The great shells . . . on bursting . . . filled the air with poisonous fumes . . .'[24]—Le Queux introduces the distant ancestor of napalm, the 'petrol bomb.' In one scene of shelling, rows of buildings become sheets of flame, 'the frightful result of those awful petrol bombs. Fire and destruction had been broadcast everywhere.'[25] Soon after, in the assault upon Poole, where civilians and Volunteer troops resist the German landing, the petrol shell (which Britain's 'unprogressive Government had so frequently refused to entertain'[26]) shows its effectiveness against row houses:

> In a flash three were well alight, and even while I watched the whole block . . . was furiously ablaze, the petrol spreading fire and destruction on every hand. . . . Surely there is no more deadly engine in modern warfare than the terrible petrol bomb. . . . In all directions the houses began to flare and burn.[27]

Upon witnessing this weapon doing its ghastly work, Le Queux's fictional reporter comments, 'In those never-to-be forgotten moments we realised for the first time what the awful horror of War really meant.'[28] This 'rumored' new munition would, of course, soon be confirmed as one of the most notorious and 'infernal' facts of twentieth-century weaponry, as was proven by the conflagrations that consumed Dresden, Tokyo, Vietnamese villages, and countless other locales.

The most predictable hindsight criticisms of Le Queux's portrayal of a German invasion—excluding its overall strategic absurdity—concern his failure to anticipate the war of attrition and the immense casualties that would stun and horrify the world only eight years later. I. F. Clarke is right to characterize the losses suffered by Le Queux's invading Germans as 'trifling;' as they prepare to initiate the sack of London (their final geographical objective) the Kaiser's forces have suffered 50,000 casualties out of an initial invasion force of 250,000. While this magnitude of carnage is, by any measure, terrible, it is minuscule in comparison with the horrific losses of World War I trench warfare. The comparatively low casualties suffered by Le Queux's invaders are even more remarkable when one considers that the German forces have staged a sea-borne landing into the very heart of a major European adversary. As Gallipoli, Salerno, and Normandy would prove, the loss of life associated with difficult and vulnerable amphibious operations often far exceeds that of comparable land battles. However, before rashly dismissing all of Le Queux's imaginings as flawed, the operational nature of the invasion campaign should be considered *exclusive* of its fundamental strategic flaws.

In attempting to explain why the Germans might invade England at all, Le Queux shows some small measure of embarrassed common sense when he tries to diminish the improbability of the offensive by asserting that 'the whole scheme of operations ... was more of the nature of a raid than a prolonged "siege".'[29] With only a quarter of a million men, the Germans could hardly have had anything else in mind; even if such a small force had somehow managed to conquer a country of tens of millions, it would have been absolutely unable to control the land or secure provisions from it. In essence, then, Le Queux's 'invasion' is a form of channel-hopping blitzkrieg; a surgical strike designed to decapitate Britain's government and cripple the will of its people with a single bold stroke. Accordingly, during the sack of London, readers learn that the Kaiser makes the recall of his invading forces contingent upon the remittance of a crippling indemnity (such as Germany was later required to pay under the terms of the actual Versailles Treaty).

Clearly, the narrative's strategic reasoning remains preposterous. However, once this is accepted, a reapproach to Le Queux's text reveals that—mostly by common sense and the process of elimination—he arrives at a number of telling anticipations regarding warfare's operational evolution toward high mobility and dispersed 'battle groups,' and away from set-piece battles and fortified lines.

Le Queux's Germans understand that it is not in their best interest to engage their enemy in a classic 'field battle:' indeed, such a contest could only end in disaster for them. On foreign soil and without hope of significant resupply or replacements, even a moderately expensive major victory would also portend imminent final defeat. The Germans must, therefore, defeat their adversary 'in detail,' by engaging and destroying the isolated army units or pockets of local resistance before these can be amassed and organized into an efficient, coordinated fighting force. This places a high premium on mobility and makes any assaults on fixed positions (always lengthy, costly affairs) highly undesirable. This is, in fact, the strategic raison d'être of the *blitzkrieg*, or 'lightning war,' used by the massively outnumbered Wehrmacht to very nearly overrun the Soviet Union 35 years after Le Queux's *Invasion* appeared.

Thus, Le Queux's portrayal of the Battle of Purleigh[30] does not anticipate the front lines in France, does not present static defenses and human wave assaults and a No-Man's Land of barbed wire. Indeed, why should it? At Purleigh, both sides have few men, much terrain to cover, and little time to prepare: the only way an entrenchment scenario could evolve would be for the Germans to inexplicably sit in bivouac for a week or more, dig trenches, wait for more English units to arrive, and then begin an incessant artillery duel. What occurs instead is a running battle much more reminiscent of the kind of World War I operations that were conducted in the Middle Eastern and Italian theaters, where the logistical realities dictated a more fluid battlefield. At Purleigh, the Germans do not advance *en masse*, nor do they move directly toward their objective; instead, they move forward in spurts, enveloping, flanking, covering each other and then advancing in sequence. This style of field operations is not only enabled, but inspired and determined, by the technological improvements in mobility and massed firepower that they possess. Their adversaries look in vain for a central thrust, a commitment of the German 'van' (the leading edge of the main attack force), but, unable to adapt in time to a style of field operations that defy conventional wisdom and, therefore, prediction, the British are ultimately driven from the field.

The invaders fare less well at the Battle of Royston, where the English are finally able to amass some of their own forces. For the first time, the Germans take losses 'by the thousands.' The same occurs at the Battle of Sheffield, and is implied at the Battles of Manchester and Birmingham, although these last two engagements are mentioned only in passing. The description of these combats—and particularly, of the rapidity with which the casualties mount—anticipates the horrific killing power of the 'new' weapons demonstrated at the Somme in 1914. For some critics, the fact that these most pitched of Le Queux's battles last only a few days indicates his inability to foresee the defining reality of warfare in World War I: an entrenched stalemate that would go on week after week, and month after month. However, Le Queux's failure to portray prolonged trench warfare does not represent a total failure in his prevision. Rather, this criticism of Le Queux may reflect a common but possibly ill-advised contemporary assumption that the Western Front combat environment of World War I constitutes the seminal or ur-reality of that conflict. The prevalence of this opinion may stem, in part, from its ubiquitous and uncritical inclusion in the memoirs of the military elites of all the major Western Front combatants. Foch, Joffre, Churchill and many others unfold their tales of the four-year tragedy in France with similar degrees of detail and restrained horror, regardless of the other ways in which their narratives might differ. By inspiring a profusion of such accounts, by producing untold terrors in unprecedented volume, and by being the decisive theater of the war, the Western Front thus became not merely an *aspect* of the war: it became symbolic of the war in its *entirety*. Just as the image of the mushroom cloud would later come to obliterate other possible signifiers of Cold War Armageddon, the image of a barren No-Man's Land, scarred by trenchworks and pocked by craters, quickly erased almost all rival images of World War I. However, much evidence suggests that the sustained and stalemated trench warfare that created this gruesome iconography was an anomalous artifact of specific conditions that existed only at that particular time and place.

The Western Front campaign of World War I was arguably the most anticipated and prepared-for conflict of the modern epoch. It was conceived and waged according to the major resources of two massive, conventionally well-prepared, Continental alliances. Furthermore, it was conducted in a region that was readily accessible by direct rail-link to the major supply centers of both sides, thereby allowing a sustained conflict. The prior concentration of forces in primary strategic positions, in addition to the ability to rapidly shift large masses of men and matériel both from front to rear and from flank to flank, meant that the dramatic, unchecked breakthroughs of earlier conflicts were difficult to achieve, particularly once the initial impetus of an offensive began to diminish. The technologies that might have broken this deadlock existed, but were either too immature, too sparsely available, or too reflexively associated with other uses to decisively disrupt the operational *rigor mortis* that settled in all along No-Man's Land. Examples of these potentially decisive technologies abound: motorized units existed, but were primarily associated with rapid shipment of supplies or translocation of artillery (or other heavy support equipment) and were never seriously considered for enhancing tactical mobility at the front. Armored fighting vehicles were conceived of early in the war, but could not be developed or procured fast enough to impel a radical shift in operational thinking. Similarly, by the time combat aircraft completed their evolution from initially fragile contraptions into robust, powerful vehicles, the war was almost at an end. Even then, they were still too primitive to deliver tactically decisive masses of ordnance upon specific battlefield targets. Increasing the individual soldier's firepower—which promised the simultaneous advantages of dramatically increased volumes of cover fire for assaults and of facilitating the rapid exploitation of any resulting breakthroughs—was also neglected until the last months of the war. At that time, both sides managed to field what were jocularly referred to as 'trench brooms:' Germany introduced the submachine gun, and America fielded prototypes of the Browning automatic rifle and the Thompson submachine gun.[31]

Lastly, it must be stressed that, once the process of stalemate had begun, it reinforced itself, and not only at the front lines. The rear areas became vast, specialized logistical staging depots, where the routines of sustained resupply, relief, and reinforcement were well in place, along with contingency plans to compartmentalize and control breakthroughs. In the final analysis, the war in Western Europe evolved into a conflict in which attrition—raw numbers—carried the slow, bloody day. Armies counted successes not by forcing and winning a decisive battle, but by grinding down the opponent's economy and resource base to the point that it was unable to maintain its field forces.

During four years of globe-spanning conflict, these conditions became the norm *only* in the Franco-German salient: this is hardly surprising, since the complex combination of underlying factors that caused it existed nowhere else on the face of the earth. Had they, similar conditions would undoubtedly have arisen and endured on some other front during World War I. Instead, military operations in Russia, Turkey, Italy, the Balkans, Arabia, and innumerable small colonial brush wars tended towards fluidity. This was inevitable in these campaigns, where the antagonists had had less opportunity for preparation, less railway and logistical infrastructure elements, and much more terrain to cover per available soldier. These conflicts had far more in common with each other than any of them had with the operational 'norms' of the Western Front. Indeed, they also had more in common with what had come immediately before—the Boer War, the Philippine Insurrection, etc.—and what was to come after: Guderian's *blitzkrieg* in Russia, Rommel's North African campaign, Patton's drive into France. In each case, mobility, combined arms, and coordination between independent units were the keystones of successful operations.

It is no different for the Germans in Le Queux's *The Invasion of 1910*: their operations in England represent a speculative vault over the trenches that were to line the Marne less than ten years later. Instead, the invaders' hypothetical romp across England is much more reminiscent of operations on the sprawling ebb-and-flow battlefields that characterized World War II, sans advanced technology. The analogy is not perfect, but it may offer more insight into Le Queux's text than a summary dismissal based on its failure to postulate protracted trench warfare. If the Western Front of World War I is, in fact, a single anomalous deviation from the evolution of warfare that both preceded and succeeded it, then Le Queux's portrayal of military operations—and in particular, mobility—seems the more plausible alternative, particularly in the context of his invaders' objectives and his defenders' resources. Le Queux's Germans are conducting a raid (not a war of conquest and occupation) against unprepared Britons, who are inventing a desperate, makeshift defense of their small, ocean-girdled homeland. Because of the differences in geography and military objectives, there are no massive rear staging areas; neither side has deep logistical pockets for sustained operations; there isn't the time to create extensive entrenchments; and finally, the ratio of troops available to square miles of potential front lines makes the very concept of 'lines' meaningless except around key strategic sites.[32]

However, Le Queux's Britons certainly understand that a war of entrenchments and static positions would be in their strategic and tactical interests: it would both slow down the Germans and favor the defenders, who lack the modern technology and mobility of their attackers. The resulting decision to make the construction of such defenses a top priority is one of the main reasons that the (marginal) British victory at Royston cannot be properly 'followed up:' the victors slowly fall back from the site of their success—thereby further delaying a renewed enemy advance—so that the rest of England's defenders will 'be able to get on with the lines of fortification that are being constructed to bar the approaches to London . . .'[33] Reminiscent of the Marne, these lines are comprised of a massive labyrinth of 'chin-deep trenches' where the troops constantly 'busied themselves improving their loopholes and strengthening their head cover.'[34]

Accordingly, the defense of London is the one episode in which both the support of a logistical infrastructure and time for preparation are available to the defenders. Not surprisingly, the pace, style, and casualties of that combat are very reminiscent of trench warfare of World War I. During a rush toward the English positions, a German officer recounts

> Seldom have I seen such a concentrated fire. Gun, pom-pom, machine gun, and rifle blazed . . . along more than three miles of entrenchments. . . . I could see the bullets raising perfect sand-storms in places, the little pom-pom shells sparkling about all over our prostrate men, and the shrapnel bursting all along their front . . . Every

forward move of the attacking lines left a perfect litter of prostrate forms behind it, and for some time I felt very doubtful in my own mind if the attack would succeed.[35]

Significantly, Le Queux repeatedly insists that, had the British been adequately prepared (enough trained men, enough weaponry, enough munitions and other logistical reserves and support) no such attack *could* have succeeded. The result would have been that of the Somme: a futile exercise in sending tens of thousands of men into a raging storm of shrapnel and machine gun fire.

However, Le Queux's most interesting—and striking—anticipations of new mobility and tactics concern the Germans' use of both cavalry and motorized units. Throughout their invasion, the Germans exhibit a radical departure from the traditional uses of cavalry. They rarely use it to screen their movements or assault a weak enemy flank, and they never use it to 'drive home a charge' in a pitched battle. Instead, they use cavalry as an instrument of tactical exploitation, exemplified by the pincer movement they employ at the Battle of Chelmsford, where all German cavalry in that salient is grouped for a wide sweep *around* the British lines. Of even greater significance, a large part of this force is actually comprised of 'motor infantry' which is equipped with 'several of the new armoured motors carrying light, quick-firing and machine guns . . .' Some of these vehicles are later precisely identified as '35–40 h.p. Opel-Darracqs, with three quick-firing guns mounted in each.'[36] Thus, Le Queux envisions light armor and motor units as the spearhead for outflanking or pincer movements, which are conducted with the intent of 'pocketing off' enemy units which can then be isolated and neutralized—a tactic that would not see routine employment until the Wehrmacht's 1941 Russian offensive, but that would forever change the conduct of war thereafter.

This is not Le Queux's only reference to machine mobility; he often emphasizes that a considerable part of the invasion force is 'motor infantry,'[37] which is key to the invaders' plans. Although the Germans are willing to leave behind their wagons and caissons, they insist on bringing their self-powered vehicles: because of the cargo limits of the invasion fleet, 'the supply of wheeled transport, *with the exception of motor-cars*, had been somewhat reduced' *(italics are mine).*[38] In addition to the comparative efficiency and durability of motor vehicles, there is also the matter of their tactical utility; prior to World War I, motorized infantry was already capable of a steady 20 mph, even over country roads: no cavalry unit could come close to matching such a feat. Consequently

> [V]on Dorndorf's motorists had been of the greatest utility. They had taken constantly companies of infantry hither and thither. At any

threatened point, so soon as the sound of firing was heard in any cavalry skirmish or little engagement of outposts, the smart motor infantry were on the spot with the promptness of a fire brigade proceeding to a call. For this reason the field artillery, who were largely armed with quick-firing guns, capable of pouring in a hail of shrapnel on any exposed point, were enabled to push on much farther than would have been otherwise possible. They were always adequately supported by a sufficient escort of these up-to-date troops who, although infantry, moved with greater rapidity than cavalry itself, and who, moreover, brought with them their Maxims, which dealt havoc far and near.[39]

Le Queux also foresees many of the profound operational changes impelled by the widespread use of machine guns, of which the Maxim was one of the earliest varieties. It could be employed as far as 500 meters with absolutely lethal effect, and had a potential effective range of up to 1500 meters. Le Queux anticipates the role these weapons would one day play in undoing mass-formation assaults when he writes 'Our Maxim served us admirably, for ever and anon it cut a lane in the great wall of advancing troops, until the whole roadway was covered with dead and maimed Germans.'[40]

Returning to the issue of tactical mobility, the British discover the value of motor transport themselves when, for want of sufficient rail transport due to sabotage and poor contingency planning, their cavalry is not able to get to the 'front' in time to conduct sufficient reconnaissance and screening operations. This deficiency in cavalry

> was made good . . . by the general employment of hordes of motorcyclists, who scoured the country in large armed groups in order to ascertain, if possible, the dispositions of the enemy. This they did and very soon after their arrival reported the result of their investigations to the general officers . . .[41]

In short, motorized troops were portrayed as being able to respond rapidly and operate independently, whereas horse soldiers were susceptible to all kinds of delays and logistical impediments. The makeshift nature of the defenders' efforts to compensate for their shortage of motor vehicles strangely anticipates the extraordinary lack of vehicular provisioning that characterized not only the British Expeditionary Force's (BEF) situation in France, but also its overall shortcomings as of 1914. This collective failure in foresight is indicated in a report written by the influential Lt. Colonel Maurice Hankey for Lord Kitchener: 'No one could have foreseen to what an enormous extent mechanical transport would be required from the first day of mobilization.'[42] On the day the war began, the British army had only '80 lorries' of its own; it had a lien on 700 additional vehicles. Hankey's report reveals that this represented an absurdly insufficient degree of equipment: 'Since mobilization over 8000 have been provided already, and this number is increasing at the rate of 250 per week. Similarly the number of motor cycles has increased from 15 to nearly 3000 . . .'[43] The rapidity with which the situation was corrected—more than a tenfold increase in three months—strongly suggests that the original shortcomings were not due to a lack of finances or availability, but a lack of foresight on the part of the army's planners. Even the BEF's crash program of 'modernization' was not able to keep up with the level of demand and associated logistical support requirements: 'The principal difficulty throughout has been the provision of motor lorries . . . . The maintenance of the vast mass of mechanical transport now possessed by the Army itself is a gigantic task.' Roughly 1 percent of the vehicles were out of action for maintenance or repair work at any given time, and there was also the further issue of procuring and distributing unprecedented volumes of gasoline: 'The fact that the consumption in the Expeditionary Force alone amounts to some 35000 gallons daily indicates the scale on which provision has to be made.'[44]

It is ironic that Hankey begins this segment of his report with the phrase 'No one could have foreseen,' when there is plentiful evidence to the contrary. Writers of future-war fiction—even those as inexpert and sensationalistic as Le Queux—*had* foreseen exactly these requirements. Indeed, basic quantitative analysis of the logistics of the coming war, in correlation with what various authors and planners had foreseen, would have predicted the need to increase the ready stocks in the British army's 'motor pool' by a factor of (at least) twenty. Furthermore, several future-war fictions portrayed the vulnerability of horses as battlefield or near-front transport assets. This should have been equally evident to actual planners, given the murderous increases in artillery and small-arm lethality. The machine gun did more than end the era of the frontal cavalry charge: it made the notion of wheeling light, horse-drawn artillery to and fro on an open battlefield tantamount to suicide.

Of course, the full horrific reality of the Western Front stunned authors and officers alike, possibly because of its anomalous and unlooked-for nature. The future-war authors proved to have at least equally flawed political foresight: an accurate anticipation of the 'hows' and the 'wheres' of the events that would lead to war eluded them. Only the most basic assessments of 'who' would fight—Germany on one side, England and France on the other—were right as often as they were wrong.

However, it is revealing that these most frequently used criteria regarding the value of a future-war fiction presuppose several arbitrary, even dubious, assumptions. For instance, these criteria imply that a 'near-future' war fiction is invariably expected to concern itself with 'predictions' about the 'next' war. However, not all future fictions aspire equally to 'prediction' *per se* and, therefore, should not all be judged according to the same criteria.[45] Admittedly, Le Queux committed himself to speculations about the 'next' war when he put his *Invasion* in a very specific, near-future frame. However, does his failure as a political anticipator validate or vindicate dismissing his technological and even tactical foresight? Le Queux's tale is not necessarily a failed anticipation of World War I, but rather, might be a marginally successful anticipation of World War II. Why then, with all the experts at their disposal, could the general staffs of the collective nations of Europe not envision technological and operational developments that a hack sensationalist newspaperman apparently could?

First, Le Queux's 'anticipations' are neither particularly innovative nor radical. He gives the Germans up-to-date technology and illustrates how the principles of warfare would evolve as a result. When his narrative is reapproached from this perspective, it is the prosecution of World War I, not the tactics of *Invasion*, which defies easy explanation.

Arguably, the historical evidence suggests that the strategists of the Great War were blinkered by a powerful mix of preexistant logistical commitment and ingrained military doctrine. Until they had their collective noses repeatedly rubbed in the corpse-choked midden heaps of the Somme and Ypres and Flanders and the Marne, the general staffs of all the great powers still included believers in defilade and enfilade, column and line: these Napoleonic concepts still described the peripheries of their flat-earth view of the military cosmos. By the time the realities of modern, machine-age warfare exploded their outdated martial paradigm with even more force than Copernicus blasted Ptolemy, it was too late to rethink or reequip. Those minds that might have been capable of revising military operations and thereby altering the face of combat were almost all pressed to the task of conducting the war with the materials and training that already existed: desperate exigency understandably ran roughshod over any inclination to experiment. The appearance of the tank, the rapid evolution of the airplane, the eventual jettisoning of the 'serried ranks' vision of warfare, the increased emphasis upon high-rate-of-fire weapons that could be carried by individual soldiers, the increased importance (and ubiquity) of fast, simple, voice-grade communications—all are evidence that there was both theoretical awareness and tangible acknowledgement of the need for change in many aspects of military operations. But the governing adage—better the devil you know than the one you don't—

necessarily delayed full-scale adoption of such decisive new technologies until the smoke had cleared and the whole debacle could be viewed from that lofty—and safe—observation post known as hindsight.

The new technological and operational realities of weaponry and mobility also brought changes to the psychology of the battlefield, changes that Le Queux was sensitive to, although not in any professional or consistent fashion. Rather, Le Queux displayed a peculiar mix of empathy for consequent changes in the experience of war and an ability to unerringly detect and depict the most titillating and/or horrifying aspects of those changes. In doing so, he unintentionally anticipated some of the mental and emotional alterations to warfare that the doctrinally obsessed experts overlooked.

For instance, Le Queux's depiction of street fighting in London is not only memorable in its lurid sensationalism, but for its prescience regarding the increased viciousness of modern urban combat; the leveling effect it has upon differences in troop quality and training; its preclusion of artillery support; and lastly, the massive confusion it generates and the resulting degradation of the command and communications advantages enjoyed by professional military units. Rather, weapons with high volumes of fire (which, in this era, meant the Maxim guns) and familiarity with the streets are the decisive factors. Ultimately, these factors give the British a better than fighting chance. Le Queux also foresees how compromised communications and control within an urban environment also lead to the problem of 'friendly fire' casualties: despite their training and superb discipline, 'in many cases the Germans were shot by their own comrades.'[46]

Le Queux's narrative also reflects a dramatic increase in the employment of 'irregular' insurgent forces akin to the Boers. Le Queux's Germans make a sharp distinction between Great Britain's uniformed soldiers—whose surrenders are always duly respected and accepted—and the local terrorist/resistance fighters (i.e. anyone not in uniform), who are considered spies and, after drum-head trial, are summarily executed.[47] In particular, the 'Frontiersmen,' a Maquis-like group, are comprised of professional marksmen, hunters, and club members who were non-military.[48] The tactics they adopt to hamper and harass the enemy—and the German response (first the penalization, and then the burning, of implicated villages)—both evolve in a manner that recalls the later conduct of the Nazis in the Balkans and the Ukraine, the US in Vietnam, and the Russians in Afghanistan: 'A party of eleven Frontiersmen, captured by the Saxons . . . were obliged to dig their own graves, and were then shot as they stood before them.'[49] Furthermore, as 'punishment for an attack on a requisitioning party, the entire town of Feltham had been put to the sword, even the children.'⁵⁰ The gulf of animosity between invaders and inhabitants—most of whom did not begin with any great personal enmity toward each other—becomes increasingly vast, intractable, and vicious. Each side slowly succumbs to the expedient barbarities of total war: assassination, execution, sabotage, preemptive strikes, and immediate reprisals. As Le Queux writes,

> Such was the system of terrorism by which the enemy hoped to terminate the struggle. . . . On the contrary, they only served to prolong the deadly contest by exciting a wild desire for revenge in many who might otherwise have been disposed towards an amicable settlement.⁵¹

In addition to illustrating how modern war tends to blur the lines by which an invader differentiates soldiers and civilians, Le Queux also depicts the death of battlefield chivalry between opposing conventional forces. However, Le Queux is inconstant in his address of this topic, suggesting that, once again, his previsions are largely unintended. For instance, Le Queux, either in an attempt to appeal to his audience or to his own romantic ideals, presents a classic example of English 'fair play' when an old, retired officer comes upon essential intelligence regarding the German invaders, and must get through enemy lines to make his report. Here's how this veteran handles his crucial attempt at slipping past a German sentry:

> Macdonald crept up slowly. If the man woke and discovered him he would be again challenged. Should he take the man's big revolver and shoot him as he lay?
> No. That was a coward's action, an unjustifiable murder, he decided.
> He would take the horse, and risk it by making a dash for life.⁵²

For his chivalric pains, MacDonald gets shot in the shoulder, and only because he is extraordinarily robust—and because his body did not intercept the sentry's bullet a few centimeters lower—does he survive to make his crucial report on the disposition of the enemy forces. This passage is particularly revealing in that it illustrates the Briton's stolid, dogged, subconscious refusal (in which Le Queux might have genuinely shared) to part with the chivalric ideals of the earlier ages of warfare. Instead, the Germans are the more accurate precursors of the modern military age, and if their autocratic and brusque control over civilians as well as military targets is seen as ruthless, it is more in keeping with military conventions which have become commonplace in the latter half of the twentieth century: 'They did the work before them in a quiet, business-like way, not shirking risk when it was necessary, but, on the other hand, not needlessly exposing themselves for the sake of swagger.'[53] In this, Le Queux announces that the epoch of the warrior is past; as would be confirmed in the rapid erosion of chivalric restraint in World War I, this is the age of the scientific soldier, for whom war is a matter of competing technological quantities, not shared virtues of honorable conduct. He also foresees a concomitant change in what is considered 'desirable' in the behavioral and psychological make-up of individual soldiers. During a discussion of the early naval engagements, Le Queux explains that

> the Germans surpassed their British rivals, not because the German officer was braver or more capable, but because he was younger taught to display initiative to a higher degree than the personnel of the British fleet, and better trained for actual battle.[54]

It is impossible to address in any brief manner the complex issues of culture and background raised by this problematic passage. If the British military initiative is retrograde because of a tendency to wait for one's social superiors to issue orders, then what of the similar class divisions that existed in Germany at the same time? What great or subtle differences in training or socialization would account for these variances? Le Queux's assertion is not supported by explanations and therefore defies detailed analysis—despite its tantalizingly proleptic echoes of the German capacity for independent operations, often in very small, detached units.

Vastly less problematic are Le Queux's representations of how improved communications result in a more timely downstream flow of orders and upstream flow of intelligence, and how the ability of individual officers to act independently was simultaneously increasing in importance. Absolute and rigid adherence to the chain of command was no longer always advisable—particularly when the tactical situation had changed more rapidly than new orders could be issued. This statement—which sounds like common sense to twenty-first century laymen—was deeply paradoxical to the more hierarchical military mindset of the post-Napoleonic era. Either chain of command *or* personal initiative had to be preeminent; both things could not be equally important. This widely held conviction was not the product of ignorance, nor even doctrinal rigidity, but it illustrates how the changes in technology had redefined war so profoundly and swiftly that the presuppositions of esteemed but aged commanders had become not merely woefully inadequate, but dangerous. In the space of two decades, senior strategists went from being experts to anachronisms; 1914 found them issuing orders and making assumptions based on a style of warfare that no longer existed, an obsolescence which they refused to acknowledge until confronted with the mute evidence of several million corpses.

The importance of time, coordination, information, and personal initiative is underscored at the very outset of Le Queux's tale: two journalists are discussing how they were both following a story from Yarmouth by telegraph and phone when the wire suddenly went dead and connection could not be reestablished.[55] This turns out to be only the first in a cascade of communications failures that effectively severs contact between the essential industrial and governmental centers inland and the continent-facing coastal areas. The attempt to check on these failures reveals cut wires and broken train rails. Thus, Le Queux starts his tale by highlighting the linked tactical and psychological importance of interdicting an opponent's key data and transport junctures, thereby simultaneously producing confusion and a sense of isolation. Le Queux's unconscious recognition of the growing importance of psychological warfare is further reflected in the timing of the German invasion: it begins on a weekend and at night, when the commanders of Her Majesty's forces are all at home in their beds. Towards the end of the first day, enraged and baffled crowds 'looked up at the many windows of the Admiralty and the War Office, ignorant that both those huge buildings only held terrified caretakers and a double watch of police constables.'[56] Le Queux underscores this lack of vigilance by explaining that this weekend was just like any other in that 'there was no one at the Admiralty—not even a clerk.'[57] The critique implicit in Le Queux's rhetoric points toward yet another change in the nature of warfare: no longer a gentleman's game, it has become a round-the-clock duel of wits, nerves, and eternal readiness. Le Queux's text thus previews a new ethos and ecology of warfare, one that would ultimately give rise to the Situation Room at the Pentagon, and the day-and-night watches manned in the air-conditioned, computer-banked bowels of NORAD. The damning stares of Le Queux's London crowds are, ultimately, a criticism of the political and military habits that their leaders have retained from an earlier, slower age. What had been a sufficient degree of vigilance only thirty years before now seems lackadaisical 'amateurism' or even criminal negligence. Thus, Le Queux's passage suggests that when the people of England placed trust in officials who were technologically retrograde—who refused to embrace the new realities of warfare in the dawning era of superpower states—the people of England placed their trust poorly.

For every rational appeal that Le Queux makes to his reader's sense of outrage and betrayal, he includes at least a dozen visceral scenes of tragedy, which constitute the emotional, and therefore most forceful, half of his argument. Predictably, he holds the most gruesome descriptions of weapons effects in reserve for his depiction of the shelling of London itself: 'The most awful sights were to be witnessed in the open streets: men and women blown out of recognition, with their clothes singed and torn to shreds, and helpless, innocent children lying white and dead, their limbs torn away and missing.'[58] The carnage continues into the night—and for a full twenty pages: '[T]he scenes of bloodshed that night were full of horror, as men fought in the ruined streets, climbing over the smouldering debris, over the bodies of their comrades, and shooting from behind ruined walls.'[59]

Although Le Queux was fond of representing Britons as the mangled martyrs of machine-age warfare, he was occasionally willing to include even the German invaders within the scope of this tragedy (although this may have been motivated more by a desire to maximize the number of sensationalistic scenes than it was by any sense of pan-humanism). For instance, a civilian mayor witnesses the shelling and collapse of a tower containing a contingent of German signal specialists, and as he and the townspeople run to the scene to search for survivors,

> I caught sight of an arm in a light blue sleeve protruding from the debris, and took hold of it in a futile attempt to remove . . . the . . . rubbish which I thought [was] covering the body of its owner. To my horror, it came away in my hand. . . . I dropped it with a cry, and fled from the spot.[60]

When compared to the most 'visceral' scenes from *The Great War of 189–*, this passage illustrates the differences between serious and sensationalistic authorship, as well as the change in what constituted appropriate (or acceptable) discursive practices *vis à vis* the representation of war. The new graphic and even gory frankness of Le Queux's narrative is a match for the grim new battlefield reality, and is a harbinger of the more unremittingly brutal battlefield depictions of Wilfred Owen, Dalton Trumbo, and countless others.

Another cultural casualty of Le Queux's war, and perhaps even more horrifying to readers than the despoliation of the countryside or the destruction of cherished Imperial icons,[61] is the absolute extinction of British civility and restraint. Like all other apparently impregnable facades, these time-honored British traits of character are no more resistant to German munitions than any other gossamer veil of culture or stone. When a panic breaks out among crowds that have attempted to take refuge in the 'Tube,' it causes a rush through these unlit subterranean dungeons in which

> women and children were quickly crushed to death, or thrown down and trampled upon by the press behind. In the darkness they

fought with each other, pressing on and becoming jammed so tightly that many were held against the sloping walls until life was extinct.[62]

Although the British nation survives, its culture—both material and spiritual—is profoundly crippled. Le Queux leaves his reader to brood over the disastrous consequences of his nation's carelessness and lack of vigilance. Also doomed—and implicated as playing a role in inviting the disaster—is the myth that British pluck, British luck, and just plain British origin are enough to save the day: 'Many a gallant deed was done . . . by patriotic Londoners in defence of their homes and loved ones—many a deed that should have earned the V.C.—but in nearly all cases the patriot who had stood up and faced the foe had gone to straight and certain death.'[63] These patriots, their city, and their nation are all, according to Le Queux, martyred victims of 'the careless insular apathy of the Englishman himself!'[64]

This passage also points to Le Queux's pronounced capacity for accepting—or missing—the logical inconsistencies in his own rhetoric and exhortations. Although here he decries the 'insular apathy' of Englishmen, elsewhere he evinces a predisposition for (or at least a willingness to pander to) the extreme xenophobia which is the prerequisite for the production of such insularity. For instance,

> The riff-raff from Whitechapel, those aliens whom we had so long welcomed and pampered in our midst—Russians, Poles, Austrians, Swedes, and even Germans— . . . had swarmed westward in lawless, hungry multitudes, and on Monday afternoon serious rioting occurred in Grosvenor Square and . . . several houses were entered and pillaged by the alien mobs.[65]

Le Queux neglects to suggest any method by which 'appropriate' suspicions of foreigners can be maintained (and acted upon) without incurring an inevitable tendency toward the blinkered, and even vicious, xenophobia that his own narrative echoes.

Le Queux identifies one other psychological feature that was to emerge in response to the unremitting intensity of twentieth-century warfare: the rapidity with which those who are perpetually at risk become inured to war's horrors:

> A very curious fact about the bombardment must here be noted. Londoners, though terrified beyond measure when the shells began to fall among them and explode, grew, in the space of a couple of hours, to be quite callous, and seemed to regard the cannonade in the light of a pyrotechnical display. They climbed to every point of vantage, and regarded the continuous flashes and explosions with

the same open-mouthed wonder as they would exhibit at the Crystal Palace on a firework night.[66]

A final review of the new psychological horrors that Le Queux anticipates is a sad and sobering commentary on the future facts of the twentieth century: the death of chivalry; the need for an inhumanly round-the-clock, machine-assisted deathwatch; the violation and disruption of bodies into disassociated parts; the new martial virtues of calm, control, and clockwork efficiency; the destruction of national edifices and traditions of civility; and ultimately, the diminished recognition or acknowledgement of the threats to one's own life within a war zone. Taking these psychological factors collectively, one discovers that Le Queux has presented a chillingly complete prevision of how both self and opponent are dehumanized when trapped within the automated charnel-house realities of modern warfare. Various elements of Le Queux's narrative anticipate the totalized effect of this grisly endgame: toward the end of the story, the British have embraced the concept of sacrificing their own people and property—reflexively and ruthlessly—in order to gain their objectives. The new leadership of England has 'decided that, in order to demoralize the enemy and give him plenty of work to do, a number of local uprisings should take place north of the Thames.'[67] These 'uprisings' consist of pitched street mêlées in which hundreds of civilians lose their lives, and to which the German commander responds by randomly selecting scores or hundreds of uninvolved citizens for reprisal executions. The tactics of the guerrilla—the grim efficiency of which were soon to be proven in the Balkans, China, and the Ukraine—find their first European enunciation in the following passage: 'every dead German has had his rifle, pistol, and ammunition stolen from him. Hundreds of the enemy have been surreptitiously killed for that very reason.'[68] A war that begins with an old man deciding not to kill a sleeping sentry with his own weapon because it is 'unsporting' ends in the official sanctioning of—indeed, dependence upon—terrorism, assassination, sabotage, and massacre. Morality and ethics are, at first, cast aside in order to achieve the nation's objectives, and then later vanish altogether, buried under the brutalities of mechanized modern warfare. No matter that the British are fighting to oust a rapacious foe; they ultimately match their foe in the ruthlessness with which they fight, and show at least as great a talent for attaining objectives through terrorism.

*****

While not all the future-war fictions of the Victorian and Edwardian epochs exercised the same influence or commanded the same sales as *The*

*Great War of 189–* and *The Invasion of 1910*, many of them did offer the kind of unintentional insights which one finds in Le Queux's decidedly purple prose. One such insight lies in the slow but steady change in the identities of 'the enemy' and 'the ally' in these anticipations of coming conflicts. It is particularly revealing that in the earlier British texts (and in the later German analogs), the US is often cast in the role of the enemy, the external threat that can be used to unify European (ultimately, Aryan) interests. This also illustrates the rapid growth of the presence of an American variable in the equations of European statecraft.[69]

However, the post-Victorian reconception of the US as an ally may also illustrate that as America began evolving into a true superpower, British authors and power elites began seeing more promise of common understanding—and common cause—with their colonial offspring than with their traditional Continental allies. It may be exactly this perceived shift in the center of international and ethnic gravity that prompted German author Karl Bleibtrau to write in his 1907 future-war narrative, *Die 'Offensiv-Invasion' gegen England*:

> every European war could only benefit the other continents of the world . . . Napoleon's old statement is truer than ever today: 'Every war in Europe is always a civil war'. . . . Only a peacefully united Europe can maintain itself against the growing strength of other races and against the economic dominance of America.[70]

Bleibtrau's attempt to realign the center of Western power to once again fall somewhere between London and Berlin was ultimately futile. A new tide was rising, carrying British interests and affinities—often haltingly and reluctantly—across the Atlantic. The mounting strength of this drift is recorded in Louis Tracy's overtly racist *The Final War*:[71]

> America arose, that second England, new home of the Saxon race, and heir to her aspirations and destiny, America, . . . developed a new type of being, more versatile still, and still more strenuous . . . [H]ow could such a race be resisted? For, wherever it penetrated, it did not languish under conditions unfavourable to its growth. With miraculous ease the Saxon remodelled himself to cover every variation of climate, every manner of sky, every form of life, till it became clear that he was no fixed irrevocable type, but of plastic mould, and reproducing himself in a hundred different shapes. The Saxon is content wherever he is; the instinct of his blood tells him that the earth is his home, and that his spirit must inform the nations and regenerate decaying peoples.
>
> Commerce bent itself to Britain and all peoples intrusted to her

their possessions. The Saxon tongue has become the speech of the world, the Saxon ensign, whether British or American, is the flag of the seas.

Thus, as life becomes more complex and harder grows the struggle, there is no escape for peoples not fitted to bear its strain. The Saxon race will absorb all and embrace all, reanimating old civilisations and giving new vigour to exhausted nations. England and America, their destiny is to order and rule the world, to give it peace and freedom, to bestow upon it prosperity and happiness, to fulfill the responsibilities of an all-devouring people; wisely to discern and generously to bestow.

This vision, far-off it may be, already dawns; and in the glory of its celestial light is the peace of nations.[72]

The grotesquely twisted Darwinism that Tracy weaves through this passage as both justification and glorification of 'Saxon' preeminence ironically identifies one of the genuine points of commonality between both England and America: a radical and systematic tendency to regard peoples who are oppositional or obstructive as 'Other.' It is certainly true that dehumanization of opponents is fairly common pre-conflict behavior in most social groups, and that other Western nations (such as Hitler's Germany) made extensive use of it themselves. However, possibly because of the pluralistic traditions that are so deeply rooted in both Britain and America, the discursive procedures whereby they engage in such 'othering' are characterized by convoluted ethical rationalizing. It is as though these nations, in order to engage in the othering process, must first 'find' malicious intent in the group to be 'othered,' particularly if that group had previously been an ally. Consequently, from 1900 onwards, Britain turns its considerable xenophobic energies upon formerly approbated Germany, rapidly reversing two centuries of Francophobia in order to ready itself for a new era of Teutophobic conflict. Evolving as an irregularly gathering consensus rather than as the conspiratorial product of some star-chamber of elites, this 'othering' was registered and reinforced through various discursive mechanisms, but the 'spy-scare' may have been the most powerful. As was true for dozens of his fellow future-war fabricators, the threat of a German 'army in waiting' not only initiates Le Queux's tale of Britannia downfallen, but motivated him to write it in the first place.[73]

America, in its later years as a Cold War superpower, would engage in very similar discursive procedures of self-brainwashing, having already had ample practice vilifying the Japanese in World War II. That an intervening ocean does nothing to diminish the strong Anglo-American parallels in the general practice and specific processes of such 'othering' warrants attention, for it is further evidence of the passing of the 'superpower baton' that linked Great Britain and the US. In both societies, the most alarming outside threat is embodied in the agent of a known rival power, whose menace is not proximal or immediate, thereby providing an inexhaustible (and impossible to disprove) source of spy scares. The physical manifestation of this danger is usually a male *agent provocateur*, duplicitous as he is ruthless, his apparent identity a sinister masquerade. He also is often depicted as secretly greedy for the material benefits of the country he threatens. That desire—filled with symbolic and often literal connotations of sexual violation—invites readers to perceive their homeland as too innocent and naive to suspect the evil motives and machinations that lurk like unseen daggers behind the cloak of amiability adopted by such infiltrators. Of course, this innocence is all at once proof of the ethical superiority, but also the tragic unpreparedness, of the home nation: in this manner, cultural self-affirmation and dire warning are mixed into a titillating encounter with that most dangerous of radical 'others,' the spy.

In summary, by analyzing the content of Colomb's and Le Queux's texts, and by delineating the affiliated strands of power that joined many of England's military leaders, politicians, authors, and editors into a cat's cradle of common interest around the turn of the nineteenth century, there is ample evidence for the assertion that future-war fiction exerted considerable political influence upon the military imagination and agendas of the period. Furthermore, the social dynamics that engendered, shaped, and responded to these texts suggests that the Empire's political preoccupations and praxes were consistent with those ascribed to and associated with later superpower states: active information management, opinion formation, technophilia, and ideological cooption of popular discursive forms.

However, another hallmark of such states is that they are not content with merely controlling their present and a few years beyond: they aspire to create their own future—and they frequently imagine, design, and rehearse it through war fictions that envision bold new technological advances and the socio-political revisions they might impel. These procedures not only informed, but were implicit within the narratives of, the next Edwardian wave of Britain's future-war authors.

*Chapter 3*

# Promoters of the Probable, Prophets of the Possible: Technological Innovation and Edwardian Near-Future War Fiction

Drill for oil? You mean drill into the ground to try and find oil? You're crazy.
> Drillers whom Edwin L. Drake tried to enlist to his project to drill for oil in 1859

This 'telephone' has too many shortcomings to be seriously considered as a means of communication. The device is inherently of no value to us.
> Western Union internal memo, 1876

The wireless music box has no imaginable commercial value. Who would pay for a message sent to nobody in particular?
> David Sarnoff's associates in response to his urgings for investment in the radio in the 1920s

Senior experts may be the best persons to consult regarding the immediate technological state of affairs in their own field, but there is ample historical evidence that the most important innovations do not occur at the senior levels of an industry at all. Rather, new ideas often emerge from younger, unconventional, even iconoclastic members of that hierarchy, or they arrive—unsought, unbidden, and initially unwelcome—from without. The conception and initial tactical assessments of the three most important new weapons technologies introduced during World War I— the tank, the submarine, and the airplane—are attributable to just such persons.

The least technologically ambitious of these devices—the tank—was, paradoxically, the only one that did not already exist when the war began. Although the basic principle had been explored (the Opel-Darracq armored cars of Le Queux's *The Invasion of 1910* really did exist), and although the constituent technologies were available (caterpillar treads were already being used in agricultural machinery), few people had foreseen the grim advantages that might be derived from combining an armed and heavily armored chassis with a rugged, all-terrain propulsion system. However, the story of—and stories by—those same few, farsighted people constitute a particularly illuminating illustration of the connections between intentional technological innovation in near-future war fiction and political influence.

The idea of an armored fighting vehicle has a long pedigree. The Hungarian war-wagons of the Renaissance, Da Vinci's designs, numerous nineteenth-century proposals for steam-powered gun carriages, and French illustrator/futurist Albert Robida's *blockhouse roulants* all testify to a long-standing desire to marry weapons, armor, and mobility in a single stable platform. However, as with so many weapon technologies that are now commonplace, the first detailed and technologically reasonable articulation of the 'idea' of the tank came from the often-prophetic pen of H. G. Wells. His 1903 story 'The Land Ironclads' was inspired by the mechanical possibility of a new weapon, but it also offers an anticipatory response to the stalemate of 1914.[1] Looking across a flat killing-field at the enemy's trenches, the protagonist (a young war correspondent) exclaims: 'And this is war!' 'No,' replies the young lieutenant with him, 'it's Bloch.'[2] Although this response—offered without footnote or explanatory context—can only perplex and mystify a contemporary reader, it immediately framed the political and military significance of the story for any relatively well-read Edwardian Briton. The lieutenant's reply— 'it's Bloch'—is a reference to Jan Bloch's *Modern Weapons and Modern Warfare* (1900), the first systematic attempt to integrate a quantitative assessment of weapons technologies, statistical analysis, and measures of industrial output to predict the course of a 'modern' twentieth-century war.[3] Bloch's conclusion was a direct, almost flawless prevision of the 1914–1918 stalemate on the Western Front: the increased lethality of weapons and the increased level of production could only result in a battlefield environment so deadly that no attacking force could survive in sufficient numbers to make a decisive breakthrough. Bloch asserted that the conflict would settle into a protracted war of attrition, in which logistical exhaustion, not battlefield defeat, would determine who lost.

Wells' 'The Land Ironclads' is, therefore, not merely a depiction of a new weapon, but a proposal for disrupting Bloch's equations.[4] Wells adds a decisive new technological variable: a land ironclad that can survive the approach across No-Man's Land and carry home a decisive assault. This is exactly what Wells' caterpillar-treaded armored fighting vehicles achieve, thereby ending the entrenched stalemate and ushering in a new era of warfare.[5]

However, as was frequently the case with Wells, his extraordinary gift for 'macroscopic' anticipations of trends in scientific innovation surpassed his ability to translate these visions into specific shapes conducive to technological actualization. Accordingly, there are significant distinctions between his iron leviathans and the first actual tanks. Wells' land ironclad is 'eighty to a hundred feet long . . . its vertical side was ten feet high or so, smooth for that height, and then with a complex patterning under the eaves of its flattish turtle cover.'[6] This is many times larger than the largest tank ever built. Also, although the *strategic* objective to be realized by Wells' vehicle is identical to that of the first actual tanks—breaking an entrenched military stalemate—its *tactical* means of achieving that end are radically different. Whereas the first actual tanks were designed to breach enemy lines and either suppress or destroy machine guns, Wells' ironclad is employed in the systematic destruction of enemy troops, driving parallel along the line of entrenchments and gunning down the defenders. To give Wells his due, this error may have been caused by too much foresight, rather than too little. Shortly after its inception, the tank began evolving into a more generalized infantry and vehicle killer. This was facilitated by the end of trench warfare (the specialized 'line-breaching' function of the tank lost much of its emphasis) and by improvements in weapon stabilization and fire control technologies. Wells foresaw these last two innovations with startling clarity: 'Their rifles . . . were . . . automatic, ejected their cartridges and loaded again from a magazine each time they fired, until their ammunition store was at an end . . .'[7] On tanks, self-loading main guns were not to appear until the late 1970s. Furthermore, Wells' weapons are almost unerringly accurate, having 'the most remarkable sights imaginable,' which Wells describes in great detail, and which, in many ways, anticipate all-weather targeting scopes.

Unquestionably, Wells' story is the first serious anticipation of modern armored fighting vehicles. When it came time to award laurels and royalties to those most responsible for the tank's creation, Wells' contributions were the first discussed. The chief discussant, who obviously had been aware of and impressed by Wells' prophetic acumen, was also one of the tank's earliest, most enthusiastic, and influential supporters: Winston Churchill.[8] He offered the following testimony at the opening of the inquiries:

> (Commission Chairman) 2. I want to ask you, first of all, one or two questions of a general kind. At the close of the year 1914 was there any novelty about the idea of an armoured vehicle travelling across country and passing over trenches?
> (Churchill) No, I do not think there was. You may remember that Mr

H. G. Wells, in an article written some years before, had dealt very fully with that and practically exhausted the possibilities of imagination in that sphere . . .[9]

Were this the end of the story of the tank, it would be significant enough: Wells' fiction was clearly known to, and influential upon, those Imperial elites who actually developed, produced, and deployed the world's first armored fighting vehicles. However, contrary to Churchill's sweeping assertion, the full story of the political influence exerted by fiction writers who had foreseen the tank picks up where Wells' involvement ends.

One cannot inquire very deeply into the origins and development of the tank without encountering the name of Ernest D. Swinton. Despite some opinions to the contrary,[10] Swinton's claim before the same Royal Commission that he deserved *'a very large share* of the credit, *and so far as the Army is concerned the sole credit* for the introduction of the Tank' is fundamentally valid.[11] He pursued this claim vigorously, averring that he was not interested in the (rather modest) monetary reward, but in justice. There is, however, a third motivation that Swinton did not directly address, but which his various writings and activities recommend to our consideration: prestige.

Whether as military engineer or political adventurer, Swinton was quite sensitive to the importance of politically advantageous associations and accomplishments. His autobiographical works, *Eyewitness*[12] and *Over My Shoulder*,[13] are at least as much self-congratulatory exercises in name-dropping as they are records of significant historical events—and Swinton has plenty of names to drop. All the larger-than-life figures of his era are there and in personal contact with him: Kitchener, Lloyd George, Churchill, Northcliffe, Balfour, and others. However, Swinton's contact with these persons ultimately arose not from his expertise as an officer in the Royal Engineers, but from his work as 'Ole-Luk-Oie,' the pseudonym he employed when writing his many future-war fictions for *Blackwood's Magazine*.[14] As a result of these 'scribblings,' he was asked to serve as the BEF's official war correspondent at the Front, and it was in the course of these duties that he saw the need for what he would later call a 'tank.'[15] The primary cause of this need was the extensive use the Germans made of machine guns, and hence, Swinton conceived of a tracked 'machine-gun destroyer:'

> The idea of developing a petrol driven caterpillar tractor in a climbing machine capable of traversing barbed wire and carrying forward a crew under bullet proof protection for the express purpose of meeting the highly developed system of defence employed by the

Germans by means of destroying the factor i.e., the machine-gun—upon which it chiefly depended, was conceived by me at the beginning of this war in September, 1914.[16]

The evidence in support of Swinton's claims is too varied and voluminous to reproduce here.[17] In brief, Swinton returned from France in October 1914, and with the political aid of the Secretary to the Committee for Imperial Defence, Lt. Colonel Maurice Hankey, and the engineering assistance of Captain T. G. Tulloch, he began a two-year campaign that would—after considerable confusion, bureaucratic dithering, and interdepartmental in-fighting—result in the creation of the first tank. Codenamed Mother, this vehicle was rhomboidal in shape, and only '31 ft. by 8 ft.,' although it was 13 feet wide when the dismountable side gun sponsons were added. Mother 'could traverse with ease a 9 ft. gap after climbing a perpendicular parapet of 4 ft. 6 in.'[18] Much smaller and less powerful vehicles than those proposed by Wells, tanks akin to the Mother design were to have a major impact in the latter half of the war, and have often been credited with contributing significantly to the German admission in 1918 that their front-line situation had become untenable. The most striking and convincing evidence of this (and therefore, of the immediate political influence of the tank) is to be found in German sources:

> These powerful armored cars, which were first used by the British, are undoubtedly the most wonderful weapons which modern tactics have revealed in warfare . . .[19]
> 
> Lieutenant-General Baron von Ardenne in the *Berliner Tageblatt*

> The Tank . . . is doubtless a factor seriously to be reckoned with, all the more when it appears in great masses. . . . [The writer calls for] the further construction of Tanks and special defence artillery. . . . Readiness is everything—The Tank has a future.[20]
> 
> 'The Tank as a Tactical Factor,' *Die Wien neue Freie Presse*

> [T]here is . . . no longer any prospect of forcing the enemy to accept peace. Decisive for this conclusion are two factors: [the first being] the Tanks . . .[21]
> 
> A Statement from the Supreme Command of the German Army to the Party Leaders in the Reichstag, October 2, 1918

Swinton, however, was not eager to share the glory that might be associated with the success of 'his' brainchild. He politely but pointedly asserted that even though Wells had written 'The Land Ironclads' in 1903, the then worldfamous author could not be said to have 'invented' the tank, because:

> [T]hose soldiers who gave the impulse for this innovation did so without any knowledge of Mr Wells' brilliant forecast written in 1903. . . . So far as the writer is aware, the first definite proposal for a fighting machine on the lines of the existing Tanks was due to the appearance of the Hornsby-Ackroyd Caterpillar Tractor, which was tested for military traction purposes in England in 1906–1908. It was made by a military officer, and was carried up to the stage of the preparation of sketch drawings, when the project died for want of support.[22]

However, in his editorial appendices to *The Tale of the Next Great War*, I. F. Clarke points out that, some time later, Swinton's strident claim that he and his associates acted in complete ignorance of Wells' work was shown to be somewhat excessive: '[H]e said later that he had read Wells's *The Land Ironclads* in 1903, "but had looked upon it as pure fantasy and had entirely forgotten it."' Also, 'Sir Basil Liddell Hart observed in his obituary notice on Swinton (*The Times*, 17 January 1951) that vestigial recollection probably remained.'[23] Clarke doubted Hart's hypothesis regarding Swinton's source of inspiration, and had good reason to do so: one of Swinton's close friends, who died in 1908, had written a future-war story in 1907 in which a tracked, petrol-powered armored vehicle called 'The Snail' was used to breach an adversary's otherwise unassailable entrenchments. The title of the story points directly to the raison d'être of this machine's creation: 'The Trenches.' Clarke hypothesized that, in all probability, Swinton had not been as influenced by Wells as he had been by his friend and fellow Royal Engineer, Captain Vickers. If this is true, then two unanswered but tantalizing questions present themselves: how much influence did each of these two future-war fictions exert upon Swinton's 'invention' of the tank, and, why is Vickers' name so conspicuously absent from any of the official discussions thereof?

The first question is the easier to answer, since Swinton's tank, Mother, seems to have emerged from the engineering ideas that Vickers encapsulated in his Snail. To begin with, Wells' and Vickers' respective stories are fundamentally dissimilar. In comparison to 'The Land Ironclads,' Vickers' tale is of modest scope, and is ultimately more focused on the evolutionary process that brings such a vehicle to the battlefield than a detailed examination of its use. Whereas Wells' story takes place in one location and as one extended episode, Vickers narrative advances from the War Office (where the vehicle is first encountered and procured from an American salesman), to Staff Headquarters in a subsequent campaign that has become hopelessly bogged down in trench warfare, and finally to the site of the vehicle's decisive contributions in breaking the stalemate. Each new location also brings with it a new set of characters. Thus, Vickers' 'Snail' is the central character of his story; Wells' land ironclad cannot claim a similar centrality, even though it is his story's dramatic focus. Furthermore, Vickers' device is comparatively humble, both in dimensions and operational expectations. Since it cuts—and can be concealed by—trenches, it cannot be more than 15 feet wide, for this was generally the maximum trench width. This is much more in keeping with the dimensions of the first actual tanks, which were only 10–13 feet in width. Furthermore, this compact 'trenching machine' achieves its objectives not by killing the enemy but by digging a 'covering trench' that protects friendly infantrymen as they approach the enemy. Moreover, whereas Wells' story—and rhetoric—is structured to surround his vehicles with initial mystery, then exoticism, and finally, awed wonderment, Vickers' tone is utterly matter-of-fact, almost dismissive of the drama of such an innovation:

> [I]t seems such a simple, almost obvious, notion to evolve a machine that shall dig trenches, that shall be able to move unconcernedly across open ground where no man can show himself scatheless, secure under its turtleback of steel, inconspicuous, minding all the hail of lead as little as rain, patient. They have nicknamed it The Snail, but it can burrow forward like a mole![24]

In keeping with this more sober, limited portrayal of an armored combat vehicle, Vickers also depicts the Snail as being susceptible to enemy fire: several are knocked out by enemy artillery, and they conduct the majority of their work at night, to minimize the possibility of being targeted. This device is not, therefore, the invulnerable juggernaut that Wells' land ironclad seems to be, nor is its purpose to decimate the enemy. Rather, if an 'approach is secured'[25] for infantry units, it has achieved its objective—and it accomplishes this goal not by operating independently, but as part of a combined arms effort.

All the aforementioned factors reflect Vickers' military—and specifically, engineering—background. Unlike Wells, Vickers is not sanguine about the robustness of even moderately complex machinery on a battlefield, doubts that any single weapon can produce victory, and is acutely aware that a huge investment in untried weapons (such as Wells') is not in keeping with the *modus operandi* of the procurement branch of the War Office. Vickers' wryly depicts the routines of this office with the masterful and authoritative grace of a seasoned insider, while also echoing Wells' overall assessment of how war is changing: '[T]he men march, they fight, they struggle, the guns roar: wounds, carnage, it is all but part of the working out of a calculation; men, guns, battalions, companies, horse, foot, and artillery, all are merely the bits which go towards making up the pattern. The machine has begun to dominate war.'[26] In another shared fictional anticipation of fact, both Wells and Vickers posit that the preparation and employment of such vehicles will be kept secret until they actually rumble across the battlefield. The use of the tank as a surprise weapon also suggests the two authors' awareness of the inevitability of countermeasures, and that—given enough advance warning—the enemy could devise such machines of their own and thereby rebalance the strategic equation. This is, of course, exactly what began to happen toward the end of World War I.

In terms of size, operational parameters, and tactical objectives, the tanks that Swinton brought into being are much more akin to Vickers' Snail than they are to Wells' land ironclads. Furthermore, the details of the interview and procurement process at Vickers' fictionalized War Office are key pieces of evidence in establishing Swinton's probable earlier exposure to his co-worker's prevision of the tank, for it was through this venue that Swinton had his contact with Vickers. Not only was Swinton a fellow Royal Engineer, but he was also Vickers' immediate superior officer at the War Office during the period 1905–1908—the period during which 'The Trenches' was written. This fact leads naturally —inevitably, even—to a more puzzling inquiry: why was Vickers never mentioned in any of the official discussions regarding the origin of the tank? Could it be that, despite their proximity in the same room at the War Office, Swinton never saw Vickers' story? Or that the friendship that Swinton implies existed between them in his obituary for Vickers (in *The Royal Engineer's Journal*[27]) is merely empty rhetoric and artifice? Or that, somehow, even though Swinton had seen the story, he had forgotten both it and Vickers during the intervening years? The answer to all these apologetic alternatives is negative, for there is now conclusive evidence to the contrary: as will be proven in the following pages, Swinton did read Vickers' story, his friendship with this fellow officer was genuine and enduring, and reminders of that friendship (and by logical extrapolation, Vickers' work) endured for years after Vickers' death. This leaves only one plausible reason why Vickers' name never appears in the official records pertaining to the invention of the tank: Swinton deliberately elected not to mention him to the Royal Commission on Awards to Inventors (just as he failed to mention his good friend in any of his later autobiographical writings), fearing that his own claim as the genuine 'inventor' of the tank would be weakened, even ruined, if Vickers' contribution became known.

Vickers, who graduated top of his class at the Royal Military Academy, was awarded the Pollock Medal and many other prizes. He was a graphic artist, arguably a more gifted writer than Swinton, and at least as inventive an intellect. Swinton, however, seemed to have a pronounced gift for ingratiating himself in various social and political spheres, and for creating productive synergies among his many diverse contacts. One of Swinton's earliest, and profoundly productive, contacts was with the editor of *Blackwood's Magazine* who actively cultivated the military as a source of new writers. Shortly after Vickers arrived at the War Office as a Headquarters Staff Captain in April 1905, he began collaborating with Swinton on various short works of future-war fiction for *Blackwood's Magazine* (referred to by its devotees as 'maga'). The evidence for this is found in Swinton's letters to the editor (and owner) of *Blackwood's*. In an undated letter from October 1906, Swinton talks about a recent submission as having been written 'about 1½ years ago, by myself and a brother officer. We sent it to various magazines last year.'[28] If the 'brother officer' is Vickers, then this indicates that they started writing together almost immediately, since Swinton's post-dating reference of 'about 1½ years ago' coincides with Vickers' posting to the War Office—April 1905.

Although it is impossible to prove that the 'brother officer' is Vickers, there is strong evidence to suggest such a conclusion. For instance, in his December 29, 1906 letter to Blackwood, Swinton writes of another recent, jointly authored submission, entitled 'An Eddy of War': 'About the yarn you have by you now, we are neither of us proud of it, and I am not surprised that you like the others better, but before we threw it away, we wanted an expert's opinion. We are both grateful for your reading it.'[29] Although no mention is made in this letter of the specific identity of the other author, subsequent communiqués indicate that the future-war 'yarn' in question is eventually accepted for publication after a rewrite. Swinton returns the corrected manuscript with a letter (March 11, 1907) that contains the following passage: 'I return proof of "An Eddy of War" corrected. I need hardly say that both my pal (Capt. Vickers R.E.) and I am delighted at your taking for Maga.'[30] Beyond referring to Vickers as his 'pal' (not the way most British field-grade officers of higher social station referred to their middle-class subalterns), the letter holds manifold significance. First, it establishes Vickers as the co-author of 'An Eddy of War.' Secondly, since Swinton's earlier letter indicates that 'An Eddy of War' was received by *Blackwood's* sometime before December 29, 1906, Vickers obviously began collaborating with Swinton by November–December of that year (at least). Furthermore, Swinton remarks in his letter of December 29 that he is not surprised 'that you like the others better, but before we threw it away . . .[etc.].' The persistent use of the pronoun 'we' rather than 'I' indicates that, given the number of jointly authored stories in question, their collaboration had been going on for some time. It is of course possible that these two friends sat down one long weekend in late November and, without pausing to sleep, managed to draft and submit a passel of publishable stories. However, this is so unlikely as to be absurd, particularly since staffers at the War Office did not have generous allotments of spare time. The logical and reasonable conjecture supported by all these communiqués is that Vickers and Swinton had been collaborating for quite a while.

The biographical evidence for their ongoing collaboration is further supported by the content of the narratives themselves: in one of the apparently jointly authored stories—'The Joint in the Harness'—the first dialogue between the two main characters goes as follows:

> 'Well, my Captain of Plumbers, how goes it? Aren't you across yet?'
> 'Hullo, Shunter-in-Chief, is that you? What are you doing down here, away from your beloved yard? What is your grumble now? Come, talk with me a while and learn something.'[31]

The jocularly derogative titles that these two characters adopt for each other suggest Swinton's and Vickers' own areas of professional specialty, respectively. Swinton's work concerned construction, fortification, and structural engineering, and he was frequently called away to inspect installations throughout England: he was a 'Captain of Plumbers.' Vickers specialized in railway matters, and in the Boer War, served as a traffic superintendent, railhead traffic officer, and finally, deputy-assistant of railways: he was a 'Shunter-in-Chief.' Of course, it may be that the similarity of characters to authors is coincidence, but we see a matching model in Vickers' own 'The Trenches,' which begins with two officers wading through paperwork in the War Office. The senior of the two, 'Major Swann,'[32] is 'a man of plans' who is inundated with 'plans and drawings' nestled near drawers 'labeled with names of fortresses and barracks.'[33] The reader also learns that Swann has 'spent a good deal of time on the Indian frontier,' which is where Swinton was born and later served. In both texts, therefore, each author playfully used a character resembling his coworker and fellow-officer. But furthermore, it suggests that each consulted the other when a field-specific narrative matter required an expert opinion or perspective, which indicates that Swinton probably involved rail-expert Vickers in his publishing efforts not later than mid-1906 (the submission date of the railway-focused 'Joint in the Harness') and possibly well before. Thus their collaboration was neither brief nor unsuccessful and therefore, it should have been important—and memorable—to Swinton.

There is every indication that it was. In addition to advancing his own interests, Swinton was keen on promoting those of reliable friends and subordinates. In a letter of March 28, 1907, he thanks Mr Blackwood 'for your thought in sending a copy of "Maga" for Capt. Vickers. I will give it to him today.'[34] It does not take a great deal of reading between the lines to conjecture that Swinton's frequent mentions of his collaborative 'pal' Vickers were intended to encourage Blackwood to express interest in Vickers' own work.[35] By sending the Captain a complimentary copy of the magazine, Blackwood was also sending an invitation.

It was not long before Vickers responded with a finished manuscript. On October 10, Vickers wrote a letter of thanks to Blackwood: 'It is hardly necessary to say that I feel very pleased you think "The Trenches" worthy of a place in "Maga." It is the first writing of my own you have accepted, though "An Eddy of War" was partly mine (with Swinton).'[36] Swinton was quick to include a supporting promotional note in a letter of December 12, 1907: 'I was pleased to hear from Vickers (Capt RE) that he has had a story accepted by you and I am keen to see it. It sounds a good one.'[37] However, it is the next letter from Swinton to Blackwood that establishes Swinton's reading of 'The Trenches' as fact. Swinton writes in his letter of January 8, 1908: 'I like Vickers' yarn. . . . Why will our powers at home not consult the people who *know*, a little more?'[38] Although Swinton does not refer to 'Vickers' yarn' by its title, he is unquestionably referring to 'The Trenches,' since it is the only story that Vickers ever published while alive. Furthermore, the date of Swinton's letter corresponds to the release date of the issue of *Blackwood's* which contained 'The Trenches.' However, the 'powers at home' had little time to realize that Vickers was one of those 'people who *know*': a month later, Vickers had died of complications arising from pneumonia-necessitated surgery—and it was Swinton who made the funeral arrangements for his 'pal,' writing to Blackwood on February 9, 1908 that 'The funeral procession starts from 41 Oakley Street at 3:45 tomorrow . . .'[39]

Clearly, Swinton—the man who 'invented' the tank—had been exposed to Vickers' prevision of the vehicle, to its uses in breaking the kind of stalemate that would necessitate its development, and had a clear sense of its impending importance. Swinton even reveals that he considers these anticipations of Vickers' to be particularly foresightful and valuable when he laments 'Why will our powers at home not consult the people who *know*, a little more?' It is also clear that Swinton and Vickers were not merely professional acquaintances, but 'pals'—and the uncharacteristically glum tone of the remainder of Swinton's letter of February 9, 1908, suggests the sorrow of a man who has lost a close friend. Finally, a letter from Vickers' sister Emily to Blackwood indicates that, as of late 1909, Swinton was still handling Vickers' affairs, overseeing the posthumous publication, and reediting, of his work, 'The Shunting Puzzle.' She writes to the editor that '[I] am sure . . . that Major Swinton will do anything you might think necessary.'[40] Therefore, the proposition that, from the beginning of the tank project in 1914 to the Commission hearing in 1919, Swinton did not once recall his 'pal' Vickers and his prescient 'tank story' seems implausible, if not preposterous. Since Swinton is never reported as suffering from amnesia, it is difficult to understand how such a pointed and prolonged lapse of recollection might have occurred. Furthermore, the demonstrated acuity of Swinton's memory, writing, and self-marketing acumen argue against any such diagnosis. More logically, Swinton realized that the price of political advantage was silence—thereby demonstrating that within the Edwardian military hierarchy, future-war fiction possessed the power not only to shape organizational, but personal, agendas and actions.

Further doubts about Swinton's claims of invention emerge when one considers that, in the years 1905–1908, according to Swinton's own pamphlet 'The Tank,' the Royal Engineers (Swinton's own branch of the service) tested 'the Hornsby-Ackroyd Caterpillar Tractor,' which eventually took part in the Royal Review of 1908, at Aldershot.[41] There it received the particular attention and interest of King Edward, and made front-page headline news (complete with photographs) in the *Daily Mirror* of May 19, a paper claiming the second largest morning circulation in the nation. This device was modeled after the American Holt tractor, which the then Colonel Swinton first claims to have encountered in Belgium in the summer of 1914. The description of the Holt vehicle (various, similar models of which had been in existence for more than ten years) is suspiciously like the machine that gives rise to the 'Snail' of 'The Trenches,' which Major Swann procures from an American salesman in a scene that is rife with inside jokes and other tell-tale signs consistent with a faithful adaptation from actual events. Did an American 'josser' actually barge into the War Office one day, accosting Swinton and Vickers with the wonders of his Holt caterpillar tractor? It would certainly explain much about the War Office scene that initiates Vickers' story, the source of its inspiration, and the similarity of the 'Snail' and the Holt machine (which was equipped to dig broad furrows, if not trenches). This constellation of facts and highly probable deductions establishes the presence of caterpillar tractors in military publications in the period 1905–1908. It also makes Swinton's claims that such a machine was not known to him until 1914 even more suspect. At the very least, his own correspondence establishes that he read 'The Trenches' and felt that the potential of such vehicles was under-appreciated by the General Staff and government. More important, all evidence indicates that Vickers' foresightful story influenced Swinton, who in turn brought the tank into existence, and thereby, had a major impact on the conduct of World War I.

\*\*\*\*\*

Another vehicle that was under-appreciated by both military and government experts in the Empire was the submarine. They were not alone in doubting that this very new technology could ever have a major influence upon the outcome of a war. Even H. G. Wells claimed that submarines would remain too unreliable to make satisfactory weapons. It was left to another well-known writer of speculative fiction to predict and illustrate the tremendous impact of the submarine upon warfare.

That writer—Arthur Conan Doyle of Sherlock Holmes fame—wrote the proleptically titled 'Danger!' in 1914, a mere two months before the commencement of hostilities. In it, submarine commander John Sirius informs the King of his unnamed Continental nation that he can win the impending war with England 'within a month, or six weeks at the utmost.'[42] His method: systematic destruction of merchant ships—both English and neutral vessels—that bring food supplies to the island nation. Sirius predicts that this unprecedented sinking of scores of unarmed merchantmen will create a food shortage in England, which will in turn precipitate runaway inflation and financial chaos. The unnamed King agrees, Sirius sails, the cargo ships sink by the dozens, and—despite international outrage—the scheme works. Although the scale of success and destruction that Conan Doyle depicts in his imaginary U-boat campaign is more accurately reflected in the German 'wolfpack' predations of World War II,[43] it is nonetheless a very reasonable and sober prediction of how an essentially new weapons technology would soon play havoc with the anticipated course of events of World War I.

Before World War I, it was almost universally assumed that no nation would intentionally attack civilian or neutral targets, even those that might be supplying an opponent's war effort. If this seems strangely naive to modern readers, it is, in part, because future-war fictions served as inoculations against popular rejection of the tactic, thereby acculturating Western society to a new 'infernal machine' and the horrible mode of warmaking it portended. Arguably, this acculturation was itself proleptic of another trend which has grown prodigiously ever since submarine tactics destroyed the presumed inviolability and safety of 'civilians': superpower presumptions of, and accommodation with, 'total war' have not only taken hold of, but have come to dominate, modern political consciousness. In total war, the concept of 'non-combatants' borders on the oxymoronic, because resources and social infrastructure, not merely military formations, come under attack. Consequently, commerce, utilities, and communication facilities must be eliminated or interdicted, and, with a flourish of semantic necromancy, casualties among nearby civilians are conveniently transmogrified into mere 'collateral damage.' Only a few decades after Conan Doyle first alerted readers to the 'Danger!' of total war, actions that were once considered unthinkably brutal and barbaric had become blithely accepted norms.

However, whereas Conan Doyle anticipated the new level of wartime barbarity and dehumanization that first surfaced along with the sub, the tradition-bound experts could not (or perhaps refused to) foresee this development. Admiral Penrose Fitzgerald, whose observations were included in an appendix of commentary that *Strand Magazine* published along with 'Danger!', remarked that 'I do not myself think that any civilised nation will torpedo unarmed and defenceless merchant ships.' Another commentator, Admiral Sir Algernon de Horsey, had a similar reaction, characterizing Conan Doyle's tale as 'a very interesting, but, as most would say, fantastic account of an imaginary war.' Admiral Sir Compton Domvile felt 'compelled to say that I think it most improbable, and more like one of Jules Verne's stories than any other author I know,' and Admiral William Hannam Henderson dismissed the notion that 'territorial waters will be violated, or neutral vessels sunk. Such will be absolutely prohibited, and will only recoil on the heads of the perpetrators. No nation would permit it, and the officer who did it would be shot.'[44]

More crucially, the most senior members of the British defense community, the Committee for Imperial Defence (CID), simply could not believe that so seemingly fragile and untested a technology as the submarine could bring such changes to their long-held strategic and tactical assumptions about the conduct of maritime warfare. As CID Secretary Lt. Colonel Maurice Hankey[45] writes in a personal letter appended to a 'Private and Confidential Letter' from the CID of June 11, 1915,

> It may, of course, be contended that in future wars, when the submarine has been still further developed, our communications with the outer world might be seriously threatened by German submarines. It appears far more probable, however, that as the submarine develops, so the antidote will develop. Even in the present war, although at the outset we had made no attempt to combat submarines, we have limited its activities, so that, in fact, they do us no more harm than the French privateers did in the Napoleonic wars after the Battle of Trafalgar.[46]

As Hankey wrote this, the rapid increase in German submarine activity had already started, and in another week or two, was making itself felt as a dramatic new factor in a war that had already proven itself to be full of grim surprises. Written only two weeks later, Hankey's 'Secret Report' from the CID to Kitchener includes the following recommendation:

> Our main preoccupation will be in dealing with the attacks of the enemy's submarines, which it must be anticipated will increase very rapidly in number. It is . . . essential that the strength of our mercantile fleet should be preserved unimpaired. . . . So great have been the losses from the depredations of the Germans' cruisers in the early part of the war, and the activities of the enemy's submarines during recent months, that for the first time for very many years the amount of British tonnage available is at present below that of twelve months ago.[47]

This rapid change in the assessment of the 'Danger!' posed by the submarine underscores how insightful Conan Doyle's story was, particularly in comparison with the assumptions of the 'best' military minds in the Empire. Considering the massive purchases of key war matériel arriving from America and Canada, the initially blithe dismissal of a threat to England's transoceanic logistical lifeline can only be considered a product of unfounded optimism or blinkered traditionalism. Since the decisive naval battle at Jutland had not yet been fought and mastery of the seas was still uncertain, the military establishment's dismissal of the submarine seems to have derived from an inability to envision the consequences of new technologies, rather than strategic stupidity. Ultimately, lessons such as those learned from the unexpected power of the submarine revealed the necessity of remaining current and even imaginative in matters of military technology, and thus, paved the way for the characteristically superpower reconception of weapons research as big business, and the evolution of what Eisenhower was to dub 'the military/industrial complex.'

*****

The most dramatic and revolutionary of the three technologies investigated in this chapter—the airplane—was, predictably, the one most blithely and routinely dismissed by 'experts.' Their self-assured, negative prognostications concerning aircraft now read as comic aphorisms of misperception: 'Heavier-than-air flying machines are impossible'—Lord Kelvin, president, Royal Society, 1895; 'Airplanes are interesting toys but of no military value'—Marechal Ferdinand Foch, Professor of Strategy, Ecole Superieure de Guerre. However, one keen observer of innovation in military technology foresaw a world in which

> Every country was hiding flying-machines. They [were] fighting in the air all over Europe—all over the world. . . . [T]he whole atmosphere was the Seat of War, and every land a cockpit.
>
> H.G. Wells, *The War in the Air*[48]

Once again, it is a speculative author's 'rumors' regarding the consequences of an imminent 'infernal machine' that anticipate history as it has unfolded. Indeed, the preceding passage from Wells' 1907 *The War in the Air* is the only one of the three citations that is not so profoundly and comically wrong as to elicit a rueful smile. Yet the first two statements were made by, respectively, one of England's most respected scientists and one of France's most esteemed generals, thereby recalling the chapter's initial proposition: that new ideas, new technologies, and new tactics are most likely to arise from the middle ranks (or from outside) of a nation's official hierarchy, not from its upper echelons. Furthermore, it also highlights the fact that these ideas almost inevitably first come to the public consciousness—including that of officials and political elites—through works of speculative fiction, not ready-to-build blueprints.

Although Wells' *The War in Air* may be the definitive prevision of military airpower, humbler anticipations preceded his. Two in particular are worth mentioning because, as was the case with 'The Trenches,' they arise not from a novelist or a hack journalist, but from the imagination of a military officer whose connections both with the defense and journalistic communities illustrate the extensive interconnections that exist between the domains of popular discourse and political influence. The stories in question are 'The Kite' and 'The Joint in the Harness'—and both were written by Ernest D. Swinton of tank-inventing fame.

Whereas Wells' slightly later envisioning of aerial war and combat technologies is grand both in its scope and radical imagination, Swinton—with the same studied, engineering sobriety evinced by his 'pal' Vickers—advances a very modest proposition: that small heavier-than-air craft, properly designed for special, narrowly defined missions, could make themselves a major new variable in both tactical and strategic combat equations. 'The Kite' is just barely predictive: as Swinton writes to Blackwood on May 10, 1906, it is 'an anticipation of what may quite possibly happen in the use of kites and Q.F. guns which are existing weapons now . . .'[49] The story is nothing more than a vignette that depicts these two fledgling technologies in combination—much to the consternation of the opposing forces. Swinton probably sensed that because such an idea was dangerously non-traditional, it was not necessarily advantageous to his military career to have his name connected with the manuscript. Instead, he used his pseudonym 'Ole-Luk-Oie,' a precaution which Blackwood apparently suggested: in his letter of May 28, 1906, Swinton extends his 'Thanks for your hint about not publishing my name. I think you are right, especially as my yarn may open some people's eyes as to *possibilities*.'[50]

These 'possibilities' apparently did attract some attention—of a most unusual nature. Shortly after the story appeared in *Blackwood's Magazine*, a London newspaper ran the following article:

COMMAND OF THE AIR—NAVIGABLE KITE TO DESTROY BRIDGES IN WAR

In any future war the British Army will have a surprise in store for the enemy.

A clever sapper has invented a navigable kite—an airship in miniature—which so far has answered all the purposes required of it.

This machine is not intended for heavy warfare in the air, but can carry sufficient weight in dynamite or other powerful explosive to make it of use over an enemy's lines of communication.

Thus it could be utilised to destroy a railway bridge or pontoon. Charges heavy enough to destroy earthworks cannot be carried, as the maximum navigable weight for this aeroplane is only small.

The destruction of vital points on a line of communication is a powerful aid to a force in the field, and the army that can employ a destructor of this kind is assured of many successes, even against greater numbers.[51]

There are several fascinating implications hidden within this apparently straightforward article. In the first place, the British army had not, as of 1906, commenced any investigations into the airplane as a potential weapon: that would not occur until 1911.[52] Furthermore, the article is peculiarly short on evidentiary details. No trials are mentioned, and neither names nor dates are given; indeed, no facts are provided other than what would seem to constitute a conceptual outline of a new, untested, and possibly incomplete piece of technology. The only concrete information provided is that the 'inventor' is a 'clever sapper.' In British military parlance, a 'sapper' is an engineer—and so of course was Swinton.[53] This apparent coincidence is made more suspicious by additional improbable correlations: the device in the article is (like Swinton's) also called a 'Kite' and its capabilities match (and in some particulars, exceed) those of the proto-aircraft depicted in Swinton's yarn. Most unusual of all, the ways in which the aforesaid 'Kite' exceeds the performance of Swinton's proposed vehicle precisely anticipate the increased performance of the aircraft that he depicts in his very next story, 'A Joint in the Harness,' which he had already submitted to *Blackwood's* by mid-October.

While the inferential nature of this evidence makes any conclusive assertions impossible, the likely explanation is that a sympathetic editor had not only read 'Ole-luk-Oie's' yarn in *Blackwood's Magazine*, but learned that the author was a member of the Royal Engineers who had already penned another air war yarn that envisioned further operational capacities for a similar aircraft. However, concocting a 'news article' out of such material would require an editor who was sympathetic to the idea of military air power, aggressively nationalistic (probably a Conservative), willing to obscure the boundary between current facts and future-war fiction, and powerful enough to shrug off any accusations of journalistic improprieties. There is only one editor of a London paper in 1906 who embodied all these traits, and who would soon begin running a regular feature entitled 'Man in the Air:' Lord Northcliffe. The powerful and hawkish yellow journalist was one of Britain's first, most ardent, and aggressive proponents for air power. Beginning in 1906, his technological interest in flying machines became amplified by nationalistic anxiety. In the success of Santos-Dumont's French flights, he foresaw a German threat to England. 'ENGLAND IS NO LONGER AN ISLAND' his headlines pronounced, followed by his assertion that 'There will be no more sleeping safely behind the wooden walls of old England with the Channel our safety moat. It means the aerial chariot of a foe descending on British soil if a war comes.'[54]

Northcliffe was not content with being the only eminent Edwardian raising the clarion call of air power: influential officials such as Haldane, Esher, and Beresford were regular recipients of his pro-aviation exhortations. To popularize the technology, he virtually sponsored Bleriot's flight across the Channel, and then commissioned an article of news commentary by H. G. Wells, who wrote, 'It means . . . that the world cannot wait for the English. It is not the first warning we have had . . . in spite of our fleet, this is no longer, from a military point of view, an inaccessible Island.'[55] Northcliffe's involvement also included posting cash prizes (some as high as £10,000) for aerial achievements, and eventually, appointments to air-related positions in the war years, including a personal stint as Director of Propaganda in Enemy Countries (which was, in large part, conducted by dropping leaflets from aircraft).

So, although it is impossible to prove that Northcliffe reacted to Swinton's tale by converting the core of it into a news article, or that he acquired knowledge of 'The Joint in the Harness' even before it was published, it seems almost certain that someone in a position analogous to Northcliffe did precisely this, and it is hard to find any other editor whose nationalism, air enthusiasm, and influence are all so auspiciously combined to both facilitate and predict such an act of yellow journalism.

A close analysis of Swinton's 'A Joint in the Harness' actually recommends it as the most probable source for the article in question. As Swinton explains in a letter to Blackwood, his tale

> ... is about war, and a wee bit of an anticipation because it deals with flying machines which, of course, are coming soon. It relates how an army was started and beaten owing to the action of these 'flies' acting upon the sore spot in its line of communications. The sore spot is a large broken railway bridge which is being repaired against time, but the sore is kept open (by the flies hovering around and dropping explosives every night) long enough to starve the army ahead.... I think whether dropping explosives from the air is forbidden by any international convention or not, the nation that can fly will do it.[56]

Swinton adds to the drama of the piece by placing the 'flies' not in the hands of the British, but the curt, ruthless 'generalissimos' of an unidentified nation, which has engaged the more sympathetic (and British-accented) army with their 'Western Force.'[57] However, the 'flies' themselves are ultimately the focal point of the manuscript, and Swinton anticipates and combines several aeronautical developments into these craft. In the first place, these 'flies' are capable of hovering: 'You see, we have to hover anyway to aim, and that's the difficulty. That's what the secret gear and auxiliary-lifting propeller are for . . .'[58] This does not describe any of the aircraft which, in ten years time, would be dueling over the trenches in France; instead, it leaps ahead to envision what we would now call an ultralight autogiro:[59] 'Each was supported by a sort of dwarf bicycle and tied down. They were skeletons, with great flat awnings of membranous material and queer shape stretched taught on light frames stayed with wire. . . . [T]heir spidery appearance . . .', along with their ability to hover, inspires the nickname of 'flies.'[60] Swinton's prevision also includes napalm bombs: inquiring as to the munitions with which the aircraft will be provided, one of the mission-planners asks 'Can't we set anything alight? I'm stocking a splendid line in incendiary bombs, pretty things of petrol and celluloid, that look like capsules?'[61] Swinton's understanding of how airpower will generate terror, anxiety, and sleeplessness finds articulation through another of the planners: 'Afterwards, if any machines are left unexpended, we might further assist their hunger-bred fantasies by flying over them and dropping a bomb or two, or even by flying over them and showing a light.'[62] These considerations of the tactical and psychological opportunities implicit in control of a battlefield's tactical airspace constitute not only astute military anticipation, but literary prophesy as well: today's best-selling future-war technothrillers are incomplete if they do not include an obligatory 'command of the air' discussion early on.

Last, in response to the logical question of whether Swinton was actually trying to anticipate technologies—and thereby exert a covert form of cautionary political influence—or whether he was just trying to spin a yarn and earn a shilling or two, we have Swinton's own explanation of his motivations. In a letter written as early as December 29, 1906, and speaking of a future-war story with a tragic ending,[63] he writes,

> I have been accused of being a pessimist and ending my stories very dismally. I do not know whether this is good art or not, but I do know that the more the bulk of the British nation realizes what war <u>can</u> be, the better for us. I don't want to let things end all happily.
>
> I don't know whether you agree with my ideas, but it is at the back of all my yarns that you have seen.[64]

Despite their heated battle over the origins of the tank in the 1930s, Wells was in agreement with Swinton on this last point: influencing the perspective of the nation—or, in Wells' case, the world—was certainly 'at the back of all his yarns,' as well. Wells was convinced that fiction was 'the only medium through which we can discuss the majority of the problems which are being raised in such bristling multitude by our contemporary social development.'[65] However, whereas Swinton's focus was trained narrowly on immediate technical innovations and tactical opportunities, Wells' perspective was comparatively panoramic. His interest was compelled by the larger military, political, and ultimately social, consequences of combat aircraft. Accordingly, Wells did not trouble himself over-much with the mechanical particulars of the diverse aircraft that flit in and out of the pages of his air-war stories. For instance, in *The War in the Air*, Wells offers up a bizarre cornucopia of airborne oddities, ranging from massive German zeppelins, manta-shaped Chinese dirigibles, one-man Japanese ornithopters, American biplanes, and more. The air-to-air combats feature rifles and larger guns, but they also involve grapples to rend the sides of dirigibles and—the most improbable of all—boarding actions between the larger, slower airships. Clearly, Wells' technological interests were primarily excited by the many possibilities, rather than by one specific form, of aerial technology.

Even though air power was the dramatic focus for many of his narratives (including, but not limited to, *The War in the Air*, *Filmer*, *Things to Come*, and the apocalyptic *The World Set Free*), Wells was neither the most prolific, nor the most prophetic, of this subgenre's authors. He was, however (as even George Orwell conceded), the most influential by several orders of magnitude.[66] His works were as well known and talked about as Swinton's were obscure and often unremarked. However, from the most conservative speculators of almost-invented technologies through to the bolder visionaries of a further future, there was a consistent —and often heavily intertexualized—motivational thread: to educate. Many of these authors avow a deliberate attempt to encourage a social predisposition to 'air-mindedness.' As Paris' *Winged Warfare* amply illustrates, these future-war fictions 'exerted considerable influence on the pre-1914 mind, especially on . . . the pioneers of military aviation. . . . [Through them,] the flying machine as an additional weapon in the technology of war . . .[was]. . . established in the public imagination as a future certainty . . .'[67]

Without question, the most influential of these many texts is Wells' *The War in the Air*. Despite its almost comical assortment of weird flying contraptions, it articulates with almost pedagogical thoroughness and clarity the strategic and social consequences of the introduction of combat aircraft. These lessons were particularly relevant to a profoundly technocentric nation that was just awakening to thoughts of global influence and concomitant military restructuring: the already-'air-minded' United States of America. In hindsight, it is tempting to hypothesize that one of America's unrecognized conceptual primers for evolution into a superpower was *The War in the Air*'s practical examination of what would soon become the hallmark of US military might, combat aircraft. As Wells explains in the preface written for the novel's reissue in 1921,

> [W]ith the flying machine war alters in its character; it ceases to be an affair of 'fronts' and becomes an affair of 'areas'; neither side, victor or loser, remains immune from the gravest injuries, and while there is a vast increase in the destructiveness of war, there is also an increased indecisiveness. Consequently 'War in the Air' means social destruction instead of victory as the end of war. It not only alters the methods of war but the consequences of war. After all that has happened since this fantasia of possibility was written, I do not think that there is much wrong with this thesis. . . . I am inclined to think very well of myself as I re-read the entirely imaginary account of the collapse of civilisation under the strain of modern war which forms the Epilogue of the story. In 1907 this chapter was read with hearty laughter as the production of an 'imaginative novelist's' distempered brain. Is it quite so wildly funny to-day?[68]

Wells' self-congratulatory conclusion reflects a fragile authorial ego that was notoriously sensitive to criticism of any type, and from any quarter. But he does not misadvertise the visionary accuracy of his fiction. *The War in the Air* is the story of Bert Smallways, whose humble everyman background and pedestrian intellect matches his name. As a consequence of initially comic misadventures which place him in exactly the right places at exactly the wrong times, Smallways unwillingly becomes witness to the collapse of civilization as a result of the first air war. Spirited away by a German aerial armada that is flying to launch a sneak attack on the United States, he sees the sinking of fleets, the bombing of Broadway, a sprawling air duel over the East Coast, and the invasion of the US by rival Japanese and Chinese airfleets. This piecemeal annihilation of America is a cipher for what is transpiring throughout the world, as one nation after another takes to the air in a domino-effect frenzy of preemptive strikes, score-settlings, and genocidal campaigns of subjugation and extermination.

Despite the grand scope of the story, Wells wisely keeps his focus more or less centered on the hapless (but decreasingly comical) Bert Smallways, whose simple-minded and inoffensive good nature is the most intimately dramatized casualty of the war. Although he does not revel in killing, Smallways becomes accustomed to violence, so much so that, at the end, in order to secure domestic tranquility upon his homecoming, he soberly carries out the ambush and assassination of a local troublemaker. (He has apparently picked up the tactic of 'bushwhacking' an opponent from his grim experiences in America.) He regrets the deed, but his belief in its necessity—and the inuring effects of years of war and then wandering in a turbulent, violent world—make this killing just another regrettable incident in Bert's thoroughly blasted life.

It is Wells' ability to trace the steady accumulation of horrors that change Bert, while simultaneously depicting the social effects of a global air war, that constitutes the most noteworthy narratalogical achievement in the text. However, the most clever thematic sleight of hand in the novel is Wells' depiction of how these two processes are inextricably linked. Ultimately, both individual psyches and social orders decay not merely because of the physical damage of the bombs, but because of the dehumanization that inheres in this new type of warfare. A memorable example of this thematic synthesis occurs when Bert witnesses—in horribly graphic detail—the destruction of the American Atlantic fleet by aerial bombardment:

> Smash! came a vast explosion in the forward part of the flagship, and a huge piece of metal-work seemed to lift out of her and dump itself into the sea, dropping men and leaving a gap into which a prompt *drachenflieger* planted a flaring bomb. And then for an instant Bert perceived only too clearly in the growing, pitiless light a number of minute, convulsively active animalculae scorched and struggling in the *Theodore Roosevelt*'s foaming wake. What were they? Not men— surely not men? Those drowning, mangled little creatures tore with

their clutching fingers at Bert's soul. 'Oh, Gord!' he cried, 'Oh, Gord!' almost whimpering. He looked again and they had gone, and the black stem of the *Andrew Jackson*, a little disfigured by the sinking *Bremen*'s last shot, was parting the water that had swallowed them into two neatly symmetrical waves. For some moments sheer blank horror blinded Bert to the destruction below.[69]

Shortly after, the Zeppelin in which Bert is riding reascends, and the carnage becomes mercifully indistinct. However, Wells reveals that such distancing only facilitates another of the great dangers of aerial warfare: detachment from the human consequences of one's aggressive actions. With the possible exceptions of rocketry or long-range artillery, no weapon places such immense physical and psychological distance between an attacker and his victims. As a result, no other weapon is so conducive to an attacker's fantasies of self-rationalization and delusional beliefs in the ability to restrict destructive energies to 'military targets.'

Before long, the Zeppelins descend again, this time in order to conduct a precision bombardment of New York's Broadway, an action that is both a reprisal and an attempt to 'pacify' the city's populace. In order to bomb precisely, the Zeppelins swing low over their target—affording captive Bert Smallways a traumatically intimate view of the carnage that results:

> The catastrophe was the logical outcome of the situation created by the application of science to warfare. It was unavoidable that great cities should be destroyed. . . . And so our Bert Smallways became a participant in one of the most cold-blooded slaughters in the world's history, in which men who were neither excited nor . . . in any danger, poured death and destruction upon homes and crowds below.
>
> He clung to the frame of the porthole as the airship tossed and swayed, and stared down . . . into the twilight streets, watching people running out of the houses, watching buildings collapse and fires begin. As the airships sailed along they smashed up the city as a child will shatter its cities of brick and card. Below, they left ruins and blazing conflagrations and heaped and scattered dead; men, women, and children mixed together as though they had been no more than Moors, or Zulus, or Chinese.[70]

Wells' placement of this scene of devastation in that utterly American megalopolis which was already, in the globe's collective consciousness, outpacing London as the First City of the world, is a clever and effective narrative choice for several reasons. First, it is a sound marketing ploy, maximizing the immediacy of the story for Wells' second largest English-language audience. Also, Wells' decision to have the Germans pulverize New York City highlights the fundamental alteration to warfare and politics that is manifest in warplane technology: the era of geographical isolation as a guarantee of national security had come to an end. Wells' enunciates the consequences of this change in one of his more didactic passages:

> The essential fact of the politics of the age . . . was a very simple one . . . The development of Science had altered the scale of human affairs. By means of rapid mechanical traction it had brought men nearer together, so much nearer socially, economically, physically, that the old separations into nations and kingdoms were no longer possible, a newer, wider synthesis was not only needed but imperatively demanded.[71]

However, since this demand went unheard or unheeded by the great powers of the world, Wells concludes, the air war that followed was inevitable. Aircraft represented a new opportunity to project power, but, when possessed by a rival, they also represented a new vulnerability to that rival's identical capacities. The result—an escalating war inflamed by fear and hate, and excused by the rhetoric of preemption and manifest destiny—was as unavoidable as it was tragic. Although he concludes with an appeal for a world government (a recurrent theme), Wells is also foreshadowing the superpower state's evolution toward transnational praxes. Wells points to the dissolution of borders, and suggests that the only reasonable response is to expand, stabilize, and integrate the peripheries of social control across these old boundaries—and in so doing, he anticipates a 'mature' superpower's methods (if not objectives) of conquest and control.

Wells anticipates another evolution in politico-military strategy when he reveals why the Germans decide to initiate the global air war with an attack upon America. The Kaiser is convinced that he must begin by eliminating not the largest, nor the most proximal nation, but that one which is his closest *technological* rival. It is not enough that 'Germany was by far the most efficient power in the world, better organized for swift and secret action, better equipped with the resources of modern science, and with her official and administrative classes at a higher level of education and training.'[72] These advantages would only be decisive if they were also exclusive, so Germany must eliminate any nation that has the technological acumen and infrastructure to create a force with the same attributes. Inevitably, therefore, the Kaiser decides to 'strike America swiftly, because there, if anywhere, lies the chance of an aerial rival.' Mindful of the combat planes that the Americans are evolving out of 'the Wright flyer,' the Germans decide boldly to 'fling a great force across the Atlantic heavens and bear America down unwarned and unprepared.'[73] Here, as in World War II, and in the Cold War that followed, the decisive struggle is increasingly defined by the opposition of technological rivals. By attacking America first—even though it is a distant and difficult target—Wells' Germans anticipate the new strategy of technological interdiction and preemption that will become the new standard operating procedure in the planning and conduct of modern war between superpower technocracies. Wells might have been reading the Kaiser's mind when he wrote this. According to Lord Haldane's synopsis of a subsequently suppressed 1912 interview granted to Dr. William Bayard Hale of the *New York Times*, the German monarch did, in fact, attach great significance to America's rapid technological and industrial ascendence. He was careful to include that he 'was very friendly towards the United States because the march of progress and the degeneration of Great Britain showed that the two dominant world forces of the future would be Germany and the United States.'[74] It is tempting to speculate that in Kaiser Wilhelm's aggressively competitive mind, the term 'two dominant forces of the future' was merely a polite synonym for 'future rivals.'

In Wells' narrative, America's response to the aerial actualization of the German threat is no less revealing and anticipatory of its own eventual praxes as a superpower at war. Specifically, America's reaction illustrates the practical disjunctures and philosophical dissonances that arise when its democratic ideals must adapt to the waging of a true mechanized war. Wells observes that

> One of the most striking facts historically about this war, and the one that makes the complete separation that had arisen between the methods of warfare and the necessity of democratic support, is the effectual secrecy of the Washington authorities about their airships. They did not bother to confide a single fact of their preparations to the public. They did not even condescend to talk to Congress. They burked and suppressed every inquiry. The war was fought by the President and the secretaries of State in an entirely autocratic manner.[75]

This is one of the most subtle, impressive, and chilling anticipations in this narrative: the demands of 'technowarring' (to adapt a term from Buckminster Fuller) not only prove to be at odds with, but immediately predominant over, the basic principles of democratic government. Furthermore, this usurpation of power reveals itself first and foremost in terms of information control.

Continuing his pattern of juxtaposing the social and personal effects of the war, Wells reveals that the technological threat to democratic principles has an individual dimension as well. In excusing America's ineffectual civilian outcry and defense preparations, Wells' omniscient narrator explains that 'The balance of military efficiency was shifting back from the many to the few, from the common to the specialised. The days when the emotional infantryman decided battles had passed by for ever. War had become a matter of apparatus, of special training and skill of the intricate kind. It had become undemocratic'—and inhuman, both in terms of the predominance of infernal machines, and in the routine acceptance of brutalities that, half a century earlier, would have been considered not merely barbaric, but indicative of a sociopathic absence of empathy and compassion.[76]

In addition to air power's impact on societies and individuals, it also brings revolutionary changes to the strategic conduct of war: 'The . . . peculiarity of aerial warfare was that it was at once enormously destructive and entirely indecisive . . . [since] both sides lay open to punitive attack.'[77] Although Wells' assertions regarding the absolute indecisiveness of air power are somewhat simplistic, the radical rethinking required when war is no longer 'an affair of fronts' but of 'areas' is anticipated with remarkable clarity in *The War in the Air*. Furthermore, he illustrates that although the airplane may be the ultimate offensive weapon, its ability to be decisive in any conflict is dependent upon absolute operational freedom: without 'uncontested air superiority'—without freedom from interdiction by rival airforces—the outcome of a war remains uncertain, even though the concomitant devastation has increased a hundredfold.

Of course, Wells failed to anticipate a number of important features of air combat, particularly those that apply to tactical air operations. He did not anticipate the evasiveness of ground targets in difficult terrain, or the development of sophisticated anti-aircraft countermeasures and adaptive strategies, both of which were integrated and raised to a grim but effective art form by the North Vietnamese during the Vietnam War. However, as Thomas Scortia observes in his article 'Science Fiction as the Imaginary Experiment,' even General Westmoreland still had something to learn from Wells. Writing during—and with obvious reference to American tactics in—the Vietnam War, Scortia points out that Wells shrewdly foresaw 'that, while aircraft may interdict territory to the enemy, they cannot hold ground to become the decisive force in a war. . . . This is a remarkable insight for one writing in 1908, an insight that has not yet been granted to our leading military minds in the Department of Defense.'[78] The irony of Scortia's barbed conclusion doubles when an historical assessment reveals that Wells was given greater credence by Edwardians who were less well-prepared to understand (let alone believe) his insight, and was ignored or forgotten by post-war Americans, whose reality was daily evolving into the one which he had foreseen.

H. G. Wells' contributions to the Edwardian social consciousness were not restricted to his literary efforts: he was also a considerable source of expert opinion. While his powers of speculation functioned as a multifocal lens through which his society's consciousness often first approached and considered new variables, his web of acquaintances served as the discursive equivalent of a telephone switchboard, facilitating exchanges, debates, ideological alliances, and philosophical juxtapositions across a wide realm of technologically oriented social ideas and concerns. In addition to the many acquaintances that Wells enjoyed with eminent Victorians and Edwardians, his active membership in the Empire's pro airpower lobby placed him in contact with individuals as diverse as Lord Roberts, Hilaire Belloc, Eyre Crowe, and William Joynson-Hicks. In many cases, Wells' influential personal associations could be traced to the impression his previsional fictions of flight had made upon the boys who would one day be the young men pioneering military aviation. Indeed, Wells seems to suggest that ideological acculturation is strongly facilitated by military speculation when his narrator reveals that future-warfare narratives are a key preparatory element for the Germans in *The War in the Air*: 'A considerable literature of military forecasts beginning as early as 1906, with Rudolf Martin, the author not merely of a brilliant book of anticipations, but of a proverb, "The future of Germany lies in the air," had, however, partially prepared the German imagination for some such enterprise.'[79] It is interesting and significant that Wells presents the idea of 'preparing the imagination' as an integral part of the 'enterprise' of warmaking: social preparation and propagandizing proved to be indispensable to numerous superpower aggressors over the course of the twentieth century.

As Michael Paris recounts at some length in *Winged Warfare*, almost all the major names in the pioneering days of flight attributed their interest to one or more speculative fiction authors. If their inspiration wasn't Wells, then it was usually Jules Verne: Santos-Dumont, Geoffrey de Havilland, John Dunne, Joubert de la Ferté, and G. E. Livock all made major contributions to the evolution of military aircraft and all attribute their initial interest to Verne.[80] This phenomenon of inspiration-through-fiction would be repeated with increasing frequency as the technocratic roots of superpower practice took firmer hold in the West, culminating in the almost incestuous relationship between fiction and fact that characterized the origins and early days of the United States space program.

The species of political influence that resulted from the combination of Wells' discursive talents and social contacts is also observable in diminished fashion in the careers of more obscure historic figures, such as Swinton and Vickers. They too were part of an influential discursive community and saw themselves as working within the more restrained subgenre of near-future war fiction that begins with Chesney's 'The Battle of Dorking' and which they—and their contemporaries—continued and shared. In the collaborative 'An Eddy of War,' Swinton and Vickers chide those who have belittled or ignored cautionary tales, facetiously lampooning the attitudes of resistance and scorn that their own yarn might encounter: 'Who had ever taken seriously such vain tales as "The Battle of Dorking," or any of the numerous subsequent imitations written by alarmists and hare-brained military faddists?'[81] The community of near-future cautionary discourse was not only alert to new contributions, but to how they compared to earlier efforts: on January 29, 1909, Swinton writes to Blackwood of 'the successful play in town called "An Englishman's Home" which is the Battle of Dorking in less heroic form on the stage.'[82]

The many points of overlap and interconnection that exist between the domains of military technology policy and future-war fiction are illustrated not merely by the content, but the 'history,' of Swinton's and Vickers' fiction, and their simultaneous membership in both groups. Indeed, their careers and correspondences almost suggests that full membership in these two discursive domains of genuine military innovation depended upon interest in, and familiarity with, relevant future-war fictions—a subculture phenomenon that is still frequently observed in today's analogous community of military engineers and designers.[83]

A final consideration of technologically inspired near-future war fiction —particularly Wells' *The War in the Air*—should not, however, end on a narrow note, but with an appreciation of the broad bell-toned warning that Wells wished to send reverberating through his 'fantasias of possibility.' Wells offered possibilities, not prophesies, and if his subject was often future war, his theme was even more frequently human survival. *The War in the Air* is a warning, which he summarized thus:

> But mechanical invention had gone faster than intellectual and social organization, and the world, with its silly old flags, its silly unmeaning tradition of nationality, its cheap newspapers and cheaper passions and imperialisms, its base commercial motives and habitual insincerities and vulgarities, its race lies and conflicts, was taken by surprise. Once the war began there was no stopping it. The flimsy fabric of credit that had grown with no man foreseeing, and that had held those hundreds of millions in an economic interdependence that not many clearly understood, dissolved in

> panic. . . .[W]hile the collapse of the previous great civilisation, that of Rome, had been a matter of centuries, had been a thing of phase and phase, like the ageing and dying of a man, this, like his killing by railway or motor-car, was one swift, conclusive smashing and an end.[84]

Ultimately, Wells' greatest fear was not inspired by new weapons technologies, but by the probability that humanity would not heed—or could not see—the first danger signs in time to prevent the all-consuming disasters that these innovations enabled. Shrewdly anticipating that the apocalyptic end of civilization would not stimulate tears so much as stunned muteness, he envisions not a blowing-up, but a caving-in, of society. Indicting the blind overconfidence created by the 'steadily accelerated diastole of Europeanised civilisation,' Wells' warning is reminiscent of Yeats' in *The Second Coming*:

> Three hundred years of diastole, and then came the swift and unexpected systole, like the closing of a fist. They could not understand it was a systole. They could not think of it as anything but a jolt, a hitch, a mere oscillatory indication of the swiftness of their progress. Collapse, though it happened all about them, remained incredible. Presently some falling mass smote them down, or the ground opened beneath their feet. They died incredulous . . .[85]

In this description, Wells anticipates the linked syndromes of denial and shock that photographic history has recorded on the blank faces of the victims of carpet bombing, of Dresden, of Hiroshima—and which would ultimately be projected onto hypothetical survivors of the fictional apocalypses that were to coalesce into the 'nuclear aftermath' subgenre in Western (but particularly American) fiction after World War II. However, even this genre had its start in a novel by Wells—*The World Set Free*—in which the ultimate offensive war vehicle, the airplane, is married to the ultimate weapon: the atomic bomb. In conjoining these technologies, Wells anticipates the answer to the question that he indirectly posed in *The War in the Air*: how can combat aircraft achieve what he called 'an initial knockout blow?' His query would later dominate the consciousness of a superpower, and would evolve into an oft-pondered nightmare question, carefully couched in the sanitized parlance of the Pentagon: how does one launch a successful 'preemptive first strike?'

*Chapter 4*

# H. G. Wells: The Far-Future War Prophet of Edwardian England

> Everything that can be invented has been invented.
> Charles H. Duell, Commissioner, US Office of Patents, 1899

As if to underscore the severity and magnitude of the error in Charles Duell's turn-of-the-century pronouncement, two of H. G. Wells' most terrible visions—the strategic bomber and the atomic bomb—synergized into a single, terrible reality in the skies over Hiroshima on August 6, 1945. Wells, however, was not surprised at this confirmation of his worst fears: in the preface to the 1940 edition of *The War in the Air*, he proposed that his bitterly vindicated epitaph ought to be, 'I told you so. You *damned* fools.'[1]

The claim implicit in Wells' admonishment—that both the physical and psychological realities of nuclear war existed in the form of narrative speculation long before the bomb itself was built—could not be more true, or more pertinent. As H. Bruce Franklin observes in *War Stars*, 'Before nuclear weapons could be used, they had to be designed; before they could be designed, they had to be imagined.'[2] And imagined they were, with startling proleptic clarity. The politico-military influence of these visions is not a matter of conjecture, but record. Indeed, the reality of the bomb might properly be said to have arisen from anticipatory fictions of the bomb, rather than vice versa.

In 1914, Wells completed *The World Set Free*, in which the Earth is brought to the brink of destruction by weapons that Wells labeled 'atomic bombs.' Although references to weapons based on atomic principles appear in earlier texts, no prior narrative exhibited a comparable degree of focus upon these (literally) 'infernal' weapons, so accurately foresaw their ghastly consequences, or depicted their employment in such detail. The proleptic power of *The World Set Free* is reflected not only in its ideas, but even in its dates: in both fact and fiction, the power of the atom is first harnessed in 1933. By this actual date, *The World Set Free* had already gone beyond anticipating the future: it had begun to shape history. In 1932, Leo Szilard, a Hungarian physicist working at the University of Berlin's

Institute of Theoretical Physics, had read Wells' book and was profoundly impressed—and distressed. Fleeing Germany when Hitler came to power in 1933, he continued to reflect upon the scientific ideas in *The World Set Free* and succeeded in describing the laws that govern a weapons-grade chain reaction within a year: he flatly attributed that accomplishment to inspirations gleaned from Wells' novel. He also took inspiration from the cautionary aspect of Wells' tale: in order to keep the chain-reaction theory a secret, he patented it and assigned the patent to the British Admiralty. He later wrote: 'This was the first time, I think, that the concept of critical mass was developed and that a chain reaction was seriously discussed. Knowing what this would mean—and I knew it because I had read H. G. Wells—I did not want this patent to become public.'[3] It may be that Szilard not only gained a more profound appreciation of the consequences of atomic weaponry from Wells' narrative, but that he also internalized a sense of responsibility from it. Szilard's patent and secrecy precautions echo those pondered by Holsten, Wells' inventor of weapons-grade nuclear matter,[4] when he realizes the magnitude of his discovery:

> He had a vague idea that night that he ought not to publish his results, that they were premature, that some secret association of wise men should take care of his work and hand it on from generation to generation until the world was riper for its practical application.[5]

Wells' narrative is but one piece of evidence (out of many) that the men who built the first bombs did not move forward innocently or ingenuously, nor were their researches conducted in a formless fog that obscured the theoretical or social implications of their discoveries. To adapt a metaphor from Thomas Kuhn, they were already operating within a powerful new paradigm that had been established by future-war fiction. These narrative vehicles of change carried them over the comfortable borders of known science and into uncharted lands where the old cartographer's label 'here be dragons' was not only apt, but held deadly new meaning. In the years that followed, after Leo Szilard composed his famous letter with Einstein apprising Roosevelt of the consequences and probable imminence of the Nazi attainment of atomic weaponry, he successfully urged that the American scientists of the Manhattan project be given two texts to read. Neither one of them were on physics. Rather, both were futuristic fictions portraying the consequences of atomic war, and one of them was H.G. Wells' *The World Set Free*.[6]

Szilard's choice of Wells' dystopian/utopian synthesis narrative may have been responsible for establishing it as the ur-text of nuclear war literature, but it is equally valid to assert that Szilard's choice was simply the first of many famous recognitions of the ways in which Wells' imagistic portrayal of nuclear war was to blaze a path for so many others to follow. The sheer destructive power of the bombs, the duration of their effects, and their unprecedented capacity to shred the delicate weave of civilization first appear in this seminal text. Conversely, time has turned many of Wells' predictions into quaint anachronisms: his airplanes and weapons are extremely primitive; his 'constantly exploding' atomic bombs evince a voracious China syndrome effect; and atomic reactors/engines are optimistically compact. Still, the central premise of the story and the anxieties it expresses have aged remarkably well. Wells' graphic prevision of the aftermath of a nuclear strike is an example of this, and even if some of his imaginary details are well off the mark, what is most noteworthy is the enduring general accuracy of his description of the inner blast zone at Paris. Wells' omniscient narrator describes ruins

> lit by a strange purplish-red light, and quivering and swaying with the incessant explosion of the radio-active substance. Whole blocks of buildings were alight and burning fiercely, the trembling ragged flames looking pale and ghastly and attenuated in comparison with the full-bodied crimson glare beyond. The shells of other edifices already burnt rose pierced by rows of window sockets against the red-lit mist.
> 
> Every step further would have been as dangerous as a descent within the crater of an active volcano. . . . Few who adventured into these areas of destruction and survived attempted any repetition of their experiences. There are stories of puffs of luminous, radio-active vapor drifting sometimes scores of miles from the bomb centre and killing and scorching all they overtook. And the first conflagrations from the Paris centre spread westward half-way to the sea.
> 
> Moreover the air in this infernal inner circle of red-lit ruins had a peculiar dryness and a blistering quality, so that it set up a soreness of the skin and lungs that was very difficult to heal . . .[7]

Wells' description of the infernal afterground of an atomic blast is surprisingly accurate. The last sentence even offers a preview of radiation sickness and its dermatological effects, which Wells associates with sites where 'The radiations eat into people's skins.'[8] Furthermore, his description of a world where 'Power after power about the armed globe sought to anticipate attack by aggression' certainly anticipates the reality of nuclear proliferation and the doctrine of preemptive strikes.[9]

Consequently, whether or not subsequent authors on both sides of the Atlantic were directly influenced—or even aware of—Wells' images of a world immolated and teetering on the edge of a new dark age, his text represents the first comprehensive attempt to represent the physical and social destruction of an all-out atomic war. Wells also foresaw how the combined effects of unremitting anticipatory terror and misplaced faith in the prophylactic strength of a 'first strike' would make such weapons inherently destabilizing to any hope of world peace or even manageable coexistence. Wells knew that each nation would become obsessed with the objectives and arsenals of its neighbors, all tremblingly poised to make attacks that would ultimately prove to be suicidal. Wells anticipates the endgame of such a war of nerves in terms that still ring with significance:

> They went to war in a delirium of panic, in order to use their bombs first. China and Japan had assailed Russia and destroyed Moscow, the United States had attacked Japan, India was in anarchistic revolt with Delhi a pit of fire spouting death and flame; the redoubtable King of the Balkans was mobilizing. It must have seemed plain at last to everyone in those days that the world was slipping headlong to anarchy. By the spring of 1959 from nearly two hundred centres, and every week added to their number, roared the unquenchable crimson conflagrations of the atomic bombs, the flimsy fabric of the world's credit had vanished, industry was completely disorganized and every city, every thickly populated area was starving or trembled on the verge of starvation. Most of the capital cities of the world were burning; millions of people had already perished, and over great areas government was at an end. . . . Even though the shattered official governments now clamoured for peace, bands of irreconcilables and invincible patriots, usurpers, adventurers and political desperadoes, were everywhere in possession of the simple apparatus for the disengagement of atomic energy . . . The stuff exercised an irresistible fascination upon a certain type of mind. Why should anyone give in while he can still destroy his enemies? Surrender? While there is still a chance of blowing them to dust? The power of destruction which had once been the ultimate privilege of government was now the only power left in the world—and it was everywhere.[10]

This may be the single most remarkable passage in the entire body of Wells' work. Not only does it anticipate and illustrate the nature and scope of a global thermonuclear catastrophe, but it affirms the subsequent, contemporary threat of the bomb as the tool of 'political desperadoes,' 'irreconcilables,' and fanatics. Were Wells writing today, he might well have conflated all these subtypes of renegade bombers into political 'terrorists,' whose possible possession of such devices makes lasting international stability impossible. Wells also foresees the grim proposal (and inevitable operational denouement) of the monstrous strategy of Mutual Assured Destruction: even if one side has been obliterated, and stands to gain nothing by retaliation, it will still strike back rather than capitulate. To be prepared to do anything less indicates a fatal lack of resolve in this hair-trigger nuclear version of Mexican-standoff. Wells anticipates that, by its very nature, the atomic bomb must invariably promote a strategic philosophy that is tantamount to global suicide. Such weapons can achieve no reasonable political end if launched in retaliation. Arguably, then, their deployment is an ultimate observance of the same intricate rituals of threat and counter-threat that are used to determine outcomes in primitive struggles for patriarchal dominance.

Wells' critique of these irrational, primal tendencies is an overt thematic component of his narrative. At the conclusion of the first chapter, Wells reveals the close links between the desire for knowledge and the desire for power by asserting that the primitive beginning of human speculative thought is triggered by a desire to set a 'snare that shall catch the sun.'[11] This recurrent image—that of attempting to capture the sun—also concludes the book: as Karenin, the character symbolically linked with the evolution of a 'new humanity,' lies dying on a veranda in the Himalayas, he watches the sun sink behind the mountains, and then exclaims,

> 'I've talked to you before, old Sun, I've talked to you a million times, and now I am beginning to remember. Yes,—long ago, long ago, before I had stripped off a few thousand generations, dust now and forgotten, I was a hairy savage and I pointed my hand at you and—clearly I remember it!—I saw you in a net. Have you forgotten that, Old Sun?'[12]

Beyond the interesting Jungian implications of collective speciate memory, this articulates the connections Wells perceives between lofty desires for knowledge and social growth and the risk of social disaster. Far-sighted Karenin, who can even conceive of a world in which both gender and sex is eliminated in order to create a more perfect harmony, is nonetheless still held in the thrall of the simultaneously wondrous and hazardous quest for power and knowledge: 'Old Sun . . . Well may you slink down behind the mountains from me, well may you cower . . .'[13]

The simultaneous promise and threat of unlimited power is the key social conundrum that Wells turns over and over in his narrative, a speculative worrystone that has implications far beyond the bomb. Wells' concern is not limited to the consequences of atomic weapons, but engages the broader problem of perpetual advancement in the physical sciences, and the changes it portends for an often blind, warlike humanity:

> They did not see it until the atomic bombs burst in their fumbling hands. Yet the broad facts must have glared upon any intelligent mind. All through the nineteenth and twentieth centuries the amount of energy that men were able to command was continually increasing. Applied to warfare that meant that the power to inflict a blow, the power to destroy, was continually increasing. There was no increase whatever in the ability to escape. Every sort of passive defence, armour, fortifications and so forth, was being outmastered by this tremendous increase on the destructive side. Destruction was becoming so facile that any little body of malcontents could use it; it was revolutionizing the problems of police and internal rule. Before the last war began it was a matter of common knowledge that a man could carry about in a handbag an amount of latent energy sufficient to wreck half a city.[14]

This passage—already remarkable for its prevision of backpack nukes, terrorism, and the concomitant problematization of both international and domestic security—is most striking for its broader theoretical insights. Wells notes that further inroads made into the physical sciences translate into an ever-increasing surfeit of destructive power, rendering defense—whether by armor or evasion—futile. The portability, concealability, and lethality of weapons will only increase, leading to an endgame in which the forces of global destabilization may be carried in a suitcase, or a pants-pocket.

Wells links this inevitable progression with an increasing mania for advanced weapons. The utopian discussants at the end of the narrative, whom claim to have risen above such a primitive protective reflex, ponder this obsession and the society which was ultimately unmade by it:

> The whole system was rushing toward bankruptcy. And they were spending every year vaster and vaster amounts of power and energy upon military preparations, and continually expanding the debt of industry to capital.[15]

—and, in the process

> 'mankind made three million big guns and a hundred thousand complicated great ships for no other purpose but war.'
> 'Were there no sane men in those days' asked the young man, 'to stand against that idolatry?'[16]

The solution that Wells proposes for this war-wearied world of 'desperate hope and protesting despair' is a world government that is a great deal less believable than the catastrophe that necessitates its creation.[17]

Wells' new global rulers are a self-appointed board of proto-technocrats whose government is 'representative' in only the shallowest sense of the word. Furthermore, once securely in place, this organization's methods of ensuring social control are suspiciously materialistic:

> Once the world was released from the hardening insecurities of a needless struggle for life . . . it became apparent that there was in the vast mass of people a . . . passion to make things. The world broke out into making, and at first mainly into aesthetic making.[18]

This sudden celebration of material comforts, art, and leisure sounds pleasant, but it also reeks of placebos and seduction. Wells' argument that this postwar cornucopia of beautiful objects and ideas will quickly produce international moral goodness depends on developments and value-systems that veer perilously in the direction of Huxley's *Brave New World*.[19] Put another way, Wells' argument anticipates the key strategies of domestic social control employed by a superpower. Indeed, upon close inspection, this new government installs itself, secures its position, and maintains control using the methods favored by superpower autocrats. Thus, Wells' final (unintentional?) conclusion is that such massive, impersonal states will—even must—emerge and become dominant in a world where the danger of atomic weaponry can be moderated only through coordination between two or three such powers, or from a central, universally approved polity. Wells begins by pointing out that the old political and national assumptions that held the world poised on the brink of self-destruction had to be eliminated, and that 'Perhaps the most dangerous of those outworn traditions were the boundaries of the various "sovereign states," and the conception of a general predominance in human affairs on the part of some one particular state.'[20]

Furthermore, in this very first nuclear text, Wells explores the strategy and political consequences of centralized weapons control. In addition to ensuring that atomic weapons cannot be used in an 'international' dispute, centralized control indirectly causes the agency or organization charged with the responsibility of caretaking these weapons to become immediately and incontestably dominant. The passage in which this arms control strategy is proposed foreshadows the American attempt to appoint itself as the sole 'atomic policeman' immediately after World War II: '"And next," said King Egbert . . . "we have to get every atom of Carolinum and all the plant for making it, into our control."'[21]

Even though this absolute power does not apparently corrupt absolutely, Wells does reveal that it will be used to ruthlessly exercise—and excuse—the state's new security precautions: another superpower characteristic that inevitably leads to an institutionalized routine of covert operations. Consequently, Wells' otherwise pleasant King Egbert[22] unilaterally determines that the one autocrat who has attempted to retain an independent atomic arsenal must be firmly—and permanently—punished for his deviation from the new world order. Consequently, the renegade King of the Balkans is followed by the new government's agents to his secret cache of illegal atomic weapons. With only moments to spare, two of Egbert's operatives discover the Slavic monarch perched over a bomb:

> For a moment in that shivering circle of light the two men saw the king kneeling up in the cart and Peter on the barn floor beside him. The old fox looked at them sideways—snared, a white-faced evil thing. And then as with a faltering suicidal heroism he leant forward over the bomb before him they fired together and shot him through the head.
> The upper part of his face seemed to vanish.
> 'Shoot them,' cried the [government] man who had been stabbed. 'Shoot them all!'
> ... They shot [the Balkan King's accomplice] Peter even as he held up his hands in sign of surrender.
> [Accomplices] Kurt and Abel at the head of the ladder hesitated for a moment, and then plunged backward into the pit. 'If we don't kill them,' said one of the sharpshooters, 'they'll blow us to rags. . . . Here they are. Hands up! I say. Hold your light while I shoot . . .'[23]

The bombs are secured and the world is safe, but the method of accomplishing these laudable goals—the cold-blooded execution of the perpetrators, even those who try to surrender—is founded upon dehumanization of one's enemy: the same psychological process that facilitates, and ultimately validates, the use of the bombs themselves. The motivations for, and scope of, these two forms of dehumanization may be as different as the weapons themselves (pistols versus atomic bombs), but both derive from the same perspective of superpower *realpolitik* as surely as two separate fingerprints from a murderer's hand still belong to the same culprit.

Arguably, Wells' previsions tend to lose focus beyond the mushroom-clouded horizon of the Atomic Age. In particular, he did not foresee the extent to which scientific weapons research would become a formalized and stable social obsession that often drives, rather than is driven by, the needs of technophilic superpowers. However, this did not prevent him from imagining weapons beyond the nuclear threshold, as well as their consequences. Indeed, he had already done so sixteen years before *The World Set Free*, for it is an even bolder and more proleptic military thought-experiment that explodes from the pages of Wells' most famous—and, in the broadest cultural sense, influential—future-war fiction: *The War of the Worlds* (1898).

In many ways, Wells' *The War of the Worlds* represents the radical extreme of his technological and military inventiveness. Although dismissed in 1898 Britain as pure fantasy, a modern reader may find his descriptions of the Martians' weapons suffused with contemporary relevance. As numerous critics have pointed out, the Martian heat ray is in many ways premonitive of laser weaponry. The earliest of these comparisons were being drawn in the late 1950s, in the first years of the laser's development, when such an assertion was as uncertain of viability as the laser itself. Now, such a comparison is so obvious as to be pedestrian: the US military has already tested lasers in anti-missile and anti-aircraft roles, and some of these prototypical 'heat rays' are portable and rugged enough to be mounted in aircraft and armored ground vehicles. The articulated tripod 'walkers' with which Wells' Martians stride about England's Home Counties also have modern analogues, that are, ironically, scheduled to invade Mars early this century: some of the remote-controlled vehicles now being considered for the exploration of the Martian surface are based on a multi-legged 'walker' design.

However, in the early years of the twentieth century, *The War of the Worlds*, along with other radically innovative anticipations of future-war technology, was regarded as pure fantasy by the same doctrinaire military hierarchs who could not foresee the slaughter at the Somme and the stalemate that would follow. Their blindness is not surprising: unable to foresee the consequences of already- or near-extant technologies, they could not be expected to realize that Wells' Martians were not merely invaders from across interplanetary space; they were harbingers from humanity's own industrialized future, prefigurations of the shapes and horrors of actual wars to come.

In anticipating humanity's vastly increased destructive power, Wells' Martians also presage a change in tactics. Historically, from the 1930s onward, emerging in parallel with increases in mobility and portable firepower, the concept and use of small assault teams grew dramatically. New technological capabilities made the tactic of 'surgical strikes' against an opponent's key industrial, communication, and transport nexi a realistic military option. Accordingly, the Martians 'do not seem to have aimed at extermination so much as at complete demoralization and the destruction of the opposition. They exploded any stores of powder they came upon, cut every telegraph and wrecked the railways here and there. They were hamstringing mankind.'[24] When the Martians attack London, they do not use their massively destructive heat rays, but instead they 'discharge enormous clouds of a black and poisonous vapour by means of rockets.'[25] This not only points toward the standard technocratic strategy of conquest by interdiction, terror, dislocation, and demoralization, but also anticipates the tactical reasoning behind the development of non-persistent nerve agents of the mid-twentieth century, such as Sarin. Indeed, even the method whereby the Martians deliver their gas attacks (rockets) anticipates the tremendous Soviet development of and investment in just such weapons. FROGs, or Free Rockets Over Ground, armed with chemical warheads, were considered by the Kremlin to be an essential part of any Soviet offensive in Western Europe. Accordingly, although the Soviet Union was willing to entertain proposals regarding the reduction or limitation of nuclear arsenals, it almost universally dismissed any suggestion regarding similar negotiations on the issue of chemical warfare stockpiles. Their reasons for this 'chemical dependency' were akin to those evinced by the Martians: the option to eliminate opposition without destroying or permanently contaminating *in situ* resources.

Whether they involve atomic bombs, heat rays, or gas rockets, Wells' more radically imaginative future-war fictions have several particularly pertinent psychological and social themes in common. The new weapons produce not only a maximum number of casualties, but impose a maximum degree of dehumanization upon both the victim and the attacker. Therefore, these weapons are both handmaidens of a radically new type of 'total' war, and are, in the very nature of their operation, the physical manifestations of the superpower propaganda process of othering an opponent, of transmuting living beings into objects to be destroyed or subjugated. In *The War of the Worlds*, these conjoined themes are not merely recurrent; they permeate the narrative's structure and semantics. Humans are repeatedly portrayed as inconsequential pseudo-entities in relation to the powerful, technologically advanced Martians: 'But the Martian machine took no more notice for the moment of the people running this way and that than a man would of the confusion of ants in a nest against which his foot has kicked.'[26] Later, the narrator witnesses 'people . . . scrambling out of the water through the reeds, like little frogs hurrying through grass from the advance of a man, or running to and fro in utter dismay on the towing path.'[27] Returning to the man-as-insect simile, the narrator wonders how the impotent, disjointed frenzy of humanity must appear to the virtually omnipotent Martians: 'Did they grasp that we in our millions were organized, disciplined, working together? Or did they interpret our spurts of fire, the sudden stinging of our shells, our steady investment of their encampment, as we should the furious unanimity of onslaught in a disturbed hive of bees?'[28] Later, figuring humanity as a largely witless, ineffectual herd, the narrator explains that the mass exodus from London 'was no disciplined march; it was a stampede—a stampede gigantic and terrible—without order and without a goal, six million people, unarmed and unprovisioned, driving headlong. It was the beginning of the rout of civilization, of the massacre of mankind.'[29] This metaphor, which likens 'the massacre of mankind' to cattle being driven into an abattoir, gives way to images of animal desperation and furtiveness once the Martians begin to 'settle' into their new home. The narrator, eternally in fear of discovery, explains that 'I felt as a rabbit . . . I was no longer a master, but an animal among the animals, under the Martian heel. With us it would be as with them, to lurk and watch, to run and hide: the fear and empire of man had passed away.'[30] He goes on to recount how he eventually

> crept out of the house like a rat leaving its hiding-place—a creature scarcely larger, an inferior animal, a thing that for any passing whim of our masters might be hunted and killed. . . . [I]f we have learnt nothing else, this war has taught us pity—pity for those witless souls that suffer our dominion.[31]

This last passage offers a bridge between Wells' representation of 'man' as inferior animal and the related theme of Western 'man' as the colonized, not the colonizer. Wells often entwines these related concerns, as when the narrator gives an ironic account of his own angry but impotent reaction to the initial depredations of the Martian 'colonizers,' who seemed poised to bring about the extinction of the human race: 'So some respectable dodo in Mauritius might have lorded it in his nest, and discussed the arrival of that shipful of pitiless sailors in want of animal food. "We will peck them to death tomorrow, my dear."'[32]

It could be reasonably argued that Wells' text is about invasion, not colonization. However, as the preceding citation indicates, one of the most arresting ideas that Wells advances in *The War of the Worlds* is that any distinction between the two is, at best, dubious. Wells' narrator says of the Martians:

> And before we judge of them too harshly, we must remember what ruthless and utter destruction our own species has wrought not only upon animals, such as the vanished bison and dodo, but upon its own inferior races. The Tasmanians, in spite of their human likeness, were entirely swept out of existence in a war of extermination waged by European immigrants in the space of fifty years. Are we such apostles of mercy as to complain if the Martians warred in the same spirit?[33]

As always, Wells' empathy for colonized peoples is problematized by his simultaneous marginalization of the dominated native populations with which he sympathizes, here characterized as 'inferior races.' However, despite his inconsistencies, there is a distinct and undeniable anti-colonialist thread woven into this tapestry of humankind downfallen. By returning to this topic at numerous points throughout the text, Wells establishes it as both the narrative's thematic impetus and touchstone. He later wrote in a 1920 article for *Strand Magazine*:

> The book was begotten by a remark of my brother Frank. We were walking together through some particularly peaceful Surrey scenery. 'Suppose beings from another planet were to drop out of the sky suddenly,' said he, 'and begin laying about them here!' Perhaps we had been talking of the discovery of Tasmania by the Europeans—a very frightful disaster for the native Tasmanians! But that was the point of departure.[34]

When Wells' humans-as-vermin analogy is considered within the context of his anti-colonialist observations, the trajectory of the narrative's political commentary seems to aim well beyond the mere suggestion that as the Martians are to humans, so Westerners have been to ants, frogs, dodos, and Tasmanian natives. Rather, a closer consideration of this analogy reveals that physical power has not been the primary prerequisite for the imposition or expression of these speciate or ethnic hierarchical presumptions. Instead, it is the ruthlessness and inscrutability of purpose with which the colonizers go about their grim business that most distinguishes them from their colonized victims. Like the Martians, Western colonizers arrived not only with means, but also motivations, of conquest that were unfathomable to native peoples. Europeans often sought land for tilling which was of no use to indigenous hunters, gatherers, or terrace-farmers; they razed the trees and bushes that primitive hunter-gatherers associate with sustenance; they were willing to suffer considerable expense and casualties in order to control worthless mountain ranges —only to dig out even more worthless lumps of rock (coal, iron, copper, gold). From a native viewpoint, therefore, European colonizers often ignored many or all of the strategic objectives that the local culture would strive for in a war, such as readily arable land, livestock, or tribal preeminence. Consequently, the Europeans' strategic and social objectives were (like those of the Martians and modern superpowers) as alien and mysterious as the technology with which they conducted the wars to secure them.

In this regard, *The War of the Worlds* not only anticipates future technologies, but political trends, and in so doing, it moves in the direction of what would later come to be identified as a postcolonial perspective. Appropriate to a text that traces the fate of a colonized people, Wells illustrates that the first of the many violences perpetrated by colonizers in general and superpowers in particular is often not a bodily assault. Rather, the brutal first blow is the eradication of original cultural identity, achieved by the systematic erasure of history, language, customs, and traditions in order to make way for imposed substitutes. Although the Martians seem little disposed to alter human culture selectively, they do seem dedicated to its eradication. This is implied by their decision to land in a pattern that allows them to immediately converge upon and destroy London — the self-appointed First City of the world, and repository of human history and culture.

Wells carries another postcolonial theme — that of colonizers depending upon the colonized for both material sustenance and purpose — to its symbolic extreme when the narrator's fellow-survivor and comrade, a no-nonsense artilleryman, reveals that the Martians are not just consuming Earth's resources, but its inhabitants as well:

> 'It's just men and ants. There's the ants builds their cities, live their lives, have wars, revolutions, until the men want them out of the way, and then they go out of the way. That's what we are now — just ants. Only . . . we're eatable ants.'[35]

In returning to this 'humans-as-ants' simile yet again, Wells presents the Martians' carnivorism of homo sapiens as the inevitable zenith of the inscrutable alien horrors to which humanity bears witness. And from here, it is but one more modest step in the logical progression of the artilleryman's thought to posit an endgame in which humans become complicit in the degradation and demise of their own species. Characterizing the great mass of working, unquestioning Victorian society as being more interested in comfort than freedom or self-determination, the artilleryman says:

> 'Well, the Martians will just be a godsend to these. Nice roomy cages, fattening food, careful breeding, no worry. After a week or so chasing about the fields and lands on empty stomachs, they'll come and be caught cheerful. They'll be quite glad after a bit. They'll wonder what people did before there were Martians to take care of them.'[36]

The artilleryman then takes his convincing prediction of human cooperation with the new colonial masters to its ineluctable end: active collaboration —

> 'Very likely these Martians will make pets of some of them; train them to do tricks — who knows? — get sentimental over the pet boy who grew up and had to be killed. And some, maybe, they will train to hunt us.'

'No,' I cried, 'that's impossible! No human being–'
'What's the good of going on with such lies?' said the artilleryman. 'There's men who'd do it cheerful. What nonsense to pretend otherwise.'[37]

This brutally frank analysis of Earth beneath the Martian heel (tentacle, actually) recalls in only slightly exaggerated form how colonized populaces were (and still are) kept in subjugation and 'consumed' through learned dependencies—the preferred colonialist carrot of comfort and security, backed up by the hidden but ever-ready stick of machine guns and embargoes.

The final discursive thrust of Wells' interrelated themes of dehumanization, subjugation, colonialism, and intranecine betrayal ultimately invalidates any simplistic formulae that would identify either the Martians as 'evil' or advanced technology as the source of their amorality. Rather, Wells advances a much more unsettling, two-part proposition: first, that the root of Martian 'evil' is not species-specific but resides in the ubiquitous 'social instinct' to impose one's will upon others; and, second, that increases in technology only amplify and reify this universal primal reflex. Therefore, the blood-sucking Martians are not merely symbols, but ciphers, for the social and cultural vampirism that communities of the strong inflict upon communities of the weak. Similarly, the magnifying effect that Martian technology has upon the invaders' own primal instincts for power is merely an exaggeration of a congruent process in human superpowers: subjugation by, and to, the machine is arguably their fundamental political dynamic. Thus, *The War of the Worlds* becomes a mirror held up to human nature, revealing it not only in the figurative guises of heroic human survivors and implacable Martian invaders, but in the much less appealing form of slaves, collaborators, traitors, and appeasers.

Humanity's alternative—resistance against the Martians (or the superpower paradigms they represent)—may be more ethically satisfying, but Wells depicts it as no less dehumanizing. The artilleryman, who has sketched out the course such resistance must take, projects the consequences that extended Martian subjugation will have upon the human race:

'The tame ones will go like all tame beasts; in a few generations they'll be big, beautiful, rich-blooded, stupid—rubbish! The risk is that we who keep wild will go savage—degenerate into a sort of big savage rat . . .'[38]

In a horrible prevision of the survivalist strategies and attitudes that were to become the commanding imagery of both anti-machine dystopias and post-apocalyptic nuclear-war fictions, the ever-practical artilleryman offers images of a reduced, almost Morlockian humanity:

> 'You see, how I mean to live is underground. . . . under London are . . . hundreds of miles [of] main drains . . . And . . . railway tunnels and subways . . . [W]e form a band—able-bodied, clean minded men. We're not going to pick up any rubbish that drifts in. Weaklings go out again. . . . Those who stop, obey orders. Able-bodied, clean-minded women we want also—mothers and teachers. . . . Life is real again, and the useless and cumbersome and mischievous have to die. They ought to die. . . . It's saving our knowledge and adding to it is the thing. . . . There's books, there's models. We must make great safe places down deep, and get all the books we can; not novels and poetry swipes, but ideas, science books.'[39]

The narrator is sympathetic to this, but not without reservation: it is an ugly future, brimful of social regression, spartan sacrifice, and ruthless utilitarianism. It also suggests a reproduction of the technophilic, Machiavellian power structure of the Martians: a classic case of becoming that which one is dedicated to destroying.

Whether one reads *The War of the Worlds* as a proleptic allegory of a coming world war, as an anticipatory nightmare of the dehumanizing power of modern weapons and superpower politics, as a symbolic expression of terror regarding the colonized 'alien' races of the developing world, or even as a damning critique upon human nature, it is clear that Wells took great pains to site the difficult issues surrounding the social place and process of 'radical Othering' at the thematic center of his text. Unlike many of Wells' later 'utopia-or-oblivion' narratives, *The War of the Worlds* offers no panaceas for these crises, and, in an important reversal of his tendency to reserve a place of pride for superior technology and technologicists, Wells suggests that the cost of extremely advanced evolution may be further dehumanization. In the Martians, this takes an overtly physiological form:

> [T]he Martians were absolutely without sex, and therefore without any of the tumultuous emotions that arise from that difference among men. A young Martian . . . was found attached to its parent, partially *budded* off, just as young lily bulbs bud off, or the young animals in the fresh-water polyp.[40]

The symbolism invoked in this passage is complex and crucial. In portraying the Martians as propagating themselves through asexual reproduction, Wells eliminates a basic reason for, and force in, communal relations, love, compassion, selflessness, and sensuality. Wells' consequent summation of the Martian species is unsettling, suggesting that in them we might see our own future, simultaneously filled with both promise and warning: speaking of the human trend toward cognition over emotion, the narrator contends that 'in the Martians we have beyond dispute the actual accomplishment of such a suppression of the animal side of the organism by intelligence.'[41]

Therefore, Wells' Martians are the ultimate technocratic soldiers: creatures without family, empathy, altruism, or mercy, dedicated only to self-interest and efficiency. The Martians may experience the last, pallid stirrings of passion only through their acts of aggression, suggesting that a frustrated or vestigial sex drive might only find re-expression through violence and domination. The generative process of 'budding off' suggests homogeneous replication more than heterogeneous reproduction, producing a race of largely identical creatures whose physical inception and development is rich with implications of egoism, narcissism, and intolerance for the different. Wells' Martians may be exemplars of ultimate Otherness, but they also are uniquely well-prepared to engage in Othering themselves. They lack the emotional or physical bonds of community that would impede an absolute dissociation of self from another being.

Wells reinforces this assessment of the 'Martian character' by portraying them in close, possibly direct neural, contact with their machines. The narrator wonders, 'did a Martian sit within each, ruling, directing, using, much as a man's brain sits and rules in his body?'[42] One of the traits commonly associated with contemporary depictions of such 'cyborgs' is their decreased or compromised humanity and empathy: another is their speed and efficiency—particularly when it comes to killing. This trend in the depiction of cyborgs is as old as the genre of science fiction itself; starting with the homicidal Creature in Shelley's *Frankenstein*, similar images of artificial beings as destroyers become and remain a staple of the speculative fiction narrative. Fritz Lang's *Metropolis*, Philip K. Dick's *Do Androids Dream of Electric Sheep?* (and the film version, *Blade Runner*), Crichton's *The Terminal Man*, and the *Terminator* series of movies (along with its innumerable and often insufferable imitations) collectively represent only the tip of the veritable iceberg of evidence which indicates that Western culture expects ruthless, efficient, and absolute warmaking to be an inherent trait of artificial beings. As one of the earliest previsions of military uses of cyborging, Wells' Martians not only illustrate the physical and psychological characteristics of half-mechanized technowarriors, but imply the sexless, loveless, egoistic social ecology that might produce them.

Wells develops this theme of mechanized humanity in other works as well. Even when depicting far less radical applications of the machine to warfare, he foresees the increased mechanization of warfare as moving in an evolutionary direction akin to that of the Martians of *The War of the Worlds*. Even in so humble a speculation as 'The Land Ironclads,' Wells' correspondent-protagonist becomes aware of the fundamental antagonisms between animal essence and automation:

> 'Manhood versus Machinery' occurred to him as a suitable headline. . . . He surveyed [the prisoners] and compared their sturdy proportions with those of their lightly built captors.
> 'Smart degenerates,' he muttered. 'Anaemic cockneydom.' . . . 'I'll call my article . . . "Mankind versus Ironmongery" . . .'
> And he was much too good a journalist to spoil his contrast by remarking that the half-dozen comparatively slender young men in blue pyjamas who were standing about their victorious land ironclad, drinking coffee and eating biscuits, had also in their eyes and carriage something not altogether degraded below the level of a man.[43]

There is no simple way of summarizing Wells' work in the field of future-war fiction, let alone speculative fiction. Although he made seminal—and influential—contributions to the anticipation of radically changed weapons, warfare, and warriors, his interests and the implications of his work defy any attempt at compartmentalization. Wells not only integrates detailed human analysis with broader political perspectives, and considers the (often regressive) influences technology can have upon society and vice versa, but also traces out the numerous lines of linked opportunity and threat that arise from these factors. Taken as a whole, these themes combine to give Wells' work a continuing contemporary relevance. It is hardly surprising that Wells' warnings about the coming revolutionary changes in the technologies and tactics of war initially fell upon mostly deaf Edwardian ears: his version of the future meant the end of their world, and all its traditional ideas of war, relationships, and economy. Consequently, as England stumbled into World War I with slightly outdated technologies and thoroughly archaic notions of strategy and tactics, few were capable of sharing Wells' far-future perspective.

*****

However, as readers grew accustomed to the idea of mechanized warfare —a process dramatically accelerated by the horrific revelations of World War I—so too did they grow accustomed to the idea of wars as struggles that were not so much battles between national armies as they were between rival scientists, and in particular, between their new proxies: innovative, even automated, weapons of ever-increasing power. Although Wells' depiction of the Martians in *The War of the Worlds* may not have directly inspired any new technologies, it certainly alerted readers to a new type of warfare. Whereas the atomic bombs of *The World Set Free* conjured up associations with already-extant myths of indiscriminate and absolute destruction (hence the terms nuclear `Apocalypse' and/or 'Armageddon'), *The War of the Worlds* invoked a scenario and a sensation that was without precedent. The idea that wars could—and would—be fought by faceless, mechanized opponents, unadorned by the banners, valor, or passions that were the inevitable appurtenances of all prior armies and conflicts, was a new and chilling revelation. Human values and ethics had been 'factored out' of the brutally efficient equations that directed combatants who were increasingly the servitors, rather than the wielders, of their weapons. Consequently, *The War of the Worlds* did not evoke earlier associations for there were none to evoke. Rather, it became the standard and the ur-myth against which the subsequent actualization of this kind of war was measured and with which it was rhetorically associated. Thus, the first, and possibly most profound, political influence exerted by *The War of the Worlds* was its emergence as a new metasymbol in the rhetoric of war, politics, and history. Consequently, when the Nazi panzers began crushing Europe beneath their clanking treads, Stuart Cloete was able to write in *Yesterday is Dead* (1940):

> The novelists are justified. The war is waged on a Jules Verne basis. It is *The War of the Worlds* that Wells wrote . . . . Until a thing happens it is fiction. . . . No one believed . . . that the Orson Welles program . . . would be duplicated so terribly, so accurately, or so soon.[44]

It is, perhaps, not merely coincidence that—as the Orson Welles reference reminds us— Wells' tale of ultimate war and destruction found a more enduring presence in the popular culture and consciousness of America than it did in Great Britain. Countless reprints in the early days of the science fiction pulp magazines, a film version, and then a television series all stand as testimony to its continuing influence upon, and presence in, American imagination and media-mythology. Although America's first reaction to Wells' most startling vision of future war and humanity downtrodden varied, two common themes characterized the initial critical response. First, whether reviewers were aesthetically compelled or repelled by the text, they almost invariably found the description of war as waged by the Martians to be gripping in the most literal sense of the word, seizing their imagination with a cold terror that was as vivid as it was enduring. The (largely dismissive) review in *The Critic* categorized the text as 'an Associated Press dispatch, describing a universal nightmare' in which humanity is 'beaten by superior mechanical genius.'[45] Similarly, the mostly positive assessment in *The Nation* refers to *The War of the Worlds* as 'one long banquet of horrors,' presided over by aliens who are '"vast, cool, and unsympathetic intellects," who are all brain and hand,' and who, since they arrive 'by smiting with heat-rays, and choking out life with tubes of liquid black smoke, make mere powder and shell household pets by comparison.'[46]

This last characterization points toward the second discursive thread that seems to run through the otherwise diverse commentary that arose from the ranks of America's first reviewers: regardless of whether they championed or chastised the text and its liberal use of imagination and invention, none scoffed at the technology with which Wells equipped his invaders. As Sydney Brooks wrote in *Harper's Weekly*, '*The War of the Worlds* is not only a tale of capital interest, it has the precision and reasonableness, the sense of distance and proportion, that are the foundation of imaginative literature,' a foundation which Brooks felt stemmed from the fact that Wells' ideas were 'founded on knowledge, and will bear the seal of scientific analysis.'[47] However, it was Clement Shorter, reviewer for the New York edition of *The Bookman*, who was most overt in drawing parallels between the imagined alien depredations and foreseeable human conflicts: 'It set me thinking that if the Martians did not war on the world [then] some human enemy armed with those heat-rays might . . . until London became the silent empty city that Mr Wells's imagination has pictured with so much force.'[48] It would seem, then, that the American mindset was already receptive to the possibility, even the plausibility, of this ultimate fusion of two of its most cherished ideals: technological innovation and military omnipotence.

Wells' story also began a new trend in far-future war fiction, one in which the capabilities and consequences of new technologies received more attention than either the historical or heroic outcomes of such tales. *The War of the Worlds* opened the door for serious, systematic assessments of imaginary weapons, while also serving as a matchmaker between two passionate patriarchal obsessions: technophilia and militaria. The traditional male interests in both machines and martial facts and finery now fused into a single, extraordinarily powerful popular force. Fiction, reportage, and even cinema all discovered that—more than ever before—there was a large audience of 'weapon buffs' eager to buy into the burgeoning mythologies and icons of technowar. Nowhere was this trend so powerful, or so rapidly ascendant, as in the United States. Indeed, the first fulfillment of these expressly male fantasies was realized in a response to Wells' tale of humanity downfallen. Only months after *The War of the Worlds* was serialized in US papers, Garrett P. Serviss rebutted with a tale of humanity (but especially America) triumphant. This action-oriented yarn was 'Edison's Conquest of Mars,' in which the unflappable wizard of

Menlo Park builds a space fleet, takes the war to the Martians, and decimates them with weapons even more amazing and awful than those possessed by the former invaders of Earth. However, as H. Bruce Franklin shrewdly observes, this text may have heralded more than mere post-adolescent technophallic fantasies, for ultimately:

> [T]he arms race of the twentieth century has been so spectacularly successful that if those Martians imagined by Wells in 1897 were to arrive today with their line-of-sight heat beams, clumsy three-legged armored fighting machines, ponderous automata, and primitive aircraft . . . it is their weapons that would be mere bows and arrows against our thermonuclear bombs, intercontinental missiles, and automated guidance systems . . .[49]

Whether or not Wells' Martian mechanisms inspired any actual technological ideas or emulations, they certainly awakened a powerful appetite for, and obsessive interest in, bigger, better, and more spectacularly devastating weapons. Such a mindset was the natural, and perhaps necessary, social and political precursor to the evolution of America's military-industrial complex. Even though Wells never specifically forecast such a fusion of technology, military planning, and superpower industrial strategy, he did predict that the human resources and social commitment to conduct such activities would be the deciding factor in future conflicts of all types:

> The nation that produces in the near future the largest proportional development of educated and intelligent engineers and agriculturists, of doctors, schoolmasters, professional soldiers and intellectually active people of all sorts . . . will certainly be the nation that will be the most powerful in warfare as in peace, will certainly be the ascendant or dominant nation before the year 2000.[50]

As I. F. Clarke points out, 'It took the British people fifty years of slow change, two world wars, and half a dozen reports on educational reform before they began to catch up with the Wellsian proposition.'[51] However, three other nations exhibited much more alacrity in appreciating and actualizing these prerequisites for ascension to true superpower status. Significantly, all three were, in one important sense or another, 'new' nations. Russia reinvented itself in the shape of the Soviet Union, which ideologically embraced new technology and infrastructure improvement. However, the practical implementation of these objectives was intermittent and plagued by the rigid and finally incompatible structures of its philosophical foundations. Germany underwent a gruesome rebirth into the Third Reich, determined to remake itself, compensating for its population limitations by expecting more of each individual. This was a natural corollary to Wells' proposition that worker quality was becoming vastly more important than worker quantity. However, the Nazis' linked assumption that Germany was also a nation of undefeatable *ubermenschen* led ineluctably to the insane, ethnocentrically engendered arrogance that both built the gas chambers at Auschwitz and crushed the Fuhrer's bunker in Berlin.

However, it was the United States, emerging from its chrysalis stage of isolation and domestic consolidation into the vast expanses of global affairs and power, that fully embraced the priorities and criteria set forth by Wells. Increasingly aware of its own restless searchings for national identity and culture, America's arrival in the ranks of world powers occurred at the very cusp of the information and atomic ages. Its longstanding national assumption that technology would lead to utopian attainment was the ultimate marriage of a simultaneous (and often conflictual) commitment to both material utility and social idealism. This national belief not only prepared, but also presaged, the United States' evolution into the world's first true superpower state.

*Chapter 5*

# Hard Numbers, Hard Cases, Hard Decisions: Politics and Future-War Fiction in America

In the very instant that Wells' proleptic nightmare vision of nuclear war and global turmoil rose up as a reality over Hiroshima, America's identity as the globe's first true superpower was confirmed. Already in the early stages of the Information Age, the United States demonstrated not just a working atomic bomb, and the willingness to use it, but an implicit reliance upon the tangible products and dispassionate ethical accounting procedures of a true technocracy. This, in combination with the America-as-export subtext of the Marshall Plan and a globe-spanning film industry, confirmed that America's hegemony was both political and cultural, and that its international penetrations and growing atomic arsenal marked it as a true 'super'-power.

This was not the stable sociocultural post-atomic endgame that Wells had hoped for. Rather, it reflected American visions of manifest destiny and world leadership that had been a growing component of the nation's collective subconscious since the turn of the century. In this particular vein, American fiction writers had been remarkably successful in envisioning (and possibly imprinting) their nation's future. One of the myriad Japanophobic future-war fictions published before World War II, John Ulrich Giesy's *All for His Country*[1] is particularly notable in that, after the Japanese initiate the mass bombing of civilian targets, America finishes the fight by devastating the Japanese homeland using a huge aircraft called a 'Peacemaker.' In 1945, the B-29 Superfortresses which conducted the majority of the bombing against Japan, and which dropped the first atomic bomb on Hiroshima, were given a new 'product name' by their Boeing marketers. The B-29 became the 'Peacemaker'—and proceeded to blast Japan into peaceful submission, just as its fictional counterpart had done thirty years before.

However, there is good reason to ask if this *is* merely coincidence. From World War II onward, there is considerable evidence suggesting that the top dogs of America's international policy were being wagged by the 'tales' of future-war fiction they had imbibed in earlier days. Young readers in the first two decades of the twentieth century matured into the policy makers at Potsdam and in the Pentagon, and their wartime decisions suggest that they may have acted in accordance with speculative images and ideas accrued in their youth. This process, in which ideas concretized in fiction become indirect but forceful impetuses for later policy decisions and technological initiatives, warrants detailed attention and analysis.

Even more than Britain, America has a long history of fascination with advanced weaponry and its battlefield applications, a superpower tendency that is reflected in American science fiction from the late nineteenth century onward. Much of the American trend in this direction may have been initially influenced or even imparted by British future-war narratives,[2] but it quickly became a distinct and separate literary phenomenon. The American trend was more extensive, technology-oriented, and ultimately, more enduring. The science fiction magazines of the 1930s and 1940s, the sudden burgeoning of serious novels of nuclear dread in the 1950s and 1960s, the exacting 'nuts and bolts' tales of war and space in the 1970s and the closely related 'techno-thrillers' of the 1980s are all mute testimony to America's unremitting and often dark romance with weapons, warfare, and the future. Narratives as politically diverse as Robert Heinlein's *Starship Troopers* (1959), Poul Anderson's *Kings Who Die* (1962), and Joe Haldeman's *The Forever War* (1974) all reveal the intensely technophilic utilitarianism that underlies the tradition of American future-war fictions. This utilitarian ethos is not an 'invention' of the authors, but reflects the interests and cultural legacies that they, and their readers, inherited. This helps to explain the unusually influential place that future-war fictions, and their authors, hold in the American military establishment, especially when it comes to 'far-future' anticipations of weapons technology and warmaking. This official sanction is not a matter of conjecture but record: the US military uses science fiction authors as think-tankers in research colloquia sponsored or encouraged by the air force, the army, and other branches of the nation's defense apparatus.

It is both ironic and significant that many of the 'far-future' nightmares of Armageddon and annihilation that Wells explored in *The World Set Free* and *The War of the Worlds* became contemporary reality within forty years. However, the actual waging of a true nuclear war has remained an object of 'near-future' speculation, rather than actualization, and thus, nuclear war narratives remain—thankfully—speculative. Even in these harrowing previsions of a world laid waste, characteristically American thematic and rhetorical predilections are evident. Compared to Wells' earlier tales of social horror and collapse, America's profuse nuclear war literature evinces a greater interest in technical detail. However, the narrative focus that many American future-war authors maintained upon the apocalyptic endgame of Cold War brinkmanship suggests that this popular literature exerted a consistently humane, widespread, and ultimately anti-war upward pressure against those official fingers that might have otherwise pressed downward upon the fateful buttons of Armageddon.

Although nuclear war narratives are not typically associated with 'hard' science fiction, they do share most of the same defining parameters. Indeed, post-World War II nuclear war tales are arguably the least speculative of all future-war fictions because they introduce only one novel element to the narrative environment: a nuclear exchange. They are, therefore, arguably the most serious and careful conjectures to be found among America's many 'rumors of war.' Like other hard science fiction, nuclear war fiction's potential for shaping politically significant opinions and informing both elites and laypersons of impending (or overlooked) technologies and their consequences is not merely a claim advanced by its authors. It has been regularly confirmed and acted upon by the technocratic power elite of post-World War II America.

America's experience with this phenomenon of literary and political synthesis is not unique, but it is more pronounced and enduring than in other twentieth-century polities. As the preceding chapters on British future-war fiction have illustrated, the most influential and often foresightful future-war narratives employed greater, not lesser, degrees of technological speculation, thereby keeping pace with the accelerating processes of modernization. Even in the realm of political 'shock' narratives, such as Le Queux's *The Invasion of 1910*, the emphasis on new technologies had become more consistent and pronounced than it had been 14 years before, when Colomb produced *The Great War of 189–*. The sheer growth of Wells' popularity and influence may be seen as another telltale sign of the growing technophilia that characterizes the emergence of a true superpower, and that portends concomitant changes in literary content, reader interests, and political realities.[3]

A similar trend is observable in the other two superpower states of the post-World War I era. The Soviet Union's ultimate failure to endure as such a polity did not prevent 'hard' science fiction from achieving rapid growth in both popularity and influence within the Soviet Union, as is evinced by the official interest in the genre, its ready and non-pejorative inclusion into the discursive domains of the space program, and its careful policing by the Party apparatus.[4]

What may be less well known but ultimately more significant is that the Third Reich was even more interested and invested in future-war and science fictional discourse than the Soviet Union. The reasons for the Nazi fascination with these genres are too numerous and complex to treat here in any great detail.[5] However, it is particularly interesting to note that many of America's post-war visions of space, energy, and weapons technologies find proleptic resonance in future-war fictions of the Weimar Republic and the early Reich. Given the objectives and results of Project Paperclip, this may not be mere coincidental crosscultural confluence, but a premeditated and direct attempt to appropriate the Reich's technomilitary aspirations along with the relevant apparatus.[6] However, the US had analogous dreams and previsions of its own long before the Weimar's technophilic fantasists set to work. This may partly explain why, in Germany's pre- and proto-Nazi fictions, the recurrent, and usually most dangerous, enemy is America—a nation that appreciates and employs innovative technology, is relatively efficient and technocratic, and industrially energetic. In short, although it saw many other nations as enemies, Germany perceived America to be its only serious rival. This recalls the same motivations that propel Wells' fictional Kaiser to attack America first in *The War in the Air* as well as those which informed the actual Kaiser's identification of America as the only other ascendant world power in his notorious 1912 interview with Dr. William Bayard Hale of the *New York Times*.[7]

History, of course, proved the Nazis to be right: without American industry and technology, the outcome of World War II might have been considerably different.[8] This suggests that America's identity as a superpower was, at least for the Germans, evident prior to the commencement of World War II. Accordingly, any exploration of the roots of the US's evolution into such a polity must necessarily reach back beyond the 1930s—far beyond.

Arguably, this evolutionary direction was woven into the earliest fabric of American culture. As Howard P. Segal observes, America's tendency to associate new technology with 'progress' may have been an inevitable consequence of the circumstances and characteristics of its settlers: a diverse, diasporic population of individuals who willingly abandoned traditional hegemonies in order to found their own. The underlying validation and valuation of self-reliance, new ideas, and new devices, in conjunction with the utilitarian requirements of survival in a new land, combined to create a technophilic trend that was already implicit in the work and writings of Franklin and became explicit in the Utopian visions of Lowell and others who followed. As Segal asserts, 'the technological utopians took these convictions to their logical finale: they equated advancing technology with utopia itself.'[9]

It may be, therefore, that the very nature of the American experience preordained the nation's eventual evolution into a technophilic superpower, into a state motivated more by pragmatism than by tradition, more interested in the future than in the past. If we are to believe the cultural commentary of George Steiner (in *Real Presences*), America's evolution may be more a matter of cultural predisposition than post-World War II inheritance. Speaking of the '[t]wo principal impulses [that] energize the American spirit: immanence and egalitarianism,' Steiner asserts that 'The crux of American time is now. The past matters in direct reference to its usability in and by the present.' Therefore, according to Steiner, Americans tend 'to invest remembrance not in historicity but in utopia. Transcendence itself is made pragmatic; the definition of tomorrow is that of the empirical realization of substantive dreams.'[10] In essence, America's legacy is ultimately not to be found in its past, but in its technotopian future. Consequently, according to Steiner, no other culture has so fused the idea of an 'empirical realization' of dreams with a technological approach to 'the definition of tomorrow.' From this perspective, America's growing fascination with, and development of, future-war fiction appears causally and inevitably linked to its increasing technocentrism. It also suggests an explanation for the sudden burgeoning of this literature in America after World War I. Although America's interest in machines, technology, and warfare is almost as old as the nation itself, two new variables in the post-World War I world may have contributed to the sudden fusion and codification of these 'affinities' into a specific, increasingly ordered, and increasingly influential discursive domain. The first of these variables was the decline of Great Britain as a viable global empire. The resulting power vacuum was an invitation as obvious as it was irresistible. America could acquire a position of world power simply by absorbing the influence of a globe-spanning, English-acculturated hegemony. This was a dream certain to whet the appetite of a young nation just emerging from more than a century of isolation and domestic consolidation. However, this carrot came along with a stick: the keenly felt threat of 'world communism.' The self-proclaimed global ambitions of Bolshevism meant that England's fragmenting empire could not be ignored, could not be allowed to splinter into dozens of independent and potentially vulnerable polities, all ripe for penetration, persuasion, and political integration under the red banners of communism. From the predominant American perspective, the political consequences of international inaction were, at best, dire.

The second variable that abetted America's inter-war ascendance was the expanding matrix of interconnections among the areas of scientific research, technological innovation, industrial output, quantitative analysis, and the conduct of war. World War I proved that the age of the warrior was over and notions of chivalry as outdated as the armored-plated knights from whom the term originally derived. The twentieth century ushered in the age of the technologically competent and mathematically directed soldier. It was also the age of integrated efforts of faceless masses, not personal heroism and accomplishment. This ultimately influenced the priorities—and fictions—of an emerging America. There was a decided movement away from tales of heroism and valor and toward narrative explorations of new weapons, new tactics, new technology.

Consequently, American future-war fictions rapidly came to reflect different values (e.g. technophilia), and purposes (e.g. fiction as a test bed for new technological concepts) than their British precursors. These differences were so powerfully amplified in the twentieth century that they became the defining characteristics of a new style of extremely technocentric and weapon-focused future-war fiction.[11] The older narrative trope of the 'lone genius'—the source of most innovation in Victorian 'scientific romances'— slipped from narrative dominance about the same time that real science was rewriting the book on the conduct of war all along the stalemated trenchlines of the Western Front. In a crowning irony, the human catalyst that sparked the consequent change in the innovation and development of American weapons was the most individualistic of all its inventive geniuses: Thomas Edison. Accepting an offer to become the Naval Consulting Board's principal adviser on July 7, 1915, Edison later claimed that he felt the nation should equip itself to fight wars

> in which machines, not soldiers, fight . . . America is the greatest machine country in the world, and its people are the greatest machinists. They can . . . invent machinery faster and have it more efficient than any other two countries. It is a machine nation; its battle preparation should be with machinery.[12]

H. Bruce Franklin's exhaustive review of the relevant literature of that time reveals that Edison and the authors of America's earliest future-war narratives anticipated, and possibly abetted, a number of key political processes that would support the evolution of a military-industrial complex: increased Executive control, war-footing economy, secret budgetary allotments for 'super weapons,' information management and restriction, and Red-scare rhetoric.[13]

Just as Germany foresaw the US as its primary competitor for superpower primacy, the growing ranks of Americans interested in science fiction in the 1920s and 1930s saw Hitler's Reich—not Stalin's Russia—as the primary danger to their nation's interests. The authors and readers of 'hard science' future-war fictions identified technology, not ideology, as the dominant variable in calculating and assessing emerging international threats.[14] Once again, history bore them out: the scientific acumen and military aggressiveness of the Nazis placed them in a neck-and neck race with American scientists to develop both atomic bombs and the means of delivering them. The Russians, despite their own subsequent development of such weapons, were (history has proven) not overly ready to employ them as instruments of policy. On the other hand, it is hard to imagine that Hitler or any of his genocidal cabal would have maintained a nuclear stalemate for over forty years.

When America took stock of its post-World War II reality, it could not help but perceive a world in which it was the only nation that was arguably stronger than it had been before the war began. It occupied Japan, was funding the rebuilding and reculturalization of most of Western Europe, had sole possession of the atomic bomb, possessed or had the cooperation of all the best scientific minds of the West, had seasoned and lavishly equipped military forces, and had a behemothic industrial sector that was capable of spewing out unprecedented quantities of high-quality—and comparatively high-tech—products in remarkably short periods of time. Furthermore, America's position as the world's leading creator and distributor of popular culture (books, magazines, and especially movies) had also been reinforced by the war, since the comparable industries of all the European countries were either in tatters (as in Germany and France) or were hobbled by devastated national economies (as in Great Britain). America entered World War II as a nation of vast potential but uncertain direction: it emerged from the conflict with both the predisposition and material power to direct and dictate much of the world's political ecology. This necessitated a sudden reification of an already developing trend toward the official implementation of futurists and games theory. America's new position required newer and faster means for assessing policy options, establishing long-range goals, and anticipating opportunities and problems. In short, it compelled the national penchant for informal prognostication to rapidly mature into codified epistemologies and methodologies of prediction and problem solving, later collectively labeled 'futurology.' Proponents of this new style of forward planning rose to positions of prominence: for instance, General Curtis Le May was appointed as Deputy Chief of Air Staff for Research and Development largely on the basis of his purported strengths in these areas. Subsequent developments led to the creation of the RAND corporation,[15] which later became a civilian contractor to the air force and the world's best known promulgator of games theory, scenario analysis, and outcome predictions. Another of these 'think tanks,' the Hudson Institute, provided the background whence the controversial, but also highly influential, nuclear scenarioist/strategist Herman Kahn emerged.

Consequently, in the immediate post-war years, a convergence of international and political factors made official prognostication on future weapons and warfare not merely important, but crucial to national security. In *The Future of the Future,* futurist John McHale details the forces that propelled the growth of the 'large industrial-government research facilities' that now order and initiate a great deal of contemporary weapons procurement and futures prediction:

> [They] were set up originally as weaponry analysis centers for maintaining scientific and technological parity in the cold-war phase. As captive institutions, their more directly prophetic work in the social sciences has been largely concerned with politico-military scenarios in which the various aspects of the compelling world-power systems are analyzed and projected so as to forecast necessary developments in weaponry, counterinsurgency and intelligence systems, and logistic and resource allocations.[16]

Accordingly, these scenarios—these rumors of the future—and the men (almost exclusively) who imagined them wielded tremendous influence over international policy, military strategy, and the shape and direction of cutting-edge scientific research. This use of games theory and prediction is not restricted to strategic planning: it is an essential component of tactical training, weapons innovation and redesign, and mission preparation. According to critic Chris Hables Gray, these war games and predictive scenario analysis have been crucial to US military planning and operations for over a century, and when those 'games' include considerations of new or untried weapons, they become de facto works of future-war fiction.[17] Gray goes on to contend that the inverse process—of science fiction directly influencing the planning and development of military technologies and strategies—is a relvatively recent phenomenon. If so, it is recent only insofar as it exists as an officially sanctioned and integrated military resource: critics such as Thomas Scortia and Reginald Bretnor began reporting such codification in 1960s.[18] Consequently, official dependence upon, and cultivation of, fictional military futures does not represent a revolution in American thought and political process: quite the contrary, it represents the formalization and intensification of a long-standing confluence between both military and literary trends. Today, highly ordered extrapolation and speculation is routinely promulgated and validated at the very highest levels of government, by the most prominent officials, and on the broadest possible strategic topics. As recently as 1996, Caspar Weinberger, Reagan's Secretary of Defense, and Peter Schweizer collaborated on a text titled *The Next War*.[19] In essence, it is an anthology of near-future war scenarios for the US. Extrapolating along lines familiar to, and used by, authors of 'hard' science (and future-war) fiction, Weinberger and Schweizer systematically trace the cause-and-effect chains that could bring the US into conflict with one of five 'likely' adversaries (China, Russia, Mexico, Japan, Iran). They continue by following and assessing the key factors that would then govern the prosecution and scope of the resulting war, its probable outcome, and long-term sequelae.

Thus, just as it was in Victorian and Edwardian England, future-war fiction remains a vehicle for political advocacy, as well as a means of conducting *gedankenexperimenten* into technical and tactical innovations. However, whereas many future-war scholars succumb to the temptation to label all such military speculations as explorations of 'the *war* to come,' this not quite the same as exploration of 'the *warfare* to come' or 'the *weapons* to come.' Whereas the phrase 'war to come' is general and is often associated with political extrapolation, rumors of 'warfare' or 'weapons' to come are more profoundly speculative, and have gained greater prominence as America's technological preeminence has become more entrenched. They also tend to receive more attention whenever politically focused predictions of near-future wars languish for lack of an imminent conflict with a likely adversary (e.g. Russia, *the* imminent threat in the 'Cold War,' was the focus of forty years of America's political future-war fiction). Consequently, when the immediate political threats and anxieties decrease, future-war fiction directs itself toward the methods and machines of warfare, rather than the causes and combatants. In the last twenty years, however, an increasing focus on new hardware seems to be an unflagging trend within this fictional domain. Even at the end of the Soviet era, technothrillers such as Tom Clancy's *Red Storm Rising* and Harold Coyle's *Team Yankee* devoted greater attention to the operation and instrumentality of war than to the underlying strategy and policy issues. Whereas future-war projections such as Hackett's *The Third World War* (a best-seller in the 1970s) used occasional analyses of tactical situations and technologies to illustrate its larger strategic and political points, the now-dominant technothriller reverses this relationship, using strategic and political situations primarily to provide a stage for the real objects of narrative focus: the machines and methods of modern warmaking.[20]

Arguably, the most important distinction between American future-war narratives of the post-World War II era and their British forebears is the almost ubiquitous US obsession with automation and computers. These novels' incessant ruminations upon the military role of information technology underscores, even defines, America's status as a 'mature' superpower. Computers—and the various ways in which they facilitate information distribution, assessment, and management—are vital to the modern state's intelligence services, international exchange, and military operations. Indeed, even in a non-military domestic environment, computers are essential to a superpower, since they undergird the day-to-day social control and political influence of the power elite. Information technologies not only orchestrate the machinery of national and global telecommunications, but also facilitate the statistical analyses used by advertisers, manufacturers, politicians, and other technocrats to optimize the depth and breadth of their media influence.

This scenario, in which the peacetime superpower state shifts away from a policy of compulsion via missiles and toward a policy of coercion via media, is not novel, nor hypothetical, nor lacking in direct military implications. Computer-moderated information exchange and a pervasive media culture may offer unprecedented levels of interconnectivity and stimulus, but they also facilitate social control, centralized information management, even operant conditioning of users. Recast in military terms, a computer in every home is more likely to ensure social obedience than a garrison in every town. As Raymond Williams warned, the natural affinities between global media access and the technocratic dynamics of superpower control threaten a scenario in which, 'para-national corporations, with their attendant states and agencies, could reach farther into our lives, at every level from news to psycho-drama, until individual and collective response to many different kinds of experience and problems became almost limited to choice between their programmed possibilities.'[21] Frank Elwell carries this dystopian premonition one step further, pointing to the almost Wellsian manner in which citizens might slowly, but surely, be simultaneously converted into 'cool and unsympathetic' intellects reminiscent of the Martians, and also into docile, interchangeable, and unwitting sheep. Elwell asserts that as 'bureaucracies satisfy and satiate us with their output of goods and services, they also shape our mentality.' Increasingly detached and self-interested, we excuse our moral apathy through 'rationalization [which] involves dehumanization —the elimination of concern for human values. The assembly line is designed to eliminate human variability . . .' Ultimately, this culture-wide trend promotes the increase and eventual preeminence of *Zweckrational* or technocratic thinking, 'in which the goal is simply to find the most efficient means to whatever ends are defined as important by those in power.'[22]

However, even while post-World War II future-war fiction tacitly and explicitly championed the 'techno-' component of American technocracy, it also began challenging and decrying the concomitant social and political costs of this trend. Perhaps one of the most striking and foreboding examples of this can be found in 'Cold War' by Kris Neville (1949). Written before there were hydrogen bombs, ICBMs, or a space program, the premise of this short story is that the US has achieved global mastery, maintained and ensured by its unilateral possession of a space station armed with nuclear weapons. This tense situation has led to extreme international acrimony, particularly with the Soviet Union. As the story begins, the reader learns that the US can no longer maintain its space station and must keep this change in defensive (or more aptly, offensive) capability a secret, lest the vengeful Soviets exact thermonuclear revenge for a past American 'preemptive strike.' Neville's portrayal of the official steps taken to ensure that this secret does not become common knowledge (due to the discoveries of investigative reporter Adam Kregg) are as darkly prescient as his anticipations of orbital fusion weapons:

> Adam Kregg knew, he lived in a democracy. And the government tactics did not include—
>
> He tucked the column into his coat pocket. He was going to take it to the syndicate personally. He was going to see it go out over the wires. . . .
>
> He . . . started across the sidewalk.
>
> A huge, black car hurtled around the corner and flashed by him. Two shotgun blasts erupted from it.
>
> He fell, his chest torn away. He squirmed once and died.
>
> Almost immediately, a plainclothes agent was bending over him. The man removed the bloody sheaf of typed paper. He stood up and flashed his badge to the crowd.
>
> 'This man is dead,' he said.[23]

Neville's technological and strategic foresight encompasses the tense brinkmanship of 30-minute mutual annihilation and the pros and cons of unilateral deployment of nuclear weapons in orbit. While both are noteworthy, it is his clear, cynical appraisal of the effects of such weapons on democratic principles that is particularly chilling and proleptic. Written just before the 'feel-good' 1950s, 'Cold War' seems more consistent with the ruthless *realpolitik* that is the dramatic staple of contemporary narratives such as *The X-Files* and other current 'conspiracy-obsessed' offerings. Ultimately, Neville's vision is more grim than its modern-day equivalents, which usually represent the *highest* levels of government as being essentially innocent and ignorant of such cold-hearted and brutal tactics. Sinister violence is usually associated with rogue elements of the bureaucracy, or small star chambers of political fanatics. However, in Neville's story, the orders, the execution—and hence, the abrogation of the most fundamental principles and guarantees of American democracy—come right from the top. The shot that kills Kregg is fired by (or at least with the cooperation of) the FBI, acting on behalf of the President. But Neville's narrative is not merely a simplistic denunciation of Machiavellian tactics; it also explores the ethical quandaries of superpower leadership by placing the reader in the Oval Office. There, as the President and his advisers weigh the life of one reporter against the world's continued existence, the simplistic archetype of amoral government autocrats dissolves, leaving readers face-to-face with a profound moral dilemma: what would we choose, to spare an individual or to save a world? From this perspective, Neville's scenario presents his audience with an ironic and pitiless polarization of alternatives characteristic of Classical tragedy: the bombs are the superpower's instruments of dominion, but they are also the source of its hamartia. Just as the bombs protect Americans by (potentially) destroying others, now an American must be destroyed in order to protect the peacekeeping 'power' of the bombs. Confronted with this sudden and horrific inversion, readers may thus discover themselves grappling with the same ethical conundrum that arises in *Oedipus, Antigone*, and other tragedies: who, ultimately, are the culprits? The intrusive press, the FBI assassins, the ruthless President—or the unexploded bombs that set off this chain reaction of anti-democratic actions? Neville, by leaving this question unanswered, goads readers to face the final, stark challenge implicit in 'Cold War': will America's new weapons destroy the society they have been built to protect?

The highly ordered extrapolation that underlies both the authorship of hard science fiction war stories and the creation of strategic scenarios is essential to the military and political life of the modern superpower state. At the same time, however, a reliance upon prognostication poses problems and even subversive challenges to that same military-political order. Confidence in the state increasingly rests upon the supposed accuracy of such predictions, yet readers can never *know* whether they are perusing visionary truth or pure fantasy. The reliability of both futurists' and fiction writers' extrapolations are further complicated by the narrative equivalent of Heisenberg's principle: has the political influence exerted by these predictions changed events so that what was predicted will not, or even cannot, come to pass? Is an unrealized cautionary prediction evidence of successful proscriptive influence, or simply botched soothsaying? How can one be conclusively distinguished from the other in any given case? Ironically, this aspiration to predictive 'failure' is exactly the hope and faith at the core and inception of all cautionary tales: if a dire 'predicted' future fails to materialize, then the warning has been heeded and is a success. However, even those future-war (and science) fictions that propose to alert us to approaching dangers are not purely and solely warnings: they are also a form of training and testing in the virtual reality of a literary laboratory. They are conceptual rehearsals, practices, thought experiments —motivated not by a prior commitment to reject a specific future, but by a desire to shop among possibilities, to browse democratically through the stalls of the marketplace of futurist ideas.

However, for the Pentagon, this shopping expedition may occasionally become an orgy of impulse buying in an overstuffed mall of military maybe-machines. This preoccupation with constant acquisition of new weapons and support technology now occurs with an unparalleled openness and avidity. The consequent patterns of procurement are as radical a departure from military precedent as the technological and tactical changes that impelled it and which predict, even compel, its continuance. Every new technological twist entails a new tactical turn, expressed as new weapons, new vulnerabilities, new capabilities. Each new battlefield capability cannot help but perpetuate the cycle, for military analysts must anticipate the possible ripostes to the new equipment and tactics: it is their job to imagine the next technological response, to foresee how it might be constructed and also countered. The contemporary reality of developing new technologies of annihilation is therefore a perpetually spinning motor of innovation—and the fuel that makes it run is imagination.[24]

Nowhere is that fuel available in such plentiful supply and diversity as the domain occupied by science fiction writers. This is not a recent phenomenon. The veritable 'grandfather' of popular science fiction in the US —Hugo Gernsback—launched the first 'sf pulp' with a public declaration of his interest in publishing stories that presented views of future technology, not those which embraced the aesthetic standards of *belles lettres*. Writers such as Robert A. Heinlein, Isaac Asimov, Arthur C. Clarke, Poul Anderson, Jerry Pournelle, Frank Herbert, and Frederick Pohl have achieved intellectual and social stature by being asked to share their expertise as lecturers and consultants to the government and its proxies. For instance, Asimov and Clarke both testified before a Congressional subcommittee that was investigating the future options of the space program. This was not an exceptional incident for science fiction authors, but only part of a larger pattern of official involvements, both with government and industry. Clarke has lectured around the world, and his consultancy skills have been sought out by Bell Telephone Labs, General Electric, and Hughes Aircraft, where one unnamed scientist avowed that 'In one bull session with Clarke, we get more ideas than many companies get from two years of management meetings.'[25] Many of these authors also enjoyed entrée to official circles as a result of their prior associations with the military. Clarke was an RAF officer overseeing radar deployment and development in World War II. Isaac Asimov (initially as a civilian) and L. Sprague de Camp (eventually a Lt. Commander) were engineers for the navy in high-tech and, on occasion, secret projects. Robert Heinlein, an ex-navy officer, was involved in the same hush-hush Philadelphia projects, where, as de Camp recounts, 'Heinlein had an Annapolis classmate, Commander A. B. Scoles, with whom he had kept up. . . . Scoles wanted to lure to his unit a few science fiction authors with technical backgrounds, to see what they could do' as engineers and advanced concepts designers.[26] Indeed, one apocryphal story (often attributed to Heinlein) has it that, during the war years, one room at the Pentagon was reserved for a junior officer whose sole duty was to comb through science fiction texts in search of useful ideas for weaponry. According to Frederick Lerner, '[t]he bazooka was allegedly designed by an engineer who had read imaginary descriptions of rocket launchers,' ostensibly in the *Armageddon: 2419 AD* stories of Philip Nowlan.[27]

Such a collection of author-experts poses something of a challenge to Foucault's model of discrete 'domains of discourse,' at least in so far as these are considered separate communities that can be clearly and conclusively staked off from one another. The challenge implicit in the example posed by such authors is not to Foucault's general concept, but to its orderliness in application, for these authors occupy a domain that exists only *because* it overlaps with several others. Authors of future-war fiction have positions, and proactively participate, within the discourses of popular literature, high literature, military thought, and scientific exchange. Their activities and discursive production indicates that the membrane between these different 'domains' of discourse is, at the very least, extremely permeable.

Arguably, the permeability of this interdiscursive membrane is what facilitates, even enables, the singularly lively flow of concepts and figurations from one domain into others. This, in turn, suggests that these multivalent authors and this membrane of exchange are one and the same: it implies that they facilitate a two-way flow of information between different political communities. This function is an intrinsic property of even the earliest future-war authors: as I. F. Clarke observed, 'The Battle of Dorking' was unique in that 'Chesney had by chance introduced a new device in the communications between a specialist group and a nation.'[28] This is the most important aspect—and most radical literary departure—of the 'Dorking' episode. Chesney became the conduit between the official, expert review of relevant facts, and a readership made up of the majority of Britain's credulous body politic. Arnold-Forster furthered this flow of accessible expert discourse by offering a guided tour of the crucial minutes of battle experienced 'In a Conning Tower.' American future-war fiction, particularly of the hard science fiction variety, is simply the formalized, widespread, and increasingly influential descendant of these early efforts to bridge crucial gaps between expert and lay discourses of new (or future) warfare and weaponry.

However, as is the case with cell membranes, osmosis rarely occurs in one direction only. If such narratives represent a 'trickle down' of information from lofty expert discourse, they just as often enable a 'trickle up' of unofficial opinions and ideas. Like water moving up a tree, the reactions, fears, and even technological inspirations that condense in the grassroots of the body politic may flow from an author's pen and rise to the attention of the political elites who read these narratives. It is largely through this process that most serious speculative narratives articulate, and thereby nourish, democratizing, radical, or even subversive alternative visions of the future.

So where are the writers located in this trickle-down/trickle-up model of discursive exchange? Are they securely nested in the upper branches of government association, or nestled in around the popular base of the society? The answer would seem to be that, by having access to both, they cannot claim exclusive membership in either: they must exist somewhere in between. They are, as the permeable membrane metaphor suggests, a medium of exchange that pervades, and thereby links, many discursive entities. They are not spokespersons so much as they are synthesizers of future possibilities, occasionally inventing, often reconfiguring or recontextualizing, but always facilitating a two-way exchange between the expert and lay components of a constantly changing and growing society.

Before moving from this metaphor of a tree of knowledge to a consideration of its deadly fruit, several further clarifications are necessary in order to finish illustrating its function. The downward trickle of information characteristically carries information on projected policies and actual technologies. This is the source of the more conservative, extrapolative elements of science fiction, as authors organize and narratively synthesize anticipated military actions with the performance statistics of the new technologies that will be employed. Conversely, the upward trickle is mostly speculative: authors propose their own near- or far-future innovations, often in combination with alternatives culled from non-official sources, resulting in a rich, imaginary stew of new technological and political possibilities.

Naturally, the flow is cyclic: if the trickle-up ideas are pursued, they may engender new technological capabilities, which then need to be disseminated back 'down' to the body politic once they are achieved. Similarly, as the components and consequences of official policy and projections trickle down to the grassroots, laypersons consider the anticipated outcomes, react, and express their opinions—which flow back up to inform new policy. The discursive foundations of science (and particularly future-war) fiction are, therefore, (in)vested in the same pluralistic ideals and rhetorical value systems that underlie, and ultimately enable, America to function as a Federalist-inspired 'marketplace of competing ideas.' Arguably, such fictions may bridge the widening rhetorical and informational gap between expert and layman that results from what George Steiner calls the specialist's 'jargon of vehement obscurity.'[29] Therefore, just as the flow of information enabled by future-war fiction is bidirectional, its potential for political influence is bivalent, for it simultaneously confirms and contests the praxes and purposes of America's technophilia even as it reaffirms their cultural valuation.

*Chapter 6*

# An Imperfect Future Tense(d): Anticipations of Atomic Annihilation in Post-War American Science Fiction

> There has been a great deal said about a 3,000 mile high-angle rocket . . . I don't think anyone in the world knows how to do such a thing, and I feel confident that it will not be done for a long period of time to come . . . I think we can leave that out of our thinking. I wish the American public would leave that out of their thinking.
> 
> Dr. Vannevar Bush, testimony before Congress, 1945

> The only defense against the weapons of the future is to prevent them ever being used. In other words, the problem is political and not military at all. A country's armed forces can no longer defend it; the most they can promise is the destruction of the attacker.
> 
> Arthur C. Clarke, 'The Rocket and the Future of Warfare,' 1946

> If we don't end war, war will end us.
> 
> A line from the Wells/Menzies film, *Things To Come*, 1936

> Peace is our profession.
> 
> Motto of the Strategic Air Command, United States Air Force

On March 6, 1990, *The Bulletin of Atomic Scientists* set back its famous 'Doomsday Clock,' signifying, for the first time in many years, that humanity had moved away from, rather than closer to, the horrors of a nuclear midnight. This readjustment of the 'atomic clock' anticipated the brighter dawn of a post-Cold War world, and the longer, happier hours of what might be called day-*life* savings time. However, this resetting of an epochal clock also stands as mute testimony to the pervasive influence of metaphoric imagery in nuclear discourse. Symbols, icons, allegories, all manner of rhetorical short-hand have been pressed into service in the attempt to communicate about global destruction, and to adequately illustrate physical and social consequences so vast and uncontainable that they defy finite terms. As a result, the speculative narratives that ventured into the nightmarish realms of nuclear inferno and aftermath not only influenced technological understanding and awareness, but also established the psychological and discursive tropes that would shape American discussions and beliefs about the bomb.

The tendency to resort to the qualitative richness of imagery over the quantitative precision of statistics predates the use of the atomic bomb. After witnessing the successful Trinity test at Alamogordo, Oppenheimer's commentary was neither technical nor laudatory: 'I am become Death, the destroyer of Worlds.' This phrase, one of Krishna's most fateful utterances in the *Bhagavad-Gita* (Book XI), initiated a search for adequate imagery, a quest which has problematized the semantics and semiology of nuclear-centered discourse for the past half century. Oppenheimer's proposed first use for the bomb once again transmogrifies it into a primarily discursive object: he and other leaders of the Manhattan Project suggested that the first bomb be dropped on a purely industrial site, to demonstrate its power without causing undue loss of life. As nuclear historian/commentator Spencer Weart explains, 'The first atomic bombings would be an act of rhetoric, a science fiction image aimed less at the enemy's cities than at his mind.'[1]

Arguably, the bomb itself was the end result of science fictional discourse. Not only were literary anticipations of this weapon midwives to its actualization, but were also the source of its name: it was H. G. Wells who labeled it an atomic bomb. Formalized, technical rhetoric was to prove particularly useless in any attempt to grapple conceptually with the possible consequences—social, psychological, and physical—of the bomb, leading Weart to conclude that 'By the 1980s it was clear to all careful thinkers that nuclear policy had less to do with the physical weapons than with the images they aroused.'[2] Hence, the discourse of nuclear literature has traditionally relied upon images because a personally meaningful quantitative assessment of the bomb's annihilatory powers is impossible. Its size dwarfs and makes mute any discursive attempt to establish a connection between individual experience and the overwhelming total reality of a nuclear explosion. Consequently, humans may only approach this superhuman event through symbols and imagery: a mushroom cloud climbing toward the heavens, a roiling incandescent fireball ravening outward at its base, skyscrapers tumbling like dominoes. Through the medium of these unforgettable images, the instruments of Armageddon are eternally exploding in humanity's consciousness, made real by imagination and anticipation. In this context, the bomb may have already been as devastating culturally as it has been physically.

Long after the exposure levels in Hiroshima and Nagasaki had dimmed, narrative byproducts of the blast still continued to collect in a fallout of bomb-obsessed future-war fictions. More than television news commentators, learned physicists, or even impassioned activists, the nuclear war narrative has had the greatest success in imparting a tangible shape to the unimaginable. Even an abbreviated list of the most important and commonly known texts in this subgenre suggest how extensive it is: *On the Beach, Alas Babylon, 1984, Ape and Essence, Fail-Safe, Level Seven, A Canticle for Leibowitz, Riddley Walker, Fiskadoro, Down to A Sunless Sea, Warday*. The ever-expanding blast radius of the image and idea of the bomb propagated even more chain reactions in popular literature. It is the balance of nuclear power which finally propels and preoccupies *Smiley's People* and the rest of Le Carré's Cold War creations, has Russians and Americans racing each other to reach MacLean's *Ice Station Zebra*, deranges an American general during *Seven Days in May*, and motivates the technothrills in Clancy's *The Sum of All Fears, Red Storm Rising, The Hunt for Red October*, and *The Cardinal of the Kremlin*.

Many of the most powerful and enduring anticipations of the bomb are those that employ actual images, particularly nuclear war films that depict not only the explosions but the post-Armageddon actualities. But such noteworthy films as *The Day After, On the Beach, The War Game, Threads, Five, Testament, The World, the Flesh and the Devil, The Bedsitting Room*, and *Dr Strangelove* are not the only cinematic representations of atomic catastrophe and threat. More numerous are 'bomb-sploitation' films as diverse as *Terror in the Year Zero, Mad Max* and its various imitators, *Terminator* and *Terminator 2*, and innumerable puerile espionage-adventures, of which the James Bond series is the exemplar.

Images of atomic apocalypse also speak directly to primal human obsessions with titanic forces of death and destruction: logically, a large part of any culture's consciousness and imagination will coalesce around that which can utterly destroy it. It is not surprising, therefore, that the bomb is the thematic engine of so much popular and futurist fiction, and that these fears and fantasies of Apocalypse have commuted into other genres, such as poetry. Atomic war and its horrors seethe at the center of Swedish Poet and Nobel Laureate Harry Martinson's 103 cantos of nuclear allegory 'Aniara,' and give shape to the diminished world of Edwin Muir's 'The Horses.' Similar concerns find expression in Robert Lowell's and Denise Levertov's work, which, although not overt advocacy, nonetheless constitute significant contributions to the anti-nuclear discourse.

However, the most direct and wrenching depictions are still found in nuclear war fiction, which has often been noteworthy for the inventive rhetorical strategies its authors have employed to intensify the immediacy of both its theme and unique narrative environment. One of the most ingenious and psychologically daring of these approaches can be found in James Kunetka's and Whitley Strieber's *Warday*.[3]

A fictional documentary, *Warday* chronicles a journey across a devastated America, undertaken by the two authors—who have cast themselves as the first-person protagonists in a near-future world where the US and Russia have stumbled into an exclusive nuclear conflict. Written in chapters that mostly alternate between the narrative voices of the two 'author-characters,' the record of their travels is ostensibly a journalistic project, an attempt to report and reflect upon the new, horribly crippled America that is still limping unsteadily out of the ruins of its former greatness. However, between and beyond their interviews with local power brokers, their contact with British relief services, their observation of paramilitary Japanese incursions in the Southwest, and their clandestine efforts to enter the xenophobically separatist paradise of a well-preserved California free-state, the two authors are also completing a spiritual Columbiad. The sum of their contacts and encounters reveals an America bereft of its earlier optimism, suspicious of expansionistic talk, uncertain of its future, yet more spiritual—though it is difficult to discern whether the increased emphasis upon religion is part of a bright new revelation or a recidivistic retreat from a world of broken dreams and bitter realities.

However, the novel's most evocative narratological twist is in what the authors reveal, not what they discover: they themselves are the most subtle, yet telling, registers of the changed America. Although each alteration to the nation's pre-war culturescape is boldly dramatized in one or more of the locales which they survey, the journeyers evince modest versions of the same modifications in their own post-war identities. They are changed men, living changed lives in a changed nation: Strieber and Kunetka use their fictive selves as mirrors of the world in which they must exist.

The overlapping strands of narrative reflexivity that join and yet contrast the actual authors with their projected post-war selves is a particularly unsettling and effective literary device. If *Warday* is the fictional dissection and diagnosis of the aftermath of a superpower, it is also the genuine confrontation of two men with their alter egos, a shadow-boxing tournament in which both the authors' actual and imagined selves become indexes for the social and psychological failures of the two worlds. Prewar ingenuousness, idealism, and material insatiability prove no better and no worse than the inverse post-war characteristics of suspicion, cynicism, and self-protective parsimony. Yet both epochs—and the persons they created and reflected—are neither models nor monstrosities: whether exploring a group or an individual, the narrative consistently returns to the human struggle to make sense of, and make a living in, the world they made, yet, paradoxically, did not foresee. Through this unblinking critique of the limitations of the authors' real selves and society, in constant comparison with their projected alter egos, Strieber's and Kunetka's narrative is not only invitingly intimate, but strangely authoritative. Although the world of *Warday* exists only as an imaginary future, by casting themselves as characters within it—characters who have suffered the same losses and brutalizations as their neighbors—the authors attain a peculiar form of credibility. The resulting fusion of self-revelation, confession, and psychological exhibitionism creates a narrative that is edgy, compelling, and, at least at points, devoid of the contrivance of 'constructed character.' The 'personal' authority that Strieber and Kunetka accrue through this narrative strategy then spreads, by subtle association, to their depiction of post-nuclear America, thereby shrewdly enduing the novel with an unusually 'realistic' feel.

*Warday* is only one (albeit distinct) example of how nuclear war fiction's narrative innovations—in conjunction with arresting imagery—have influenced readers. In the early, optimistic days when the word 'atomic' was usually associated with the promise of 'power,' rather than the threat of 'bombs,' many of the young men who took up the challenge to split the atom recalled their initial inspiration as coming from books. Speaking of the various groups that were working to split the atom in 1939–1940, Spencer Weart reports that members of the Paris team paralleled their work to the spirit of Jules Verne's novels in general, and more specifically to H.G. Wells' *The World Set Free*.[4] In addition to finding inspiration for his work on a chain reaction in Wells' text, Leo Szilard also indicated that it was a primary reference in his first report on the design of reactors.

This influence was even more profound and widespread among young American males. The editor of *Astounding Science Fiction*, John Campbell, spent the 1930s recruiting writers who were also scientists or engineers—including Heinlein, de Camp, and Asimov—to write 'hard' science fiction stories which speculated upon imminent breakthroughs in crucial areas of technology. Atomic power was one of the most important of these areas, and stories about it attracted, influenced, and elicited enthusiastic responses from young science majors or high schoolers who were eager to embark upon a career in 'atomics.'

The New York office of *Astounding Science Fiction* also witnessed the government's ultimate admission of the political importance it placed on such literature. In 1944, alarmed by Cleve Cartmill's atom bomb-construction story 'Deadline' (*Astounding Science Fiction*, March 1944), army intelligence officers barged into John Campbell's office and brusquely instructed him not to publish any new stories concerning or even mentioning atomic bombs. This intrusion had been preceded by a surprise visit to, and interrogation of, Cartmill, whose imaginary bomb design was based solely on available prewar publications. It was accurate in many of its particulars, but its only claim to significant (and possibly dangerous) prevision was the way in which Cartmill proposed to combine the probable elements of an atomic bomb design: otherwise, the short story contained no unforeseen innovations. In the end, Campbell was allowed to continue soliciting and publishing 'atomic weapon' stories after he pointed out to the intelligence officers that the sudden discontinuation of such fictions would attract more, not less, Nazi attention, and would likely lead the Germans to conclude that the increase in secrecy indicated that America was close to producing a workable bomb.[5]

This episode was only one small part of a massive official censorship and secrecy operation that surrounded the bomb. Beginning in the fall of 1940, the US government decided to eradicate any textual trace of atomic weaponry from the American culturescape. Any and all words with atomic connotations—cyclotron, fission, fusion, etc.—were prohibited in the media. The continued distribution of old articles, books, or films that mentioned such topics or objects was frowned upon, and their authors were monitored and even compelled to silence. One of the most extraordinary episodes in this mania of secrecy involved Philip Wylie, who would later write a number of important nuclear war narratives. In 1945, he submitted his novella *The Paradise Crater*—in which uranium 237 was posited as the bomb's primary warhead substance—to *Blue Book*. The magazine's editors, obeying official directives, duly forwarded it to the government for review. The result: Wylie found himself under house arrest and with an unwelcome guest—an army intelligence major who informed the stunned author that he was prepared to kill Wylie if that was what it took to ensure his silence and, thereby, protect the secrecy of the bomb.[6]

This campaign to effect an *ex post facto* eradication of information was more successful than one might wish to believe: the explosion of the bomb at Hiroshima came as a profound surprise to a great many, even a majority, of the American people. If George Steiner is correct when he asserts that censorship is the ultimate proof and litmus test of literature's political influence, then nuclear war fiction must have struck military elites as particularly important for them to impose such extraordinary protective measures.

In later years, even after the need for complete secrecy had passed, the West still frequently engaged in, or seriously considered, censoring nuclear war narratives, particularly films. Now, however, these efforts at surreptitious information control were overtly and exclusively motivated by domestic politics. When Neville Shute's harrowing *On The Beach* was faithfully and effectively produced by Hollywood veteran Stanley Kramer, it was neither audiences nor critics that objected to his haunting tale of atomic endgame, but the US government. Fearing the film would weaken the nation's resolve in the ongoing Cold War game of nuclear brinksmanship Eisenhower's cabinet met to consider how they might diminish its success and exposure.[7]

Official misgivings over graphic depictions of nuclear war are not, however, an exclusively American phenomenon. The British government had a similar reaction to *The War Game* (1965), and, in conjunction with the BBC, prohibited the airing of the film. As James M. Welsh recounts in 'The Modern Apocalypse: *The War Game*,' filmmaker Peter Watkins strove for, and achieved, a reality which the BBC felt was 'too effective for public consumption, and banned it from television because [it] feared the possible consequence of mass panic and suicide.'[8] The government's reasons may have included those claimed by BBC, but its first motivation was political: the film and its frankly depicted horrors (which evoke memories of the Blitz) were perceived as 'lending support to the Campaign for Nuclear Disarmament.'[9] The political potential inherent in this film was realized in its rapid adoption as the cinematic rallying-banner for the anti-bomb movement in England, France, and, to a lesser degree, all of Europe.[10]

By the mid-1960s, the now-pervasive imagery of the bomb and its effects appeared in countless other narratives. Public sensitivity to any infringements of civil liberties or freedom of expression made official silencing impossible. There was a dramatic increase in discussions about alternatives to atomic weapons and a steady growth in anti-nuclear movements, many of which spread their message through fictional narratives. These proved to be at least as effective as fact-filled pamphlets and air-base protests. Despite a slew of utterly forgettable bomb-sploitation films, productions such as *On the Beach*, *Dr Strangelove*, and *The Day After* left a lasting imprint on America's consciousness. Indeed, all indicators suggest that the imagery and vicarious experience provided by such films had the greatest anti-bomb influence upon the general populace. Weart cites a 1982 survey that 'confirmed that the people most active in opposing nuclear war were motivated not by technical statistics but by concrete personal images, charred bodies of people and the like.'[11] These narratives were perceived by anxious (often young) adults as warnings about a horrible tomorrow —but it was a tomorrow that could be averted by taking political action today. After the initial shock of the images, viewers would often express indignant, horrified rage at the existence of such weapons and the men (overwhelmingly) who created and controlled them. Although the activism generated by the evocative imagery of these media depictions was neither particularly focused nor articulate, it was vehement and sincere—and, since authors and readers still exist to discuss and analyze its effects, perhaps that was enough.

By combining the 'if this goes on' extrapolations of imminent doom with 'what if' speculations on possible paths away from nuclear holocaust, American nuclear war fiction borrowed and synergized science fiction's two primary rhetorical modes in maximizing its discursive force against the threat of Armageddon. However, exposition of the fearful consequences of what might occur 'if this goes on' are clearly the more powerful of the two modes, as was proven by the considerable research conducted immediately after the first airing of the made-for-TV movie that subsequently became the bellwether of the American anti-nuclear movement, *The Day After* (1983).

To this day, *The Day After* still holds the record for being the single most widely seen nuclear war narrative, and also holds the distinction of having generated the greatest amount of unsolicited public response. When it aired on November 20, 1983, it set the record for being the television program with the single largest audience ever recorded; it also engendered an unprecedented firestorm of debate and analysis. The cover story of that week's issue of *Newsweek* (November 21) covered the issues and controversies raised by the film. Then-President Reagan, who screened the film a month before the air date, recorded in his personal journal,

> I ran the tape of the movie ABC is running Nov. 20. It's called 'The Day After' in which Lawrence, Kansas, is wiped out in a nuclear war with Russia. It is powerfully done, all $7 million worth. It's very effective and left me greatly depressed. So far they haven't sold any of the 25 ads scheduled and I can see why . . . My own reaction: we have to do all we can to have a deterrent and to see there is never a nuclear war.[12]

Although some polls were divided regarding the social effects of *The Day After*, one result seems consistent: those persons who already had even modest nuclear fears experienced a major intensification of these anxieties. When polled before the film, only 26% of the viewers-to-be expressed a fear that nuclear war was imminent; after seeing the film, 88% of those polled said that they felt it to be a severe threat and a source of considerable worry and concern.

Less debatable is the discursive weight this film still exerts upon nuclear discourse. *The Day After* (and to a lesser degree, *On the Beach* and *Threads*) are frequently cited, referred to, and have generally evolved not only into icons of an entire political movement, but have come to function as ideographs for specific discursive exercises within the broader domain of the nuclear debate.[13] Yet, despite their diverse previsions and rhetorical strategies, the major works of nuclear war fiction have a compelling similarity: all offer images and textures of a possible future that is impossible to accept. And in rejecting each vicariously experienced world, readers and viewers alike echo and re-echo the resolve that, whatever the unfolding plot of human experience may hold in store, this is an event that must not, and cannot, be accepted.

In addition to providing a preemptive, imaginative inoculation against the impulse to proceed down the path to Armageddon, nuclear war fiction played another, equally important sociopolitical role: it disseminated information concerning changes in the technology of nuclear weaponry and the concomitant threats to political stability. As authors (such as Heinlein) and futurists (such as Toffler) have suggested, one of the major social benefits of 'hard' science fiction may be its capacity to distribute an accessible overview, and awareness, of new technological achievements — and threats. This may be increasingly true in superpower states, where, long before the 'cutting edge' of either theory or mechanism falls under the eager gaze of the public eye, it may have profound political and social consequences. Few domains of discourse have illustrated these linked issues of providing politically crucial information and anticipations so dramatically and clearly as nuclear war fiction. The Victorian readers of Arnold-Forster's 'In a Conning Tower' had not heard of and did not understand the ramifications of new innovations in the naval technology of their day. The changes that have occurred in the realm of nuclear weapons are still less accessible to the American body politic. In addition to the major innovative steps—the atomic bomb, the hydrogen bomb, the ICBM, the MIRV—there have been numerous, smaller technological changes that have amplified the probable speed, irreversibility, pervasiveness, and horror of a projected nuclear conflict. An extremely abbreviated list of the most important of these developments would still have to include the introduction of technologies such as performance changes in intercontinental bombers; in-air refueling; intermediate range ballistic missiles; atomic artillery rounds; anti-ballistic missiles; sub-launched ballistic missiles; all-weather, all-angle radar; MARVs; cruise missiles; neutron bombs, satellite-killer rockets; both ground-based and orbital anti-satellite weapons; and the many technologies explored under the Strategic Defense Initiative. One would also have to consider the military applications/implications of almost every major technological advance or innovation produced by the space program, including satellite telecommunications; sensor development (i.e. light-amplifying, infra-red, thermal, spectrographic); changes in launch capacities and reliabilities; orbital transfer vehicles; laser-guidance and ground positioning (e.g. GPS); and look-down/look-up airborne radars. This list, while long, is nonetheless merely a scratch upon the surface of the diverse array of weapons and support systems which has had major impacts upon the probable outcome of any nuclear conflict.

There are further complicated, often counter-intuitive, variables to be considered: for instance, although it is tempting to believe that each new technological adornment to the nuclear armamentarium could only ensure faster, more absolute destruction, this is not the case. One example of this is improvements in orbital sensors, which allowed both East and West to engage in unilateral verification of not only their opponent's launch sites, but probable alert status. Therefore, certain technological developments had (and still have) a significant stabilizing effect. Alternatively, these same 'stabilizing' technologies often produce a reassessment and shift in the 'distribution of probability' *vis à vis* the most worrisome or likely escalation scenarios. For instance, it could be argued that as sensors became more advanced, the probability of the all-out 'sneak attack' scenario diminished considerably. However, this meant that new emphasis had to be placed on the innumerable 'foreign escalation' scenarios, in which various global flashpoints were perceived as being the new primary threats that could lead to a deterioration of relations and an increase in the defense posture and nuclear alert status of a potential adversary. In these scenarios, the delicate management of intimidation and concession, antagonism and amelioration, became as important—and far less predictable or controllable—than the nuclear weapons which spawned the harrowing game of 'brinkmanship.'

What are the realistic prospects for the body politic of America—or any other pluralistic state—to maintain a reasonably detailed and current understanding of this bewildering matrix of shifting technologies and tactics? A particularly avid newspaper reader—after struggling through political doubletalk, military technospeak, and pert acronyms—might be able to appreciate and integrate all these new factors into a revised 'total scenario.' However, individuals with the time, ability, and inclination for such an exercise are likely to comprise a small minority of the reading public. Furthermore, even if those individuals faithfully and competently undertook such 'scenario revising,' their adjusted understandings would be of altered quantities, not new, *qualitative* changes—which can only be vicariously experienced through the medium of an imaginative narrative.

*****

Arguably, the most striking examples of nuclear fiction's public influence concern its dissemination of those coldest facts of the Cold War: the instruments, odds, and outcomes of Armageddon. Indeed, changes in the technologies of doomsday often provided new inspiration (and sales) for writers and publishers: new realities in weaponry often meant new depictions of what a nuclear war would be like. For instance, only a few years after Neville Shute portrayed a world-destroying doomsday cloud moving south to finish off Australia in *On the Beach* (1957), Pat Frank gave America its first major, and best-selling, survivalist tale, *Alas, Babylon* (1959).

In the two years that separated the publication of these two novels, changes in rocketry and space technology had caused major re-evaluations of how a nuclear scenario might be played out. Shute's final war is, as it only could be in 1956–57, a war of bombers. This creates what military slangsters have called a 'use-it-or-lose-it' scenario. Before the advent of satellites and rockets, the only useful strategic nuclear weapons were the ones that were airborne before an attacker arrived. Faced with the prospect of waves of incoming bombers, the options were either to immediately initiate a response in kind or a blithe acceptance of annihilation without retaliation. Shute's scenario is predicated, therefore, on a full exchange of cobalt-enhanced nuclear weapons. Shute does not directly mention this, and he did not need to; most of his readers understood it. However, the text did impart something new to them, something even more urgent than cognitive understanding: it gave readers a vicarious yet visceral experience of the human impact of such a war. Naturally, later fictions not only revised the probable 'world's-end' scenario to keep pace with technological changes but also reflected advanced understandings of meteorology, distribution of fallout, and other ecological insights which have subsequently shown Shute's scenario to be extremely unlikely. However, the symbolic value of the descending cloud remains undiminished: although the text has lost scientific plausibility, it has retained pertinence and meaning as an allegorical tale.

In contrast with Shute's 'use-it-or-lose-it' scenario of total extinction, Frank's 1959 narrative, *Alas, Babylon*, postulates a sharp, brief war of missiles, submarines, and survivors (at least 50 million in America alone). Frank—the pen-name of Harry Hart—was not a neophyte when it came to strategic issues: his professional service record included an appointment to the Allied Political Warfare Council and a position with the UN mission in Korea. Frank's scenario reflects the extraordinary changes in technology that had occurred by 1959: early warning systems were much more advanced, and the commitment to a retaliatory strike no longer required such a long lead-time. Frank's near-future world was also one in which nuclear attacks had become unstoppable; missiles could now fall out of the sky with extraordinary precision and at speeds that defied any reasonable hope of interception. It was also a world in which the distribution of fallout was understood to be widespread, but highly variable and uneven.[14] Therefore, the projected aftermath of Armageddon no longer resembles Shute's uniformly dying world, but is a chaotic melange of utter devastation and serendipitous survival. This is the scenario, and the premise, that allows Frank to weave his story around the resourceful and doughty people of Fort Repose, Florida, who manage to survive the first year after the war, eventually to be recontacted by the remains of the US government. In this war, however, the American counter-strike, and dubious 'victory,' was not effected by aircraft: the agent of the 'new' government explains that 'The subs saved us, I guess. The subs and solid fuel rockets and some of the airborne missiles.'[15] Significantly, this passage informs Frank's readers that America's 'win-from-behind' game of mutual annihilation has been won by three technologies that either did not exist, or were in their operational infancy, when Shute wrote his narrative. Solid-fuel rockets were an important new technology insofar as rapid response to an incoming threat was concerned. Conventional, liquid-fuel rockets required a pre-launch fueling interval, since the fuels could not remain in their on-board tanks indefinitely. In contrast, a solid-fuel rocket's propellant is an inert, solid substance that becomes immediately active upon ignition, resulting in an almost instantaneous response time and no fueling delays: such weapons are eternally ready for immediate, unstoppable retaliation. Frank's reference to 'airborne missiles' indexes the simple 1959 precursors of today's ultra-sophisticated cruise missiles—another 'new' counter-strike option which could not be eliminated by a surprise attack. Lastly, 'the subs' refers to new submarines capable of launching Polaris nuclear missiles, and which were generally immune to detection until they actually carried out their strikes.

Because of these technologies, even the aftermath of the war is different. The first, sharp exchange of blows in *Alas, Babylon* is focused primarily on military targets, and the Soviets, evidently crippled by the American response, are unable to resume their attack. However, America's victory is decidedly Pyrric: the government official explains that the US is only 'a second-class power now. Tertiary would be more accurate,' although help is on the way from various nations in the southern hemisphere.[16] He goes on to reveal that Russia has been 'clobbered' and, by implication, is wholly unsalvageable.

The relative hopefulness of this aftermath—both in terms of international outcomes and the successful struggle of individuals to survive in good health and dignity—suggests that Frank's book is not primarily intended to be a rigorous projection or anticipation. The wish-fulfillment fantasies that Frank gratifies by siting his protagonists in a wholly unravaged region, coupled with a return to more traditional values and the efficacy of direct, personal action, anticipates the perverse, dark romanticism of the 'nuclear frontier' ethos that emerged in later decades and endured until the 1990s. Frank does explain in his closing pages that the conditions in Fort Repose are exceptional and possibly unique. The rest of the nation seems just barely to exist under militarily enforced rationing and martial law. However, the subtextual message of reassurance and reclaimed virtue was obviously one that American audiences wanted to hear, and may explain the book's longevity and success.[17] In summary, *Alas, Babylon* illustrated and explored a number of significant alterations to the probable experience of nuclear war, and, if we are to believe Frank's foreword, his primary motivation for writing it was a desire to give Americans a better understanding of the probable scope and devastation of a such a war.

Frank's proposition that survival in the aftermath of a nuclear war would entail a precipitous plunge in the quality of life was to become a staple of American nuclear war fiction. It certainly informs the blasted, neo-medieval environment that Walter J. Miller postulates in *A Canticle for Leibowitz*.[18] Although published the same year as Frank's book, *Canticle* could hardly be more different in style or conclusions. Set in a distant post-apocalyptic future, it documents the inexorable return of the nuclear Satan a thousand years after 'The Flame Deluge' of the twentieth century consumed most of humanity and even more of its knowledge. The last remains of this knowledge are kept, copied, and recopied by the Church. Miller does not offer a reader any look at new weapons technologies in connection with the devastating war: in fact, war is never depicted. Instead, Miller imagines a new, horrible future in which the consequences of an all-out nuclear war would be a veritable return to the Stone Age. Miller's nuclear war results in a physical, mental, and spiritual decline of unprecedented proportions; hope, charity, and innovation are supplanted by cynicism, brutality, and bitterly lethal Ludditism. In short, Miller offered Cold War readers a third, highly detailed and highly distinctive scenario of nuclear aftermath: not Shute's headlong plunge into rapid (but essentially 'clean') extinction, nor Frank's celebratory portrayal of humanity precariously recovering its footing at the brink, but a thousand-year night of ignorance, stupidity, and species-wide degradation.

Ironically, the next 'landmark' nuclear war narrative inverted the scale of Miller's sardonic, century-leaping romp across post-nuclear badlands, presenting instead an intensely focused and detailed account of how a nuclear war could occur purely as a result of a small oversight. This examination of both human and machine error is arguably the most memorable and chilling revelation in Burdick and Wheeler's *Fail-Safe* (1962). Written only three years after *Alas, Babylon*, the authors were very conscious of their role as the public's purveyors of new, politically important technological information, as well as the consequent changes in outcomes implied by the altered strategic scenario. As they write in their preface:

Although science and technology have been harnessed to the American defense system in a miraculous way, most people are unaware of even those portions of the miracle which have been declassified and discussed openly in technical books and journals. Thus, paradoxically a fictional portrayal employing declassified information may seem like science fiction to the layman and ancient history to the expert. . . . The authors have . . . taken some liberties with what has been declassified. Usually this amounted to attributing improved or more powerful performances to control and weapons systems. . . . The events in this story are thought of as taking place in 1967.[19]

As history revealed, the technological improvements Burdick and Wheeler postulated were far more humble than those that had actually accrued by 1967. The sophistication of rocketry (particularly ICBMs), sensors, and command and control mechanisms had far outstripped their previsions. However, they were generally accurate in their observation that as the nuclear response system grew in complexity and size, its reliance upon automation increased exponentially, and that the possibility of an irreversible machine error was mounting steadily. In their preface, Burdick and Wheeler explain:

[A]ll too often past crises have been revealed to us in which the world tottered on the brink of thermonuclear war while S.A.C. commanders pondered the true nature of unidentified flying objects on their radar screens. . . . Men, machines, and mathematics being what they are, this is, unfortunately, a 'true' story. The accident may not occur in the way we describe but the laws of probability assure us that ultimately it will occur.[20]

The malfunction in *Fail-Safe* that jeopardizes the future of the human race is unspeakably minor—which is one of the greatest strengths of the novel. By illustrating how the most minor breakdown can initiate a rapid descent into global annihilation, an outrageously disproportionate relationship is established between simple mechanical failures and unthinkably catastrophic effects. This in turn thrusts the reader into a bizarre, nightmarish world where pedestrian assumptions of a fundamental balance between actions and consequences prove to be unreliable, thereby undermining the very foundation of most human logic and planning. Were it not written in such straightforward, and often uninspired, prose, *Fail-Safe* could alternatively be read as a dark absurdist comedy. For instance, just as one of the main characters, Colonel Cascio, is in the process of informing official visitors that the automated 'Fail-Safe' system which controls nuclear attack and response is 'infallible,' contradictory events are transpiring in the room where the 'Fail-Safe Activating Mechanisms' wait in eternal patience to set in motion the clockwork gears of Armageddon:

> At about the moment that Colonel Cascio said the word 'infallible' a sergeant sitting at one of the desks stood up and walked around the bank of machines.
> 'Frank, how are you fixed for cigarettes?' the sergeant asked. 'I'm out.'
> Frank tossed him a pack of Chesterfields. The sergeant reached to catch them. At that moment in Machine No. 6 a small condenser blew. It was a soundless event. There was a puff of smoke no larger than a walnut that was gone instantly.
> The sergeant sniffed the air. He turned to Frank. 'Frank, do you smell something?' he asked. 'Like something burning?'
> 'Yeah, that's me,' Frank said. 'You bumming cigarettes all the time and then not paying me back, that burns me.'
> They grinned at one another. The sergeant returned to his desk. Things returned to normal . . . almost. A small shield hid from the sergeant's view the tiny knob of burnt carbon on top of the disabled condenser. No instruments on the table indicated a malfunction.[21]

The ludicrous nature of this malfunction makes the outcome all the more ghastly. When, as a result, an American bomber cannot be recalled from its raid on Moscow, the US president must sacrifice New York in an act of atomic expiation and good faith, a massacre that must be carried out by an American warplane. The scenario, and the implications of deadly ghosts in the ever-growing nuclear machine, were roundly decried by officials and military experts. Significantly, these same experts usually declined to comment on the accuracy of Burdick and Wheeler's portrayal of the nation's defense technologies and controls—a paradoxical refusal indeed, if the authors were so completely off the mark. In the end, however, the official reaction to the narrative did not prevent it from becoming one of the best-known and most widely discussed novels of the early 1960s, spawning numerous reprints in the process, as well as a film version in 1964, and a teleplay remake as recently as 2000. Nor did the counter claims and reassurances of government representatives prevent life from imitating art several times in the following years, when hauntingly similar minor failures almost led to catastrophic results. On June 3 and June 6, 1980,

> A computer in the North American Air Defense Command set off signals that Soviet missiles from submarines and Russian land bases were flying toward targets here.

The alarm caused American duty officers to order strategic bomber crews to their planes to start the engines, to have battle-control aircraft prepared for flight, to have one in Hawaii take-off and to bring silo-based missiles closer to the stage of firing.[22]

The cause of all this panic? In a strangely close parallel to the source of the *Fail-Safe* error, 'a failure in an electronic component about the size of a dime and worth 46 cents caused the two false alarms that put United States strategic nuclear forces on alert . . .'[23]

Another major change in the nuclear technoscape began emerging in the late 1960s when, in conjunction with the successes of both the American and Russian space programs, the venerable 'science fiction' concept of orbiting missile platforms—such as those postulated in Neville's 'Cold War'[24]—began to emerge as a crucial strategic issue. This new concern with space-based weapon systems was quickly taken up by future-war authors, who had long envisioned and predicted such devices. However, these writers reacted with as much cautionary reserve as technophilic zeal. In one notable speculation on how such weapons or defense systems could critically destabilize an already hair-trigger international situation, Ben Bova's 1976 novel *Millennium* depicts a world poised on the brink of destruction due to the rapid accumulation of orbital weapons, defenses, and countermeasures. Amplifying the danger, the interconnections between the diverse systems are so intricate and fragile that tensions cannot help but increase. As theoretical defensive and offensive scenarios become more uncertain, war anxiety—and likelihood—mounts. In the end, the solution is not found on the Earth, but on the Moon, where the leaders of the American and Russian bases—fearful that their logistical lifeline from Earth will soon be severed by a globe-consuming thermonuclear conflict—arrange a codominium in order to share vital resources and survive in isolation. Joint secession from their terrestrial masters leads to bolder action: pooling all their technical and intelligence resources, they engineer a takeover of the anti-missile laser satellites of both sides and unilaterally declare peace. Bova's narrative provides not only an interesting foreshadowing of the technologies that would be studied and developed under the Strategic Defense Initiative, but also of the high potential for destabilization inherent in either unilateral or bilateral deployment of orbital weapons. This possible instability, even more than economics, was an urgent issue in the debate over Reagan's misnamed 'Star Wars' scheme.

Another noteworthy aspect of *Millennium* is its 'spaceman as deus-ex-machina' theme, which is a recurring motif in both the future-war and 'hard SF' discursive communities. In addition to the obvious symbolism of characters from the 'heavens' as somehow transcendent, or even Christ-like (the protagonist of *Millennium* dies ensuring a new era of peace), there are reasonable arguments underlying anticipations of extra-terrestrial settlers having far more in common with each other—experientially and politically—than they would with the citizens of their terrestrial lands of origin. Most significantly, long-term survival in space requires a careful husbanding of resources. It also requires an extremely high degree of security, since the environmental viability of space habitats can easily be ruined beyond repair. Unless somehow excluded from attacks, space communities would almost certainly be targeted in the first moments of any such war, due to their strategic value, and—being so fragile—they could do virtually nothing to prevent their destruction.

The thorny issue of orbital defense systems as a destabilizing factor emerges once again in Whitley Strieber and Jim Kunetka's *Warday*, in which general readers were exposed to the consequences of what the authors described as a limited nuclear conflict.[25] In this narrative, the unilateral American deployment of the first component in the 'Star Wars' defense system reintroduces a much more complex version of the 'use-it-or-lose-it' strategizing that informed Shute's *On The Beach*. *Warday* addresses a defensive technology conundrum that has plagued arms limitations negotiations for thirty-five years: if one side has sole possession of even a marginally effective anti-missile deterrent, the opposition is likely to conclude that its long-term safety requires immediate preemption. Thus, in Strieber and Kunetka's near-future Third World War, the Soviet Union becomes terrified when the principle of mutual assured destruction begins to lose its mutuality—due to American defense satellites. Accordingly, Russia cripples the US with a preemptive nuclear strike, but in so doing, is even more horribly savaged by the American counter-strike. However, Strieber and Kunetka's fundamental thesis is that the concept and term 'limited' nuclear war, is, at best, a dubious distinction, and more properly categorized as oxymoronic. *Warday* demonstrates that the effects of nuclear weapons continue to radiate outward—through space, time, lives, genetics, and attitudes—long after the blast has passed. The fictional Strieber lives with the statistical probability that the rads he received during and after the attack will produce early and inoperable malignancies. Throughout the US, education is rudimentary, leisure almost nonexistent, publicly shown art an affectation from an earlier epoch. Owning firearms is no longer seen as suspicious or even atypical, but advisable, even essential. Personal loss of numerous family members, friends, lovers generates a web of personal tragedy so wide and deep that it entraps, and strangles the affect out of, many survivors. The accumulation of these recurrent reminders of the fateful 'war day' becomes an emotional mosaic that reveals the insufficiencies and inaccuracies of the term 'limited war.' Instead of preaching against the dangers of such conflicts, Strieber and Kunetka let their fictive world bear witness to the proposition that 'limited nuclear war' is not just a flawed, but a dangerously misleading, concept—precisely because it utterly fails to express the infinitude of loss and suffering that will define life in its aftermath.

*****

From hydrogen bomb to Star Wars, from cobalt-induced global die-off to long-term horrors and tragedies that drag grotesquely behind a body politic crippled by a limited atomic exchange, nuclear war fiction has, over the past fifty years, routinely and repeatedly reexamined and grappled with the changing realities and probabilities created by new weapons technologies. Whether or not these narratives enumerate and explain the specific improvements in weapon performance and the changes in probable effects and outcomes, the tangible, human consequences of these changes are subsumed into and experienced through the images and stories of the narratives. What begins as mathematical assessments by weapon designers and expert commentary by military professionals is translated by future-war authors into a non-specialized social discourse that surveys the potential effects of new weapons through the infinitely more accessible medium of vicarious experience. This is, of course, the most pronounced example of the 'trickle-down' effect adduced in the prior chapter. Nuclear war fiction cannot function as a viable source of entertainment, activism, or education unless it successfully converts the recondite and specialized cants of technical experts into terms and narrative experiences that make cognitive, emotional, and physical sense to laypersons. But this same domain of nuclear discourse is also noteworthy for facilitating the 'trickle up' of new ideas, new policies, even new self-assessments of the psychological and social consequences of life lived on the brink of absolute annihilation. In particular, it enabled the articulation of the public's perpetual anxiety of imminent Apocalypse, a culturally deranging condition that might reasonably be labeled 'silo-psychosis.'

*Chapter 7*

# Nuclear Fiction and Silo Psychosis: Narratives of Life in the Shadow of a Mushroom Cloud

According to conventional wisdom, the atomic bomb, along with information technology and manipulation, are two essential national prerequisites for 'true' superpower status. However, the nuclear sword of Damocles comes equipped with a second edge—one that cuts into the consciousness and cohesiveness of the superpower itself, even as that state uses the bomb's physical and psychological power to expand its hegemony across previously impermeable cultural and national borders. Ultimately, the radiation of a nuclear warhead is social as well as physical, mutating not merely the culture of those who fear the wielders, but that of the wielders themselves. As such, 'we'—the whole of humanity—are at risk in mind as well as body.

*****

The Cold War psychology—and often, psychopathology—of American culture was frequently acted out, and tellingly disclosed, through narrative articulations of its nuclear stream of consciousness. Indeed, it is possible to diagnose America's nuclear anxieties by studying the narrative imagery that dominated the symbolic shadow-plays of new weapons and maybe-wars with which it both amused and indoctrinated itself over a long period of mushroom-clouded MAD-ness. A rigorous and revealing inquiry into American obsessions with, and representations of, the bomb will also benefit from a cross-cultural comparative analysis, since the contrasts revealed thereby will bring the unique characteristics of US nuclear nightmares into high relief. Particularly appropriate to this project, comparisons between British and American images of the bomb and its aftermath can be used to highlight the key features of America's nuclear psychology, to explain the uniqueness of those features, and to reveal the influence of nuclear weapons upon the consciousness of both the nation's political elites and general public.

In British and American narratives, images of the actual moment of nuclear destruction are notable mostly for their similarities. This is hardly surprising, since the actual conflagration is virtually the only aspect of the nuclear question that is (mostly) congenial to straightforward, objective analysis: the physics are not subject to contextualization. However, in British versus American nuclear war films, the selection of what to frame and how to frame it is subtly different.

In *Threads* (1984), as in other UK films that envision the moment of atomic incineration, the portrayal of the blast effects is frank, fast, even brutal.[1] However, in keeping with the tradition initiated by Wells' ur-text of nuclear conflict, *The World Set Free*, the intensity of these visual examinations is leavened by a marked degree of circumspection, by an unwillingness to voyeuristically step back and acquire a macroscopic view of the calamity.[2] Accordingly, in *Threads*—and also in *The War Game* (1965) and *The Bedsitting Room* (1969)—the audience is never provided with a bird's-eye look at the end of the world. The scale at which viewers witness the effects of the bomb never exceeds the devastation of individual buildings; the scope never expands to show a larger landscape. As in *The World Set Free* and its British progeny, the human effects of the blast are shown, but each view is intimate, immediate. Hence, it might be said that integral to many British portrayals is a marked reluctance to look too deeply or too long into the atomic inferno. Therefore, if one were to categorize British cinema's psychological posture *vis à vis* nuclear war as either 'approach' or 'avoidance,' it would seem that 'avoidance' is by far the dominant tone.

The exact opposite holds true in the United States. Indeed, the American tendency to approach—and reapproach—images of Armageddon is pronounced and unsettling. The most striking aspect of US depictions of the moment of atomic incineration is the strange mix of shocked horror and compulsive fascination that seems to underlie these representations of larger-than-life destruction. US films, as epitomized by *The Day After* (1983), present detailed visual dissections of the detonation and offer expansive views of mass destruction.[3] More disturbing still, this fascination often becomes an obsession in American films, one that reaches its grim zenith in the action/sf film genre. For instance, the nuclear blast sequence from *Terminator 2: Judgment Day* (1991) is horrible, even repulsive, culminating in the protagonist's flesh being burned and blasted off her blazing skeleton. However, the obsessive nature of these visuals—the attention to detail, the dilation of time to permit an almost clinical assessment of the annihilating effects of the bomb—additionally suggests a sensual, almost erotic, fascination with the spectacle of destruction.

It would be unfair and inaccurate to suggest that graphic depictions of Armageddon are simply indicative of an American willingness to pander to the sensationalistic and dramatic. As Patrick Mannix points out in his incisive and extensive examination of Nicholas Meyer's *The Day After*, the cinematic scaling and framing of nuclear devastation is at least as much informed by rhetorical objectives as it is by a perverse hunger for lethal spectacles: 'Because Meyer wants to show the effects of nuclear war on a cross-section of people, he must keep cutting from one character to another in the large cast, never concentrating on one long enough to develop any real psychological depth.'[4] Mannix's exfoliation of the tactics underlying this technique is important and incisive enough to warrant inclusion here. The most provocative of Mannix's observations on the film is that, instead of education,

> fear seems much more crucial to its rhetorical strategy. Meyer begins by insuring the maximum level of identification for an American audience through his choice of setting: Lawrence, Kansas, almost the exact center of the nation. . . . [F]armers harvest corn in the nearby fields; children play in a park; workers in a milk plant run their bottling machines; students go to classes at the university. . . . [T]hese are meant to be glimpses of the lives of people like us—lives that are about to be destroyed by a calamity that threatens us daily. Through this identification, Meyer is conditioning us to feel the sense of imminent danger that fear demands.[5]

Further evidence supports Mannix's contention that Meyer's narrative constructs are designed to generate a growing sense of fear and helplessness. The onset of the nuclear conflict is foreshadowed through an accumulation of half-heard television and radio reports on escalating international tensions, clues of the coming apocalypse that viewers understand with clarity and certainty, but which most of the characters in the film either ignore or discount. Consequently, as they proceed to their doom, we experience a growing sense of dread akin to that which is generated when a slasher movie's ingénue enters the house in which the inevitable pathological killer is lurking. We are unable to deter the sacrificial starlet, ready to flinch every time she enters a new room, uncertain when the blade will fall, but certain that it will. According to this formula, we are powerless to stop what will transpire, and in *The Day After*, this horror of entrapment expands from several moments to many minutes, the anxiety and inevitability of doom extending into a dreadful, slow-motion anticipation of the multimegaton lacerations soon to shred the social tissue of the body politic.

When Meyer finally does let the nuclear knife fall, its slashing is neither brief nor oblique: he capitalizes on the associations he has established between the viewer and the workaday Americans of Lawrence, Kansas by illustrating the ghastly effects of the bomb upon the town's unwitting human canvases. The montage of shots depicting the actual atomic devastation includes: the immolation of countless individuals (whose skeletons improbably persist a fraction of a second after they are vaporized); tidal waves of star-hot plasma washing away trees, animals, flesh; the disintegration of buildings; and a sustained collage of nuclear test footage showing the horrific (and often bizarre) effects of the bombs themselves. But this four-minute sequence is just the beginning of Meyer's studied (and some contend, tiresomely didactic) exercise in viewer education via emotional shock therapy: the strongest doses are to be found in his depiction of the aftermath. As Mannix observes, 'True to the facts of nuclear war—and Meyer is scrupulous in making sure that his depiction is accurate—the survivors of the missile strikes face an ongoing struggle for life.'[6] Indeed, Meyer's extended investigation into the hellish physical, emotional, and social challenges that must be surmounted in order to survive in the aftermath of a nuclear attack is atypical, in that most American films that depict a post-apocalyptic world have been 'bomb-sploitation' adventure romps. However, what does emerge as a constant—both in 'serious' nuclear war films and the countless 'Mad Max' rip-offs—is the fascination with panoramas of annihilation and destruction.

If the British narrative's tendency to avert its gaze from the heart of the nuclear horror is easy to understand, the American narrative's tendency to stare fixedly at this spectacle is not. Susan Sontag offers one explanatory postulate in her essay 'The Imagination of Disaster.'[7] Speaking only of films, and in particular, their mesmeric fixation upon scenes of destruction, she proposes that they may effect a form of catharsis, a grappling with the unimaginable in order to feel that some measure of control has been asserted over that which cannot be controlled. However, a more pertinent model may be found in Vivian Sobchack's 'The Violent Dance: A Personal Memoir of Death In the Movies.'[8] Sobchack proposes that the avid American interest in the depiction of violence is, in effect, an attempt at psychological prophylaxis against the shock we would suffer should we actually become witnesses to, or victims of, such horrors. In terms of atomic war, this would represent an attempt to prepare for the unimaginable by preemptively shocking—and partially inuring—ourselves to the horrors of the ultimate in annihilation.

Whatever the reason—dark prurience, futile catharsis, or a desperate attempt at self-preparation—American viewers seem to possess at least some, if not all, of the mixed motivations that almost certainly compelled Lot's wife to turn and consider the conflagration that consumed Sodom. American film-makers and viewers look long, hard, and possibly too deeply into the hypnotic flames, so fascinated and compelled that the normal reaction to the horrific—an impulse to look away—is overridden. In contrast, the behavior of the British viewing public seems more reminiscent of that associated with Noah, who is unsettled when he hears the profound voice, and prescription, of doom. His, and perhaps Britain's, reflexive flinch of aversion is primal, recalling fears of taboo contact and sympathetic magic, and of whispered subconscious warnings that, if the foretelling of the coming flame deluge is heard too clearly, and in too much horrible detail, then it may also immolate the consciousness of the listener.

However, the differences in British and American depictions of nuclear warfare become more pronounced—and more revealing—when the narratives move beyond the actual moments of annihilation into the horribly altered world of the atomic aftermath. In films originating in the UK, the first, and primary, focal image of this aftermath is almost invariably a city—another trend with roots in Wells' original work, as well as in the memories of the Blitz. In films such as *Threads*, *The Bedsitting Room*, and *1984* (1984), the dominant British image is that of the crushed city: masonry and girders tumbled into ramshackle streets, hollow-eyed survivors picking through the urban graveyard in search of the dead, the dying, and the shreds of yesteryear—which might have ended only a second before. It is a worldview in which the dominant themes are those of desolation and defoliation, which, if considered in the specific context of an urban landscape, may reveal the equally specific fears that underlie this trend in UK imagery.

To the British mind, it seems, the destruction of the city—not any particular city, but the sheer concept of 'city'—is the nexus of national and social terror. At one level, this may reflect the centripetal mental and cultural force exerted over Great Britain by the city of London and the revealingly named 'Home Counties.' Certainly no single city or region in the US has ever been comparably central to national consciousness, governance, and history. Consequently, it might be suggested that the loss of *a* city is actually a cipher for the loss of *the* city of London—and with it, the loss of nation, culture, identity. This is certainly gestured to in both the earliest British contemplations of apocalypse (in the ruined London of both *The World Set Free* and, particularly, *The War of the Worlds* (1898)) and in its latter-day manifestations.[9] But does this mean that the destruction of Sheffield in *Threads* is merely a cipher for a similar annihilation presumably occurring simultaneously alongside the Thames?

Such a conclusion would be both ill-advised and dangerously simplistic. Instead, the imagery of urban annihilation may indicate a specific, significant geopolitical reality that informs the British mind, but which is largely absent from American thought. This reality is that of the 'Island Fortress' self-perception—which, in the modern age of push-button apocalypse, undergoes a terrifying inversion: Britain's traditional sense of defensive security becomes an anxiety of horrible, claustrophobic vulnerability. Where once England's relatively small size and marine separation offered it a measure of impregnability, daunting onrushing Nazi armies only sixty years ago, the advent of the bomb has converted the green and pleasant land into a killing zone: a small parcel of land which can be easily blanketed by multiple strikes. In its limited confines, there is no room to run; there are no prairies, outbacks, or mountains so remote that refugees might entertain the hope of escaping the pestilential aftermath or subsequent hordes of the desperate and barbarous. Once the bombs go off, there are no longer any alternatives; there are no escapes, no distant horizons to disappear behind. The people of Britain are trapped—as are the people of a city—between shores and among streets that can only continue to be piled higher with the dead, and, after, must crumble down in unarrestable decay.

Conversely, American nuclear war narratives rarely pursue their exploration of aftermath so exclusively in cities. There is, in addition to urban perspectives, extensive consideration of the destruction of the countryside and of isolated towns—whether or not the damage there was inflicted directly by the blast or as 'collateral effects.' Indeed, much of the post-blast action of American narratives (in both text and film) takes place away from urban centers, as is the case in stories as diverse as *The Day After*, *Testament* (1983), Frank's *Alas, Babylon*, Stieber and Kunetka's *Warday*, and Miller's *A Canticle for Leibowitz*.[10]

This, on reflection, is hardly surprising. Whereas English nuclear consciousness may be informed by island-claustrophobia and a 'mind-the-gap' appreciation of the dangerously narrow separation between 'life as usual' and 'death among the ruins,' the American nuclear consciousness has been influenced by a completely different geopolitical reality, which correspondingly gives rise to completely different attitudes, reactions, outlooks, and a completely different palette of images. For want of a better term, this different geopolitical perspective might be called the frontier mentality: the inveterate American belief that there is always a new land beyond the horizon, a new mountain beyond which to start a new life, an undiscovered country ready to welcome the determined and the industrious. Whether this is infantile ingenuousness or valid optimism is difficult to say, but in apocalyptic scenarios, the comparative vastness of America often functions as a tacit sponge for atomic bombs, allowing the nation to absorb damage. As a consequence, it is often difficult to ascertain whether any given 'post-nuclear frontier' story is essentially reasonable or ridiculous due to the lack of specificity regarding the nature of the nuclear conflict that gave rise to the narrative scenario. This uncertainty is often the result of authorial reliance upon imprecise and unqualified terms—and the phrase 'nuclear war' may itself be the most notorious example. 'Nuclear war' may refer to either a 'full strike' or 'limited exchange,' yet both of these terms are equally imprecise. Is a single bomb an act of terrorism or a limited strike? What total of inbound warheads or accumulation of megatonnage constitutes a 'full strike'? The assessment of whether the American 'frontier mentality' (and its implications of resilience, survival, and rebirth) reflects extraordinary ingenuousness or reasonable optimism largely depends upon the scale of nuclear exchange posited by the author. Consequently, authorial imprecision or silence on this point not only allows, but invites, uncritical speculations upon the survivability of 'limited strikes.' This recurrent evasion has become one of the most subtle yet pernicious components of the 'popularization' of post-nuclear 'adventure' scenarios, which are fundamentally narrative accommodations of inconceivable and unacceptable future histories.

In contrast to America's hopeful previsions of existence in the aftermath, the British assessment of the probability of post-nuclear survival effectively plummets to zero the moment a missile is launched in anger. This is quite unlike its American counterpart, which describes a more gradual gradient of catastrophe. This belief in the 'survivability' of potentially 'limited' nuclear attacks seems, in turn, to promote a greater willingness to balance the concept of 'the bomb as tool' against the undeniable horrors of its use.

Hence we see an image of the bomb in American literature and film that has no analog in the UK: the bomb as prophylaxis. The entirety of Europe —so densely populated, so delicately balanced in its interconnections— shares a common awareness that the use of the bomb means the breakdown of everything. Except in extremely remote regions, there is not even enough space to establish a 'dead zone' in which to safely detonate a nuclear device. But in the American consciousness, filled as it is with images of North Dakotan prairie, Texan badlands, and Southwestern deserts (such as the one around Alamagordo), there is a pronounced temptation to think in terms of places in which it would be 'safe' to use a bomb.

Regardless of whatever purely clinical accuracy might reside within such an assertion, it propagates a potentially perilous mentality. Individuals come to see the bomb as survivable and, as a result, not as an outrage against civilization but as a 'tool'—a utility object which, under the right conditions, might be of benefit to the nation, or even the world. And it is through this dangerous doorway of recontextualization that American narratives arrive at the bomb as prophylaxis. In the George Pal adaptation of Wells' *The War of the Worlds* (1953), the Martians are introduced to (but unimpressed by) the bomb. In Larry Niven's and Jerry

Pournelle's novel *Footfall* (1983), a good-sized chunk of the American prairie is sacrificed in order to annihilate an alien landing force.[11] Numerous B-movie bomb-homages have celebrated the mushroom cloud's (supposed) potential to either disincline or discorporate threatening monsters/mutants/maladies as diverse as Godzilla, virally created zombies, and overgrown amoebae. However, as often as not, these attempts at atomic eco-control only serve to further perturb, promote, and/or propagate the threatening agency. And although these narratives are as ludicrous as they are predictable, their anxieties represent only one small discursive step beyond those found in more responsible and somber fiction: the bomb is proposed as a means of effecting widespread sterilization over an area infected with Michael Crichton's deadly *Andromeda Strain* (1969).[12] However, the research scientists learn in the nick of time that this course of action would also have undesirable results: global dissemination of the utterly lethal Andromeda virus.

Such cautionary endings notwithstanding, America's atomic utilitarianism is most noteworthy for the seriousness and influence of its most significant manifestations. The so-appropriately named MAD—Mutual Assured Destruction—strategy conceived of the bomb as the insurance, rather than antithesis, of peace. In Eugene Burdick and Harvey Wheeler's *Fail-Safe* (1962), the bomb serves as the means of redistributing international justice and balance (*à la* Hamurabi): the erroneous incineration of Moscow by an American bomber threatens global catastrophe, until America re-equalizes the scales by dropping a similar weapon on New York City.[13] This cultural perspective also informed the use of the bomb at Hiroshima itself—the use of a nuclear tool, justified by claims that it would ultimately save lives by making Operation Olympic (the planned American invasion of Japan) unnecessary.[14] Despite these alarming examples and their moral implications, it may be more important to recognize that they collectively suggest a conceptual heritage in American thought that allows a place for the image of the bomb as prophylaxis. And it may be that this mindset helped give rise—and shape—to what commentators refer to as the American Century, for the relationship between the bomb and American attitudes played a large role in defining the new political position, praxis, and identity that abetted America's evolution into a modern superpower.

This evolution was facilitated not merely by technological attainments, but by alterations to the national psychology. One such psychological alteration involved the increasing perception of other individuals as part of the 'masses.' In military matters, this is amplified to include extreme detachment from the mitigating emotions of empathy and compassion, culminating in a systematic dehumanization of other persons, often achieved through the redirection (and/or inversion) of the sex-drive. This alteration was aided and abetted (and also epitomized) by the bomb, which has long been associated with imagery that is both sexual and perversely pornographic. The perversity and pornography of the bomb might be said to inhere in its very structure and function: regardless of the political intentions of its inventors and handlers, the idea of the device itself flirts at the edges of moral obscenity. There are, inarguably, some inanimate objects in which the moral intents of their creators have been indelibly inscribed: the death camps, iron-maidens and thumbscrews, booby-trapped children's toys. These constructs are not merely objects, nor have they been created merely to destroy; they reflect an almost psychopathic fixation upon the infliction of death and pain, either in ways, or upon a scale, that breaks beyond the boundaries of what is commonly designated as merely 'terrible'. These objects imply a misanthropy so intense, and so vicious, that it warrants the label 'obscene.' While it would be wrong to claim that the bomb is a device designed to inflict such selective harm and sado-masochistically motivated pain, it may have, at times, aroused the American subconscious with darkly erotic fantasies of final consummation and annihilation.

In discussing the bomb, Jacqueline Smetak strikes a decidedly Freudian chord when she posits that 'the aim of all life is death,' and argues that whereas 'the life instinct, turns toward pleasure rather than destruction, any society intent on obliterating itself will repress or distort erotic tendencies.' However, a society so afflicted will be largely unaware of this unhealthy inversion, because it 'will also repress awareness of ... its desire to kill itself.'[15] While Smetak's conclusions may be somewhat extreme, both the sex and death drive can be rechanneled to abet the technocentric super-state's trend toward systematic dehumanization of both its own warriors and their opponents. No other object has become a more effective medium for achieving these objectives than the atomic bomb, both in terms of the psychological force it exerts and in its significance as an icon that simultaneously embodies the yin and yang of both global destruction and sexual climax.

No narrative has made more use of this dualism in the imagery of the bomb than Stanley Kubrick's *Dr Strangelove* (1964), significantly subtitled *Or, How I Learned to Stop Worrying and Love the Bomb*. The character of General Buck Turgidson is a caricature of this bizarre conflation of apocalyptic and sexual appetites. For instance, when Turgidson must leave his mistress in order to respond to the growing threat of global holocaust, he jocularly exhorts his sexual partner to 'Begin your countdown and Old Bucky'll be back before you can say "Blast off!"' Meanwhile, General Jack D. Ripper has started the world down the garden path to nuclear devastation in order to preserve the 'precious bodily fluids' of his flagging potency, and Doctor Strangelove is busy imagining his dominion over a cohort of post-apocalyptic love slaves in the subterranean shelters of the political elite.

Many have observed similar connections between nuclear weapons and sexual gratification, particularly phallic imagery. Nuclear activist Helen Caldicott's non-fiction tract *Missile Envy* (1985) contains this revealing passage:

> These hideous weapons . . . may be a symptom of several male emotions: inadequate sexuality and a need to continually prove their virility plus a primitive fascination with killing. I recently watched a filmed launching of an MX missile. It rose slowly out of the ground, surrounded by smoke and flames and elongated into the air—it was a very sexual sight, and when armed with the ten warheads it will explode with the most almighty orgasm.[16]

It would be naive to suggest that the ICBM, like the gun, is simply a phallic symbol, albeit writ in absurdly large dimensions. The more disturbing, and dehumanizing, aspect of atomic eros lies in the sheer scale of its destructive potential: the mere fantasy of using such a weapon is an obscene and supremely ego-masturbatory outrage against the ethics of most recorded civilizations and against human conceptions of scale and balance. If detonated, a nuclear bomb may vaporize millions, but even by merely existing, it shatters our ability to affix limits, to grasp the world in our accustomed framework of the finite. The fact of the bomb slays any functional faith in the preeminence of cognition, logic, law, order, morality, ethics. It is the ultimate symbol of transgression and violation, and to employ such a weapon could well be perceived as the ultimate and final act of egoistic self-gratification. Thus the bomb—being an absolute destroyer both of physical and conceptual boundaries and restraints—may also propel humans over the borders of acceptable, socialized behavior into bizarre mental topographies where Daliesque extrusions of megalomania, narcissism, and sadism burgeon chaotically, making an unmappable mockery of 'normative' experience. Burdick and Wheeler examine these obscene fascinations and perverse gratifications in *Fail-Safe*, when the nuclear expert Groteschele engages in a seductive death-dance with the sleek, predatory socialite, Eleanor Wolfe:

> When he described the Doomsday system, hinting that it was semi-classified, she closed her eyes for a moment and a light smile started at the corners of her mouth.
> 'Beautiful,' she said.
> Just that single word unaccompanied by an expression of horror

or astonishment or dismay. . . . 'What makes you fascinating and what makes your subject fascinating is that it involves the death of so many people. Quite literally everyone on earth.' She paused a moment and then spoke savagely. 'Damn it, I wish I were a man and a man who could push the button. I would not push it, you understand that. But the knowledge that I could.' She shivered in her mink coat. . . .

'Why wouldn't you push it?' Groteschele asked softly. . . .

'Because I would die along with everyone else,' Evelyn Wolfe said.

Her voice came to a queer faltering halt. Groteschele felt a very deep excitement. 'That is one statement you do not really believe,' he said with authority. 'Do you think that life is the most important thing to a person? . . . Knowing you have to die, imagine how fantastic and magical it would be to have the power to take everyone else with you. . . . The swarms of them out there, the untold billions of them, the ignorant masses of them, the beautiful ones, the artful ones, the friends, the enemies . . . all of them and their plans and hopes. And they are murderees: born to be murdered and don't know it. And the person with his finger on the button is the one who knows and who can do it.'

The sound Evelyn Wolfe made was not a moan. It was the sound of wonderment that a child makes . . . even if the child sees cruelty.

'Stop in one of those little side roads,' Evelyn Wolfe ordered.[17]

The predictable tryst that follows is, essentially, the Freudian death instinct and the countervailing sex instinct fused into one act of mutual consummation. The attraction and sexual encounter between these two characters is laced with metaphors not merely of predation, but of that most ravenous of all black magical eroticisms: vampirism.

This symbolism of not merely *de*humanized, but *in*human, creatures is also reflected in another consistent narrative theme within American nuclear war fiction: that of the linked onset of emotional detachment and madness. As the persons who must handle and control these weapons begin to adopt responses and habits that mimic the automata that are the true masters of such systems, their disassociation from intrinsic human needs, behaviors, and freedoms produces a fracturing of the self. Spencer Weart calls particular attention to Robert Heinlein's 'Blowups Happen,'[18] a yarn that *Astounding*'s editor John Campbell described as based on the very latest, laboratory-grade information.[19] Heinlein's story concerns a nuclear power plant—candidly referred to as 'the bomb' by its attendant technicians—which is risky to operate, but has become an essential energy source. However, Weart correctly avers that the core of Heinlein's story is not nuclear but psychological: 'Could any human being be trusted to operate such a plant, Heinlein asked, when one mistake might cause a catastrophe that would devastate thousands of square miles? Might not the pressure of the job drive an operator mad?'[20]

America's technocratic solution to this vulnerability was not merely the creation of machines that could do the work of men, but of men that could work like machines. The stoic, inflexible demeanor of totemic nuclear warlords such as General Curtis Le May (the architect of American nuclear strategy) and Admiral Rickover (the driving force behind the nuclear submarine) set a standard that not only 'trickled down' into their own branches of the armed services, but into the narrative characterizations of the de-libidinized machine-men who were charged with controlling and unleashing the arsenals of Armageddon. As Weart observes, there was incessant '[t]alk about steely logic, denial of feelings, and authorities controlling superhuman force . . .' The training movies of the Strategic Air Command featured flight-suited technowarriors carrying out their missions without any perceptible sign of emotion, chillingly reminiscent of those 'scenes in *Frankenstein* or *The Invisible Ray* where the scientist ignored his woman as he relentlessly pursued secret powers.' This provided the Russian propaganda machine with particularly valuable material, furnishing it with evidence that every American SAC pilot was a '"robot-soldier" who could "drop atom bombs on civilian towns without shuddering."'[21]

These inhuman standards of behavior and operational precision exacted the price that Heinlein anticipated in 'Blowups Happen.' Weart cites the case of nuclear submariners as evidence, revealing that they 'had to be impervious to sentiment if only because they literally held in their hands the keys to catastrophe. . . . [T]he crews endured months locked in steel corridors, forbidden contact with their wives; "after a while," a reporter wrote, "even their talk of sex stops."' Weart's research produces telling statistical confirmation of the claims: in addition to 'morale problems and a high divorce rate,' the pressure of nuclear sub service was such that 'in a typical year one out of every twenty-six missile submariners was referred to a psychiatrist and some had to be hospitalized for paranoid schizophrenia and other mental illnesses . . .' However, these statistics were withheld from the public, largely because '[t]he accepted image, rather, was of men who had made themselves into logical machines.'[22]

The truth, of course, was closer to what Heinlein and others foresaw: 'Blowups' do happen, particularly in the highly reactive core of the human psyche. Indeed, the association between nuclear responsibility and diminished human affect and empathy began to become one of the most common tropes in nuclear war fiction. From the emotionally inert characters populating the film version of *Fail-Safe* (1964) to the partially mechanical Dr Strangelove, nuclear war narratives (particularly films) have brooded not only upon the physical mutations caused by the bomb, but upon the psychological degeneration of those who must live in proximity to it. Whether or not such narrative representations are motivated by an authorial desire to investigate and/or critique such a phenomenon, they stand as mute testimony to the influence of the atomic bomb as a defining metaphor for the altered social consciousness—and political concerns—in post-World War II America.

\*\*\*\*\*

The imagination of the bomb and American political actions and futures are so inextricably entwined that, at times, America seemed to be searching for its manifest destiny at ground zero. For instance, H. Bruce Franklin reveals that President Truman cited Tennyson's 'Locksley Hall' as the inspiration for his faith in the war-ending efficacy of the 'final weapon,' carried select verses of the poem in his wallet, and offered them as both explanation and justification to members of the American press in 1945.[23] This is but one piece of a vast body of evidence indicating that imaginative anticipations of wonder weapons were as central to the development of the American bomb as were physicists such as Oppenheimer and Teller. In addition to Wells' *The World Set Free* being adopted as 'required reading' (on Leo Szilard's suggestion) for Manhattan Project insiders, and the scrap of poetry that Truman carried in his wallet, American periodicals were fairly littered with futuristic perspectives on the development of atomic weapons. One of these may have influenced and possibly inspired the adoption of the Baruch Proposal, a policy initiative which advocated complete disarmament—policed, at first, by a unilaterally armed United States. Franklin reveals that this idea found adherents in the White House; indeed, two presidents publicly affirmed how seriously they took their responsibility as sole owners of the bomb. One president, anticipating the use of atomic weaponry against the Japanese, counseled his advisers as follows: 'Let us bear with fortitude whatever reproaches may be heaped upon us, for we are the instruments of God.' He went on to declare that 'This most deadly machine ever conceived' should be used in 'the last great battle in history,' 'thereby ending wars for all time.'[24] The second president, speaking just after Hiroshima, called the bomb 'an awful responsibility which has come to us' and that 'We thank God that it has come to us, instead of to our enemies; and we pray that He may guide us to use it in His ways and for His purposes.' If the quotes sound very similar, they are; and if it seems that the second president 'cribbed' his speech notes from the first, he very well may have. But what may be surprising

—and possibly disturbing—to note is that the first president is a fictional character in Roy Norton's Japanophobic 1907 serial *The Vanishing Fleets*, published in the widely read *Associated Sunday Magazine*. The second president in question—Harry S. Truman—was, according to letters to his wife, an avid reader of that magazine during the period *The Vanishing Fleets* was published. The similarity—in diction, tone, and especially message—may very well be coincidence, but as one pundit has put it, coincidences like this are a somewhat rare and endangered species.[25]

Similarly, the Baruch plan, which proposed the US as a temporary, unilaterally armed guardian of nuclear peace and non-proliferation, did not first arise from seasoned consuls of state. Rather, it emerged from the pages of *Liberty Magazine*, one of the three most widely read magazines in America in 1940. This policy of nuclear Pax Americana is articulated in the form of a serialized future-war story, *Lightning in the Night*. This novel-length serial was written by Fred Alhoff, in consultation with Lieutenant General Robert Lee Bullard, Rear Admiral Yates Sterling, and others who were members of America's conservative political elite. In the narrative, Alhoff projects that America develops intercontinental bombers and atomic bombs only months before succumbing to coordinated German, Japanese, and Soviet attacks (including an imminent Nazi nuclear assault). The US unleashes its own secretly prepared atomic weapons first, devastating many cities of its adversaries and compelling them to accept America as a global policeman, with sole possession of, and discretion to use, a nuclear arsenal. This, with minor alterations, is a synopsis of the Baruch Proposal, and one must wonder whether this anticipatory accuracy indicates that Alhoff's narrative did not merely envision, but inspire, official policy.

However, the most prescient and sophisticated of the many pre-Hiroshima nuclear war narratives may be Heinlein's prophetically titled 'Solution Unsatisfactory' (1941). In this story, Heinlein not only offers a highly informative view of the technical realities of atomic research of that day, but also of the security measures that had been (often brusquely or even brutally) imposed by the US government: 'Someone in the United States government had realized the terrific potentialities of uranium 235 quite early and, as far back as the summer of 1940, had rounded up every atomic research man in the country, and had sworn them to silence. Atomic power ... was planned to be a government monopoly, at least till the war was over.'[26]

Heinlein's story does not posit an atomic bomb as the ultimate doomsday device. Instead, Heinlein foresees atomic byproducts, not blasts, as having the most profound military potential: the weapon in 'Solution Unsatisfactory' is air-dispersion of highly radioactive wastes which are lethal in even minute quantities. Although this may superficially seem to be a failure in prevision, it correctly anticipates enduring radiation effects, rather than the explosion, as the primary destructive agent in an atomic weapon. Furthermore, this is another example of information 'trickling down' to the public: Heinlein's 'weapon' was almost a direct reflection of the thinking of that day's leading weapons researchers and theorists. Once again, H. Bruce Franklin's research reveals that 'on May 17, 1941, a month after Heinlein's story appeared . . . [a National Academy of Sciences report] argued that the "production of violently radioactive materials . . . carried by airplanes to be scattered as bombs over enemy territory" might be achieved a year after a successful chain reaction, which meant "not earlier than 1943," while "atomic bombs can hardly be anticipated before 1945."' Enrico Fermi and J. Robert Oppenheimer reemphasized the viability of this approach in 1943, a further suggestion that 'Heinlein's tale may have directly influenced these schemes, for as his editor, John Campbell attested, it "was read, and widely discussed, among the physicists and engineers working on the Manhattan Project."'[27]

What is most noteworthy about this short story's various previsions, however, is that Heinlein sees beyond the seductive and dangerous simplicity of unilateral armament as the means of enforcing a global Pax Americana, as was triumphantly proposed in *Lightning in the Night*, *The Vanishing Fleets*, and countless other American wish-fulfillment fantasies. Heinlein foresaw that nuclear weapons—no matter the design—could not and would not remain the monopoly of any nation for long. Since the knowledge of the weapon 'won't remain our secret; you can count on that' and since its proliferation would translate into 'a loaded gun held at the head of every man, woman and child on the globe,' the weapon's designer, Colonel Manning, correctly foresees that 'The whole world will be comparable to a room full of men, each armed with a loaded .45. They can't get out of the room and each is dependent on the good will of every other one to stay alive.'[28] The only alternative to this inherently unstable and anxiety-producing Mexican standoff is an American hegemony. But, extending his foresight beyond this familiar (and reassuring) horizon, Heinlein realizes that this answer, like the weapon itself, is also a 'Solution Unsatisfactory':

> It seemed to me that a peace enforced by us was the only way out, with precautions taken to see that we controlled the sources of uranium. I had the usual American subconscious conviction that our country would never use power in sheer aggression. Later, I thought about the Mexican War and the Spanish American War and some of the things we did in Central America, and I was not so sure . . .[29]

Manning, a military officer, is essentially a humane and conscientious individual. Before America first uses the weapon on Berlin (which it depopulates), Manning convinces the president to warn the city's residents of the danger of the weapon, and to compel the Nazis to accept non-'vindictive' surrender terms—all without result. The post-war attempt to impose a global Pax Americana meets with violent rejection: a sneak atomic air attack against the US is conducted by the Eurasian Union. The American-Allied response is to destroy Moscow, Vladivostok, and Irkutsk in an act of enforcement, avengement, and consolidation of universal power: this counterattack eliminates the US's only remaining superpower rival. Manning and the president then labor to ensure that this new 'American Empire' is equitable and impartial, since 'imperialism degrades both oppressor and oppressed' and the threat of a doomsday device should not be used to facilitate unfair, exploitational efforts to 'protect American investments abroad, to coerce trade agreements.'[30] The magnitude of this task is ultimately too great, proving the old adage that conquest is easy, control is not. Unforeseeable events also illustrate how fragile such self-policed good will can be: after the president dies in a plane crash, a less open-minded chief executive takes his place, jeopardizing the delicate peace and world balance. Ultimately, Manning is compelled to depose the new president and take over as global autocrat, thereby politically embodying and personally experiencing how very deeply this weapon is a 'Solution Unsatisfactory.' The doomsday device he helped to develop has taken away not only his personal freedom, but has obliterated the fundamental liberties that defined America and its values. These are the same values that brought the nation into the war with the Nazis, and which, ironically, impelled the construction of the weapon in the first place. In short, Heinlein has created a grim anti-version of the O. Henry parable 'The Gift of the Magi:' an American wonder weapon has saved the world from fascism, but the price is global martial law—even for America itself.

Heinlein's later, equally troubled cautionary tales on nuclear weapons and brinksmanship were equally insightful and often explicitly written to influence political opinion. As Heinlein's wife Virginia observed 'he was preoccupied with "world saving" after the atomic bombs were dropped.'[31] This resolve does not indicate ingenuousness, however; of his authorial activities at that time, Heinlein later wrote, 'Was I really so *naif* that I thought that I could change the course of history this way? No, not really. But, damn it, I had to try!'[32]

However, Heinlein's 'Solution Unsatisfactory' may stand as his most important work of nuclear fiction since, as Spencer Weart observes, it stands at a juncture between pre- and post-Hiroshima anticipations and speculations on atomic weapons and warfare. This juncture is a critical crossroads for it is here that the overarching 'story' of all nuclear discourse —whether fact or fiction, classified or public—'divides into two streams. One stream was the public history. . . . The other stream was the secret history known to a few hundred American and British leaders . . . [where] ideas ran ahead swiftly . . . Yet at the end of the war when the two streams rejoined, the fantastic and the scientific, they would merge with unreasonable ease.'[33]

This easy confluence occurred largely because many of the authors of both future and nuclear war fiction were often as farsighted as the experts, sometimes more so. Where and when they were severed from the conduits of classified discourse, these authors employed their own intellects and researches in constructing narrative *gedankenexperimenten* on both the physical and political future of the bomb. The similarities between their conclusions and those of the actual researchers and policy makers were often remarkable, occasionally uncanny.

Perhaps these distressingly close parallels between nuclear fiction and later nuclear reality also provide clues to why American anxiety regarding the bomb is characterized by a peculiar mix of simultaneous dread and expectation regarding its use, since the nation's anticipatory experts and authors could envision all futures but one—that in which the bomb would not be used.

Even before it built the bomb, America devoted no small effort in constructing anticipatory apologetics for its use. This, in turn, suggests that given the technology and the cause, America always anticipated that it would have the will to use atomic weapons. What was uncertain were the ethical requirements. The primary question, therefore, was not 'if' the bomb should be used, but under what conditions, and for what reasons. The search for answers to these questions determined America's pivotal role in the events and unfolding of the twentieth century. Consequently, American national pride and the bomb may be entwined so closely as to be inseparable and, at times, indistinguishable. Thus, American anxieties of the bomb cannot help but consistently and unavoidably coexist with the latent knowledge that the bomb is largely responsible for making America the century's leading nation and sole surviving superpower. The US would not be what it is, could not have done what it has done—both good and bad—without an international and political environment that was, in many ways, determined by the existence of the bomb and the nation's possession of it. This is, to put it lightly, uncomfortable knowledge, a conscience-pricking revelation that Americans are perhaps more comfortable approaching obliquely, rather than head-on. Sontag suggests in 'The Imagination of Disaster' that America's bomb anxiety can even be found in monster films and alien invasion narratives, which she claims are merely symbolic discharges of nuclear anxiety.[34] It is equally possible that these films exist to distract and discharge the troubled conscience of a nuclear-armed nation that cannot decide whether to feel guilty, justified, proud—or all three. Certainly, this tripartite melange of motivations seems to have a solid foothold in the implied cultural psychology of George Pal's decidedly American reworking of Wells' *The War of the Worlds* (1953), in which images of impending Armageddon are detached from Cold War politics, but not from the apocalyptic anxieties of the times. Whereas Wells' text quietly considers, even grudgingly accepts, the interplanetary social Darwinism that posits the Martians as the would-be exterminators of *homo sapiens*, Pal's rendition of this story is fraught with anxiety and borderline hysteria over the existence and use of truly annihilatory power. Where Wells' narrator is a well-educated nondescript who keeps no remarkable company in the course of the text, Pals' protagonist is a world-famous scientist—Time's 'Man of the Year'—who regularly consorts with generals, high-level politicians, and world-class experts in various sciences. Wells, staying true to the scope and spheres associated with his narrator, never once visits the offices of state or halls of the mighty. Indeed, the Empire's military's response to the Martians is a fitful sputtering of poorly coordinated efforts, and the government's ability to exercise authority and control is shattered early in the alien attack. In contrast, Pal gives us numerous 'briefing room' scenes—governments in session, the situation room in the Pentagon, press briefings, gatherings of high-ranking military men—and thereby underlines that despite tremendous casualties there is still someone in charge. Thus the avuncular General Mann can calmly tell the president that the army's counterattack cost '90% loss in equipment, 60% in personnel.' This almost obsessive focus upon reassurances of order and organization despite destruction suggests suppressed, but subconsciously volatile, fears of social chaos and disorder associated with the possibility of nuclear attack.

Borrowing Pierre Macherey's proposition that 'obsessive repetition' of objects is often a clue to deeper structures at work within a narrative, one might also consider how Pal has inverted Wells' rather casual handling of scenes of destruction. In Wells' text, these scenes are described in matter-of-fact and economic fashion, and the narrative neither organizes itself around them, nor maximizes the number of opportunities for their inclusion. In fact, there are really only three combat scenes of any appreciable length and detail: the initial encounter with the heat ray, the skirmish between the Martians and the artillery batteries near Chertsey and Shepperton, and the invaders' engagement with the warship 'Thunder Child.' What might be seen as the greatest opportunity for a collage of carnage—the attack on London—not only occurs 'offstage,' but is not especially dramatic: the Martians depopulate the city with poison gas and the threat of their approach, not with physical destruction.

Nothing could be further from Pal's vision, in which Los Angeles, the dubious American equivalent of London, is handled a bit more brusquely by the alien invaders. Beams blast apart skyscrapers, flames leap high into the sky, the menacing delta shapes of floating Martian death machines prowl the city streets, showering anyone foolish enough to show themselves with shrilling bursts of energy that tear apart the atomic structure of matter itself.

The resolution to the lengthy montage that depicts the leveling of Los Angeles presents an equally radical departure from Wells' text; although the rest of the City of Angels is burning, choruses of praise are still rising up from undestroyed churches. This is an interesting, and telling, additional element in Pal's palette of distinctly American imagery. Despite the lavish orgy of on-screen carnage, the use of an atomic bomb that is '10 times more powerful' than any previously exploded, and the incessant scenes of death rays obliterating cars, buildings, people—despite all this, there is a constant thread of religious and biblical reference running through the film. However, when assessed from the standpoint of America's then-growing silo psychosis, this thread is included not in spite of, but *because* of, all the devastation—both as comfort against a possible apocalypse and as a reassurance that America is on the side of the angels. Wells' distinctly non-valorized depiction of religion—from the lack of deistic intercession to the less-than-laudable behavior of the curate—has been converted by Pal into an ecumenical hymn of praise that echoes throughout the entire structure of the film. The heroine of the movie, Sylvia van Buren, is the niece of a reverend who is disintegrated by a Martian while trying to initiate peaceful contact. Indeed, he is struck down not only while reciting a psalm, but at the very moment he raises his cross. This instance of incandescent martyrdom initiates and ostensibly vindicates an ineffectual whirlwind of retributory firepower from both the army and air force. Later in the film, when one of the scientists observes that he has calculated that the Martians will conquer the earth in six days, Sylvia observes—in a detached tone of voice that suggests spiritual possession—that this is 'the same number of days it took to create it.' And lastly, Sylvia's final refuge—of safety and security from all fear—is a church, where, at the very end, we hear a cleric praying for 'divine intervention.' This intervention, which, the narrator tells us is effected by 'the littlest things God put upon the earth,'[35] bacteria, is where the movie stops: dawn limns the skyline of the City of Angels, and a chorus swells in the background to pronounce the final word of the film; 'A-men.'

What is most revealing about these repetitive themes and images in

Pal's *The War of the Worlds* is that, despite biblical allusions and scenes of strong-jawed generals, the film is not particularly concerned with either religion or patriotism. Rather, it reflects a search for an ultimate refuge, a reversion to belief in, and association with, protective powers of mythic proportions. Is this simply because a visual medium such as film invites larger than life figures and forces, because the wide-screen spectacle and pageantry of Apocalypse requires equally sweeping reassurances? Or are Pal's simultaneous fixations upon the moment of destruction and the mythic forces that undergird hopes of subsequent resistance and survival suggestive of a conflict within the American psyche? If the latter, then the film may reflect a barely repressed conflict between America's competing senses of pride and regret, responsibility and avoidance and above all, potency and vulnerability. The God-fearing inhabitants of the Great Republic, inheritors of a 'New Eden' rhetoric that dates back to the Puritans, know full well what ultimately happens to those who live by the sword, and they also know all too well the lethality of the Damoclesian weapons that hang over their heads.

It may be, however, that the public's atomic anxieties find their most direct expression not in scenes of incineration, nor in the mind-withering assessment of the horrible physical consequences, but in the aftermath that would accompany all these grim alterations. The fundamental truth discovered by almost all nuclear war authors is that the potential psychological consequences outstrip the physical misery a hundredfold. Even if survivors were able to scrape out a meager existence from the scorched remains of society, they face the death of empathy, responsiveness, and even hope. Indeed, images of the mentally blasted or benumbed are one of the great commonalities shared by American and British nuclear narratives. Almost every serious cinematic foray into this nightmare includes an obligatory scene in which a major character emerges and staggers through a world suddenly shattered and insane. But it is also arguable that the impact of multi-megaton warheads is not a prerequisite for this loss of affect: the anticipation of the bombs may be enough, according to studies of those whose childhoods were spent under the unremitting threat of nuclear annihilation.

Psychologist Robert Jay Lifton, who surveyed and interviewed the survivors of Hiroshima, analyzed the withering psychological blast that radiates out from the idea of the bomb by assessing its damage to both individual and communal mental states. Commenting on this 'nuclear psyche,' he and co-author Richard Falk wrote that

> We are just now beginning to realize that nuclear weapons radically alter our existence. . . . [N]othing we do or feel—in working,

playing, and loving, and in our private, family and public lives—is free of their influence. The threat they pose has become the context for our lives, a shadow that persistently intrudes upon our mental ecology.[36]

This effect may be in part due to a fundamental shattering of boundaries between the conceivable and the inconceivable that the mere existence of the bomb and its potentials requires us to accommodate. Synopsizing Lifton's extensive interviews with the survivors of Hiroshima, Weart reports that 'they tended to merge the bombing experience with childhood images of victimization and the end of the world—images of desperation, helplessness, and annihilation. . . . The bombings seemed less like a military action than a rupture of the very order of nature, an act . . . of sacrilege.'[37]

The fear and psychological disruption that Lifton found in the aftermath of an actual nuclear attack is also engendered—in diminished and slightly altered form—by the chronic anticipation of such an event. In *Nuclear Fear*, Weart presents an overview of the psychological research that has explored this particular phenomenon, and indicates that the aggregate results suggest a complex and multi-layered psychological reaction to the persistent threat and anxiety of nuclear weapons. Although respondents may be quite likely to express concern over the issue of nuclear war *if* they feel that there is a reasonable chance—and a concrete means—of averting such a holocaust, this admission of anxiety tends to harden into denial and/or repression when the threat of that war seems uncontrollable. However, underneath this second layer of declared disinterest in nuclear issues, there remains an intense fear.[38] In younger persons, this 'second layer' of repression and denial was less firmly established and, consequently, studies that focused on this group were particularly revealing:

> A survey that said nothing about bombs, but only asked school children to talk about the world ten years ahead, found over two-thirds of the children mentioning war, often in terms of somber helplessness. In 1965 a song lamenting that we were on the 'Eve of Destruction' became the first song on a political issue to become a number-one popular tune in the United States . . . By the 1960s, observers from Teller to Dr. Benjamin Spock of SANE were reporting talks with young people who said it was pointless to study or save up money when the world might end tomorrow. In 1982 a psychiatrist, summarizing decades of studies, said that the nuclear problem had left many young people with 'a sense of powerlessness and cynical resignation.'[39]

It is sobering to consider that, for these 'children of MADness,' growth from toddlerhood to adult consciousness took place completely under a mushroom-cloud shadow, where the unprecedented terror of nuclear brinksmanship was a daily reality. They are, therefore, a unique generation in a way that no other has been before them, for they grew to awareness believing that this eternal state of tension and imminent annihilation would either continue as the basic defining fact of their tenuous existence, or would end in a short sequence of sirens, terror, fire, and then absolute nothingness—without even the consolation of imagined remembrance in the thoughts of others. Considering the effects such a grim formative environment has had upon an American generation, Jane Caputi observes in 'Psychic Numbing, Radical Futurelessness, and Sexual Violence in Nuclear Film' that there is 'a new ephemeralism which tends to undermine interpersonal and family relationships; a sense of radical futurelessness due to an expectation of annihilation in our lifetimes . . .'[40] If, to paraphrase George Steiner, hope is the source of all human and transcendent values, then such a presumption of hopelessness can only abet the emergence of behaviors that do violence to both self and others, whether in body or mind. Accordingly, whereas the Black Death gave rise to the grim medieval exhortation 'Eat, drink, and be merry, for tomorrow we may die,' the psychological plague of silo psychosis may have inspired the equally sardonic, contemporary attitude that was captured in a now-forgotten youth culture jocularism: 'live fast, die young, leave a pretty corpse.' Or it may have been The Who that articulated this half-deranged death wish most concisely (and unwittingly) in the Quadrophenic anthem of 'their generation': 'Hope I die before I get old.' If a crippled capacity for openness, empathy, and even healthy affect is one of the casualties caused by the mere existence of the bomb, it seems inevitable that its actual use would utterly disintegrate prosocial instincts and behaviors.

Another, related, constant in both American and British imaginings of a nuclear aftermath is the likelihood that history, language, and even faith in cognition would be among the first victims. Faced with both the loss of a meaningful future and the limit-rupturing scope of nuclear devastation, words, history, and thought itself would, for many survivors, become pointless. Thus, it is the desolation of the world of *1984* that makes Newspeak possible and Doublethink a reality: the accepted limits and shape of society and culture have been shattered more thoroughly than the crumbling urban waste that Winston Smith inhabits.[41] The time is ripe for stunting language's capacity for signification, so that it offers a lexicon of referents only for those objects and ideas that have survived both the explosion of atomic bombs and the implosion of thought, hope, and freedom.

This concept is also the central, organizing metaphor of Miller's *A Canticle for Leibowitz*. Here, the futility of meaning and of speech are made sadly manifest when the monks dedicated to post-war illumination of surviving documents ceremoniously apply their gold-leafed glorifications to a grocery list just as readily as to an essay on theoretical physics. Their efforts to record and preserve past realities are not only futile: unbeknownst to them, their labors are also filled with the dark certainty of rediscovering the same knowledge that led to the first Flame Deluge, of reinitiating the same apocalyptic endgame that consumed the first historical age of Earth and left only trace fragments for them to copy. And, lest readers miss his subtler points regarding the problems inherent in slavish adherence to logocentrism and unquestioning confidence in language, Miller layers his foreshadowing of the second Apocalypse with depictions of the senior monk's struggles with his new-fangled 'autoscribe,' a voice-to-hardcopy transcription and translation machine that never works correctly.

This trope of machines that fail humanity, and then continue to goad it with elusive (or should that be illusive?) promises and lost possibilities, also revolves at the center of Russell Hoban's *Riddley Walker*, exerting a subtle, centripetal force over the rest of the elements in the text. Set centuries after a nuclear conflagration has smashed civilization back to a pre-medieval level, young Riddley Walker sets out on the equivalent of a walkabout, on which he encounters and comes to an intrinsic and poignant understanding of what the ruins of an old nuclear plant and research facility once were, and what they once enabled:

> Tears begun streaming down my face and my froat akit. . . . 'O, what we ben! And what we come to!' . . . How cud any 1 not want to get that shyning Power back from time back way back? How cud any 1 not want to be like them what had boats in the air and picters on the wind?[42]

The poignancy of Riddley's insight is sharpened when his brutalized cant is compared to the rich, diverse riot of semantic possibilities in late twentieth-century English, thereby revealing how profoundly language has devolved. Despite the renewed lyricism of Riddley's rhetoric, the crudity of his language indicates that post-apocalyptic speakers have lost both the reason and will to value orderly, cognitively rigorous discourse. Hoban highlights this problem by temporally placing Riddley Walker at the dawn of a momentous, and ominous, rediscovery of much of what had come before—including gunpowder. This dire foreshadowing recalls the conundrum that underscores Miller's *Canticle*: is humanity better off without language and logic; is the glory of its rediscovery always the ironic first step back toward self-annihilation?

Although Riddley tells the reader that he writes 'in memberment,' it may be that memory and history would be of as little use to the survivors of Armageddon as the erudition modern readers take for granted. Whitley Strieber, projecting himself into the post-apocalyptic world of *Warday*, outlines the changed consciousness and discourse of such a reality: 'words like history have lost their weight. They seem as indefinite as memories and as unimportant.'[43] Anna, a character in Paul Auster's *In the Country of Last Things*, is more eloquent, observing that

> Entire categories of objects disappear. Flowerpots for example, or cigarette filters, or rubber bands—and for a time you will be able to recognize those words, even if you cannot recall what they mean. But then, little by little the words become only sounds, a random collection of glottals and fricatives, a storm of whirling phonemes, and finally the whole thing just collapses . . . Your mind will hear it, but it will register as something incomprehensible, a word from a language you cannot speak.[44]

Time and again, nuclear films also depict these effectively mute children of the Apocalypse, from Ruth's linguistically crippled daughter in *Threads* to the subverbal wild-child in *Mad Max*, appropriately called The Feral Kid.

This last appellation, reminiscent of the *noms-de-guerre* associated with American gunslingers, once again invokes the peculiarly American image of the post-apocalyptic wastes as a new frontier. In these *film noir* revisions of the Western, road warriors are cast in place of lawmen, hordes of barbarian motorcyclists stand in for cattle rustlers (or irate Apaches), and tough chicks in leather and animal hides supplant school marms.[45] Because the foregoing is such a ludicrous reinvention of the Western, it may take a second, longer look to realize how profoundly pernicious such images are. Whereas the Western embraces an ideal version of the frontier as it never was, the nuclear-aftermath action narrative attempts to convert the abhorrent into the appealing, miraculously extracting adventure and excitement from a world of desolation and despair. The new heroic motif revels in a dangerously simplistic, dark romanticism of regained virility and a return to the efficacy of action. In these post-nuclear badlands, there are unrealistically clear-cut distinctions between good and evil; the competing forces of civilization and barbarism are simplified, presented as easily distinguished polar opposites. Here, in the desert expanses of an eternally dying but never dead world, our cues to good guys versus bad guys aren't as benign as the color of their hats. Instead, the villains have jettisoned most basic social taboos—those prohibiting murder, rape, cannibalism.[46]

This nuclear wasteland as New Western image became pervasive in American fiction and cinema in the 1980s: even *Warday*, despite its brutally frank look at the US in the wake of a limited nuclear exchange, is built upon the trope of a Lewis-and-Clarke-like rediscovery of America. There are certainly significant differences: the America Strieber and Kunetka set out to cross is a depressing patchwork quilt of radioactive zones, areas of lawlessness, and patrolled safe-city borders, instead of the untrammeled vitality of undiscovered rivers, mountains, and Native Americans. But in *Warday* there remains, undiminished from earlier tales of discovery and journey, a pervasive sense of vastness and concomitant opportunity. Were the land not so large, the diversity of encounters that offer reassurance of many possibilities for survival would seem derangedly optimistic, even ludicrous. Streiber and Kunetka are certainly not proposing that the mere vastness of the US ensures resilience, but they cannot escape the link that is implicit between this geographic fact and the post-apocalyptic possibilities for continuance and community which they have mapped upon it. Consequently, their narrative is an act of imaginative cartography that seems as much a reflexive projection of America's frontier history as it does a sober assessment of a realistic nuclear aftermath.

Ultimately, the more cavalier projections of this historical myth into a dark future also attempt to appeal to a frustrated desire for individual potency. This charred cinder of a planet is also a world where—once again—a single person (usually male) with a steely resolve and equally steely gun can make a difference. This is a world that has at last re-embraced the basic truths and elemental experience of living. The bomb has given humanity a second chance to experience life directly, without the innumerable complexities of our current existence, without the incessant sense of irresolution that characterizes the postmodern hamster-wheel of our daily reality. Contrary to Sontag's theory that post-apocalyptic science fiction films are the expression of a sublimated death wish, these films may reveal a deep and recidivistic desire for the re-establishment of uncontested traditional patriarchy, small harmonious communities, and the celebration of that most independent of all male mythic heroes—the cowboy.

Given today's diminished nuclear threat-level, it is increasingly harder for film-makers to imagine scenarios which might produce this 'Rio Lobo Redux' vision of a new frontier. However, the apocalyptic temper of the American psyche seems not so much to have diminished as to have shifted gears. The anxiety over invasive threats that began emerging in Crichton's *The Andromeda Strain* (1969) has steadily increased over the past twenty years. Texts such as Margaret Atwood's *The Handmaid's Tale* (1985), Nancy Kress' *Beggars in Spain* (1994), and Robert Sawyer's *The Terminal Experiment*

(1995) are only a few examples of this trend. In film, the graphic depictions of eco/biological devastation deployed in Ridley Scott's *Blade Runner* (1982) and Terry Gilliam's *Brazil* (1985) became the seminal, tangible referents for the terror inspired by more recent films, such as *Twelve Monkeys* (1994), *The Puppet Masters* (1994), *Outbreak* (1995), and *The Rock* (1996). These premonitions of infection, epidemic, and hysteria are amplified by the growing awareness—and media explanations—of just how easy it is to create a plague: the technology to produce and deliver viruses in lethal concentrations is both simple and inexpensive, and samples from which to grow cultures of everything from anthrax to the common cold are readily available. Consequently, it is not tactical (or 'suitcase') atomic devices, but biochemical weapons, that are the true successors to the multi-megaton bomb's former monopoly on horror.

This is not so much a new apocalyptic vision as it is a return to that which predominated before the advent of atomic weapons, when plague and pestilence were the most likely sources of a global scourge. Mary Shelley's *The Last Man* (1826), Arthur Conan Doyle's *The Poison Belt* (1913), Jack London's 'The Unparalleled Invasion' (1910), and many others saw disease as the likeliest handmaiden of Doomsday. Now, however, the options for species-wide suicide are more plentiful—and more available—than ever before. This then, may be the revised image of the shattered post-Cold War world humanity could yet inhabit: not an ashen, barren corpse produced by split-second incineration, but a crippled global body, a Gaia made hideous by an eclectic collection of deformities: radiation burns, charred stumps, grotesque mutations, and neoplasms.

As always, however, the threat of nuclear war, of whatever scale, remains. As Reginald Bretnor pointed out, since weapons cannot be un-invented, absolute and eternal disarmament is impossible. This physical and political truth is nuclear war fiction's continuing discursive *raison d'être* and validating trump card. This subgenre of future-war fiction has been not merely a mirror held up to the social and technological phenomenon of nuclear armaments, nor simply a diverse collection of lenses through which its various components were studied. Rather, it has been and remains an active, and often central, part of the social discourse surrounding and determining the role, use, and elimination of these weapons. It has also been the barometer of, and release valve for, the tremendous social and psychological pressures they have generated. These narratives have influenced presidents, stimulated discussion, served as educational liaisons between expert and layman, and—most important—have been arenas for speculation and debate, for the rejection of MAD-ness and the insistence on alternatives. If they prescribed no clear solutions, it can nonetheless be averred that they were the most graphic, visceral, socially accessible, and (probably) politically effective proscriptions against the use of nuclear weapons—and as such, may have had a crucial, life-affirming influence on the most urgent techo-military issue in recorded history.

Returning to the prior chapter's initial image—that of The Association of Atomic Scientists' Doomsday Clock—we can take some comfort in the fact that recent events have turned back its hands. However, nothing can ever eradicate the need to measure our existence relative to the enduring reality of the nuclear threat. Metaphorically speaking, we cannot hope to return to the comparative innocence of hourglass, sundial, or pendulum-driven timepiece. Since 1945 the clock that ticks at the back of our minds is, in every sense of the word, an atomic clock. Even if the missiles never launch, and the bombers never wing past their fail-safe points, the cultural threat keeps expanding, compels us to consider and reconsider the ripples its shockwaves leave upon the surface of relevant narratives, and forces us—always—to keep one eye upon the clock.

*Chapter 8*

# Radio Waves, Death Rays, and Transgressive (Sub)Texts: Future-War Fiction in the Wide Black Yonder

The earth is the cradle of humanity, but man will not stay in the cradle forever.

Konstantin Tsiolkovskiy, 1903

Professor Goddard does not know the relation between action and reaction and the need to have something better than a vacuum against which to react. He seems to lack the basic knowledge ladled out daily in high schools.

1921 *New York Times* editorial concerning Robert Goddard's groundbreaking work in rocketry

I remember on the trip home on Apollo 11, it suddenly struck me that that tiny pea, pretty and blue, was the Earth. I put up my thumb and shut one eye, and my thumb blotted out the planet Earth. I didn't feel like a giant. I felt very, very small.

Neil Armstrong, astronaut

Judging from the photographic retrospectives occasioned by the recent millennial furor, history has already rendered its judgement regarding the most dramatic and significant icons of the twentieth century—and there is a two-way tie for first place. One image dates from August 6, 1945 when the skies over Hiroshima bore witness to the power of the sun brought down to the earth in a horrible fulfillment of the legendary fall of Helios. The other event—a symbolic fulfillment and surpassing of Icarus' dream—took place on July 20, 1969 when a human being first stretched a foot into the fine powder of the Sea of Tranquility and, so doing, stood upon a world other than the Earth. Apart from their mythic importance, these two events share a second kinship: both were key moments in the linked histories of weapons development and space technology. The atomic bomb impelled the development of the rocket and the associated fields of space technology: however, those technologies have continued to advance far beyond their initial roles as handmaidens to warheads. Indeed, space technology has contributed to the accelerating obsolescence of strategic nuclear missiles and—many experts hope—will lead to their eventual extinction.

Delineating the role that future-war (and hard science) fiction played in the birth and development of space technology involves tracing a history of associations: of inventors influenced by authors; of images that inspired realities; and of government and media validation, and subsequent adoption, of some of the most foresightful narrative visions of space exploration. The narratives that were the substantive products of these associations mostly illustrate the 'trickle-up' effect of speculative fiction: theirs was a unidirectional influence, originating in the ideas of individual visionaries and ending up in the councils of official agenda-setters. The predominance of this 'trickle-up' effect is not coincidental, but is a direct consequence of the fact that space travel and its associated technologies were, as little as seventy years ago, still considered pipe dreams by most respectable scientists. In short, there were no expert sources from which encouraging visions might 'trickle down.' Indeed, this chapter's epigramatic citation from the remonstrative *New York Times* editorial was typical of its day. Consequently, the images and ideas that challenged the prevailing, prohibitory scientific paradigms were not outgrowths of the upper echelons of science, industry, or government. Rather, they germinated from conceptual seeds planted by science fiction writers, which then grew to technological and political fruition in an uncommonly short period of time because of their weapons potential.

The future fiction of aerospace technology is characterized by one other peculiarity: later authors who successfully ventured beyond the gossamer veil separating their contemporary reality from future possibilities often unwittingly penetrated the black shrouds of official secrecy. Many of the speculative aerospace narratives that were authored after World War II 'anticipated' innovations that had already been achieved but remained undisclosed, thereby illustrating just how problematic the once-discrete concepts of past, present, and future have become in the heavily managed information environment of the superpower era. This, in turn, problematizes the temporal distinctions that are implicit in the genre label 'speculative' fiction, since, in hindsight, the scientific previsions of a 'speculative' narrative may prove not to be anticipation, but an extremely shrewd guess at what was already waiting behind the shroud of official secrecy. Philip A. Pecorino attempted a commonsensical answer to speculative fiction's temporal dilemmas when he observed that 'stories are either realistic fiction or historical fiction' when 'the element of speculation beyond present scientific knowledge and technology has been almost totally eliminated.'[1] Pecorino's definition is better than most, yet profound, almost unavoidable, ambiguities remain. At what point can one say that speculation has been 'almost totally' eliminated? In other words, just how close to 'totally' is 'almost totally?' In 1960, if an author wrote a narrative featuring a jet capable of Mach 10 speed, that would surely have been 'science fiction,' or even 'techo-fantasy.'[2] But what about Mach 2.5, a scant few tenths above the prevailing records of the time; would that have been 'speculative' fiction? Perhaps so, perhaps not—an uncertainty that spawns yet another question: what is the 'magic number'—proportionally speaking—at which marginal projection beyond 'known' performance statistics becomes 'speculation?'

The second questionable presupposition in Pecorino's definition is the assumption that one can know the limits of 'present knowledge and technology.' Specifically, what informational criteria define the boundaries of 'present' knowledge? That which is known to the author? That which is 'common' knowledge?[3] Or does it even include 'scientific knowledge and technology' that exists only in a classified government laboratory? Pecorino's apparent assumption regarding the ease with which one can define and identify 'present' knowledge and technology does not seem to functionally conform to the uncertain information environment in which both individuals and societies have been living since the end of World War II. The confusions and consequences generated by these conundrums are particularly well illustrated by the strange case of one of the United States' most extraordinary technological achievements, the SR-71 Blackbird reconnaissance jet. When the SR-71 commenced flight trials in the early 1960s, it was so technologically advanced that it exceeded the performance of many vehicles that were considered to be, and were being written as, not merely near-future fiction, but true 'science fiction.' At a time when the best jet interceptors were barely capable of sustained Mach 1 flight, and the (known) airplane speed record stood just in excess of Mach 2, the SR-71 was capable of cruising at Mach 3 and had a top speed somewhere in excess of Mach 3.5.[4] Consequently, the Blackbird existed as an ultra-secret reality before any author rigorously explored the scientific 'possibility' of it in a 'speculative' narrative, thereby unwittingly writing of a scientific fact as a scientific fiction. This is precisely what occurs in Dean McLaughlin's short story 'Hawk Among the Sparrows,' published in 1968 by *Analog Science Fiction* magazine.[5] The most obvious—and extreme—science fictional aspect of this story remains as wild a surmise today as it was when the story was written: a time travel mishap strands an aviator from 1977 in World War I France. However, the far more significant scientific extrapolations in the narrative are those concerning the aviator's cutting-edge interceptor. Arguably the main character of the story, the '[h]igh altitude mach 4 aircraft,' with a maximum ceiling of (at least) 135,000 feet, and VTOL capabilities was, to McLaughlin's readers, pure science fantasy—but, in fact, it wasn't.[6] America's SR-71 Blackbird reconnaissance plane had already approached the ceiling and top speed capabilities of McLaughlin's 'fantastical' aircraft six years before he penned the story, and fifteen years before it was to have taken place. When the SR-71 rolled onto the strip in 1962, the supposed world speed record for jet aircraft was just barely in excess of Mach 2. No aircraft had a cruising, or even maximum, sustainable operating speed of anything in excess of Mach 1.2. From the perspective of the 'declassified world,' to write of an aircraft with a sustainable operating speed of Mach 3 was pure science fiction at that time, and was to remain so for more than ten years. However, in 1963, the ultra-secret Blackbird achieved a Mach 3 'easy cruising' speed and a top speed which to this day remains classified: most public literature tersely refers to it as being 'in excess' of Mach 3.2 or Mach 3.5.[7] This creates a problem in determining where the limits of speculation (or even science fiction) lie, a problem that may be surprisingly commonplace, since near-future narratives may often unknowingly intrude into technical domains where the secrecy surrounding, and the vigor propelling, advanced military research are maintained at maximum intensity. Hence, future-war fiction may offer a look not only at the future, but also at the undisclosed present or still-classified past.

Moving beyond the matter of comparable maximum speeds, the similarities between McLaughlin's imaginary interceptor (named the *Pika-Don*) and the Blackbird remain striking. The *Pika-Don* is capable of attaining at least 135,000 feet maximum ceiling, since at one point the plane climbs 'up to one-thirty thousand . . . rocket launch point lay five thousand higher . . .'[8] Although the SR-71's operating specifications never claimed such an extraordinary ceiling, its rating mounted steadily as the plane passed through a series of declassification phases: its admitted ceiling has risen from approximately 72,000 feet to slightly in excess of 100,000—and the semantics of the operational specifications almost invariably leave room for (or even encourage) extrapolations of higher, undisclosed performance.

The physical dimensions of the two aircraft are also comparable. Describing his hypothetical *wunderkraft*, McLaughlin writes:

> *Pika-Don* was eighty-nine feet long. Her shark-fin wings spanned less than twenty-five. She was like a needle dart, sleek and shiny and razor-sharp on the leading edge of her wings. Her fuselage was oddly flat-bodied, like a cobra's hood. Her airscoops were like tunnels. . . .

Deveraux put his head inside one of the tail pipes. It was big enough to crawl into.[9]

The SR-71 (varying across different versions and operating conditions) has been rated at anything from 99 to 107 feet long. At 55 feet, the Blackbird's wings are notably wider, but it too was 'sleek and shiny' with a broad, flattened fuselage that tapered into minimal, cowl-like lifting surfaces extruded from the main body, rather than the long, glide-producing wings of the known reconaissance planes of that day (such as the U-2). The SR-71's two Pratt & Whitney J58 turbo-ramjets—which comprised, and were seamlessly blended into, the greater part of the wings—were easily 'big enough to crawl into.'[10] There are other interesting similarities, such as the pilot's observation that the *Pika-Don*'s 'sprawling fuselage surface prevented him from looking down at the airfield.'[11] This is consistent with pilot descriptions of the SR-71's severely restricted near-ground cockpit perspective. Lastly, although the amount of armament differed slightly (the *Pika-Don* had six missiles, the SR-71/YF-12 four), the nature, range, and deployment characteristics of the weapons were comparable.

Certainly there are differences between the two hypersonic craft, the most dramatic and significant being the *Pika-Don*'s VTOL capability, its fuel load (50,000 gallons compared to only 12,000 for the Blackbird) and an extra engine (the *Pika-Don* is equipped with three engines; the SR-71 has only two). However, in the final analysis, the operating and technical parallels between the two machines are so many and so close that a reader must wonder if McLaughlin might not have had some friends or contacts within the military or defense industry. If he did, then any attempt to assess whether his story is speculation or not becomes hopelessly convoluted. If McLaughlin had insider knowledge, then how much must he have had before his narrative should be recategorized as 'realistic' or 'historical' fiction instead of 'speculation?' Such a determination would be further complicated by the fact that McLaughlin sold his short story/novella to the world's major science fiction magazine at that time—*Analog*. Although we would be ill-advised to hypothesize about McLaughlin's authorial intentions, by selling it to *Analog* he makes his *marketing* intentions quite clear. McLaughlin was not merely willing for this story to be *possibly* perceived as technological speculation; he sold it to a market that was, and still is, overtly and exclusively dedicated to the publication of such fiction. Clearly, then, whether or not McLaughlin believed his *Pika-Don* to be speculative or not, he clearly knew that lay readers of his day would consider it as such—and radically so. The key significance of McLaughlin's narrative requires no conjecture or interpretation, however: some aeronautical technologies and performance ratings that readers—and writers—in 1968 only encountered in science fiction stories were *not*, historically speaking, actually 'anticipations.'

Hindsight reveals that numerous 'speculative' narratives paradoxically postdated the secret actualization of the 'imaginary marvels' that they proposed. Reapproached through this somewhat mind-bending conflict between history as experienced and history as revealed, it becomes evident that the speculations of such stories could only be thought of as 'radical' if the actual sum of human knowledge and achievement vastly exceeded the amount of information available to laypersons and even science specialists at that time. Because of the international technological rivalries and consequent intelligence restraints that characterize the age of superpower politics, the assumed 'line' that divides fact from fiction, and reality from imagination, is not merely blurry, but impossible to locate with certainty. Consequently, neither reader nor author can be sure whether a narrative is speculative or not until history retroactively establishes the position of this line that demarcates the actual. Indeed, even conservative-seeming 'common sense' technological projections may often be completely incorrect, particularly when they refer to small and/or counter-intuitive technological 'leaps.' This is particularly true when the nature, number, and scope of the engineering obstacles are either unknown or easily misperceived. For instance, because the jet was more difficult to perfect than the internal combustion engine, it would seem logical to assume that creating a jet aircraft capable of both high-speed level flight (like a plane) and vertical take-off and landing (or VTOL, like a helicopter) would be a much more difficult technical challenge than creating the same dual capabilities in a propeller-driven aircraft. In fact, history proved the exact opposite to be true. Today, the AV-8B Harrier (the result of successful prototype VTOL jets tested in the late 1960s and early 1970s) is a fully matured technology and a combat-proven mainstay of many NATO formations, particularly in the UK and the US. However, the first propeller-driven 'tilt-rotor' aircraft, the MV-22/OV-7 Osprey, has proven so difficult to actualize in a sufficiently reliable model that the project has been all but abandoned on several occasions, due to mechanical challenges that remained unsolvable. Although a true VTOL jet required numerous incremental technological advancements, once these building blocks were in place, the physics of the jet engine—and the greater directness and simplicity of its operation as a thrust agency—made it more readily amenable to VTOL applications. Conversely, the challenges posed by the seemingly simple propeller become exponentially more complex as it is asked to perform the more sophisticated tasks required by tilt-rotor aircraft. The problems with establishing a sufficiently rugged and reliable transmission that could synchronize, adjust, and selectively imbalance the function of two tilting motor-pods remained beyond the capacity of American engineers for more than a decade. The final version of the much-redesigned tilt-rotor MV/V-22 Osprey is only now going through final pre-procurement trials.

Similar confused (and confusing) relationships between history and expectation, fact and fiction, also complicate any attempt to determine the degree of 'speculation' actually employed in numerous narratives that (seemingly) focus on the future of space science and space technology. This phenomenon—of which numerous examples exist—is particularly well illustrated by the example of the DC-X or 'Delta Clipper' orbital interface vehicle. As in the case of the SR-71, increasingly pronounced disjunctures between the general level of public awareness and the specialized knowledge and 'cutting-edge' capabilities of the nation's leading aerospace engineers made the almost-achieved technological probabilities of the DC-X appear to be improbable technofantasies.

The 'Delta Clipper' Single Stage To Orbit (SSTO) reusable space vehicle (RSV) was an early-1990s space initiative, actively developed by McDonnell Douglas Corporation until early in 1997. The long-held 'science fictional' dream of a fully reusable space vehicle with a low operating cost and greatly enhanced landing flexibility was to be realized in this design, of which 1/4 scale prototypes had already made atmospheric test flights. However, in 1995, a fictional, fully realized Delta Clipper—painstakingly based on the promising test models—was launched into the vast expanse of the reading public's imagination: the majority of Daniel Graham Jr.'s well-promoted hard-cover science fiction novel *The Gatekeepers* orbited around the capabilities and consequences of this object of 'technological speculation.'[12] This presents another unusually tangled case of informational and temporal disjunctures. Here, the 'speculative' aspect of the narrative is (ostensibly) that the Delta Clipper exists in completed form. This is, however, not particularly 'speculative,' considering that prototypes built from proven 'off the shelf' components had already made test flights, and that (probably) a full-scale prototype of the Delta Clipper could have been built and successfully flown by 1996–1997. Ultimately, therefore, the most dramatic (and unsuccessful) speculation in the text had nothing to do with the 'science' or 'technologies' of the vehicle, but concerned the politics that governed its development, funding, and ultimately, its survival or demise: the real fate of the Delta Clipper—project termination—was a matter of political choice, not engineering obstacles. Yet, this novel was successfully (and, from a marketing standpoint, logically) marketed as 'science' (not 'political') fiction.

These detailed examples are necessary in order to underscore one crucial factor which is often overlooked or dismissed by analysts of technological progress and critics of speculative fiction: the path of machine development often follows pathways that defy logic and intuition. Consequently, uncritically trusting that 'common sense' will help one estimate where the elusive line between 'imaginary' and 'real' technology lies can be worse than useless: it promotes a false sense of confidence when trying to establish that line's location. Confusions of this type played an especially important role in the early days of space science and space technology. The emergence of practical rocketry was shrouded in layers of secrecy and ignorance and, therefore, general knowledge of it as a 'present' or 'real' technology was subject to much the same 'time lag' effects as those that retarded accurate reportage regarding the SR-71 Blackbird. Indeed, although public awareness of rocketry actually had a much shorter 'time lag' between achievement and report, the delay was in some ways more remarkable. The SR-71 was an elusive, well-concealed, high-speed, and extremely high-altitude spy plane. In contrast, neither the operating characteristics nor the effects of the first practical long-range rockets—the German V-2s—could be characterized as 'inconspicuous.'

On September 8, 1944, the first V-2s rocketed across the Channel and fell on London. However, information regarding the existence and capacities of these imprecisely understood Nazi miracle-weapons was highly restricted. It was so restricted that Jerry Shelton, a young science fiction author who was serving with the American army in Europe later wrote to *Astounding* editor John W. Campbell,

> It was nerve-wracking to be constantly saying to yourself: 'How about this? Here I am running around in a sweat trying to dodge something all us science-fiction guys have been writing and dreaming of—it's actually reality—and I'm on the wrong end, and I can't write and tell Campbell that somebody is really on the way to space!'[13]

Shelton's letter concisely and effectively articulates how superpower information control can purposefully and systematically uncouple events and innovations from their actual place in the flow of historical time. It also underscores how future-war (and science) fiction has often bypassed the muzzling efforts of official news censors, bringing crucial topics before an otherwise excluded public through the back door of popular narratives. Finally, it is a clear illustration of the growing importance of these speculative authors, whose simultaneous access to public forums and heightened understanding of nascent technologies repeatedly casts them in the role of liaisons between enigmatic experts and an uninformed public.

As Shelton points out, the V2 rocket was indeed the harbinger of the space age. The engineering breakthroughs that were prerequisites to its introduction—controlled combustion of exothermic liquid fuels, remote or automated precision guidance, gimballed thrust for course alterations—were writ large in its roaring wake, but only for those who knew how to read the technological significance of such a device. Shelton, one such expert reader, knew that a fundamental social, cultural, and political reality had changed: humankind was now capable of reaching space. However, it was he—and others like him—who had introduced the concept to the US, and later continued to speculate upon what might lie just over the next technological horizon.

The steps whereby the age-old dream of space travel became a reality may, more than any other single example, illustrate the fundamental role that science fiction can, and has, played in the evolution of science, technology, and—through them—political and military realities. This role involved not only the creation of narratives that inspired and steered scientific researches, but the articulation, refinement, and popular empowerment of a dream that became so tangible that it burst the bounds of fantasy and became reality. This model of how fictional ideas evolve into physical actualities is neither radical nor new—at least, not outside the domain of literary criticism. Among inventors, researchers, industrialists, technologists, and futurists, it is merely the codification of a well-known phenomenon. As technologist Denis Gabor explains it,

> The future cannot be predicted, but futures can be invented. It was man's ability to invent which has made human society what it is. The mental processes of invention are still mysterious. They are rational, but not logical, that is to say deductive. The first step of the technological or social inventor is to visualize by an act of imagination a thing or state of things which does not yet exist and which appears to him in some way desirable. He can then start rationally arguing backwards from the invention and forward from the means at his disposal, until a way is found from one to the other.[14]

Respected futurist John McHale, considering the 'brilliant pioneering' and 'important role' played by writers of science and future fiction, echoes Gabor's observations: 'the predictors of major changes are often their own self-fulfilling prophets, since they are also active in producing the conceptual and physical discoveries that bring about such changes.'[15]

Yet, these 'prophets' are often themselves just links in a conceptual chain—links that may have been forged by earlier fiction writers who also fused general dreams to specific strategies of actualization. It is through endless repetitions of this process that a larger movement in thought, a slow shift in amenability to a new Kuhnian paradigm of possibility, begins to occur. Space historians Fred Ordway and Randy Lieberman describe, in *Blueprint for Space*, how this process brought spaceflight into the realm of reality, and how it required a cultural leap of faith that Gerald Hawkins calls a mindstep, a phenomenon that 'takes hold slowly but relentlessly. Ideas pass from brain to brain, changing the whole thought pattern.'[16] Ordway and Lieberman accept Hawkins' model of a self-changing culturescape, and observe that 'a favorable environment' for the concept of space travel began emerging 'at the end of the nineteenth century and matured during the first half of the twentieth.' But the mindstep that would eventually end with Neil Armstrong's booted foot descending into the lunar dust was not to be completed quickly: before spaceflight could become a reality, 'it was the subject of dreams and aspirations. . . . Many prominent scientists and engineers pursued careers in rocketry and astronautics as a result of reading about space travel in the pulps.'[17]

Such was the case with Konstantin Eduoardovich Tsiolkovskiy, who gained his initial inspiration and excitement for spaceflight from Jules Verne's space novels, particularly an 1875 Russian translation of *Round the Moon*.[18] Verne's story, while seriously flawed from both the technical and literary standpoints, was nonetheless a first attempt to bring an orderly, quantitatively and mechanistically feasible approach to bear on the question of translunar flight. Tsiolkovskiy saw these flaws not as aesthetic blemishes or scientific detractions, but as a technological challenge, which he set out to solve himself.

Tsiolkovskiy's subsequent work established the dominant shapes and directions of what would come to be known as the space sciences. His half-speculative, half-scientific tracts hypothesized on solar energy, rotating space stations, orbital communications, gyroscopic guidance, and the creation of long-term habitats. Thus Tsiolkovskiy initiated a process of incremental conceptual progress that, in turn, inspired ever more refined imagery regarding how it might be practically accomplished. In conjunction, the two major domains of Tsiolkovskiy's work—as engineer and as science fiction writer—served to introduce and refine a new, orderly paradigm for both the possibility and actual practice of spaceflight. It was in the process of this diverse theoretical work that Tsiolkovskiy discovered the Holy Grail of rocket design, the 'reaction principle,' of which he wrote: 'the only possible mode of propulsion in airless space is the method based on the reaction of particles of matter ejected from a body.'[19] Tsiolkovskiy's formulae describing this revolutionary concept were first published in May 1903: this was seven months before the Wright flyer lifted precariously into the air from the sandy flats at Kittyhawk.

Tsiolkovskiy's article, 'The Exploration of Space with Reactive Devices,' enumerated additional foresightful requirements for a rocket, including 'automatic controls' for navigation and flight correction, and life-support systems for the crew compartment in the nose of the craft. Less than thirty years after being inspired by Verne's rather fanciful ideas of spaceflight and extraterrestrial survival, Tsiolkovskiy had, essentially, already written the blueprint for the next sixty years of actual space research and development. His unprecedented speculative accomplishments became legendary in the West during the last two decades of the twentieth century; however, in the Soviet Union, he had long been revered as the founding father of the Russian space program, as attested to by the laudatory pronouncements of Academicians such as A. A. Blagonravov and many others.[20]

Tsiolkovskiy was, however, not merely a scientist or a theorist; while not a particularly gifted author, he was an extraordinary visionary who understood not only the pivotal role that imaginary narratives played in his own thought processes, but how they served as a means of communicating, refining, and expanding upon new ideas. As he wrote in 'Investigation of World Spaces by Reactive Vehicles,'

> At first we inevitably have an idea, fantasy, fairy tale, and then come scientific calculations; finally execution crowns the thought. My work has to do with the middle phase of creativity. More than anyone else I am aware of the chasm that separates an idea from its accomplishment . . . But there must be an idea: execution must be preceded by an idea, precise calculation by fantasy.[21]

Tsiolkovskiy's own best known work of science fiction, *Beyond the Planet Earth* (1896), is little more than an imaginary account of the challenges faced and then solved by the world's first (and, significantly, international) team of astronaut-engineers.[22] Its prose is awkward, plot rudimentary, and science inaccurate by modern standards, yet it inspired a whole generation of Soviet space explorers and scientists, who placed a man in orbit less than twenty years after Hitler launched the first V-2.

As Tsiolkovskiy was busy turning Verne's dreams into concrete theoretical realities, a young man on the other side of the Atlantic was thumbing through the American newspaper serialization of H.G. Wells' *The War of the Worlds*. Enthralled by this first exposure to the concept of interplanetary travel, 16-year-old Robert Goddard was hopelessly and permanently space-struck and, as a result, he went on to become the inventor of the first successful liquid-fueled rocket. Without knowledge of Tsiolkovskiy's work, Goddard set out to build a rocket capable of traveling in a vacuum, and independently arrived at the same theoretical breakthrough—the 'reaction principle'—that Tsiolkovskiy did, albeit years later.[23] Goddard was not a writer of fiction like Tsiolkovskiy, but did rise to a position of prominence inside the fledgling pre-war American efforts to build rockets and missiles. His own visionary work involved considerations of solar energy systems for spacecraft, the possibility of automated interplanetary exploration vehicles, detection and avoidance of hazardous meteorites, lunar resource extraction and fuel production, compensation for weightlessness, and even navigation and orientation of spacecraft through the use of photosensitive cells. However, despite his immersion in the very real world of mathematics and machines, Goddard frequently reminded interviewers that his enduring interest in space and its technological and scientific challenges was fueled by tales such as Wells' *The War of the Worlds*.

Goddard's first articulation of the reaction theory (in *Smithsonian* magazine) ran into haughty condemnation from the *New York Times*, which declared that the rocket could not work in a vacuum since it had nothing 'against which to react.' According to the correspondent, such 'intentional mistakes or oversights' might well be the province of scientific romances such as Verne's or Wells', but were not acceptable when encountered in the works of 'a savant who isn't writing a novel of adventure.'[24] This was not the only influential naysaying that Goddard and other space visionaries endured. As late as 1935, Forest Ray Moulton, whose theory of the origin of the solar system enjoyed wide acceptance at the time, could write that, regarding interplanetary travel, 'There is not the slightest possibility of such a journey.'[25] Moulton's assertion was typical of the time. When James R. Randolph's open-minded 'Can We Go to Mars?' (1928) was first submitted to *Scientific American*, the laymen editors rejected it; it took the contrary opinions of several consulting physicists to reverse their decision.

It was, however, in the land that was to become America's most serious technological rival that these developments received both the greatest attention and keenest utilitarian interest. A German-speaking native of Transylvania, Hermann Oberth, turned his extraordinary genius to both the design and the popularization of the interplanetary rocketship. These conceptual seeds found fertile ground in thousands of minds from Berlin to Bavaria. From the very beginning, however, the cynical Oberth foresaw that one of the earliest applications of the rocket would be for warfare, whatever he and other scientists might wish. Willy Ley[26] reported that he once asked Oberth 'Do you think, Herr Professor, that there will be a need for rockets carrying a load of mail over five hundred kilometers?' Ley recorded Oberth's darkly proleptic reply: 'Oberth looked at me with the smile which old-fashioned pedagogues reserve for people whom they call "my dear young friend" and said after awhile: "There will be need for rockets which carry a thousand pounds of dynamite for five hundred kilometers."'[27] Twenty years later, this is exactly what Hitler's 'V' (for 'Vengeance') weapons would be doing.

Oberth's interests were not in weaponry, however, but exploration. He published the seminal *Die Rakete zu den Planetenraumen* (*The Rocket into Planetary Space*) in 1923, a (rather thin) science fiction narrative that Oberth used to describe the design and flight of a single-stage interplanetary rocket.[28] He painstakingly revised and refined this design before presenting it once again in his subsequent work *Wege zur Raumshiffahrt* (*Ways to Spaceflight*).[29] Oberth's spacecraft and its mission is startlingly similar to those that would be associated with the Apollo missions forty years later: Oberth's astronaut protagonists were to pilot their three-stage rocket into lunar orbit while housed in a detachable sub-craft shaped very much like the Apollo Command Module. This capsule is mounted in the nose of the third or final stage, and equipped with parachutes for its terminal descent back to Earth. The needs of the pilots also were provided for: the text includes detailed descriptions of the procedures and equipment they would use to eat meals and excrete wastes in zero-gravity, and how they would cook, clean, bathe, and maintain a 'shirt-sleeve' environment in their small home.

Given the details of Oberth's *gedankenexperimenten* narratives, his involvement with the rocket and space research societies of his day, and his mentorship of some of the most influential rocket engineers of the century, it is unclear whether he is primarily an author, engineer, or futurist. Indeed, the logical and obvious alternative is that he fulfilled the functions of all three and, as such, exemplifies the lack of concrete boundaries between these three domains of discourse and production. Furthermore, while his prevision of the means used to achieve the Apollo missions might seem extraordinary, perhaps the more instructive perspective is to consider Oberth the *source*, not the prophet, of the underlying concepts. There are solid grounds upon which to base this hypothesis, since Oberth's narratives were a direct influence upon Wernher von Braun, the mastermind and masterbuilder of the American manned space program.[30] Ultimately, science fiction was not only a means of inspiration for the forefathers of manned space flight, but an integral part of their discursive method and domain. They used it to test concepts, exchange ideas, and proselytize doubting societies. It was, in every meaning of the word, an intensely political narrative form and, ultimately, a very influential one.

As World War II came to a close, the German rocket experts were relocated (via Project Paperclip) to Fort Bliss, Texas, where their knowledge and dreams were actualized with the aid of lavish funding, vastly expanding the capabilities and prospects of the American rocket and space programs. Fueled by an already-keen appreciation of the role that rockets would soon play in the arms race with the Soviets, space technology quickly moved from the realms of public skepticism and official secrecy into the mainstream of political, military, and popular discourse. Scientist and author Arthur C. Clarke observed that 'science fiction ... was taken much more seriously by the general public ever since the V-2 had demonstrated that long-range rockets were a practical proposition.'[31] Less than twenty-five years later, Clarke, along with Robert Heinlein, Isaac Asimov, and Ray Bradbury, were four of the most celebrated and closely attended 'experts' that CBS anchor Walter Cronkite requested to interview on the day of the Apollo 11 moon landing. Cronkite's attentiveness to the opinions of these science fiction authors was as (if not more) keen and deferential as that shown to veteran space correspondents such as Henry Steele Commager and various scientists and generals. Science fiction and its leading space savants had not merely arrived in the mainstream of American culture and thought, but their speculations had merged with reality when the spindly lunar lander settled into the moon's thin coating of dust. One of the oldest and most fantastical dreams of humankind was no longer a matter of whimsy, of imagination, or even of extrapolation: it was now a matter of history. And its achievement can be traced to the impetus, insights, and innovations of science fiction authors.

Robert Heinlein's novelette, 'The Man Who Sold the Moon,' may be the most previsionally accurate of America's post-war 'man in space' stories. Indeed, Heinlein asserted that the major accomplishment of his (or any) science fiction was that it had prepared humankind, and particularly post-war America, for the new reality of space flight (the completion of a 'mindstep,' as it were). Alvin Toffler suggests much the same relationship between science fiction and new technologies/realities in *Future Shock*, as do other futurists, such as John McHale. Indeed, there tend to be few dissenting opinions on this point, even from authors who are firmly set against the militarization of space. Future-war fiction writer Joe Haldeman, who is often inaccurately represented as the political antithesis of Robert Heinlein, is certainly not an uncritical technophile, yet even he attests to the pivotal role that science fiction played in both the political and technological actualization of manned space flight. Haldeman discloses his secret obsession for these endeavors and space flight in his article 'Confessions of a Space Junkie:'

> It's reasonable to assert that there never would have *been* a space program without science fiction—or at least there would have been a hell of a lot fewer scientists and engineers in the appropriate specialties—and the role of science fiction in providing visibility and promoting public support for the space program is undeniable. Perhaps we do romanticize it, but ... I have to quote Timothy Leary, who in a rare moment of lucidity pointed out that only the US gov-

ernment could take the greatest adventure in the history of mankind and make it boring.[32]

An even more skeptical science fiction writer, the critically acclaimed Thomas Disch, made a similar (if barbed) point in 'The Road to Heaven: Science Fiction and the Militarization of Space.' Speaking of how space flight had become almost an object of religious veneration for die-hard technophiles, he wrote:

> SF writers have a legitimate claim to be considered not only the prophets of that faith but the builders of the church. If poets are the world's unacknowledged legislators, SF writers have been its unacknowledged civil and mechanical engineers, doodling their designs for rocket ships and spacesuits on that most plastic medium, the adolescent mind.[33]

These adolescent minds evolved into the engineering prodigies that turned space flight into a reality. In addition to such founding fathers as Goddard and von Braun, numerous of their young assistants and successors were avid science fiction readers, and, on occasion, writers as well. For instance, G. Edwards Pendray was President of the American Rocket Society, designed its first successful liquid-fueled rocket engine, and also wrote a number of science fiction novelettes for *Wonder Stories* in the 1930s. Fred L. Whipple, who became involved in post-war V-rocket assessments and the development of various space flight technologies, speaks of how these involvements were ultimately outgrowths of 'nearly three decades of reading, talking, and dreaming science fiction' with other early space enthusiasts/pioneers.[34] Other examples, too numerous to include, illustrate that serious interest in science fiction has been the rule rather than the exception within the ranks of the space program—a rule which remains unbroken through to the current day. One of the most recent examinations of this phenomenon can be found in Constance Penley's *NASA/Trek* (1997), which investigates (among other things) the powerful influence that the imagery and content of the *Star Trek* television series has exerted upon the personnel and public self-presentation of NASA.[35]

A similar phenomenon is observable in the defense industry. There, various references to the concepts and technologies of the *Star Trek* series comprise a noteworthy part of that community's day-to-day vocabulary. Even some of the rather esoteric engineering images from this fictional future universe have been incorporated into the discursive routines of military and technological experts, as is illustrated by the reproduced photocopy of an overhead projection reportedly used by Northrop Grumman

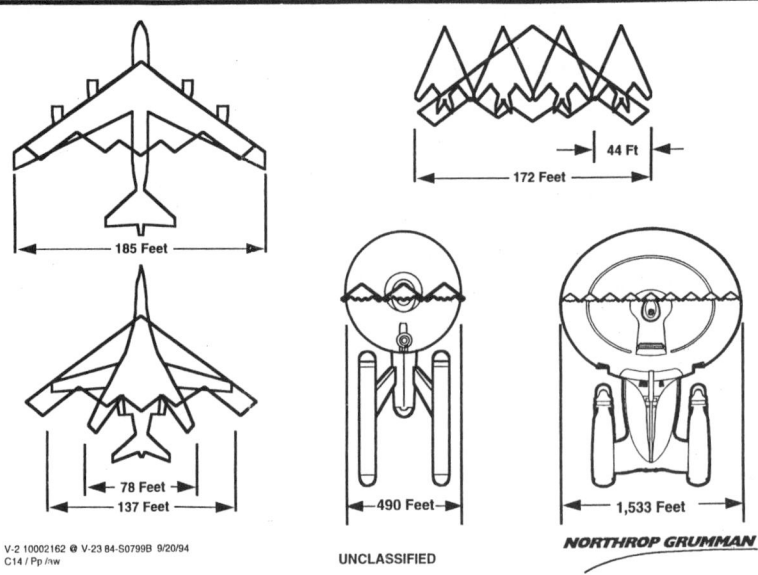

*Figure 2* Two versions of the Enterprise *starship of* Star Trek *fame are here used as size comparison models superimposed on actual military planes. The usage may be whimsical, but it is also significant. Senior defense engineers and military planners are obviously familiar with these images: the tropes and images of science fiction are not only a source of amusement, but information and measurement.*

during a 1994 briefing for government and industry representatives on its B-2 Stealth bomber (see Fig. 2).

Although one must conjecture that the primary purpose of these five size-comparison diagrams is to elicit a grin, such amusement is a response to a rather 'serious' joke. First, three of the five size-comparison illustrations superimpose the silhouette of the B-2 'Stealth bomber' upon three very real, and very lethal, aircraft: the venerable B-52 bomber, the F-117 Stealth fighter-bomber, and the B-1 bomber. Second, the last two outlines —both spacecraft from the *Star Trek* series (two different models of the now-iconic USS *Enterprise*)—are precise renderings, scaled exactly, and lifted from the four-color, lavishly illustrated, fictional 'technical manuals' sold to fans of the series. Furthermore, the coding at the lower left of the overlay, which indicates the date and reference number of the meeting, is not fictitious, and the classification warning—while certainly redundant —is no more a joke than the manufacturer's marque, which appears in the lower right corner. However, what may be most interesting about this size-comparison sheet is what it presupposes: that a room full of senior military and defense industry personnel will recognize the outlines of the 'old' and 'new' USS *Enterprise*, find these comparisons appropriate to such a meeting without needing any contextualizing references, and regard them as interesting and possibly useful.

Of course, it may be that the only 'use or interest' inherent in the *Star Trek* outlines is that the assembled experts may get a concrete idea of the size of the *fictional* vessels, rather than the actual ones. However, if this is the case, the discursive ramifications are equally significant. That this kind of 'information dissemination' is assumed to be appropriate and of interest to a large gathering of military and defense elites may be the most extraordinary proof of how great their interest is in science fictional narratives, and correspondingly, the influence it may have on their perceptions of both the technical and social implications (and shapes) of their own work and inventions. Whatever purposes informed its inclusion in an official presentation, this diagram is a singularly forthright illustration of the ubiquity of science fictional references within the discursive domain of the military and defense hierarchies, as well as the assumed validation and value of these references within those domains.

The United States government and its defense contractors are not alone in their incorporation of science fiction references into their discursive domains. The Soviet Union also did so, was even more forthright about these inclusions, and typically selected loftier, more philosophical references. As futurist John McHale observes in *The Future of the Future*, 'Russian extrapolation of the present technological development seems more literary and poetic in imagery. . . . [some] refer to Yefremov's novel *Andromeda Nebula*, and various science fiction works . . . which is not quite so characteristic of American reports in this area.'[36]

Rather, the interaction and interpenetration of American science fiction and the space program was characterized by the employment of more accessible fictional scenarios and descriptions to popularize the idea of interplanetary travel. US officials often adopted the rhetorical modes of a science fictional 'narrative' of space exploration, in much the same way that Victorian authors employed journalistic formats so that their future-war fictions acquired an added edge of immediacy, plausibility, and tangibility. Perhaps the most dramatic example of this space-age strategy of 'trickle-down' acculturation and advocacy was a celebrated series of *Colliers* articles and their cinematic spin-off, Disney's *Man in Space*. This film was, by whatever yardstick one wishes to measure, the largest of all the pro-space spectaculars produced in the 1950s: it was the most expensive, the most widely disseminated, and the most influential. It also ushered in an age of pervasive 'space consciousness' in American society, which historians Ordway and

Lieberman describe as 'a time when the public began to think of space travel in terms other than those of science fiction. The prospect of travel beyond the Earth came to hold such a grip on the public that it provided a constant theme in advertising, television, motion pictures, consumer goods, books, and magazines.'[37] This new awareness was largely due to active proselytizing through science fictional accounts of the coming adventures to be had in the last, great, star-dappled frontier. As space policy analyst John M. Logsdon notes, 'the story of the space era is not only a study of creative minds and human aspirations but also a story of the partnership between politics and dreams.'[38]

This partnership marked its first great achievement in the 1952 *Colliers* series on the conquest of space, which many analysts and historians—such as *Blueprint for Space* co-author, Randy Lieberman—credit with converting the public perception of space flight 'from science fiction to science fact.'[39] Lieberman cites the 'great amount of positive feedback from elementary through high school-age boys who had been closely following the series' as evidence of its influence, and then traces these youthful dreams through to adult realities: 'Many men who eventually went to work in the US space program attribute their initial spark of interest to the pages of *Colliers*.'[40] These pages were not only lushly illustrated but told a dramatic story of exploration, rather than simply reciting facts, figures, and capabilities. By adopting a narrative format, the authors endued these new technologies with human significance: their readers vicariously felt the trembling thrill of a thundering lift off into new realms of wonder and adventure.

The success of the magazine series carried over into its logical and characteristically American extension: film. Disney's 1955 adaptation of the series, *Man in Space*, incorporated and enlarged upon the ideas, adventures, and graphics featured in the *Colliers* series, most of which had come from the visionary and shrewd marketing mind of Wernher von Braun. Lieberman's recounting of the extraordinary phenomenon of acculturation and political influence that followed warrants full inclusion:

> The film first aired on 9 March 1955 and was well received by a television audience of nearly 100 million. An important viewer was President Dwight D. Eisenhower, who was so impressed by *Man in Space* that he personally called Disney and asked to borrow a copy of the film. He kept it for a couple of weeks, during which time it was shown to officials at the Pentagon. The show was rerun on 15 June and on 29 July Eisenhower announced that as part of American participation in the International Geophysical Year (IGY, 1957–1958), the United States would attempt to launch an Earth satellite. Prompted by Eisenhower's announcement, a third airing of the Disney film was hurriedly scheduled for 7 September.[41]

Whatever influence this cosmic-minded media confection may have had upon the opinions of a single presidential administration, its transformation of the political consciousness and interests of an entire nation were immediate and lasting:

> [V]on Braun's space vehicle designs soon appeared in movies, books, posters, even children's lunch boxes. His designs also came to life in three films produced by Walt Disney for the 'Tomorrowland' segment of the 'Disneyland' television series, which was viewed by millions during the latter half of the 1950s.[42]

*Man in Space* was only the first of the three 'Tomorrowland' space films. The other two were *Man and the Moon* and *Mars and Beyond*. All were direct adaptations of von Braun's visions of how America should evolve its presence and operations in space, all legacies of the influence of narratives by Oberth, Kurd Lasswitz, and others.

*****

Although rocketry and routine access to space are themselves of crucial military importance, it is also worthwhile to examine the influence that overt 'future-war' fiction narratives had on the conceptualization and creation of specifically *military* space technologies. There are numerous examples of this process in action, and in each of the three examined here, the original engineering concept for an important piece of space technology, as well as specific design proposals for its actualization, were first articulated by science fiction writers. Furthermore, in each of these three cases—the geosynchronous satellite, the orbital defense satellite, and a tactical version of the Brilliant Pebbles technology—the writers were officially recognized by, and incorporated into the discursive domain of, policy makers.

The first of these developments was still a 'radically innovative idea' at the close of World War II, but it is now such a commonplace component of the superpower era that its existence is taken for granted: the geosynchronous satellite, through which truly global communication was first achieved. The other advantages and opportunities afforded by such satellites are so well known and numerous that (one hopes) it is unnecessary to list them.

While these benefits seem obvious now, they were largely unanticipated in 1945, when a young, science-fiction-loving RAF officer specializing in radar applications proposed the geosynchronous satellite concept in a letter to *Wireless World*. His ideas came as a complete surprise to the readers of that journal. The RAF officer was Arthur C. Clarke, the best-known of all modern British science fiction writers, and generally held to be the father of the geosynchronous satellite. Clarke, in a typically modest dismissal of his achievement, may nonetheless be correct when he writes in *How the World Was One* (1992): 'I suspect that my early disclosure may have advanced the cause of space communications by approximately fifteen minutes.'[43]

Certainly, Clarke did benefit from the perspective he gained from standing on the shoulders of giants. Tsiolkovskiy and Goddard both envisioned objects in earth orbit, and H. Potocnik, writing under the pseudonym Hermann Noordung, described a manned space station that was able to communicate with the earth via radio link. Herman Oberth, in *Rocket into Planetary Space*, wrote in 1923 of his own hypothetical orbiting bases, the crew of which

> would be able to see fine detail on earth and could communicate by means of mirrors reflecting sunlight. This might be useful for communication with places on the ground which have no cable connexions and cannot be reached by electric waves. . . . The strategic value is obvious especially in the case of war in areas of low population density.[44]

Oberth's concluding mention of the wartime value of overhead communications and navigational platforms is extremely foresightful. It anticipates the development of satellite air traffic coordination, observation, targeting, and even remote positioning systems, such as the American GPS technology, which allows ground troops to locate their positions to within fractions of a meter, and powerfully facilitates independent operations by small units.

However, in contrast with the earlier, rather vague anticipations, it was Clarke who clearly saw how such a technological feat could be achieved, and the full spectrum of opportunities it offered:

> Back in 1945, while a radar officer in the Royal Air Force, I had the only original idea of my life. Twelve years before the first Sputnik started beeping, it occurred to me that an artificial satellite would be a wonderful place for a television transmitter, since a station several thousand miles high could broadcast to half the globe. I wrote up the idea the week after Hiroshima, proposing a network of relay satellites twenty-two thousand miles above the Equator; at this height, they'd take exactly one day to complete a revolution, and so would remain fixed over the same spot on the Earth.[45]

Clarke foresaw the communications potential in orbital platforms which are now, and must remain, the key weapon in any superpower state's cultural offensives. He also saw their reconnaissance capabilities, but hoped that such devices might be turned to the purposes of peace—

and it may well be that these humble manifestations of the space age prevented a nuclear exchange on a number of occasions. The unilateral ability to assess an opponent's nuclear arsenal, both in terms of size and readiness, allowed the Cold Warriors on both sides of the Iron Curtain to remain calm when they might otherwise have jumped to dangerously wrong conclusions in the heat of an international crisis. As Clarke points out:

> [T]he missile gap was a total illusion, destroyed when the new American reconnaissance satellites revealed the truth about Soviet rocket deployment. President Johnson later remarked that its reconnaissance satellites had saved the United States *many times* the entire cost of the space program, by making it unnecessary to build the counterforce originally planned. I would like to quote his exact words, which should be inscribed in letters of gold above the doors of the Pentagon: 'We were doing things we didn't need to do; we were building things we didn't need to build; *we were harboring fears we didn't need to harbor.*'[46]

Satellites, therefore,

> make possible such arms-control agreements as we do have, as is disclosed by the formula always used when referring to them: 'National technical means (NTM) of verification.' . . . So it is probably true to say that no large-scale military preparations or activities can ever again escape surveillance—at least by nations with NTMs.[47]

Clarke saw beyond the nuclear policing capacities of such orbital surveillance systems in the 1980s, when he exhorted a greater investment in satellites capable of detecting and discerning tactical military activities. He pleaded 'for reconnaissance satellites—watchdogs in the sky that could monitor the political (and military) state of the world. Less than a decade later, the brief but deadly Gulf war demonstrated the importance of this idea.'[48]

At the same time that Clarke was calling for greater security through satellite surveillance, other science fiction authors were echoing President Ronald Reagan's polemics about peace through superior firepower—with some of that firepower to come from satellites. The Strategic Defense Initiative (SDI) was possibly the most hotly contested, misdirected, yet misunderstood weapons scheme ever proposed, but its roots go well beyond its more popular moniker of 'Star Wars.' Even prior to the anticipatory echoes of SDI that resound in narratives such as Ben Bova's *Millennium* (1976) and Kris Neville's 'Cold War' (1949), future-war writers were considering the defensive values of holding the ultimate high ground: geosynchronous orbit. As early as 1932, Carl W. Spohr, an artillery captain in the Germany army during World War I, wrote of such possibilities in his narrative *The Final War*, in which nuclear weapons—both strategic and tactical—threaten the world. Beginning with the detonation of a single tactical nuclear warhead, war breaks out and rapidly escalates into a world-consuming cataclysm. Beam weapon defenses, in the air and on the ground, and energy shields—all defenses that anticipate and far exceed the potentials of Star Wars—are employed, but to no avail: '[T]he world was swallowed in black, raging darkness.'[49]

The idea of orbital defenses began to appear with greater frequency and in greater detail after World War II. In 1983, however, these anticipations of space-based anti-missile missiles and lasers suddenly leaped the nebulous divide between science fiction and national policy, receiving a hefty budgetary boost to clear the hurdle. SDI's first-year nonclassified budget was more than 1.5 billion dollars; estimates suggest that undisclosed additional billions, surreptitiously culled from other budget lines, were earmarked for classified projects. Total expenditures were close to twenty times the first-year budget. Arguably, it was science fiction writers who had brought these technologies and options to the military's attention and into the national political spotlight. These same authors also locked horns with each other in some of the most well-publicized and layman-accessible arguments about SDI. Hard science fiction writers lined up on both sides of the political aisle: one of the most vocal and well-known of the dissenting voices was that of Isaac Asimov, who characterized the program as a 'fantastic scheme'[50] in a fund-raising letter he wrote for the Americans for Democratic Action in the 1980s. Many other well-known future-war authors (including Joe Haldeman) also weighed in against the program. Arthur C. Clarke was also essentially negative, and, late in the debate, pointed out that

> SDI . . . comes in many varieties . . . Some make a good deal of sense, but others—especially the much-ballyhooed but now discreetly buried vision of an 'umbrella over the United States'—were pure fantasy. (Not, as some critics said, science fiction. In that case they would have been worth taking seriously.)[51]

Clarke's measured and carefully worded statement is particularly instructive regarding the confusions that whirled about the crude all-purpose label 'Star Wars.' The discourse surrounding SDI quickly seemed to take on a life of its own, propagating misunderstandings, misrepresentations, and mistrust with dizzying speed. Most responsible advocates of SDI were as insistent as Clarke in holding that an impregnable 'nuclear shield' was a pipe dream. Instead, the more responsible and knowledgeable supporters of the program—along with almost all science fiction writers who were behind it—emphasized that it only represented a proportional deterrent. The idea was that even a marginal reduction in the effectiveness of a Soviet first strike would disincline Moscow to launch such a strike at all, since they would then bear the full brunt of a largely undiminished American response. Even ardent supporters of SDI, such as Edward Teller and General Daniel O. Graham, insisted that a '100% defense' was impossible.[52]

However, certain members of the Administration (Reagan included) seemed to be so inspired by the reassuring 'good-guy' resonance of the media's facetious label for the program—'Star Wars'—that they began to use the term freely themselves and began advertising SDI as a complete 'nuclear shield.'[53] The press rapidly picked up on this improbable claim: based upon technologies that were either in their infancy or wholly theoretical, SDI became a particularly easy target for journalistic critique and ridicule. Thus, three distinct camps emerged in the whirlwind of debate over SDI: the 'impregnable nuclear shield' advocates, the press-oriented critics who felt that SDI was a boondoggle-in-the-making, and the largely ignored ranks of those who insisted that it was neither one of these things, but rather, a limited technology with a limited military value. The inherent complexities of this last position—arguably the most accurate of the three and the one that Arthur C. Clarke and others invoked—made SDI a hard sell to both the press and the American public.

Among the strong supporters of SDI was Ben Bova, whose advocacy for it appeared in his non-fictional tracts *The High Road* (1981) and *Assured Survival* (1984), as well as his novel *Privateers* (1985). Robert Heinlein wrote a number of supportive articles, and penned the foreword for Lieutenant General Daniel O. Graham's *The High Frontier*, an influential, Reagan-endorsed tract on the pro-SDI side of the debate. However, it was Jerry Pournelle who was the most outspoken supporter of SDI. Along with fellow hard science fiction author Dean Ing, he published what may be the best-known and most controversial tract of the entire SDI debate: *Mutual Assured Survival* (1984). However, in order to understand the significance and greater context of this highly technical and in many ways challenging text, it is first essential to gain perspective on its senior author.

At the time he wrote *Mutual Assured Survival*, Pournelle already had a long history of association with the US government and the defense industry. In addition to his military career and affiliations with Boeing Aerospace Corporation and Rockwell International, he wrote (along with occasional collaborator Stefan T. Possony) an ambitious technomilitary planning treatise entitled *The Strategy of Technology* (1970), in which he averred that the doctrine of Mutual Assured Destruction should be abandoned in favor of a strategy of Assured Survival. His proposal for achieving this was to adopt a policy of 'technological war' and to reorganize the nation's industrial and military structures to optimize the probability that any future conflicts would be waged in environments and at times that maximized America's technological military advantages, thereby minimizing the chances that such events would ever occur. Pournelle's exhortations recall Edison's assertions (cited in Chapter 5) that the US's primary national advantage lies in its technological capabilities, and that steps should be taken to develop this advantage to its utmost. Pournelle's organizing motto—'Technology is America's manifest destiny' —is almost an echo of Edison's own slogans, uttered more than sixty years earlier.[54] His theories are also the realizations of Wells' predictions regarding the key resources for success in future wars, which, although already cited in Chapter 5, warrants restatement:

> The nation that produces in the near future the largest proportional development of educated and intelligent engineers and agriculturists, of doctors, schoolmasters, professional soldiers and intellectually active people of all sorts . . . will certainly be the nation that will be the most powerful in warfare as in peace, will certainly be the ascendant or dominant nation before the year 2000.[55]

In *The Strategy of Technology*, Wells' previsions—particularly those having to do with professional training—are articulated as the prerequisites and key resources of a successful technocentric superpower:

> We define as technological base the sum total of resources needed to produce and constantly modernize the tools of war and peace. Those resources include scientists, engineers, laboratories, laboratory equipment, funds, information flow, incentives, etc., as well as industry and the economy as a whole, which we do not discuss in this book.[56]

However, Pournelle's greatest claim to popular fame is a long string of far-future war stories, almost all of which embrace the basic rhetorical principles of 'hard' science fiction. These narratives, many of which feature speculations/extrapolations on new weapons (although rarely of the 'doomsday' variety), were not only popular with the general science fiction readership, but with a considerable number of the individuals who were to provide the brain-power for the SDI program. When science journalist William J. Broad interviewed many of the younger weapons researchers at Livermore Laboratories for his book *Star Warriors*, he discovered that the innovator of the X-ray laser, Peter Hagelstein, credited Pournelle as one of his primary influences in conceiving of the weapon, which appears in action in the Pournelle/Niven collaboration, *The Mote in God's Eye*. Indeed, Hagelstein had invoked this, and other future-war fictions, in his daring dissertation on the topic of X-ray lasers.[57]

One of the other key young Star Warriors at Livermore, Rod Hyde, had been drawn into the field by his aspirations to design a workable propulsion system for near-light-speed starships. He asserted that his interests and abilities had been 'nurtured by a stream of science fiction, most especially by authors Gordon Dickson, Keith Laumer, and Robert Heinlein.'[58] These are three of the most influential and scientifically rigorous future-war authors of the twentieth century. Dickson's *The Tactics of Mistake*[59] and affiliated Dorsai saga is arguably science fiction's most sustained and detailed rumination upon the evolution of the physiology and ethos of the professional soldier of the future. Laumer is the author of the *Bolo* series, an insightful and often sardonic anticipation of the future integration of artificial near-intelligence into armored combat vehicles. Heinlein is arguably, along with Wells, the most influential and insightful of all future-war authors; from the interplanetary bombardment operations in *The Moon is a Harsh Mistress*[60] to the tactics and technologies of the Mobile Infantry of *Starship Troopers*,[61] his war fictions were remarkable for their identification of the future needs, devices, and practices of the military.

Although Broad never specifically mentions future-war influences upon other researchers, the mood at Livermore is pervaded by the implied presence of the genre: pictures of starships, familiarity with SF tropes and themes, and a ubiquitous fascination with far-future weapons and spacecraft all combine to suggest that such fictions were an integral part of the Star Warriors' subcultural and discursive roots.

If Pournelle's fiction provided indirect inspiration for the nation's engineering braintrust at Livermore Labs, there is ample evidence that his influence upon both the technomilitary and political domains of the SDI initiative was even more direct and powerful. Consider the following testimonial for his tract *Mutual Assured Survival* from a prominent political figure:

Dear Dr. Pournelle:

Thank you for your letter of September 24 advising me of the unanimous recommendations of your Citizen's Advisory Panel on National Space Policy. I appreciate your generous comments on my March 23rd speech, and I am greatly encouraged by your strong support for a balanced and effective strategy for the nuclear age.

You and your associates deserve high praise for addressing with verve and vision the challenges to peace and to our national security.

Efforts like this can assist us in achieving a safer and more stable future for this country, for our allies, and, indeed, for all mankind.

Thank you, and God bless you.

Sincerely,

Ronald Reagan (Dated October 27, 1983)[62]

Reagan's letter was printed in full on the back cover of *Mutual Assured Survival*. Furthermore, Pournelle had contacts and supporters within the Administration and the Pentagon, and Reagan would almost certainly have been aware that any letter he wrote in response to Pournelle's report would boost the sales of the book.

The genesis of *Mutual Assured Survival* is, in itself, a revealing example of the overlapping discursive domains of future writers, military experts, and senior aerospace figures. Although the book was written by Pournelle and Ing, the recommendations presented in it were the result of coordinated committee work by a group of individuals who examined various nuclear defense alternatives and then presented their assessments of the separate options, along with overall recommendations for implementation. This group, the Citizen's Advisory Panel on National Space Policy, included three astronauts (including Buzz Aldrin), eight science fiction writers and editors (including Heinlein, Pournelle, Gregory Benford, Larry Niven, Greg Bear, and Jim Baen[63]), four major physicists, two retired generals—and Star Warriors Rod Hyde and Lowell Wood, both of whom had been interviewed in depth by William Broad. *Mutual Assured Survival* presents assessments of the following defensive technologies: 'Multiple satellites using kinetic energy kill; Ground-based lasers with mirrors in space; Space-based lasers; Nuclear explosive-driven beam technologies collectively known as third generation systems; Ground based point defense systems.'[64] In each case, specific recommendations were made regarding the necessary research prerequisites, technology, placement, and tactical and strategic employment of the system in question. The book circulated at various official levels, and Reagan's response is probably the clearest indicator of the high regard it received—and what a useful political boost it provided to the program.

Regardless of what one thinks of SDI and the various advocates who debated it, the importance of *Mutual Assured Survival* is that it illustrates the extraordinary linkages that exist among future-war authors, military experts, and political elites. In short, the responses it generated and its mere existence and sales indicate that technomilitary advocacy can be and is carried out through popular books. Furthermore, the collaborations that produce such books are predicated upon the advantageous merging of the experiences, outlooks, and discursive spheres of the military, the government, and future-war fiction writers. Consequently, the text partly derives its authority from the affiliation of those respected military science fiction authors whose proposals initiated the technoscientific weapons projects upon which this collective advocacy is focused. The discontinuation of the SDI program does not diminish the discursive significance of *Mutual Assured Survival*, for the litmus test of its political influence is not whether it ultimately succeeded in America's marketplace of ideas, but the credence and respect it was accorded while there.

However, for every one person who read *Mutual Assured Survival*, there were (estimating conservatively) at least twenty who simply devoured Tom Clancy's *The Cardinal of the Kremlin*, a technothriller that posited the existence of a potent Soviet anti-satellite laser station.[65] Clancy not only makes the arcane accessible to a general readership, but has the uncanny instinct of a second Le Queux when it comes to sensing, and then exciting, the anxieties that drive the political pulse of the nation. As one reviewer observed,

> He is a whiz at getting his efforts into print while the media still have the subject matter before the public. Words like Dushanbe, Star Wars, Komosol, Afghanistan, ASAT (antisatellite), *perestroika*, and *glasnost* that populate our newsprint and televisions are sprinkled through *The Cardinal*. People's interests are piqued by what is recognizable, and Clancy cultivates this exquisitely.[66]

More important than the review itself is the identity of the reviewer: then Vice Admiral William E. Ramsey, Deputy Commander-in-Chief of the US Space Command and Vice Commander of the North American Aerospace Defense Command. Much as Lord Earl Roberts supported the visions of Le Queux, so too does Ramsey trumpet not only the excitement, but, more importantly, the technological and military accuracy of Clancy's future-war fiction. He then goes on to recommend the text as an operational reference book for various branches of America's military and intelligence services: his comments, while lengthy, are so pertinent as to warrant full inclusion:

> As I read *The Cardinal* I had the feeling that Clancy had been a program manager in the SDI Organization (SDIO). He has the uncanny ability to blend fact and fiction, fragments of information with published data, and develop amazingly accurate technical descriptions. The sophisticated technocrat may find some disparities, but for the most part Clancy's discussions of early-warning satellites, communication satellites, infrared sensors, laser technology, facilities,

weapons, and SDI organization are frighteningly precise. It is this facility of Clancy's that has become his trademark. Independent of plot, his technical detail gets your attention and is described in terms that laymen can digest.

This is a book that the armed services committees in Congress should read before voting for SDI funding. Perhaps they would then authorize increased funding. Well, it may or may not be read by, or to, members of Congress; but I guarantee it will be popular in berthing compartments and wardrooms throughout the fleet. All submarines will have to have at least one book in their libraries, acknowledging the role that Clancy accords the USS *Dallas* (SSN-700) in his yarn. And spaceniks will love it! Air Force Lieutenant General Abe Abrahamson, Director of SDIO, should be given a personalized copy. The CIA might even consider introducing it as a training manual for field operations.[67]

Ramsey, a high-ranking SDI insider, was not only in a unique position to attest to the accuracy of Clancy's text, but was in the position to use its popularity to help highlight his own agendas: in the same issue of *Proceedings*, Ramsey is interviewed and uses the occasion to reinforce the importance of space technology and weaponry for all services including the navy, citing Admiral James Watkins' blunt and uncompromising statement that 'Space control is sea control. Whoever controls space will control the seas.'[68]

Although these texts and the commentary on them is all a matter of historical record, the importance of their influence is not past, for SDI itself has not so much been consigned to the history books as rejuvenated under new labels with slightly new objectives. Renamed the Global Protection Against Limited Strikes (GPALS) program in 1991, and mandated to develop technologies capable of providing limited area coverage, it continued to receive considerable funding. In 1993, SDIO/GPALS was transformed into the Ballistic Missile Defense Organization (BMDO), which was primarily concerned with strategic theater defense; national defense came second.[69] However, in 1998, India conducted five nuclear tests, Iran successfully launched an IRBM, and North Korea proved its multi-stage Taepo-Dong-1 missile operational, resulting in an increasingly bipartisan outcry to shift the BMDO's mandate more into the arena of national ballistic missile defense. In 2001, the mandate became so strong that President George W. Bush encountered little public outcry when he announced Washington's withdrawal from the anti-ABM treaty it had long held with Moscow.

The weapon technologies investigated in light of this revised mandate include the Air Force Airborne Laser System (ABL) and space-based lasers for boost phase intercept of ICBMs and possibly shorter-range missiles. However, the 'low-tech' alternatives examined by the BMDO and its successors are particularly significant in that they are the modern-day myrmidons that have sprung from the speculative dragon's teeth sown in the minds of military planners by authors such as Pournelle, Niven, and Clancy. A system of enduring interest to the BMDO is comprised of 'exoatmospheric kill vehicles' delivered by 'Unmanned Air Vehicles' (UAVs), both conceptual descendants of the SDIO's Brilliant Pebbles project, development of which was terminated in 1993.[70] In light of the high 'political survivability' factor of these weapon technologies, it is tempting to hypothesize that many of America's technomilitary strategists may have always envisioned a 'secondary' use for the multi-billion dollar research and technology developed during the heyday of SDI. Indeed, the contemporary offshoots of SDI's theoretical products may soon have profound, even revolutionizing, battlefield applications. The BMDO's kinetic-kill devices began showing a marked increase in reliability and accuracy during their 2001 trials, raising the curtain on a (potentially) new era in strategic thought and planning. On November 5, 2002, at the White Sands N.M. test range, the Mobile Tactical High Energy Laser (MTHEL) successfully hit and destroyed an incoming artillery shell (which is smaller, faster, and has much lower IR signature than rockets), proving the feasibility of beam weapons in particular, and battlefield warhead interception in general.[71] This tactical applicability of the descendants of Star Wars may not be an unexpected development, but an indication that military planners have long appreciated the *tactical* possibilities resident within many supposedly *strategic* systems—an appreciation they may have gained from Jerry Pournelle and Larry Niven's 1985 alien-invasion yarn *Footfall*. In this narrative, a tactical variety of the Brilliant Pebbles is an essential part of the aliens' arsenal and is graphically depicted in action. Countering an American armored assault against one of their landing zones, the aliens respond with an attack from orbit:

> There was a roar and the sharp snap of multiple sonic booms. Harry looked up. Dozens of parallel white lines crossed the sky from the southwest. They dropped like the lines in *Missile Command*, downward toward where Colonel Halverson's force was centered. There were bright flashes at the horizon and along the line where the connecting vehicles had been strung out. After a long pause, there was the sound of thunder.[72]

The alien weapon that effects this wholesale slaughter of an armored detachment is later revealed to be a close relative of the SDI's Brilliant

Pebbles scheme. The character Wade Curtis later explains the weapon to military officials by relating it to the specific SDI offshoot technology upon which it is based:

> 'Project Thor was recommended by a strategy analysis group back in the eighties,' Curtis said. 'Flying crowbars. . . . You take a big iron bar. Give it a rudimentary sensor, and a steerable vane for guidance. Put bundles of them in orbit. To use it, call it down from orbit, aimed at the areas you're working on. It has a simple brain, just smart enough to recognize what a tank looks like from overhead. When it sees a tank silhouette, it steers toward it. Drop ten or twenty thousand of those over an armored division and what happens?'
> 'Holy shit,' Toland said.[73]

This brief excerpt warrants special mention for several reasons. First, it is remarkable as much for what it assumes of a reader's prior knowledge as for the idea it advances. At the risk of reprising facts that may be familiar from high school physics, gravity accelerates a falling object at 9.8 meters/sec$^2$. When this falling object encounters another solid object, the resistance offered by the encountered object will slow the falling object. It slows the falling object by reducing the velocity, or kinetic energy, possessed by that object. This energy is released as heat and secondary effects, such as a shock wave. In the *Footfall* scenario, a very dense object is falling at incredibly high speeds—so high, that atmospheric friction has heated it until it glows: flocks of these speeding white-hot 'crowbars' create the 'dozens of parallel white lines' that descend toward the tanks. At the end of its descent, this falling object hits an extremely dense obstacle—in this case, the armor of a tank. The armor's resistance causes the release of all or most of the falling object's kinetic energy. The result is a blast of heat that will melt and shatter metal, ignite stored munitions and fuel, generate a considerable shockwave, and leave a battle tank looking like tortured modern art.

However, what is even more interesting about this scene is the narrative identity of the character Wade Curtis and his associates: they are all science fiction authors whom the military has called in to consult on what strategies, tactics, and weaponry the aliens might use. The senior member of the group, to whom Wade Curtis shows considerable respect, is named Robert Anson, and is accompanied by his wife Virginia. These names are significant: Robert Heinlein's full name is Robert Anson Heinlein, his wife (now widow) is Virginia, and 'Wade Curtis' is Jerry Pournelle's alias when writing editorials and articles for computer magazines.[74] In short, authors Pournelle and Niven have placed themselves, their politically allied peers, and some of the recommendations from *Mutual Assured Survival* in the text.

Only dedicated science fiction readers or academic researchers are likely to discover this, and thereby discern another level of discourse braided invisibly into the main narrative. This sub-narrative is, essentially, an impatient and grimly illustrated critique of the American government's (and possibly, American public's) unwillingness to invest in more advanced weapons, including several of the SDI variety. To impertinently adapt von Clausewitz's famous adage from *On War*, it seems safe to assert that, in the case of *Footfall*, fiction is simply policy achieved through other means.

Before the SDIO evolved into the BMDO, it also illustrated the power of popular labels. The misnomer assigned to the SDI program—'Star Wars'—made it seem accessible to the general public, but also misrepresented it. Ironically, this label did not rhetorically link the project with true science fiction, but with a rollicking technofantasy adventure that was an extension of traditional mythologies, not technological advancement. However, SDI was the stuff of legends in one sense: it reflected a new fusion of powerful mythology with the superpower state's celebration of the perfectly made object. These weapons were to be the ultimate answer to, and antidote for, silo psychosis. They were to be a technology of deliverance, of permanent peace, and, therefore, of transcendence as well. They were to be actualizations of the belief at the very center of a uniquely American dream: *utopia ex machina*.

The linkage between space technology, deliverance, and transcendence continues. It finds expression in Congressional hearings on funding for the Search for Extra-Terrestrial Intelligence (SETI), hearings that were not simply democratic tolerance for schemes assumed to be of the 'crackpot' variety. As Alvin Toffler points out in *The Third Wave*, prior to SETI '[t]he United States Congress has held hearings on "The Possibility of Intelligent Life Elsewhere in the Universe." And the Pioneer 10 Spacecraft, as it streaked into interstellar space, carried with it a pictorial greeting to extraterrestrials.'[75]

The most recent example of America's fused focus upon space, deliverance, and transcendance is reflected in the dramatically increased concern over the possibility that either a 'killer' asteroid or comet might strike the Earth—a perennial staple of science fiction disaster narratives. However, with the exception of the film (1951) and book (Wylie and Balmer 1933) of *When Worlds Collide*, none of the early yarns of this variety became particularly well known, in part because the projected agency of disaster seemed extremely unlikely and unthinkably distant. In 1979, the groundbreaking (literally) 'Alvarez theory' arrived on the paleontological and geological scene, proposing that the massive planetary disruption and multi-speciate die-off that ended the Cretaceous age—and the reign of the dinosaurs—was in fact caused by such an impact. While the stir was considerable in the scientific community, public reaction was less than impressive—and a great deal less than had been generated by the serious treatment of cometary impact that appeared in Niven and Pournelle's 1977 hard science fiction novel, *Lucifer's Hammer*.[76] Even in the same year as Walter and Luis Alvarez presented their compelling theories, speculative doomsday narratives were more effective than experts and journalists at bringing such ideas into a broad public domain: the decidedly lackluster 1979 film *Meteor* focused the attention of millions on killer space rocks.

However, even as the Alvarez theory accrued near-conclusive evidence, public interest remained comparatively minor—until, that is, news and narratives began evolving into a single, symbiotically linked discourse, the kind of fusion that has characterized the most influential speculative and future-war fictions. The trend toward increased acceptance of and interest in doomsday rocks began growing when Program Spacewatch, a modest program run by Tom Gehrels at the University of Arizona, started generating disconcerting data regarding the plenitude of earth-crossing asteroids in the mid-1990s. A 1995 television documentary produced for the Sci-Fi channel (Executive Producer Ted Griggs, GGP) highlighted Gehrels' work, and used the cataclysmic Jovian impacts of the Schoemacher-Levy comet to call attention to the program's titular assertion that, somewhere, a space rock might well be 'On a Collision Course With Earth.' By 1996, the government had stepped in, occasioning coverage by *New York Times* science correspondent William Broad. His article, 'For Killer Asteroids, Respect at Last' bluntly announced that 'The Government is searching space for potential doomsday rocks' and that

> The hunt involves an Air Force telescope usually used for the surveillance of orbiting spacecraft . . . improved by the addition of a sensitive electronic camera developed by the National Aeronautics and Space Administration, which finances and runs the search for faint celestial objects that might one day turn deadly. . . .
> It is estimated that among the many thousands of comets and asteroids speeding through the solar system, up to 1,700 of those crossing Earth's path might be big enough to wreak global havoc. . . .
> The project started scanning the heavens a little more than four months ago and has already discovered four previously unknown asteroids whose orbits intersect that of the Earth. The largest of these Earth-crossers, as such asteroids are known, is 1.8 miles across, big enough to cause a global catastrophe. . . .
> The new system's high rate of discovery implies, however, that many more unknown objects zip through the void, scientists say,

making the Earth an unwitting target in a cosmic shooting gallery....

The idea is a novel one even for scientists; it has become generally accepted among them only recently, after a 15-year debate.[77]

Of course, the idea was not novel to hard science fiction authors. Indeed, 'novelty' probably had very little to do with the concept's long period of dormancy: like so many other notions introduced by speculative fiction narratives, its official acceptability and popularization only waited upon quantifiable, empirical proof.

However, Broad's article generated only a fraction of the attention—and promotion—that were lavished on the 1997 NBC mini-series *Asteroid*, in which a doomsday rock threatens earth. Although the scientific basis for the weapons used to effect the asteroid's destruction (high-altitude, laser-armed F-15 Eagles) was preposterous, much of the astrophysical information provided was not, and was a dramatic improvement over earlier offerings (such as *Meteor*) in terms of its careful consideration of the subtleties and difficulties of dealing with such an ominous extra-terrestrial threat. For instance, after the F-15s have completed their mission, and the asteroid has been blasted to bits, researchers discover, in keeping with (now) prevailing scientific theory, that instead of eliminating the menace, they have changed its form: a cloud of asteroid fragments is still heading toward Earth. This problem—that of an anti-asteroid weapon that would convert a single mile-wide cosmic cannonball into a massive meteoritic shotgun blast—has since become a critical consideration for those experts who consider and debate the values of different 'intercept scenarios.'

To return to a term introduced at the beginning of this chapter, the 'mind-step' toward the reality of killer asteroids and comets took its most dramatic, culture-wide stride forward when, in 1998, the concept of celestial cataclysm swung much closer to the national consciousness' center of gravity. Part of this boost came on March 12, when the *New York Times*' front-page leading story—placed at the head of column one, with two full-color artist's diagrams—announced that an 'Asteroid is Expected to Make a Pass Close to Earth in 2028,' and that 'there is a possibility that it would hit Earth.'[78] However, despite reporter Malcolm W. Browne's attempts to describe the consequences of such an event—'The impact ... would have devastating global effects, including tidal waves, continent-size fires and an eruption of dust that could cause global cooling and long-term disruption of agriculture'—it was once again fictional narratives which brought home the reality of such an event to the American (and perhaps global) collective consciousness.

Released within months of each other and only weeks after the factual

*Times* reportage concluded, two Hollywood extravaganzas—*Deep Impact* and *Armageddon*—depicted the horrors and desperate challenges that such a threat would entail. Of the two films, *Deep Impact* was infinitely more credible, employing NASA advisers to comment on or review almost every scientific aspect of the story. It is also the darker of the two films: Earth's biosphere escapes complete destruction only by supreme sacrifice and considerable luck, and the East Coast of the US is still savaged by a smaller piece of the offending comet. *Armageddon* was, by comparison, a marginally (and often, non-) scientific adventure yarn that often stooped to low comedy and wildly implausible plot devices. However, these films share two important features with each other—as they do with their thematic forerunners, *Lucifer's Hammer*, *Meteor*, and *Asteroid*: in all cases, there are scenes of titanic destruction and terror, and also, military involvement proves essential to managing and/or resolving the crisis.

In all these narratives, the scenes of destruction take on mythic proportions: tidal waves topple skyscrapers, blazing meteors slice clean through office buildings, cities become smoldering craters, people are vaporized, and chaos reigns. Deliverance is required—and the form it must take (in all but *Lucifer's Hammer*) involves space technology that transcends the bounds of earth and projects human hopes and dreams outward into infinity.[79] The military is always along for this ride: in *Meteor*, the offending space rock is destroyed by waves of US and Soviet ICBMs; in *Asteroid*, US air force interceptors nullify the approaching threat and later, military units oversee evacuation of populations endangered by the remaining fragments; in *Armageddon*, the craft and weapons used to stop the oncoming planetoid are designed by and originally intended for the military, which keeps representatives connected to the mission; and lastly, *Deep Impact*'s hero-astronaut is an ex-military pilot, the bombs deployed on the comet are of US military origin, and the collection of America's pre-selected survivors (in the case of mission failure) is carried out by stern-jawed army personnel.

Conceivably, this new discourse of apocalypse could emerge as a discrete subgenre of future-war fiction, much as nuclear war fiction once did. Anxieties of mythic cataclysm propel both species of narrative. Also, the source of the cataclysm in the two subgenres is not a product of 'what if . . .' speculation, but is a consequence of an 'if this goes on' extrapolation: the missiles have not yet launched, nor an earth-killing asteroid fallen (recently), but history proves the existence and persistent reality of both possibilities. Nuclear and 'killer space rock' fictions are not, therefore, 'pure' speculation, for the plot uncertainty in both revolves not around the scientific issue of 'if' apocalypse could occur, but around the historical question of 'when' (or 'why').

Lastly, and perhaps most importantly, both nuclear and 'killer space rock' fictions fuse the American penchant for advanced spacecraft and weapons into single objects of technophilic desire: missiles or makeshift space cruisers must fly to humanity's rescue. In many ways, an approaching comet is the ideal adversary for a technocentric democracy: waging war against a force of nature requires no debate on ethics, no contortionistic acts of rationalization or vindication, no daily witnessing of bodies returning home or pictures of hollow-eyed refugees. It is the ultimate future war: waged with the highest technology, which is in turn wielded by the best warriors, it is a quest to save all of humanity from an implacable and overwhelming force of nature. Indeed, even though the scientific community has viewed military participation in the detection of 'killer rocks' with some suspicion, it is difficult to see how—or why—humanity's response to an actual threat would exclude a military component. The training, equipment, discipline, and destructive/propulsive systems required would, on the contrary, seem to indicate that military participation would be prudent, even indispensable. Significantly, the military seems to think so also: in the Air Force Academy's 1996 staff planning tract, *Air Force 2025*, one of the position papers, entitled 'Planetary Defense: Catastrophic Health Insurance for Planet Earth' explains that the means of diverting such objects, referred to as 'potential mitigation subsystems'

> are as numerous as there are science fiction novels . . . Popular potential mitigation subsystems addressed by current literature include, but are certainly not limited to, rocket propulsion systems; rockets with chemical, nuclear, or antimatter warheads; kinetic energy systems; high-energy lasers; microwave energy systems; mass drivers/reaction engines; solar sails; and solar collectors . . .[80]

The anticipated astral armamentariums of SDI, BMDO, and *Air Force 2025*, are all impressive and even, conceivably, attainable. However, despite the alloyed symbolisms of myth and machine and of transcendence and technology that are associated with space weapons, the appeal of the rocket and the ray-gun must now compete with a relatively new iconic power that may be greater than the two of them combined. Bound into the precision of these machines and into the cool imperturbability of their technologies, there are also pitiless angles of automation and 'infallible' computers—superpower tools of choice for reshaping human beings into efficient soldiers—and possibly, dehumanized robot-warriors.

*Chapter 9*

# Making Man-Machines of Mass Destruction: Future-War Authors as Seers in an Age of Cyborg Soldiers

I think there is a world market for maybe five computers.
         Thomas Watson, chairman of IBM, 1943

Computers in the future may weigh no more than 1.5 tons.
      *Popular Mechanics*, forecasting the relentless march of
                science, 1949

I have traveled the length and breadth of this country and talked with the best people, and I can assure you that data processing is a fad that won't last out the year.
    The editor in charge of business books for Prentice Hall, 1957

But what . . . is it good for?
    Engineer at the Advanced Computing Systems Division of IBM,
            1968, commenting on the microchip

There is no reason anyone would want a computer in their home.
      Ken Olson, president, chairman and founder of Digital
              Equipment Corp., 1977

640K ought to be enough for anybody.
                 Bill Gates, 1981

At the end of World War II, the most powerful weapon in today's arsenal, the computer, was not a dream awaiting realization. It was an extant (albeit nascent) technology languishing for want of imaginative applications and improvement. However, even as the experts at IBM and DEC questioned the utility and marketability of such machines, more farsighted observers were predicting that the computer would revolutionize every level and sphere of society. Science fiction writer Alan Nourse's aggressive prognostication outstripped even those advanced by Alvin Toffler, Marshall McLuhan, and Raymond Williams. Nourse predicted that

> Perhaps the most revolutionary and far-reaching of all technological changes destined to take place in our society in the next quarter century will be the introduction of modern and sophisticated computer terminals into the individual home, operating on a time-sharing basis with existing telephone lines and television cables for input and output communications.[1]

Nourse's prediction proved to be inaccurate in one important regard: the 'timing' of his prophecy was off by (at least) a factor of two—because even his estimate had been too conservative. By 1987—in half the time Nourse predicted—his largely dismissed prevision was solid reality. In half that time again, the computer had become a ubiquitous part of most middle-class American homes. However, long before domestic ownership became so pervasive, the computer had already revolutionized virtually every aspect of commerce, administration, research, scholarship, transportation, and, above all, military operations.

Until the 1990–91 Gulf War, computers were not popularly associated with, much less perceived as, weapons—except insofar as they were necessary adjuncts to the monitoring and coordination of the superpowers's nuclear response capabilities. In part, this general failure to associate computers with military applications is due to the innocuousness, and often invisibility, of microprocessors and their functions. Logistics, traffic control, navigation, multiplexed communications, electronic warfare, radar and sensors, ballistics, casualty and consumables projections, missile guidance, operational coordination: all these tasks are largely invisible to an external observer, yet involve reams of figures so great that, before the computer, they defied attempts at decisive management. However, because soldiers do not trail wires, nor tote weapons bristling with inlaid microprocessors, the casual observer had little or no reason to suspect the widespread influence of automation. The Gulf War, which has been called the first war won by the microchip, changed that perception overnight. Cruise missiles, laser-guided bombs, and Patriot missiles were the media stars of Desert Storm, and all were obviously dependent upon computer guidance and coordination. Less obvious were the targeting computers in tanks and planes, the laser rangefinders and designators, 'fire-and-forget' missiles, digitally modulated night-vision sensors, remote piloted vehicles, hand-held global positioning system (GPS) sets for infantry orienteering and navigation, and a host of other applications. Ironically, almost none of these technologies were introduced in the Gulf War; it was simply the first time that their military contributions became evident to the majority of the public. Many of these 'wondrous' technologies were already in their third or fourth 'generation;' the first laser-guided bombs, personal night-vision gear, and laser rangefinders had been employed experimentally in Vietnam. Targeting computers had been introduced even earlier, as had self-guiding missiles. In essence, the nature of war had changed long before it was publicly heralded during CNN's coverage of the clash with Iraq. Indeed, the only timely, widely available, and layman-accessible declarations of these changes had not been made in the news media, but in the pages of American future-war narratives.

Can future-war authors reasonably hope to acclimatize readers to imminent or unrealized technologies? Some analysts think not, among them the eminent I. F. Clarke, who reasonably asserts that 'The further these stories move away from their traditional task of immediate admonition and earnest warning, the less they have to do with the probable shape of a future war. Although the old delight in technological marvels and the taste for aggressive adventure stories continue, there is no place left for them in the world we know.'[2] Clarke's statement commands attention not merely because of the author's expertise, but because of one subtle yet crucial distinction it invites in response. Clarke assumes that, fundamentally, the political and technological issues raised by future-war fictions are substantially disjunct. When such narratives are considered solely in relation to their contemporaneous political and international climates, Clarke's assertion is irrefragably correct: the further a tale moves into the future, the less relevance it has to immediate issues. However, those narratives that look further into the future in order to address the long-term effects of radical technological change are simply re-siting their political emphasis away from statecraft and toward sociology. Their objects of inquiry may be broader and more speculative, but they are every bit as pertinent and political. Exacting speculations upon future warfare probe beyond the affairs and fears of the moment, asking questions that ultimately have more to do with the sociopolitical consequences of technology than with the immediate impacts of specific policy decisions. This is precisely what Wells achieves in *War of the Worlds*, bounding over and beyond the comparatively narrow and evanescent questions of current affairs and into the wider yet more enduring domain of social inquiry. By sailing further out upon the seas of speculation into the deeper, less well-charted waters of the vaguely possible, Wells was able to explore advances in weaponry and the concomitant changes in warfare that seemed fantastic in his day. Yet only four decades later, it was reasonable to compare and discuss the new technologies of mechanized warfare in terms of the 'fantastical' weapons he had imagined. Analogous speculations on how contemporary warfare and weapons may change in the next twenty or thirty years are no less valuable and instructive. Indeed, the evidence suggests that since the pace of change continues to accelerate, so too will wars be waged with ever-newer technologies. Consequently, just as Wells' far-future tales often achieved superior technological and sociological insight and prevision at the expense of immediate and specific historico-political anticipation, so too might many contemporary 'far-future' war narratives.

This may be because, according to Robert A. Heinlein, a true 'hard' science fiction writer is not an armchair anticipator, but a 'synthesizing prophet.' As such, this species of author has

> another advantage over the specialist; he knows, from experience and by examining the efforts of other prophets *of his type* in the past that his 'wildest' predictions are more likely to come true than the ones in which he lost his nerve and was cautious. This statement is hard to believe but can be checked by comparing past predictions with present facts. (Show me the man who honestly believed in the atom bomb twenty years ago—but H.G. Wells predicted it in 1911.[3]) (The 'wild fantasies' of Jules Verne turned out to be much too conservative.)[4]

Although many critics and analysts have (with good reason) challenged Heinlein's forcefully enunciated conviction in the 'prophetic' powers of science fiction,[5] it is interesting to note that one of the most conservative and skeptical of all discursive communities, the military, has repeatedly placed great confidence in Heinlein's speculations. Indeed, advanced projects administrators in America's armed forces have not merely acknowledged the pertinence and influence of future-war authors, they have employed them to work in direct advisory capacities at the very highest levels of military technology assessment and development projects. This naturally invites a cautious investigator to question whether such authors are predicting or making the future. As Chris Hables Gray asks in '"There Will Be War!": Future-war Fantasies and Militaristic Science Fiction in the 1980s,' has future-war fiction been 'pretty good futurology' or 'self-fulfilling prophecies?'[6] The logical response is that both alternatives indicate the profound political influence of the genre and its authors. Either future-war fiction predicts the shape of the coming battlefield, thereby informing those who will one day fight upon it, or it helps to 'create' that battlefield through its cultural and technological influence. The most likely answer is that both processes are at work, in varying degrees, at all times.

A clear example of this potentially bi-directional discursive fusion and synthesis can be found in the career of Robert A. Heinlein. An Annapolis graduate with various technical accomplishments, Heinlein also had a keen ear for vernacular and a sharp eye for emerging trends, all of which combined to create one of the most distinctive and influential voices in American science fiction. Furthermore, his involvement with special naval projects during World War II allowed him to keep his finger on the pulse of advanced military thought and ambitions, and kept him connected with senior officers whose interests were almost as speculative and extrapolative as his own. According to Heinlein (as mentioned earlier, in Chapter 5),[7] he recruited a number of science fiction writers to work on the Philadelphia Naval Yard projects, doing so under the auspices of his old Annapolis classmate, Lieutenant Commander (later Admiral) A. B. Scoles. Heinlein himself worked on radar, the Kamikaze countermeasures study, and materials development for hypersonic aircraft.[8] There is also considerable evidence that Heinlein worked on a number of advanced weapons systems, including anti-missile missiles and weapon automation: in short, even his military research work was the stuff of which future-war fiction is made.

Heinlein's involvement with the military and aerospace communities persisted after the war ended, largely because of the fame and influence he acquired through his work as a 'synthesizing prophet.' Indeed, by the 1950s, Heinlein's creative output was already being seriously eroded by the popular attention and requests he was receiving—from military and science elites, as well as from wide-eyed adolescent males.[9] Invitations to the nation's premier technomilitary centers and special demonstrations became commonplace; among many other honors, he was a distinguished civilian guest on board the flight of an early version of the B-1 bomber, delivered the 1972 James Forrestal Memorial lecture to the cadets at Annapolis, and received the Distinguished Public Service Medal from NASA (posthumously).[10]

Given the respect accorded Heinlein by both military professionals and fellow authors, it is hardly surprising that many of his relationships and activities bridged the gaps between these two communities, thereby illustrating the influence accrued by having membership and stature in both discursive domains. Gray points out that it was particularly appropriate that the first official use of science fiction writers as military analysts was organized by Robert Heinlein, 'since several of his stories have been seminal in establishing the main themes and approaches of military sf.'[11] However, over the decades, these early, almost opportunistic patterns of interaction and exchange became increasingly prevalent and intensely codified. By the 1980s, the relationship between the science fiction and military communities had become one not merely of overt common interest, cooperation, and occasional consultancy, but had evolved into joint, institutionalized future-war 'think tanks.' There are numerous examples of this trend toward official integration of military and science fiction discourses. In 1985, a meeting called 'Futurist II' was held at Wright Patterson Air Force Base which brought together at least forty specialists in future war and weaponry—of which eight were future-war authors. This meeting, a successor to an earlier, top-secret 'Futurist I' conference,[12] addressed issues of weapons development and potential combat scenarios. It also explored the social implications of war and peace-making. Science fiction author Joe Haldeman, one of the invitees, later wrote (in the Introduction to *Space Fighters*) that 'We saw the future there . . .'[13] and that the writers and the soldiers were, in many ways, cut from the same cloth —much more so than the futurists, whom Haldeman describes as being (comparatively) 'stodgy and conservative.'[14] More recently, science fiction authors have become a regular feature at the Air Force Academy's Nexus lecture series, and Joe Haldeman and others were tapped for their expertise by the research and planning team that compiled the Air University's 1996 white paper, *Air Force 2025*.

A slightly different example of future-war authors serving as expert consultants and commentators took place at the January 1986 conference on small arms held by the Army Joint Services Small Arms program at the Battelle Institute in Seattle. Hard science fiction author Frederick Pohl attended, as well as Dean Ing (co-author of *Mutual Assured Destruction*) and other future-war fiction writers.[15] What is particularly interesting about this meeting is the subject itself: small arms development is not a field that is particularly amenable to input from 'generalists.' Rather, small arms development is a highly specialized process driven by the prevailing limits of technology and a sophisticated understanding and projection of the likely course in which small unit tactics will evolve. By implication, then, the degree of military expertise, or at least topical interest, of any attending science fiction authors would need to be relatively high for them to be of any use to the military.

It would also indicate that military and weapon experts know of and value the competence of many such future-war authors. This then is the endpoint, and decisive evidence, of the 'trickle-up' process of the genre's political influence: the formal recruitment of future-war authors who have already earned the respect of, or inspired, the leading experts in various technomilitary discourses. In order to establish a complete model of how future-war authors and texts enter and influence domains of official discourse, it only remains to illustrate how they first inspire or impress the experts within those domains. Once again, Heinlein's writing offers an excellent example of how this might occur.

Arguably, in terms of pertinent narrative content, publication history, and plentiful technologically significant 'prognostications,' no future-war text can rival Robert A. Heinlein's 1959 novel *Starship Troopers*. With considerable accuracy, *Starship Troopers* graphically and specifically anticipated personal military equipment and weapons that are the equivalent of (or still well beyond) today's most advanced systems. Thirty to forty years before they were realized, Heinlein was foreseeing not only specific combat technologies but was envisioning how they would combine to create a radically new battlefield: one that was fluid, electronic, and largely automated. In the first twenty pages of *Starship Troopers,* Heinlein (literally) drops the reader into the middle of an urban firefight. There, his narrator uses proleptic analogs of many of today's cutting-edge or experimental technologies such as a personal head's-up display (HUD) slaved to a (laser?) rangefinder, GPS equivalent, and personal computer:

> [I] thumbed the switch for a proximity reading and read it when it flashed on in the instrument reflector inside my helmet in front of my forehead. . . .[T]he work is actually going on above and back of your head. . . . [Y]ou can flip through your several types of radar displays quicker than you can change channels to avoid a commercial —catch a range and bearing, locate your boss, check your flank men, whatever.[16]

—battlefield CAD-CAM/3-D graphics computers connected to a broadcast or satellite network:

> The artist-engineer had done double sketching and the box had combined them into a stereo picture of the first thousand feet under the surface. . . . I reported it to Blackie. He cut me off . . . 'Major Landry relayed a facsimile to me.'[17]

—flip-up, flip-down night vision goggles:

> [I]nfrared snoopers let you size up terrain quite well after you are used to them. The river that cut diagonally through the city was almost below me and coming up fast, shining out clearly with a higher temperature than the land.[18]

—personal self-guided (i.e. 'fire-and-forget') missiles:

> I . . . raised the launcher to my shoulder, found the target and pulled the first trigger to let the rocket have a look at its target—pulled the second trigger and kissed it on its way . . .[19]

—multi-plexing communications with secure and encrypted channel redundancy:

> The assortment of safe circuits we had available in the new model comm units certainly speeded things up; [Sgt.] Jelly could talk to

# MAKING MAN-MACHINES OF MASS DESTRUCTION    215

anybody or to his section leaders; a section leader could call his whole section, or his non-coms; and the platoon could muster twice as fast, when seconds matter.[20]

—real-time two-way communication with rear area/staff analysts:

'I am surrounded . . . and they are still pouring out . . . Captain, do you think this could be just a diversion? With their real breakthrough somewhere else?'

'Could be,' he admitted. 'Your report is patched through right to Division, so let them do the thinking.'[21]

—and a powered exoskeletal frame that receives commands directly through biomechanical feedback sensors:

The 'muscles,' the pseudo-musculature, gets all the publicity but it's the control of all that power which merits it. . . . [H]ere's how it works, minus the diagrams. The inside of the suit is a mass of pressure receptors, hundreds of them. You push with the heel of your hand; the suit feels it, amplifies it, pushes with you to take the pressure off the receptors that gave the order to push.[22]

The actual analogs of these revolutionary pieces of equipment are only now being developed for standard adoption, are still prototypes, or are evolving slowly in the computers of designers. First-generation equivalents of the personal communications, sensors, computing, and interface technologies that Heinlein proposes are currently undergoing field trials in the Land Warrior program conducted under the auspices of the US army. The Land Warrior project's goals (cited below) are suspiciously reminiscent of the operational standards of Heinlein's Mobile Infantry:

This system will allow infantrymen to operate in all types of weather and at night . . . In conjunction with other components, a soldier can even shoot around corners without exposing himself to enemy fire.

The integrated helmet assembly is lighter and more comfortable than today's helmet . . . It has a helmet-mounted monocular day display, a night sensor with flat panel display, a laser detection module, ballistic/laser eye protection, a microphone and a headset.

The protective clothing and individual equipment subsystem incorporates modular body armor and upgrade plates that can stop small-arms rounds fired point-blank. It includes an integrated load bearing frame, chemical/biological protective garments and modular rucksack.

. . . The computer processor is fused with radios and a Global Positioning System locator. A handgrip . . . allows the wearer to

> change screens, key on the radio, change frequencies and send digital information.
>
> ... With the equipment, leaders and soldiers can exchange information. Soldiers using their weapon-mounted camera, for example, can send videos to their leaders.
>
> Finally, the software subsystem includes tactical and mission support modules, maps and tactical overlays, and the ability to capture and display video images.[23]

While the Mobile Infantry's nuclear-tipped fire-and-forget missiles have not been created (at least openly), the technology base now exists to attempt it: actual weapons like Javelin, a self-targeting anti-armor system, possess all the necessary performance characteristics other than range and nuclear capability.

Lastly, even the 'powered armor' of the *Starship Troopers* is edging its way gradually on to designer's boards. The Defense Advanced Research and Planning Agency (DARPA) currently has a technology development initiative entitled 'Exoskeletons for Human Performance Augmentation,' and although the engineering is in the conceptual stages, the concept itself is close kin to Heinlein's vision of high-tech armor, sans jump-jets.

But Heinlein's new hardware is only half of his future-war story—and it is the lesser half. Heinlein's descriptions, both of combat and training, primarily emphasize that war and warriors will—indeed, must—be forever changed as a result of these innovations. In *Starship Troopers*, the industrial-age war of attrition is a distant memory; even the Vietnam-era squad-and-platoon level of maneuver and engagement is over. In its place is a new emphasis on individual, or small team, action. This is a necessity on Heinlein's horrifically lethal battlefield, where the primary rules for survival and operation anticipated those being drilled into today's young officer candidates:

> You're always heavily outnumbered; surprise and speed are what saves you . . . never stay in one place more than a second or two, never give them time to target in on you. Be somewhere else, anywhere. Keep moving.[24]

It is a battlefield where hesitation is suicide and initiative is everything: 'As they keep telling you in Basic, doing something constructive at once is better than figuring out the best thing to do hours later.'[25] It is also a battlefield where, conforming to the trend adduced by Wells in *Anticipations*, destructive power is always greater than defensive protection. This is why Heinlein's troops are called the *Mobile* Infantry, not the *Armored* Infantry. Speed is the key to their survival, not protection: 'A

# MAKING MAN-MACHINES OF MASS DESTRUCTION   217

suit isn't a space suit . . . It is not primarily armor . . .'[26] Anticipating current personal armor design doctrine, Heinlein's suit is not designed to be invulnerable to serious direct attacks, but is primarily intended to provide adequate protection against shrapnel, blast effects, and even lower-velocity bullets:

> I took a couple of near misses with explosives, close enough to rattle my teeth even inside armor and once I was brushed by some sort of beam that made my hair stand on end and half paralyzed me for a moment . . . [S]omebody took a shot at me . . . just a slug that bounced off my armor, made my ears ring, and staggered me without hurting me.[27]

At the conclusion of the assault, Heinlein also provides an illustration of the consequences of either depending too much on one's armor, not moving quickly enough—or being unlucky: '[T]here was actually a *hole* in his armor and blood coming out. . . . Flores died on the way up.'[28]

Heinlein's narrator summarizes the military importance of this suit as follows:

> Our suits give us better eyes, better ears, stronger backs (to carry heavier weapons and more ammo), better legs, more intelligence ('intelligence' in the military meaning; a man in a suit can be just as stupid as anybody else—only he had better not be), more firepower, greater endurance, less vulnerability.[29]

One can only wonder if the exoskeleton researchers at DARPA cribbed their copy from Heinlein when they wrote their program description and solicitation papers:

> The overall goal of this program is to develop devices and machines that will increase the speed, strength, and endurance of soldiers in combat environments . . .
>
> Inclusion of exoskeleton technology into land based operations will extend the mission payload and/or mission range of the soldier. Exoskeletons will also increase the lethality and survivability of ground troops for short range and special operations. The enhanced mobility and load carrying capability provided by the exoskeleton will allow soldiers to carry more ballistic protection and heavy weaponry. To meet the challenges set forth, DARPA is soliciting devices and machines that accomplish one or more of the following: 1) assist pack-loaded locomotion, 2) prolong locomotive endurance, 3) increase locomotive speed, 4) augment human strength, and 5) leap extraordinary heights and/or distances. These machines should

be anthropomorphic and capable of bearing distributed loads, such as that generated by extensive armor protection, as well as typical pack loads.[30]

None of the technologies depicted by Heinlein existed in 1959, yet all are presented in considerable detail—and in the first twenty pages of *Starship Troopers*. These twenty pages did not languish in obscurity. Never out of print since it was first published, *Starship Troopers* went through 14 printings in its first nine years, inspiring all manner of slang references in the defense industry and, most significantly, leaving readers with a vision of what the future of combat technology might be like. Given the extraordinary similarity between the technologies proposed in *Starship Troopers* and those currently in use or development, it seems that Heinlein either was expert at extrapolating how the technology of 1959 would evolve, or influenced the evolution of such technologies by creating an exacting, if purely imaginary, portrayal of their future development. Heinlein's own stated authorial intentions support at least the first hypothesis. In a letter to his agent, Lurton Blassingame, Heinlein explained that 'My real claim to being a student of the future, if I have a claim, lies in noting things going on now and then in examining speculatively what those trends could mean.'[31]

On closer consideration, Heinlein's extrapolative expertise implies that he may also have created images that shaped actualizations. Just as Saussure suggests that humans are unable to hold or manipulate concepts without having words to describe them, perhaps the human capacity for technical invention is analogously dependent upon guiding images from which to proceed. Certainly, Thomas Kuhn's arguments regarding the essentiality of suitable analogical images for the advancement of science suggests that the necessary ideational precursors for technological innovation might similarly emerge from future-war narratives such as *Starship Troopers*. It is easy enough to propose a model for this: contemporary 1959 technologies enabled Heinlein to envision vastly evolved offshoot devices. Heinlein then sited these advanced devices within a narrative, giving them a 'pseudo-reality' via imaginary but empirically consistent technological and sensory details. Finally, readers of this narrative, particularly those who were willing to suspend disbelief and accept the 'pseudo-reality' of the advanced devices, had detailed images of technologies that might one day be created. The specificity of these images imparts a form of solidity to the projected devices. It also privileges these devices in the memory of readers, for amid the almost infinite field of other possible technological developments, these few have been given shape, weight, color, operating parameters, even limitations and quirks: a set of discrete properties that

MAKING MAN-MACHINES OF MASS DESTRUCTION 219

may become a murmuring voice at the back of those minds which will actually conceive or create the next generation of technological advancement. And imaginative voices such as these often speak most loudly and most frequently within the technocratic domain of the military-industrial complex. Whether an exact duplicate—or even vaguely corresponding analog—of such fictional devices result from this form of narrative influence is not the point: that an image has the power to influence those who direct techno-military research is all that is implied by this model. That such images are often recapitulated in the form of actual devices years later, and that future-war authors are asked to participate in the creation of these devices, suggests both the direct and tangible presence of this influence.

This model enjoys the additional benefit of having evidentiary corroboration. In gathering evidence that might confirm or disprove this hypothesis, I conducted extensive interviews with two highly placed design and development personnel at McDonnell-Douglas Corporation in March 1996.[32] In the interest of brevity, the relevant highlights of only one of those interviews is included here, in an attempt to shed light upon how such narrative influence might 'trickle up' from speculative authors to actual engineers.[33]

The interview in question was conducted on March 7, near the McDonnell-Douglas complex in St. Louis, Missouri. The interview subject was Jerry McClellan, Chief Program Engineer for incorporating new technologies into the (then new) 'E' version of the F-18 fighter aircraft. Prior to this assignment (which he had been in for three years), he was the Director of Active Signature Technology (in San Diego) and before that had spent several years as the chief designer for new technology on the 'ATF' or 'Advanced Tactical Fighter' project. Prior to his employment at McDonnell-Douglas, he had worked for Lockheed, mostly providing field service management for clients, but he also had contact with the SR-71 Blackbird project. It was understood in advance that Mr. McClellan might have to decline answering any questions that touched on classified matters or materials. This limitation arose frequently—and at extremely telling moments.[34]

Mr. McClellan proved to be an avid reader of future-war fiction, whether of the hard science fiction or technothriller variety. At one point (because he occasionally could not recall the name of a specific text or author), he quantified his interest by remarking that 'We should have done this at my house . . . [I] . . . [p]robably have 800–1000 books in my bookcase; . . Probably 70–80% of those are science fiction . . . [and] . . . I've got all of Clancy's.'[35] McClellan's greatest interest was in 'hard' science fiction; he explained that his 'favorite author . . . is Asimov. The guy had

. . . extremely novel ideas about future worlds.'[36] Indeed, a writer's credentials as either a scientist or a painstaking researcher were very important to McClellan, both in his choice of favorite authors and in the credence he accorded their ideas: 'that's one of the reasons that Asimov's one of my favorites. Technically there's very little if anything wrong . . . I mean, things that he describes can be done. . . . [H]e doesn't talk about time passage or wormholes where you just step in and bang, you're out the other end, 85 million light years in half a second travel time. . . . In his writings, . . . it's feasible.'

Conversely, among the subcategories of speculative fiction discussed, McClellan was least interested in non-scientific fantasy. Instead, after giving a brief response to the fantasy inquiries, he abruptly changed the topic, commenting, 'You know, I've read everything of Clancy's and I really liked his stuff.' McClellan noted that his level of interest and his choice of favorite topics within future-war fiction are not particularly unusual among workers within his industry. When asked to comment on whether or not any coworkers shared similar interests, he indicated that 'about 25–30%' had a discernible interest, and almost all of these evinced 'roughly the same' degree of intensity and seriousness in their preferences.[37]

The next part of the interview was particularly revealing, and was strongly confirmatory of this project's 'trickle-up, trickle-down' model of narrative influence. McClellan was asked whether he had seen 'operational capacities' (rather than the underlying technologies), that had formerly been the province of science fiction, 'become reality.' He answered, 'Not first-hand, but . . . Yeah, definitely some of that. . . . I definitely see that going on,' and later indicated that he had been not merely a witness to, but a participant in, such incidents. An edited selection from that portion of the interview follows:

> Interviewer: How similar were the technological methods whereby the [originally imaginary] operational capacity was actually realized versus the way it was represented in science fiction?
> McClellan: I guess the only instances that I can remember *are* in the classified world and I can't talk about them.
> Interviewer: What about predictions that touch upon *your* areas of expertise? Have you witnessed any changes . . . that were first postulated as science fiction?
> McClellan: I definitely have but I really can't go into anything about them.
> Interviewer: How do you feel about the hypothesis that science fiction images set a goal, start areas of inquiry, and shape the responses? Unlikely? Likely?

# MAKING MAN-MACHINES OF MASS DESTRUCTION    221

McClellan (nodding to indicate an affirmative to the 'likely' alternative): Absolutely. I wouldn't say every science fiction book does, but I would say that definitely a lot of it comes from there.

Interviewer: Have you ever experienced that yourself in your work, or in terms of hearing people talk [about their work]?

McClellan: There have been some. Yes, but— (Interviewee shakes head, declining further comment with a gesture that refers back to the earlier agreement regarding answers prohibited by the classified nature of the subject matter).

Interviewer: So [you claim that] images set a goal. Have you *seen* it set a goal?.

McClellan: Yeah! I, I know specifically things like that have happened. (A long pause; the interviewee does not elaborate.)

Interviewer: And this, again, is an area you can't talk about?

McClellan: Right.

(Then, in a later attempt to reapproach the topic after the interviewee begins speaking of the influence of such fiction on 'the next developments' in military aerospace—)

Interviewer: [What about] weapons technology?

McClellan: Can't talk about it.

Interviewer: Can you remember any of these 'next developments' that you've been talking about?

McClellan: Yes, some of them: most definitely.

Interviewer: Can you remark what books [inspired them]?

McClellan: Uh . . .

Interviewer: You don't have to mention specifics, such as 'Oh, I saw this [innovation] in that work.' But I mean just a sense of . . .

McClellan: No, 'cause I'm afraid if I talk about the specific piece of science fiction, it's fairly easy to [infer the relevant innovation].

Interviewer: Have your own science fiction readings given you ideas regarding technical . . . innovations?

McClellan: Yeah, but unfortunately it's always been what you can do in the classified world with it.

Interviewer: Pardon me?

McClellan: (restating) Because the ones that I've specifically done that with [i.e. ideas imported from narratives to the actual workplace] have all wound up in the classified world.

As revealing as the preceding responses may be, McClellan's most interesting and decisive comments arose not in direct answer to any interview question, but as spontaneous additions of his own. When responding to a question about whether or not he thought there was a 'predictive' component to science fiction, McClellan remarked that he had never really thought of science fiction as prediction. Instead

> I think . . . you get a certain class of science fiction writers that can make leaps of technology and can write very interesting stories about whatever that thing is. And then you get engineers or physicists that read, see, hear about it, and then start turning it into reality, so I don't know that you can call that a prediction. It's kind of a cause-and-effect, rather than a prediction. . . . The way I . . . viewed it . . . is that you have two kinds of creative people. You have the abstract creative people; I guess those are the kind of 'hard core' science fiction writers that are . . . coming up with wild ideas—something that no one has thought of before. And then you've got the more logical but creative class of people, the engineers, that don't seem to be capable of making that leap into . . . the abstract, but once someone exposes them to an idea, then they can start to put together different things in a very creative way to make some of that stuff happen.

What is most striking about this commentary is that McClellan is actually suggesting that science fiction's power to directly *shape* research, technology development, and the political agenda to pursue them is more tangible, more important, and ultimately, more influential than are its postulated *predictive* qualities. Coming from a senior design engineer who has been involved in some of the nation's most important and classified weapons development and research projects, this assertion is not only extremely provocative, but extraordinarily authoritative. Who but an insider can testify to the prevalence and influence of such narratives on the actual processes of engineering discourse, design, and actualization that take place within the technomilitary communities? Given William Broad's revealing and corroborative interviews with SDI's young Star Warriors at Livermore Labs, McClellan's comments support the proposition that this discursive dynamic is the rule, rather than the exception, within the military R&D community. Indeed, most of the other defense industry engineers that I polled (informally) were at least as emphatic in asserting a 'cause-and-effect' relationship between the ideas and images presented in hard science fiction and the actual research and development initiatives undertaken by the military-industrial complex.

Although McClellan made no extensive mention of Heinlein, he was quite familiar with *Starship Troopers* and considered it a landmark text, not only in terms of technological imagination, but social foresight. This points to another process whereby such texts and authors exert influence over the military-industrial complex: they reinspect, and even reimagine, the prevailing military ethos. Certain science fictional assessments of the changing social perspective upon war and warriors are not only well known to military personnel, but have become significant referents for their professional discussions upon the same topic. This suggests that those authors who evince expertise in both scientific and military domains may have the potential to exert a particularly powerful form of combined influence over certain elite readers. Colloquially put, if a military reader listens with increased attentiveness to a military author, just as a technician listens to a technically adept author, then an author with both familiarities (and a gift for breezy, engaging, prose) may have an influence upon both scientists and soldiers that is both sweeping and enduring. There is compelling evidence that this is the case with Heinlein: certainly the VIP status of his later years suggests it. Furthermore, the influence and authority of his future-war fictions seem to be growing. In their extremely authoritative and influential 1996 text, *The Future of War: Power, Technology and American World Dominance in the 21$^{st}$ Century*, George and Meredith Friedman invoke the image, doctrine, and even equipment of Heinlein's Starship Troopers as the model for the resurgence of 'The Poor Bloody Infantry.'[38] In a similar vein, the Mobile Infantry of *Starship Troopers* is invoked as an ideal model for the next century's soldiers in *Air Force 2025* (1996): in his keynote paper 'Brilliant Warriors,' Lt. General Jay W. Kelley, USAF, asserts:

> [W]e have taken people already committed to the warrior profession and must train and educate them in such a way that by 2025, as compared to today, they will be brilliant—smart, adept, agile, savvy—professional warriors. Take away the gizmos of Robert Heinlein's *Starship Trooper* [sic] and use that image to envision the best in tomorrow's warriors. They should have all the attitudes and behaviors that allow them to survive, succeed, and lead others in whatever future we find ourselves. They must be lifelong learners, thinkers, and prudent risk-takers.[39]

That same year, an even more telling example of the influence of *Starship Troopers* (37 years after it was published) appeared in what is arguably the most august, conservative, and buttoned-down of all military journals. In the November 1996 issue of the *Proceedings of the US Naval Institute*, there appeared an article entitled 'We Can Make Real Starship Troopers.' The headlining picture showed a recent copy of Heinlein's classic protruding from the back pocket of a Marine's camouflage fatigues (Figure 3). The author, Captain Robert Smullen, USMC, assesses Marine training and readiness against that of the star-hopping Mobile Infantry—and finds his own service lacking. Smullen's solution: use Heinlein's elite troopers as literal models for an overhaul of the Corps' training programs:

*Figure 3  Heinlein's* Starship Troopers *appears to have become an almost ubiquitously used (and accepted) master-metaphor and referent within the discursive domains of American military organizations, particularly since 1990—more than thirty years after it was first published. This photograph is from an article in* Proceedings.

MAKING MAN-MACHINES OF MASS DESTRUCTION   225

The Infantry Officer Course and the School of Infantry for enlisted marines are only the start in creating a real 'Starship Trooper.' One of Robert Heinlein's futuristic warriors, a Starship Trooper is someone who can think and act independently, with self-discipline and the will to complete missions without coercion. He masters information technology to apply its combat efficiencies at the tactical level, while still appreciating the operational art of war and understanding his contributions at that level. . . .

The marine infantryman of the 21$^{st}$ century will have to . . . operate as part of small, isolated groups on a dispersed and dangerous battlefield. . . . [H]e will be more than a technician who just mans systems. He will be what he has always been—a warrior who has deliberately become a sophisticated user of such systems.

What technology promises is greater combat efficiency on a man-for-man basis. This makes each infantryman even more valuable, hence the focus on cohesion and the time investment necessary to create units that can live up to the standards of the *Starship Troopers*.[40]

One reader of Smullen's article was Alan Brown, a Commander in the Coast Guard Reserve and a member of the Science Fiction Writers of America, who observed that

I have always known that there was an affinity between military personnel and the science fiction audience (the folks at the local Waldenbooks tell me this has been measured through market research, science fiction sells better near military bases). But I never imagined that such a respectful reference to science fiction would be found in an otherwise conservative professional journal.[41]

Smullen's article is most significant not for its content, nor for the 'respect' it accords Heinlein and *Starship Troopers*, nor even for the purposeful attempt to promote Heinlein's 'cap troopers' as the technological and psychological model of the new Marine. Its most significant feature is this: published without preamble or extensive contextualization in the *Proceedings*, the article's author and editors expected that a sizable majority of the *Proceedings* subscribers have read and remember Heinlein's 1959 future-war novel. Their expectations were evidently correct: no confused letters or protests were stimulated by Smullen's article. In light of such evidence, it seems very reasonable to assert that *Starship Troopers* has not merely crossed into the realm of military discourse, but is an integral, even fundamental, part of it. A quick search of the web offers further confirmation of this: using only two commonly available search engines (Alta Vista and Google), testing for the terms 'Heinlein' and 'Starship Troopers,' and excluding those sources already cited, nine separate government or military websites (i.e., '.gov,' '.mil) contained references to this author and this particular text as the basis of an argument or in support of a given proposal.[42] Numerous other sites belonging to professional theorists or commentators (i.e. those with official connections or military rank) were also discovered. Scholarly or serious references that exist outside of the net cast by these search engines, or in print format alone, can only be a matter of speculation, but it seems very likely that numerous examples would exist.

As was the case with Heinlein, most serious future-war authors evince high levels of familiarity with, and even expertise in, diverse aspects of military doctrine, tactics, and technology. The far-future battle-stories in John Dalmas' *The Regiment*, David Drake's *Hammer's Slammers*, and many others are supplemented by extended technical descriptions of imaginary infantry weapons, often included in special appendices rather than within the narrative itself. For instance, of the 274 pages of Drake's *Hammer's Slammers*, 23 are 'Interludes' that provide basic technical information on 'Supertanks,' 'Powerguns,' and a regimental 'Table of Organization and Equipment,' just to mention a few of the topics.

However, the great preponderance of the future-war genre's foundations are rooted in the weighty mass of very-near-future technothrillers produced by authors such as Tom Clancy, Larry Bond, and Harold Coyle. These texts, which are much more contemporary in their focus on policy issues and incipient technologies, exert a different variety of political influence. Whereas far-future war fiction posits radical new technology and tactics, the technothriller is often little more than a primer on current military capabilities, given dramatic impetus by a single, speculative 'what if—?' change in the international or technological realities of the current day. The political influence of such texts is therefore mostly of the 'trickle-down' variety: a dissemination of new technological information, an investigation of one (or more) global flashpoints that could erupt into conflict, and the combat conditions and consequences that result when the aforementioned new technology is employed in the latter conflict. Once again, many technothriller authors have military or defense industry backgrounds (e.g. Coyle and Bond), although this is hardly a prerequisite for popularity or credibility among the military community. Clancy, who has no significant military background, has become a much-admired and much-courted figure in the defense establishment, and is particularly respected for his painstaking and extremely accurate technomilitary speculations.[43] This enthusiasm is apparently undimmed by the occasional national security problems created by his 'speculative disclosures' of classified capabilities, or by the obverse possibility that much of the 'extrapolation' may in fact be based on information leaks. For instance, interview subject Jerry McClellan professed an extremely strong appreciation of Clancy's works, even though he felt that 'When I read *Red Storm Rising*, it was clear to me that man somehow found out about classified information, because there were some systems that he described in that book that I had access to when I was in the Air Force, that were—when *I* was "in" [the service]—classified and were still classified when that book came out.' McClellan was then asked, 'Do you think it's impossible for someone to get that data by reading between the lines, by inferring technological specifics as a result of a thorough strategic analysis of the assumed operational capacities of a given military unit?' McClellan responded, 'Some of the descriptions he gave were too accurate, too specific for that. . . . You had some "bar talk" [i.e. indiscreet disclosures of classified information while intoxicated] in there someplace.'

Bar talk or not, former Secretary of Defense Caspar Weinberger wrote a glowing review of Clancy's *Patriot Games* for the *Wall Street Journal* (which was subsequently reprinted in the *Friday Review of Defense Literature of the Pentagon*) and ex-Vice President Dan Quayle paid *Red Storm Rising* the supreme compliment when he invoked it as evidence while participating in a debate on developing military technologies. Fortunately, Quayle's questionable military perspicacity and/or ability to distinguish fact from fiction are not, ultimately, the issues here. Rather, as James William Gibson has commented, the major significance of Quayle's remark is that he assumed—and the nation did not question—that *Red Storm Rising* was an authoritative source upon which to found discussions of national policy.[44]

Whether or not technothrillers or far-future war fictions are authoritative, they also are believed to wield considerable influence over many individuals involved in the military's rapidly increasing investment in automation, computers, and even the prospects of direct man–machine interfaces (or 'cyborging'). As Gray remarks, 'Today, on the cutting, "hairier" edges of computer science . . . sf plays a major role in defining what is possible, and just as important, what is interesting. . . . It is also an integral part of real policy-making as well.'[45] What is currently of greatest interest to the key shapers of the day-to-day political ecology of the American military-industrial complex is the idea of the man-machine, the ultimate fusion of sophisticated thought and processing speed.

One of the best illustrations of this highly detailed interest in how man–machine interfaces might alter the future battlefield is found in S. M. Stirling's 1988 short story 'Necessity.'[46] This same narrative is also noteworthy for the manner in which it simultaneously employs both 'trickle-up' and 'trickle-down' discursive strategies, depicting combat technologies that are partly drawn from today's cutting-edge research, and partly fabricated from more radical speculations upon future innovations. Set several hundred years in the future, 'Necessity' begins with an entry from a fictional technical reference, *McGraw's Encyclopedia of Military Science, 82nd Edition (New Aberdeen, 2628)*, which reads like a listing in a *Jane's* military reference book.[47] Through this narrative conceit, Stirling introduces a small arm—'the DZ-7 Light Assault Rifle'—in compelling detail. One meter in length and three kilograms when loaded, Stirling's weapon is partly imaginary, but also incorporates the latest contemporary achievements in small arms design. Its pertinent statistics are

> Ammunition: 7mm × 20mm caseless. Crystal monofilament core, treated glass sabot.
> Muzzle velocity: 2,800 meters per second
> Range: 1,000 meters maximum; 800 meters soft targets; 300 hard targets. . . .
> Sights: Electro-optical; passive light-enhancement, random-variable laser designator, infra-red (with computer display analysis of subsurface structures). May be programmed for burst selection or slaved to master computer.[48]

These specifications are particularly interesting when compared with those of the Joint Service Small Arms Program's projected replacement for the aging M-16A2 assault rifle, the Objective Infantry Combat Weapon (OICW):

> The OICW combines the lethality of novel 20mm air bursting munitions, 5.56mm NATO ammunition, and a full solution fire control system to produce a leap-ahead capability in small arms system effectiveness. The OICW's 20mm ammunition includes a miniature electronic fuze that permits the projectile to air burst at the appropriate target range. This capability enables the successful defeat of both exposed and defilade targets (individuals behind cover, within trenches, behind trees, on rooftops, etc)- a capability which current individual weapon systems cannot effectively provide the users. . . .
> The OICW fire control is the 'brains' behind the system and includes an accurate laser range finder, ballistic computer, direct view optics, video camera, electronic compass, thermal module, and an automatic target tracker. . . . This combinatorial weapon system will provide decisively violent and suppressive target effects out to 1,000 meters [49]

The DZ-7 and the OICW have identical range and extremely similar targeting, sensor, and data processing capabilities. The primary distinction is in the 'weaponry mix:' while Stirling's ammunition is a far-future technology in terms of its composition and penetration performance, he has

# MAKING MAN-MACHINES OF MASS DESTRUCTION

*Figure 4* The Objective Infantry Combat Weapon (OICW) is a shoulder-weapon that incorporates many unique design and performance features first contemplated and 'auditioned' in hard science fiction narratives. The weapon's smart munitions, micro-grenade launcher, integral laser range-finder/designator, and computer/sensor interface options were the domain of authorial invention before they became engineering actualities.

selected a 'conventional' rifle design that utilizes only a single type of ammunition and a single barrel. The OICW is a more radical, dual-barreled weapon, combining a 20mm grenade launcher with a standard 5.56 mm rifle: a very ambitious, and deadly, design (Figure 4).

Continuing through Stirling's technical briefing, the reader learns that the DZ-7 is frequently issued in conjunction with the five-kilogram, one-piece 'chameleon suit,' a computer-permeated armor which offers the following features:

(a) Protection. Multiple layers of nemourlon with boron fiber/ceramic inserts at strategic points. Full NBW protection with filters and overpressure. Will stop all shell/grenade/mortar fragments, conventional small-arms ammunition, and hypervelocity assault-rifle rounds at more than point-blank range. Filters effective against spores, etc.

(b) Sensor. Helmet contains microcomputer, 100mb RAM, AI software, option for direct neural input. Heads-up display for maps, schematics, weapon aiming points, etc. Microphone pickup for sounds, directional taps in electromagnetic communications, cryptographic and encoding capacity. Satellite links. Millimetric-wave and laser tracing, counterbattery ballistic calculations. Passive and active nightsight devices.

(c) Concealment. Fiber-optic surface and computer-scan duplicate background, incl. thermal output. Absolute match while still, high degree in motion.[50]

230    RUMORS OF WAR AND INFERNAL MACHINES

*Figure 5    Land Warrior—or Starship Trooper? Seen here with the OICW integrated into the computer-pervaded Land Warrior battle dress, the next era of infantry evolution may not boast the powered armor of Heinlein's military SF classic, but fully realizes the sensor and intelligence technology possessed by the novel's Mobile Infantry.*

Last, but most interesting, is the 'Bonephone,' a one-gram, featureless ovoid implanted behind the mastoid process and microfiber-linked to the central nervous system. This mentally activated cyborg implant provides:

(a) Communications. Acts as a medium-range radio link— 'artificial telepathy.' Multi-channel with data-linkage capability.
(b) Information processing. Limited read-write storage capacity (maps, etc.); can also interface with machinery, mainframes, etc., which have data linkage capacity. 'Picklock' tapeworm program for breaking into other systems. Can be networked to provide intelligence-enhancement programs.[51]

Once again, not all the components of Stirling's futuristic-sounding battle-garb are made from the gossamer of dreams: analogs of the major-

MAKING MAN-MACHINES OF MASS DESTRUCTION 231

ity of the 'fictional' components of the 'chameleon suit' are currently undergoing trials as part of the US Army's much-publicized Land Warrior combat dress (Figure 5). For instance, the dress includes

- A lightweight helmet with integral ballistic/laser eye-protection, monocular computer display, day/night target sensor unit, adaptable chemical/biological mask;
- Mission-tailored computer software;
- Modular, load-carrying unit [back-mounted] with integrated computer and battery, soldier and squad radios, global positioning system, video-picture capture unit;
- Thermal sight, special close-combat optics, and;
- Modular body armor, chemical/biological garments.[52]

There was even specific overlap in the materials used for ballistic protection:

[T]he armor system[s] . . . with the highest performance to weight ratio were based on the more expensive boron carbide ceramic with a high performance fiber-based (Kevlar, Spectra) composite backing.[53]

However, the greatest power of Stirling's narrative is not its combination of 'trickle-up' anticipation and 'trickle down' information dissemination, but its nature as a *narrative*. 'Necessity' does more than provide readers with a technical specifications manual that predated both Land Warrior and OICW by ten years: it brings this deadly combination of technology to life by showing it—and its cyborg-symbiot user—in action. This character, Jan Marais, is portrayed waiting to fire the weapon's

[h]ypervelocity bullets, a glass sabot wrapped around a monofilament crystal penetrator rod; the rod would blast through light armor or thick concrete, with the glass vaporizing as a lubricant. In a soft target, the glass shattered explosively and tumbled the monofilament into a small, infinitely sharp circular saw.

Snuggling the carbon-filament stock to his cheek, he squinted through the sight. Instantly the crude handwelds of the door sprang into view, mottlings of color indicating the underlying structure. Panning across, he found the hinges. . . .

Humming silently, he adjusted the rifle to six-round burst with a mental command through his bonephone, regretting that there were only a dozen of the 150-round drums left. Full auto lasted only a second and a half, but you could saw through boulders with that.

*ready,* he commanded the weapon. A red laser spot appeared in the sight; random-phased frequency shift would make the dot invisible to anyone not looking through this instrument. And the rounds would strike *exactly* where the spot lay; it even allowed for the spread on auto-fire.[54]

Significantly, when Jan fires, it is by a command sent directly through his computerized implant (the 'Bonephone'):

> *jan. now.* His finger stroked the trigger once, twice. Light erupted from the hinge areas, incandescent fragments of crystal and steel, too small to do damage. A third burst cut the bar.[55]

Stirling's somber depiction of the DZ-7 and its computer-interpenetrated and dependent wielder not only provides a powerful illustration of the distinctions between serious future-war fiction and the swashbuckling ray-gun romps of Flash Gordon and Luke Skywalker, but furnishes non-expert readers with a purposeful, detailed exploration of the latest thinking in small arms and cyborging, right down to the sensory experience of using such a combined weapons system.

Stirling's narrative also underscores how the extreme content interpenetration between science fictional and military discourses has led to their increasingly inextricable political entwinement as well. To recast this observation in terms of the now-familiar 'trickle-up/trickle-down' model, these complementary streams of expert opinion and revisionist thought, and of popular reaction and policy assessment, are now flowing so close to each other, and so interdependently, that it becomes increasingly difficult to distinguish them. Indeed, the only discursive task that remains the sole province of either of these discursive bodies is that of mainstream dissemination of information on imminent technological breakthroughs. This is left almost entirely to speculative authors, whose representations of the wars, warriors, and weapons to come reach far larger and less specialized audiences than the intermittent articles that appear in specialty journals or technical magazines such as *Popular Science* or *Proceedings of the Naval Institute*.

*****

Moving from micro- to macro-automation, the extension of the military's automation interests into the realms of remote piloting, robotics, and even artificial intelligence (AI) may also represent a very canny response to the increasing social concern over the human costs of military actions—a political sore spot for all modern democracies, but particularly for American commanders still haunted by the public outrage over Vietnam. Partly in response to changes in the rules of engagement, and the constant need to assess whether there is adequate public support for a conflict, the military has begun to appreciate—as did Edison and

Tesla at the beginning of the century—that if the casualties in a conflict were machines, not humans, the political consequences of waging war would diminish considerably. This logic, which underlies technologies such as cruise missiles, remote piloted vehicles (RPVs), and unmanned air vehicles (UAVs), was prophetically articulated by Nikola Tesla in 'The Problem of Increasing Human Energy.' In a truly mechanized war, he hypothesized that

> The loss of life will become smaller and smaller, and finally, the number of the individuals continually diminishing, merely machines will meet in a contest without bloodshed, the nations being simply interested, ambitious spectators. When this happy condition is realized peace will be assured . . .[56]

But before that 'happy condition' can be realized,

> a radical departure must be made . . . a principle which will . . . turn the battle into a mere spectacle . . . machine must fight machine. But how accomplish that which seems impossible? The answer is simple enough: produce a machine capable of acting as though it were part of a human being—no mere mechanical contrivance, comprising levers, screws, wheels, clutches, and nothing more, but a machine embodying a higher principle, which will enable it to perform its duties as though it had intelligence, experience, reason, judgment, a mind![57]

From a contemporary standpoint, Tesla's suggestion contains two rather discomfiting assumptions. First, although Tesla suggests engineering achievements that, by his era's standards, seem nothing short of miraculous, he seems to ignore or dismiss the peace-making possibilities inherent in such technological advancement. Tesla's projected level of automation might also enable humankind to eliminate or at least diminish the disparities in resources that underlie most international conflicts. Second, if we momentarily ignore the imponderable theological implications of being 'born' versus being 'made,' Tesla is espousing that 'thinking' machine-beings be given the gruesome task of annihilating each other for the detached interest and ambitions of their human creators. It would seem that if a machine were to become capable of 'performing its duties as though it had intelligence, experience, reason, judgment, a mind,' that one cannot rule out the possibility that such results might only be achieved through the creation of a form of machine sentience, or 'AI.' Although the concept of a self-aware machine seems almost as distant now as it did then, Tesla's cheerful willingness to condemn such a 'device' to a grim existence of gladiatorial combat suggests a certain cavalier ruthlessness, as well as a disregard for the troubling moral issues raised by creating 'thinking' machines to serve as lightning rods for humanity's undiminished penchant for destruction and conflict.

By the 1960s, the US military was beginning to make considerable progress in the general direction of Tesla's dubious ideal. Subversive responses to this trend were not long in coming from future-war authors who, in large part, seemed not to revile the basic principles of military automation so much as they feared the extremes to which it might be taken. This is illustrated in the work of Keith Laumer, who savagely critiqued the military's fascination with AI, often employing black humor to highlight the dangers implicit in a purely cybernetic 'solution' to the age-old problem of war-waging. Laumer's well-known 'Bolo' series postulated a future in which

> [b]y 1989 the direct ancestor of the Bolo line had been constructed by the Bolo Division of General Motors. . . . a bigger and better conventional tank, carrying a crew of three and, via power-assisted servos, completely manually operated, with the exception of the capability to perform a number of preset routine functions such as patrol duty with no crew aboard. . . . [this,] in time, gave rise to the . . . final . . . advance in Bolo technology: the self-directing (and quite incidentally, self-aware) Mark XX Model B Bolo *Tremendous*.[58]

The central point of Laumer's series is not merely the military potential of such automated machines, but the apocalyptic problems posed by this unexpected sentience, which the designer blithely dismisses:

> 'I concede that I did not anticipate the whole new level of intracybernetic function that has arisen, the manifestation of which, I am assuming, has been the cause of the unit's seemingly spontaneous adoption of the personal pronoun in its situation reports—the "self-awareness" capability, as the sensational press chooses to call it.'[59]

However, the press's alarm is well founded. The Bolo's self-awareness is not really of a human variety, for it has arisen in a being/machine that has been given only one purpose, one drive, and one instinct: to fight. The Bolo's response to impending combat is an ominous foreshadowing of the disasters to come:

> *'This is a most satisfying development. Quite abruptly my Introspection Complex was brought up to full operating level, extra power resources were made available to my Current-Action memory stage, and most satisfying of all, my Battle Reflex circuit has been activated at Active Service level. Action is impending, I am sure of it. It is a curious anomaly: I dread the prospect of damage and even possible destruction, but even more strongly I anticipate the pleasure of performing my design function.'*[60]

But the designer of the Bolo's now-sentient computer is unaware of his monster's desires, and of the grim denouement that must surely follow:

> '... I see no cause for the alarm expressed by those high-level military officers who have irresponsibly characterized the new Bolo Mark XX Model B as a potential rampaging juggernaut, which once fully activated and dispatched to the field, unrestrained by continuous external control, may turn on its makers and lay waste the continent.'[61]

The last line of Laumer's 'A Short History of the Bolo Fighting Machines' gives the lie to such technophilic overconfidence: written in the bleak centuries after these deadly and unstoppable Bolos were unleashed, the narrative reveals that:

> Many of these machines still exist in functional condition in out-of-the-way corners of the former Terran Empire. At this time the program of locating and neutralizing these ancient weapons continues.[62]

Laumer's black comedy is, therefore, a cautionary tale for modern-day Teslas who foresee only potent, unquestioning servitors as the result of their efforts to create increasingly cyberneticized soldiers.

This type of radical reassessment of the nature and consequences of combat in light of fundamental technological changes reflects the kind of extrapolation that Reginald Bretnor calls for when he exhorts his fellow authors of future-war fiction to construct 'responsible prophesies.'[63] Bretnor places particular emphasis upon the expanding significance and danger of cybernetics and 'thinking' weapons. His final comments on the subject combine exhortation with genuine anxiety: 'When we think about the special weapons, the special enabling devices, the special warriors of the future, we must always try to foresee the unexpected.'[64] In part, the military has done this by investing its interest and ingenuity in the new fields of automation and man–machine interface—the ideational descendants of Tesla's proposals. As Gray points out, the military community's interests are paralleling those of the future-war authors, in whose narratives 'artificial intelligences are a staple. As smart tanks, planes and spaceships, they buzz through all the military futurist writing, often accompanied by general purpose robots or even warbots.'[65]

Apparently, these technologies will not be 'futuristic' for very much longer. Remote operations, robotics, and limited AI devices are rapidly moving from drawing board, to proving ground, to battlefield. For instance, in the wake of the terrorist attacks against the Twin Towers and the Pentagon, the Predator RPV was rapidly moved from the classified shadows into the media spotlight, first as a reconnaissance, and later as a light weapons, platform. However, the

*Figure 6* With practical proof-of-concept provided by the success of the Predator UAV in its roles as both sensor and (retrofitted) weapons platform during 2002, the Boeing UCAV (seen here in an artist's impression) moves ever closer to becoming another example of military science fiction transmogrifying into military science fact.

most ominous of these imminent airborne Bolos may be Boeing's much more massive Unmanned Combat Air Vehicle (UCAV) (Figure 6), which

> includes a stealthy, tailless 27-foot-long vehicle with a 34-foot wing span; a reconfigurable mission control system with robust satellite relay and line-of-site [sic] communications links for distributed control in all air combat situations; and a supportability approach that includes long-term, compact storage, periodic systems testing and re-assembly for flight in just over an hour.
> 
> . . . Rich Alldredge, program manager . . . [says] 'Removing the pilot eliminates the need for pilot systems, interfaces and training, and allows for a smaller, simpler aircraft. The vehicles can also be placed in flight-ready storage for years, eliminating consumables, maintenance and personnel requirements.'
> 
> . . . The weapon systems are envisioned for the post-2010 battle-space to augment manned forces on high risk, high priority missions. The first such planned role is conducting suppression of enemy air defense missions ahead of the manned air combat force.[66]

An even more ambitious, ground-warfare analog of Boeing's UCAV project is the Defense Advanced Research Project Agency's (DARPA)

MAKING MAN-MACHINES OF MASS DESTRUCTION    237

*Figure 7   While there is no chance that Darpa's Future Combat System could achieve 'sentience' as do Keith Laumer's Bolos, the operational and motivational parallels between the two are striking. Unmanned vehicles, operating either in ROV (remote operated vehicle) or semi-autonomous mode, may become increasingly important and ubiquitous on 21st century battlefields.*

'Future Combat Systems' (FCS) where robotics is not merely a part of the multi-vehicle system, but the linchpin of its entire operational concept:

> The first concept will be for a network-centric, distributed force that will include a manned command and control element/personnel carrier, a robotic direct-fire system, a robotic non-line of sight system, an all-weather robotic sensor system, coupled with other layered sensors.[67]

To simplify the mathematics of the FCS's machine-to-human ratios, it can be described this way: of the four vehicles directly deployed along with a mechanized infantry squad, only one vehicle—the squad's APC and command vehicle—would have human occupants (Figure 7). All the rest would be remote- (or partly self-) operated—rather like Laumer's Bolos.

*****

But is this desire to follow technological prevision with industrial production, and to 'foresee the unforeseeable,' as uniformly successful as its chrome-plated achievements suggest? Is the production of new technologies—even those which save lives—the only qualitative measure of success in such cutting-edge endeavors? There is evidence that points to new human costs arising as a consequence of an automated battlefield, costs that cannot be measured in terms of combat casualties, but in intracultural conflicts. It may be that the greatest challenge implicit in the technological actualization of automated warfare does not concern successful anticipation of the next tactical or technical change, but involves a wholesale reconceptualization of our cultural concepts of 'war' and 'warriors.' As Reginald Bretnor suggested in many of his essays, humankind, and particularly superpowers, must be prepared to address the long-term consequences of these fundamental revisions. Therefore, one of the unanticipated influences of future-war fiction may rest in its possible ability to foresee how changes in military technology induce changes in culture, including new narratological and iconographic predispositions that might follow in the wake of new wars.

*Chapter 10*

# Cultural Casualties as Collateral Damage: The Fragment-ing/-ation Effects of Future-War Fantasies vs. Fictions

Automation and the mechanization of warfare have already imposed new shapes and tropes upon narratives aspiring to portray the social and personal experience of modern combat. Specifically, the personal battlefield epiphanies that were common to works as culturally and thematically diverse as Crane's *The Red Badge of Courage,* Tolstoy's *War and Peace,* Remarque's *All Quiet on the Western Front,* and Trumbo's *Johnny Got His Gun* are disappearing, along with many other traditional trappings of combat portrayals. Emerging in their place are images of the fast-paced, mechanized mayhem that came to the West's collective consciousness in the Gulf War and initiated viewers into the reality of information-age technolethality. Whether today's images simply project the immediately plausible, such as Clancy's *Red Storm Rising* and Coyle's *Team Yankee,* or push the envelope of imaginary annihilation into barely foreseeable future conflicts, the new narrative emphasis is on staccato-paced sequences of computerized carnage and mass-murdering munitions. Whether a gatling-wielding Terminator, a Starship Trooper bounding along in powered armor, or a pre-programmed Forever Warrior laden with doomsday devices, the somber introspective intervals that long characterized combat narratives have been replaced with images of incessant, instantaneous overkill. There is no time to engage in the comparative luxuries of philosophical reflection or even fear: there is just enough time to breathe in the smell of cordite and ozone before plunging back into the double-time frenzy of the postmodern firefight.

*****

Traditionally, war narratives have woven ruminations on ethics, morality, politics, ontology, and even religion into their depictions of combat. The marriage of these psychological and physical crises is often consummated as the bullets are flying. That is when Crane's Henry Fleming in *The Red Badge of Courage* realizes that after all, the 'great death' is only death, and when Paul of Remarque's *All Quiet on the Western Front* reminisces about the pastoral beauties of home.

This tendency to inject reflection and commentary into the middle of mortally dangerous experiences attains both a thematic extreme and aesthetic zenith in Hemingway's *A Farewell To Arms*. Here, during an artillery strike, Frederic Henry somehow has the extraordinary presence of mind not only to record various split-second sensory details with great precision, but to indulge in metaphysical reflection:

> Through the other noise I heard a cough, then came the chuh-chuh-chuh-chuh — then there was a flash, as when a blast furnace door is swung open, and a roar that started white and went red and on and on in a rushing wind. I tried to breathe but my breath would not come and I felt myself rush bodily out of myself and out and out and out and all the time bodily in the wind. I went out swiftly, all of myself, and I knew I was dead and that it had all been a mistake to think you just died. Then I floated, and instead of going on I felt myself slide back. I breathed and I was back. The ground was torn up and in front of my head there was a splintered beam of wood.[1]

Hemingway's impressionistic focus on personal experience typifies older representations of armed conflict. Narrator introspection and retrospection are not only possible, but integral to this experience, so that — even while a protagonist is being tossed about by the impact of an artillery shell — readers still receive a measured but very personal assessment of events.

By comparison, more recent fiction — particularly that written since the dawn of the information age — usually presents a less philosophical perspective on warfare. These new combat narratives have a markedly diminished personal component. This almost clinical detachment also advances a different aesthetic objective; whereas the earlier, 'personal' narrative was amenable to intensely subjective character study, these newer war narratives redirect their descriptive energy into an overwhelmingly male-oriented fascination with the grim technologies, swift consequences, and chilling impersonality of modern warfare. Ultimately, however, it is not the images of carnage and horror that are new, but rather their ubiquity and frequency in the narrative, unleavened by the remorse or introspection that even Le Queux admixed with his startling and graphic descriptions of civilian suffering during the shelling of London in *The Invasion of 1910*. This late twentieth-century trend toward the pitiless and relentless depiction of technowar at its most inhuman is well illustrated in the following passage from Harold Coyle's *Team Yankee* (1987), where an American infantry unit speedily, efficiently, and remorselessly dispatches a Soviet probing force:

# CULTURAL CASUALTIES AS COLLATERAL DAMAGE 241

> The men, clearly visible through Polgar's night vision goggles, were ready and like himself, tense. . . . When the lead Russian came to within ten meters, Polgar slowly released the safety on his M16, raised it to his shoulder, and fired. The single shot knocked the Russian back and unleashed the well-rehearsed and deadly ambush drill. Three of the infantrymen hit the antipersonnel mine detonators, causing thousands of small round pellets to rip through the Soviet column. The machine guns opened fire along set sectors with a withering cross-fire that knocked down those still standing after the mines had detonated. The grenadiers plunked out 40mm grenades in their sectors. The riflemen surveyed their areas and, like the grenadiers, marked their targets and took them out. . . . [T]hose lucky enough to be in the rear of the column withdrew back down the trail, pursued by a hail of bullets. Some made it.²

Although this passage from Coyle's tale of tank warfare depicts a close-quarters infantry ambush, the attack is a wholly mechanistic and depersonalized undertaking. Polgar's ambushers do not 'kill men' or 'slaughter humans;' they 'survey their areas' and then activate their 'ambush drill,' having 'marked their targets' and focused on 'their sectors' of specific responsibility.

Another passage—this one from Tom Clancy's *Red Storm Rising* (1986)—illustrates what happens when narrative description becomes completely detached from a human viewpoint; personal, sensual elements are almost completely replaced by a vivid, but more distant and horrific, tableau:

> German *Staatspolizei* had held back civilian traffic and allowed the armored units to pass, but this changed when Soviet artillery began bursting in the air close to the river. The Russians had hoped it would impede traffic, and it did. Civilians who had been late to follow orders to leave their homes now paid for their error. The artillery did scant damage to fighting vehicles but thoroughly wrecked civilian cars and trucks. In minutes, the streets of Alfeld were jammed with disabled and burning cars. People left them, braving the fire to run for the bridges, and the tanks trying to make their way to the river found their way blocked. Their only escape was over the bodies of innocent civilians . . .³

Whereas Coyle's first passage places the narrative focus someplace between the protagonist's personal experience and the observations of a more distant, omniscient narrator, the Clancy excerpt has moved entirely to the latter perspective. Clancy's cataloging of weapon effects and consequences lacks any reference to personal sensory or emotional experience. This often impersonal narrative is also devoid of any character whom we can truly designate as a sentient 'hero.' The only narrative objects with mythic stature in technothrillers such as Coyle's and Clancy's are the tanks, bombs, and guns that wreak wholesale havoc. Meanwhile, vulnerable humans scurry around like so many frantic ants, trying to dodge the descending iron boot of modern military technology.

Consequently, unless readers can associate as easily and willingly with machines as with people, the reader-as-human is being written out of these stories; the world of warfare is no longer substantively a human world. From a cultural standpoint, the choices are to quit this discursive field, or to change it so that a human element can—somehow—be reintroduced, despite the apparent insupportability of the underlying premise: that mere flesh may endure where swift steel reigns supreme. Many modern war narratives nonetheless undertake just such a desperate narrative mission: to rescue, or perhaps rehabilitate, the concept of the hero. Unfortunately, technothriller efforts to effect this 'rehabilitation' often produce protagonists who are less likable—and seemingly less human—than the machines they both depend upon and struggle against. Attempts to humanize such characters are almost inevitably ineffectual, mawkish, or hackneyed. As James William Gibson points out in *Warrior Dreams: Paramilitary Culture in Post-Vietnam America*, the 'heroes' of these tales are killers first and foremost: families, lovers and old friends are simply an encumbrance upon their ability to complete warrior quests as spies, soldiers, or commandos.[4]

Furthermore, from a narratological perspective, authorial attempts to humanize such characters are hopeless upstream struggles against the overwhelming thematic current—and marketing rationale—of the technothriller: action and violence. Character is built upon exchange and reflection: combat action is propelled by alternations of destruction and evasion. These are two diametrically opposed rhetorical masters: few authors can successfully serve them both. Therefore, the (inevitably male) technothriller protagonist—even though he may perform heroic deeds—is usually too blood-stained, too socially disconnected (or unconvincing) and too morally compromised to be a 'hero.' He is, at best, a seemingly impossible hybrid creature: he is a prosocial killer-hermit.

Consequently, we should not be surprised that future-war fiction seems to be bifurcating dramatically. One subgenre is defined by Clancy-esque technothrillers where chrome, computers, and well-groomed killers rule. The other, which has been the domain of thoughtful and socially challenging 'far-future' war fictions, is slowly succumbing to an onslaught of semi-mythic cinematic fusions between less exacting science fiction adventures and war stories. These new technofantasies tell of a land just over the temporal horizon where heroes might live once again. However, this return to the icon and image of the individual hero, exemplified by films such as *Terminator 2: Judgement Day* and the *Robocop* series, seems to be at odds with the dominant trends in military reality. This deviation also seems much more pronounced in film rather than text narratives, and usually features a hero who is simultaneously superior to, but lacking communal affiliations with, humans—thereby making him a 'double outcast.' Consequently, Hollywood imagery may be the most appropriate place to commence an inquiry into today's dominant mass media future-war trope—the male cyborg warrior-hero.

Since the hero in question is always a warrior, his weaponry is all important: it is not only his primary tool, but also his symbol, the locus of his power. Therefore, it is interesting that in these cinematic technofantasies of hero worship, there is an almost total absence of what are known as area-of-effect weapons: artillery, mines, flamethrowers, and rockets are rarely if ever encountered. There is one notable, and very important, exception to this generalization: the machine gun is not merely present in such narratives, it is ubiquitous. However, as it appears in these films, the machine gun is not used as an area-saturation weapon but as a direct-fire weapon, aimed at numerous, visible, and specific opponents whose deaths are noted individually. Consequently, one consistent weaponry pattern does emerge in these cinematic tales of cyborg soldiers: the 'new' future-war narrative avoids weapons that obscure the causal link between firer and target, between the attacker's actions and their effects. Maintaining the identity (and celebrity) of the triggerman—and the corresponding 'credit for the kill'—is all-important. Personal offensive power is being rehabilitated via explicit body-counting. It is not surprising, therefore, to discover that the dominant icons and objects associated with these warrior heroes are personal and unique in nature, rather than impersonal and generic. This is a complete reversal of what predominates in contemporary technothrillers, where Coyle's American ambushers and Clancy's unseen Soviet artillerists are simply faceless and unremarkable cogs in a greater military machine, crewing weapons made mundane by their ubiquity. Obversely, the major combatants in most recent future-war films are generally larger than average and possess tremendous physical strength; they sport impressive armor; they make use of—or have been altered to include—advanced automation or robotics; and their weapons of choice are of the automatic direct-fire variety. The epitomes of this new icon are those characters in which all these elements are present. When they are, the protagonist transcends the role of a mere soldier, even surpasses the idea of a hero. The end result is the cyborging of the Reaper, a mythic new part-man/part-machine death totem that has evolved rapidly through films such as *Terminator 2, Aliens,* and the *Robocop* series.

Even in those characters where such a synthesis is not fully realized, the male epic warrior is now identified almost entirely through his personal equipment. Although in this regard the genre may seem a departure—and a relief—from today's grim technothrillers, this focus on personal gear is not a movement forward; it is, traditionally and mythically speaking, recidivistic. It marks a return to the classical idea of the Hero, who stands not only above the crowd, but stands out from the crowd, and it is his individual iconic possessions—the symbols of his superior ability to absorb and inflict damage—that identify, personalize and, ultimately, mythologize him. Arthur is defined by Excalibur, Thor by his hammer, Achilles by his (almost) impervious flesh. In the future-war film, the identification and distinction of heroes is enabled by their unique personal attributes (e.g. size, looks, demeanor), but more especially by their characteristic equippage. Yet viewers know that each separate item of equipment is not *sui generis*, but *e pluribus unum*; one of many thousands or millions of identical units that have come spewing out of some unknown factory. So it is not the individual item of equipment itself, but its characteristics, which now mark it as a hero-grade object. In Western European myth and legend, this role usually fell to the sword, the symbol of nobility, dominion, and puissance. However, in today's future-war film, the new hero does not—indeed, cannot—embody these same chivalric values and endure. Instead, he must somehow rise above the realities of today's battlefield. Consequently, where valor and righteousness once ruled, lethal efficiency now sits enthroned, and in place of a single thrust of the sword, there is the torrential terror of machine guns.

Orgies of autofire annihilation figure prominently in many futuristic combat films, from the swashbuckling sprays of lead that seem to punctuate every scene change in *Total Recall*, to the more high-tech, and more lethal, weapons in *Aliens*. In the latter film, automatic weapons have become not only bigger and badder but some have been slaved to an automated system, which keeps the heroes removed from the enemy, yet allows them to witness their handiwork via television. Thus, the human soldiers still remain connected to, and in control of, the action, making the fire-control computer not so much a surrogate as a servitor (and thus, an almost complete realization of Nikola Tesla's vision).

Although not a military scenario *per se*, the street warfare waged by *Robocop* also illustrates the progressive amalgamation of cinematic hero icons: the half-hardware hero now has internal fire-control circuits and is encased in powered armor. Thus, the relationship between man and machine is advanced to the next level: true cyborging. Indeed, it is hard to tell where the human Officer Murphy ends and his mechanical half—Robocop—begins. What is quite clear, however, is that various scenes in the film are simultaneously homages to, and parodies of, the Western shootout. But even the parodic qualities are ultimately dependent upon the grim contrasts between Marshal Robocop's virtuoso firearm gymnastics and the pitiable human responses he encounters as he shoots his way through an inner-city version of the OK Corral.

All these new iconic values coalesce and reach their epitome in the most famous of all futuristic robotic reapers: the prosocial cyborg from *Terminator II*. Truly an infernal machine, it is here that the new cyborg death totem stands fully realized: no longer is the vulnerable man on the inside, protected by a hard external skin. Now the inverse is true: a nearly indestructible mechanical interior is coated by a convincing, but thoroughly artificial and expendable fleshy exterior. However, even though the Terminator is a machine that has been physically and behaviorally humanized, it is still impervious to bullets, doubt, and remorse. Its advanced target detection and acquisition system seeks out and destroys targets—both animate and inanimate—with the ultimate in portable automatic weapons: the electronic, 3000-round-per-minute XM214 rotary machine gun. Here, then, is the postmodern Achilles, Arthur, and Thor—all rolled into one.

There are tactical reasons that necessitate the inclusion of each of the iconic components of this new consummate warrior. Armor is certainly a necessity if the hero is going to be able to 'stand up' on the battlefield and be counted as something other than a casualty. Viewers do not have to be ballistics experts or physicists to appreciate the incredible lethality of contemporary man-portable weapon systems. Consequently, if a hero is to be at all plausible, he/she must have some degree of highly enhanced protection. Since such near-invulnerable armor would be too heavy for an unassisted human, common sense tells us that the armor must be powered (or 'self-propelled'), thereby conferring superhuman physical strength as well.

Similarly, the new hero would not be complete without various automated systems. Today's audiences know that nothing is quicker than machine processing. Therefore, they also know that a viable contemporary hero needs this edge in speed, since, as the modern military aphorism has it, there are only two types of combatants: the quick and the dead. Fortunately for the creators of this new information age folk hero, computer control systems are particularly amenable to integration with human-directed weapons systems.[5] Thus, two of the primary icons associated with the postmodern martial hero—computers and high-power weapons—are inextricably bound together in a marriage of automated calculation and control.

Last, but most important, is the heroic weapon itself: an almost deified version of the machine gun. Mixing equal measures of dark allure and gleaming technology, the automatic weapon is, arguably, the perfect phallic icon for the postmodern cinematic warrior. Certainly, automatic weapons both sound and look daunting, but their most impressive feature is the sheer volume of damage they can deal out. Furthermore, the nature of that destruction is not the result of some cleanly cauterizing futuristic beam, nor a hazy disintegration of matter, nor an indistinct immolation of a target. Machine gun slugs tear through barriers and shred beings: the weapon marries physics to deconstruction in an orgy of gore and mutilation.

An automatic weapon is also comparatively indiscriminate, thereby dehumanizing its victims. To borrow and amplify the tone of detachment that resonates from Coyle's *Team Yankee*, people become 'targets,' attacks become 'firing solutions,' all of which reflect and reinforce the utterly inhuman, but also the high-tech, qualities of this type of weapon. The drawn bow, shouldered musket, unholstered six-shooter: all are ergonomically and physiologically congruent in that the release of one string or the squeeze of one trigger produces one attack. Each perpetration of an assault is connected to a single, discrete, volitional act. The automatic weapon explodes that boundary, breaks the one-to-one relationship that has traditionally obtained between the intent and the actualization of each assault. Now, depressing a trigger initiates a generalized wash of destruction, a spray of death-intent in a widening cone. The psychological necessity of repeatedly initiating violence is removed, although the attacker still has a direct line-of-sight interface with each target. In the cyborgs who wield such weapons, a grim union of technology and physiology has unfettered the soul of the attacker from the moral consequences of each life he/she takes. This then, is the image of the new warrior, the next step in the evolution of the soldier and his equipment—or is it?

On the contrary, all technological indicators, military projection, and responsible future-war fiction[6] argue that these images are the exact opposite of what we might reasonably anticipate. This is largely because these mythic narratives are not motivated by 'responsible prophesy,' as called for by future warfare author/editor Reginald Bretnor.[7] Instead, they are desperate attempts to preserve Western culture's traditional plenipotent, personal, and patriarchal mythic heroes by 'upgrading' them with select modern components. Therefore, although these narratives may be set in the future, they are actually reworkings of the same tired 'dominant' forms and ideologies, rather than of new, 'emergent' devices and values.[8]

Although not all (or even many) of today's combat-oriented science fiction texts are free of the 'dominant' mires of traditional forms, values, and martial visions, many serious future-war narratives at least attempt to extricate themselves from the quicksand of conventional assumptions. What is most striking about the collective prevision of such works is that it anticipates future warriors, weapons, and warfare that are the antithesis of what is customarily presented in today's mythic cinematic offerings.

For instance, contemporary combat armor is (as S. M. Stirling suggests in 'Necessity') light, flexible, and primarily designed to stop shrapnel and low-power rounds. The main reason for the absence of the heavy armor that is so frequently featured in films is that the inevitable losses in speed and agility are a poor trade for the increased protection. To once again cite H.G. Wells' still-pertinent 1914 observation, '[T]he amount of energy . . . [a]pplied to warfare . . . meant that the power to inflict a blow, the power to destroy, was continually increasing. . . . Every sort of passive defense, armour, fortifications, and so forth, was being outmastered by this tremendous increase on the destructive side.'[9] Or as weapons instructors aphoristically inform army inductees throughout the US, 'If you can see it, you can hit it; if you can hit it, you can kill it.'

Automation has indeed produced rapid increases in target acquisition and assessment, but it will be some time before these advances become available on an individual, neurally interfaced (i.e. cyborged) basis. When they do, they will make the need for individual speed and stealth even more urgent. Furthermore, even if these developments were available today, they would still not constitute automation's greatest contribution to the character and ecology of the modern battlefield. Computer-controlled data exchange, multiplexed communications, signal intelligence, and electronic countermeasures are fundamental to today's combined arms tactics and closely timed operations. And, if one wishes to assess the ways in which robotics are likely to change the personal experience of battlefield combat, it would be wise to look not for titanic cyborg heroes, but for diminutive giant-killers. In 1996, two small, mobile, automated anti-personnel mines were being developed at MIT. The more promising of the two—nicknamed Genghis—was only 4–5 centimeters long, weighed less than 5 grams (approximately 1/6th of an ounce), was coated with infrared-proof paint, and homed in on the body heat and/or speech sounds of its targets. Once it has acquired its target, it scuttles spider-like into close proximity and detonates its payload of several grams of warhead—enough to kill or seriously wound a person.[10]

Finally, while it is true that automatic rifles are standard issue for most militaries, the correct use of these weapons is radically different from what is depicted on theater screens. In operations conducted by well-trained troops, most auto-weapons are routinely kept in the semiautomatic fire mode. If used at all, 'autofire' is concentrated upon a small number of individually selected targets. The tactical objective of such fire is not to saturate a broad area with slugs, nor to annihilate adversaries in droves, but to generate a higher hit percentage on individually selected targets, while simultaneously requiring less time to aim. Also, where appropriate and possible, such weapons are fitted with silencers and flash-suppressors; genuine combat troops make every effort to remain undetected for as long as possible. Therefore, the professional employment of modern automatic weapons stresses focused, coordinated, and (if feasible) unobtrusive attacks. It violates all contemporary and foreseeable tactical wisdom to slew such weapons from side to side, using them as eye-and-ear catching bullet-hoses.

Why then are there such profound discrepancies between the actual and projected employment of modern personal combat technologies, and their depictions in high-profile future-war films of the past twenty years? Much of the answer may lie in the nature and economics of film-making itself. While paperback battlefield technothrillers and superior future-war fiction may feature exactly faithful narrative previsions of modern, impersonal combat, this is not the stuff of which heroes—or big Hollywood profits—are made. However, films in which new high-technology tools enable a single male hero to climb to new heights of personal glory are the natural complements to what Hollywood producers call a 'star vehicle.' Film stars, like heroes, need to be seen, to stand impressive and impassive before the threats they oppose. However, even lay audiences realize that, today, such a hero needs armor to survive. Furthermore, he needs computerized speed and reflexes, as well as broadly death-dealing weaponry, if he is to achieve the personal potency associated with traditional heroes.[11]

It may well be that, independent of Hollywood economics, the nature of the cinematic medium induces armor and automation discrepancies as well. For instance, automation—particularly that which allows the rapid sharing of battlefield intelligence—is virtually absent from film portrayals, but is often well and richly represented in the better future-war texts. On the one hand, this might be because authors—and readers—of texts are more interested in accurate technological speculation than iconically rehabilitated heroes. However, this difference may also reflect a difference in the media: in prose, suspense depends much more on ideas and much less on specific images. Readers do not 'see' threats in novels the way they do in a film; in prose, the reader's conception of a threat is based on the information received, and often tactically dissected, by a character. For possibly similar reasons, the automatic weapon has not accrued any particularly noteworthy place in future-war prose. This is not surprising: the features that make the automatic weapon so noteworthy in film—sight, sound, visibly lavish destruction—are all imparted directly as physical stimuli. In a novel, where imagination must fill in such sensory blanks, there is nothing inherently more striking about one weapon over another.

Indeed, serious future-war texts rarely incorporate any of these overblown icons, focusing instead on the military's increasing emphasis on speed, stealth, and versatility. What contemporary future-war prose does tend to extrapolate and speculate upon, therefore, are the genuine emerging trends in warfare, weaponry, and the accelerating evolution of the soldier into a highly specialized, non-heroical craftsperson. These trends are consistent across many future-war texts, even those as politically opposed as Heinlein's *Starship Troopers* and Joe Haldeman's *The Forever War*. For instance, one of Heinlein's characters attests that 'A private soldier today is a specialist so highly skilled that he would rate "master" in any other trade; we can't afford stupid ones.'[12] Haldeman's protagonist characterizes his elite peers as 'fifty men and fifty women, with IQs over 150 and bodies of unusual health and strength . . .'[13]

These two texts also point to the increasing expense of the individual soldier. Heinlein's Sergeant Jelal reminds his squad that 'each and every one of you has cost the gov'ment, counting weapons, armor, ammo, instrumentation, and training . . . better'n half a million. . . . So bring it back! We can spare you, but we can't spare that fancy suit you're wearing.'[14] In *The Forever War*, Haldeman postulates a state that has a similarly protective attitude toward its investment in the 'average' soldier. Protagonist William Mandella and his comrades are told by their superiors that 'I am glad you're taking good care of yourselves, because each of you represents an investment of over a million dollars and one-fourth of a human life.'[15] In both cases, the message is the same: soldiers and their equipment are expensive commodities, not to be spent indiscriminately on cinematic cyborg heroics.

As the protagonists of these texts move from their backstage encounters with the economics and logistics of future warmaking into the harsh, spotlit realities of the super-modern battlefield, the drama intensifies, but the accent on pragmatism and quantifiable results remains undiminished. In this one regard, both Heinlein's and Haldeman's texts are close kin to technothrillers. Their protagonists are not mighty heroes but machine operators, vulnerable individuals who may wield devastating area-of-effect weapons but who still strive to avoid direct confrontation with the enemy, and who prize mobility and speed over armor. The following scene from Starship Troopers illustrates this, as well as the pronounced degree of psychological detachment possessed by the protagonist/narrator:

> I jumped . . . over the next row of buildings, and while I was in the air, fanning the first row by the river front with a hand flamer. They seemed to be wood construction and it looked like time to start a good fire — with luck, some of those warehouses would house oil products, or even explosives. As I hit, the Y-rack on my shoulders launched two small H.E. bombs a couple of hundred yards each way to my right and left flanks but I never saw what they did as just then my first rocket hit — that unmistakable . . . brilliance of an atomic explosion. It was just a peewee of course, less than two kilotons nominal yield, with tamper and implosion squeeze to produce results from a less-than-critical mass — but then who wants to be bunk mates with a cosmic catastrophe? It was enough to clean off that hilltop and make everybody in the city take shelter against fallout.[16]

Although Heinlein's narrative has been dubiously labeled as 'pro-war' and Haldeman's simplistically called 'anti-war,' both narrators enact their orders with the same bloodless efficiency, carry similarly awe-inspiring arsenals, and relate their stories in similarly genial yet detached prose. For instance, when not using 500 microton grenades fired from a clip-fed launcher, the Elite Conscripts of Haldeman's Forever War resort to high-intensity lasers that reduce alien adversaries to depersonalized heaps of dead meat:

> One Tauran died trying to run through a laser beam. . . . It was slaughter . . . They kept coming without faltering, even when they had to climb over the drift of bodies and parts of bodies that piled up high, parallel to our flank. The ground between us was slick red with Tauran blood — all God's Children got hemoglobin — and . . . their guts looked pretty much like guts to my untrained eye.[17]

Another recurrent theme in better future-war fictions is the purposive dehumanization of enemies as a means of furnishing combat personnel with moral prophylactics against guilt, hesitation, or remorse. Haldeman offers the most striking examination of this phenomenon when, immediately prior to combat, his Elite Conscripts are primed through post-hypnotic suggestion. Protagonist William Mandella knows that he is under the influence of brainwashing, but

> that didn't make it any less compelling. My mind reeled under the strong pseudo-memories: shaggy hulks that were Taurans (not at all what we now knew they looked like) boarding a colonists' vessel, eating babies while mothers watched in screaming terror (the colonists never took babies; they wouldn't stand the acceleration), then raping the women to death with huge veined purple members

(ridiculous that they would feel desire for humans), holding the men down while they plucked flesh from their living bodies and gobbled it (as if they could assimilate the alien proteins)... but while my conscious mind was rejecting the silliness, somewhere much deeper, down in that sleeping animal where we keep our real motives and morals, something was thirsting for alien blood... I knew that it was all purest soyashit, and I hated the men who had taken such obscene liberties with my mind, but I could even hear my teeth grinding, feel my cheeks frozen in a spastic grin, blood-lust . . .[18]

Heinlein's Mobile Infantry doesn't seem to need the hypnotic pre-indoctrination with which Haldeman's Elite Conscripts are prepared. Narrator Johnny Rico accepts killing—even when his victims might be civilians—as just a moderately unfortunate part of his job:

I ... opened my eyes and stared straight at a local citizen just coming out of an opening in the building ahead of me. He looked at me, I looked at him, and he started to raise something—a weapon I suppose. . . . I didn't have time to fool with him . . . . I still had the hand flamer in my left hand; I toasted him and jumped over the building he had been coming out of . . .[19]

Rico's off-hand remark that 'I toasted him' has, on numerous occasions, been taken to indicate Heinlein's callous disregard for life. However, it is just as plausible (and indeed, more consistent, given the thematic complexity of much of his work) to assert that Heinlein was simply remaining consistent with the scenario and characters he had set out to explore. Johnny Rico is neither evil nor stupid but, at only 18 years of age, he has been trained to become a professional, elite killer. His job description includes being dropped from orbit in a one-man capsule onto a planet full of inscrutable and implacable foes. His reflexes, value structures, and social acculturation is largely reinscribed by the Mobile Infantry (most of the novel concerns itself with his training) in order to prepare him for this task. While Heinlein does not decry this practice, neither does he leave it unproblematized. As Johnnie's callous remark points out, there are unavoidable psychological costs connected with preparations for war, and the more lethal and high-speed the anticipated conflict, the worse those costs.

This concern with the dehumanizing effects of increasingly automated conflicts—in which humans ultimately become servitors to machines—is perhaps the single most prevalent thematic thread that runs through America's post-World War II far-future war fiction. One of the most chilling of these tales of man–machine military synthesis, Poul Anderson's novella *Kings Who Die*, posits a future in which eternal war between a capitalist West and communist East has settled into a comfortable, stalemated ritual. In an attempt to break the stalemate, the East develops a direct man–machine interface: a human brain enhanced, amplified, and accelerated through direct connection with a computer. This first true cyborg, Rostock, rapidly evolves an awareness that transcends the political conventions of his time. He perceives that the endless war has become a form of sacrifice to the status quo, analogous to the ancient Aztec practice of offering up their youngest, best, and brightest to appease the Sun God that they believed controlled the natural balance of their world. Rostock resolves to end this cycle of violence and attempts to recruit a Western officer, Diaz, to his cause. Rostock is on the verge of success when another man–machine symbiot interferes. This is Diaz himself, whose subconscious has been post-hypnotically programmed to activate, under the right mental conditions, a powerful electromagnetic scrambler embedded in his body. Proximity to Rostock, who is obviously a key enemy command-and-control asset, triggers this post-hypnotic suggestion and activates the scrambler against Diaz's will. As a result, Rostock is killed, Diaz escapes—and the story ends where it began; the narrative's last line is identical to the first, echoing the endless cycle of war in which Diaz, and humanity, is trapped: 'Luckily, Diaz was looking the other way when the missile exploded.'[20] Anderson's prevision of war is therefore a bleak nightmare view of computer-assisted carnage and of men reduced to machine-dependent puppets who have created a brutal, unbreakable ritual of battle and death.

Anderson's *Kings Who Die* is only the most overt of many fundamentally subversive warnings against the slow encroachment of military automation and dehumanization within the superpower state. However, in contrast, the media magnates of that state evince enthusiasm for representations of distinctly non-subversive (and nonsensical) cyborg warrior-heroes. For the media (and, according to some, the power elite it 'serves'), this serendipitous 'new' image is simply a convenient reworking and updating of the patriarchal forms of the 'dominant' hegemonic interests which it represents. For Hollywood, this new technofantastic folk hero means a revitalization of the types of characters and stories that capitalize upon what films do best: hypnotize audiences with non-stop action, dazzling special effects, and heroes who hold out the false promise of invulnerability, even in an age of overwhelming destructive energies.

On a cultural level, these cinematic narratives may be an attempt at social self-reassurance against overarching feelings of vulnerability. The portrayal of the future warrior as an impregnable hero may be the only way to prevent the elimination of the heroic warrior role model in Western culture and consciousness. Without the technological aids that have become the stock fixtures of cinematic future-war fantasies, no character could hope to endure the monstrous destructive powers unleashed on today's battlefield. More to the point, without extraordinary technological capabilities and weapons, individual deeds would not even be noticed. Machines, not men, have become the objects of notoriety. The fighting abilities and personal characteristics of individual, noble warriors are obsolete, quaint ideas. In their place, today's professional soldiers are portrayed as accountants of death, ruthlessly calculating odds and weapon efficiencies, skulking in shadows, waiting for the opportunity to ambush an adversary from behind. The cultural need for the warrior-hero image leaves no choice but to invent a new one, just as these films have done. This reassurance, however, is almost sure to be increasingly incompatible with reality, continuing a trend of denial that has been intensifying since the end of World War I, when the discrepancy between old chivalric values and the proven realities of warfare became obvious, and the rate of divergence between the two began accelerating. In a desperate attempt to seal this breach, modern cinematic cyborg-heroes have been laden with reassuring technomagical talismans in the form of powered armor, precision automation, computer interfaces, and massively destructive personal weapons. It is, however, all a sham: even if such technologies were available, such personal enhancements would not significantly ameliorate the annihilatory powers of the swift, overmastering weapons that populate the modern battlefield.

In summary, it is not surprising that future-war texts that soberly address issues of military automation and man–machine interface have fallen so deeply into the shadow of their spectacular cinematic relatives. Tools such as today's integrated heads-up displays, multiplexed communicators, and thermal imaging goggles may be technologically impressive, and decisive, but they are not dramatic enough to become cultural icons. Information may be the most important factor on today's and tomorrow's battlefield, but the technical and behavioral means of gathering it are not heroic, are not in keeping with the 'dominant' forms of the warrior myth. Indeed, they run counter to traditional expectations of the daring, stand-alone hero.

However, the divergent textual and cinematic representations of future war are still related in one very important way: they both identify technology as the determining factor on any modern battlefield, regardless of the type of advancements they propose or the ethos they ascribe to its use. Identifying this common point between otherwise disjunct narrative sub-genres once again suggests that even when the marriage between future-war fiction and the superpower state's technocratic ideologies is tempestuous, it remains a powerful and influential partnership. On the one hand, it is almost immaterial whether automation's contributions to the modern battlefield are presented as positive or negative, as empowering or overawing. Whether its iconic proxies are male cyber-reaper heroes, or quick-and-dirty hetero-gendered commando teams, advanced weapons technology is overwhelmingly associated with high enemy body-counts. Therefore, the use of such technology is evidence that the state has both the will and the ability to exert increasingly decisive political power. Furthermore, high technology also means high profits. It may well be that, as Poul Anderson speculates in *Kings Who Die*, taxpaying and military budgets are a form of social sacrifice, ritualized acts of obeisance and self-mutilation that are collective homages to the modern equivalent of our war deities. If so, it stands to reason that we would wish to have evidence that our devotions are recognized and efficacious. These narratives may be both proof and validation of our sacrifices; the power of the techno-heroes we raise up upon the pedestal of our tax monies affirms that we are not following a false god, that ours is a mighty deity—and a real one—in today's otherwise demythologized world. Ultimately, it does not matter whether specific items of high technology are very plausible or insanely improbable: what is significant is the pervasive reinforcement of technology's preeminent position in contemporary society. These tales revel in and celebrate new technological heights, new innovations, and the new extents of power that come along with them. They are narratives that both affirm in their content and confirm in their ubiquity an enduring superpower truth: new infernal machines *are* rumors of war in and of themselves, and we may learn much by reading between the imaginative lines that engender them.

On the other hand, *textual* future-war narratives also evince deep wells of dark skepticism regarding the uses and consequences of military technology. They explore issues of dehumanization and depersonalization, and investigate increasingly complicated and problematic relationships between potentially opposed values such as civil rights and civic duties, democratic process and military necessity, conscience and combat efficiency. These conflicts often form the thematic axes of such narratives. These are, therefore, inherently political texts, that paradoxically both validate and question the technophilic superpower ethos that fostered them. They eschew the ultimately evanescent questions that preoccupy near-future technothrillers—the where, and when, and why of the 'next great war'—in order to explore the enduring and socially profound actualities of *how* future wars will be waged, with *what* machines, and *whose* lives will be changed—soldiers and civilians alike—as a result.

In works such as Heinlein's and Haldeman's, then, there is a species of political influence that pushes beyond the orderly 'trickle-up/trickle-down' and expands outward as culture-challenging ripples. Certainly, these novels (particularly Heinlein's) may have had technological 'trickle-up' effects, possibly providing the master images and/or impetus for engineers to actualize what the authors could only imagine. Similarly, for a general public whose idea of warfare was shaped by images gleaned from World War II movies, the previsions that 'trickled down' through these authors' pens may have shattered illusions, awakening lay readers to an emerging battlefield reality that was as physically and psychologically terrifying as it was technologically wondrous.[21] However, at their most subversive, future-war fictions are, ultimately, challenges to our cultural traditions and values, for by questioning the role of the individual in a time of war, they also call attention to the ways in which we are socially shaped to serve the ends of the state itself—even though the state, in theory, exists to serve us. By stimulating and enabling such critical discourse, the best future-war fictions cut to the quick of the social contract, question our assumptions about human nature, and silently present us the goading, double-edged sword of progress for periodic reassessment.

# Afterword: On Conducting a Literary Reconnaissance in Force—and in Earnest

It may be interesting, even entertaining, to investigate the increasingly symbiotic relationships between certain subgenres of speculative fiction and military imagination and innovation. However, it would be morally irresponsible, if not reprehensible, to fail to acknowledge that the vindication for such a study must not reside in the details of the relationships, but in their social and cultural portents. As John Gardner observes in *On Moral Fiction*, critics may reasonably choose to see their work as gamesmanship, and to retain a detached indifference to their objects of study—even to the point of trivializing the objects and their choice of them. Gardner admits that he 'can think of no good reason that some people should not specialize in the behavior of the left-side hairs on an elephant's trunk.'[1] However, Gardner adds a crucial proviso when he avers that 'Fiddling with the hairs on an elephant's nose is indecent when the elephant happens to be standing on [a] baby.'

Like millions of others, my two 'babies'—sons, aged five and three—live in the ever-widening shadow of that elephant's descending military-industrial foot. That mammoth institution—and all of the cultural reproduction and revision systems that it influences and is influenced by—can represent either a means for achieving increased global security or a tool of annihilation, can evolve into either a well-honed force for peace or an instrument of aggression. The stakes are not merely high, but ultimate: nothing less than the survival of the planet is at issue. Consequently, even though detached gamesmanship may persist as 'academic vogue,' responsible scholarship must also, finally, assert that some issues cannot be trivialized or rendered 'value-neutral' without committing an atrocity against the most basic precepts of human rights and the sanctity of life. This project, then, is not a species of gamesmanship. Defects or oversights in authorship may undermine the validity of its conclusions, but are powerless to diminish the criticality of the topic: the interplay between human imagination, innovation, and future war-waging.

Naturally, no single report, book, study, or speech could possibly be endued with so penetrating and complete a power of revelation that the dynamics of these relationships will become clear, uncomplicated, or indisputable. The issues of how and why we change the way we wage wars are as multi-faceted and fluid as the processes that produced the changes. However, in light of the human propensity for war and its constant cultural presence in either ritualized rehearsal or active practice, it seems that we can safely begin with at least one commonsense hypothesis: a society's prior conceptions and anticipations of war and weapons inform, and possibly determine, the actual wars it fights, and the machines with which it fights them. Were this hypothesis reflective of a social anomaly peculiar to our epoch, were this a fading phenomenon, perhaps one could argue that the issue is not an urgent one. However, the events of the past half-century have destabilized earlier military ideas, images, and practices more than all the rest of human history combined. Our grandparents waved farewell to armies of millions that departed on armadas of ponderous troopships; today, dual-gendered battalions of hundreds receive 12-hour activation alerts and fly unseen and unannounced from night-time airstrips. A modern ten-person infantry squad carries more firepower than two World War II era 40-man platoons, and the squad's capacity to call, direct, and capitalize upon air and artillery support is infinitely greater. Indeed, any comparison between the modern soldier and his/her antecedents must be misleading, because it erroneously suggests that a useful basis of comparison might actually exist.

Similarly, although war (to paraphrase von Clausewitz) remains an extension of political force, the purposes for which that force is used, and the scenarios into which it is projected, are radically different. Strategically, tactically, and experientially, World War II was arguably the last great 'industrial' war: millions of conscripts were hastily trained, moved, and committed *en masse* to campaigns that surged back and forth across continents. Although the props were different, this titanic clash between rival empires was a drama that would have been quite familiar in its scope and in its goals to Napoleon, Caesar, and Alexander.

Those days are gone. We live in the era of backpack nukes, automated battlefields, surgical strikes, black operations, strategic misinformation, psychological warfare, remotely piloted vehicles, laser-guided bombs, plausible deniability, orbital interdiction, and ten-year planning, development, and budgeting cycles. Today, weapons are being designed, tested, and redesigned that will not be completed for another ten, even fifteen years. For every war fought, a hundred are hypothesized, are subjected to games-theory analysis, are prepared for—and then forgotten as the technological horizon continues its high-speed approach, often invalidating yesterday's tactical wisdom before it can be thoroughly articulated, promulgated, and 'tested.'

Therefore, despite the thaw that ended the Cold War, and the decreasing likelihood of another truly global conflict, war has only changed shape, not vanished. Like other unwanted weeds in the garden of human hopes for a better world, it is persistent, hardy, and infiltrates at the unattended borders of our care. Where we have been unsuccessful in cultivating justice and safety, there it will find opportunity to break out into new, riotous growth. So—as with any other perennial pestilence—if we would control, eradicate, or alter the growth of war and weapons, we must begin by knowing them from seed and germination onward. We must assess how imaginings of them root into the fertile imagination of the body politic and how the consequent ideas are nourished, starved, or mutated as they come into contact with different discursive and political catalysts. And we must never forget that our observations should not merely be grist for the disinterested mills of empirical research, but should also be acts—and therefore, testaments—of human compassion and hope for change.

# Notes

### Notes to the Introduction

1 Variations of this phrase exist earlier but failed to inscribe themselves so forcefully and generally into the language as to become a stock colloquial phrase. 'Infernal engine' can be found in prior centuries, often relating to artillery or, more euphemistically, armed forces. A well-known example of this is Thomas De Witt's use of this phrase in his 1787 'Anti-Federalist' letter to the *American Herald*. Another variant—'infernal apparatus'—appears in Falconer's *Dictionary Marine* (1789), and refers to the employment of unforeseen (and therefore, unethical) naval weapons.
2 Darko Suvin's *Metamorphoses of Science Fiction* (New Haven: Yale, 1979) is arguably the most significant typology of the subgenres of speculative fiction, and is, in its own right, a cornerstone in the formation of critical theory on science fiction. In it, Suvin characterizes 'true' science fiction as being distinguished by the presence of a 'novum . . . validated by cognitive logic' (63).
3 Marshall McLuhan, *Understanding Media: The Extensions of Man* (New York: Signet, 1964), 300.
4 Joe Haldeman, *The Forever War* (New York: Ballantine, 1980).
5 Poul Anderson, *Kings Who Die. 8th Annual Edition: The Year's Best S-F*, ed. Judith Merril (New York: Dell, 1964).
6 The term 'salience' is used here in the context of an object that is deemed worthy of social consideration and display. This usage is common in various works that assess the connections between media representations and audience behavior, such as Comstock et al's pivotal television meta-analysis, *Television and Human Behavior*—George Comstock, S. Chaffee, N. Katzman, M. McCombs, and D. Roberts, *Television and Human Behavior* (New York: Columbia University Press, 1978).

### Notes to Chapter 1

1 The full story of 'Dorking's' reception by, and impact upon, Victorian society is authoritatively recounted in I. F. Clarke's *The Tale of the Next Great War, 1871–1914: Fictions of Future Warfare and of Battles Still-to-Come* (Liverpool: Liverpool University Press, 1995), 14–15. Clarke's footnotes in *Voices Prophesying War: Future Wars, 1763–3749* (Second Edition. New York: Oxford University Press, 1992) are also illuminating, particularly his inclusion of various remarks made by Gladstone upon 'Dorking' and the public furor it generated.

2 *Annual Register*, 1871, pt. I, 108.
3 Clarke (ed.), *The Tale of the Next Great War, 1871–1914*, 15.
4 Ibid, 16–17. Clark perceives a similar division in Victorian future-war fiction.
5 Ibid, 16–17.
6 Kennedy Jones, *Fleet Street and Downing Street* (London: Hutchinson & Co., 1920), 198.
7 'The Passing Hour,' *Black and White Magazine*, No. 48, Volume III, Jan 2, 1892.
8 Until the German naval expansion commenced in the 1890s, English war (and, particularly, invasion) fears were mostly focused on the French. 'The Battle of Dorking' was therefore something of a fluke—but it also presaged the later downturn in Anglo-German relations and indicated the military quality and modernity that had to be associated with a projected foe in order for a tale of imaginary war to possess the potential for immediate political impact.
9 The 1893 war scare was simply one in a long series of English anxiety attacks over a possible Franco-Russian alliance, and the joint invasion force that these two powers might project into Victoria's green and pleasant land. Such fears were, to put it mildly, almost entirely groundless.
10 Clarke, *Voices Prophesying War*, 58.
11 Ibid, 58.
12 Lay usage often conflates the words 'tactical' and 'strategic' into fully interchangeable synonyms. However, there is an essential distinction between these two terms. 'Tactical' signifies small-unit actions and the operation of both machinery and personnel in pursuit of discrete battlefield objectives; it is the 'zoomed-in' perspective on military activities. Conversely, 'strategic' refers to a 'zoomed-out' perspective on theater-wide military operations and the realization of regional, even national, objectives.
13 Hugh Oakley Arnold-Forster, 'In a Conning Tower' (1888), quoted in Clarke (ed.), *The Tale of the Next Great War, 1871–1914*, 16.
14 Ibid, 142.
15 Ibid, 143.
16 Ibid, 144.
17 The last noteworthy instance of successful ramming between capital ships was at the Battle of Lissa, during the Austro-Italian War of 1866.
18 T. A. Brassey et al., *The Naval Annual: 1892* (Portsmouth: J. Griffin and Co., 1892).
19 P. H. Colomb, *Naval Warfare: Its Ruling Principles and Practice Historically Considered* (London: W. H. Allen and Co., 1892).
20 Brassey et al., *The Naval Annual: 1892*, 551.
21 P. H. Colomb, J. F. Maurice, F. N. Maude, Archibald Forbes, Charles Lowe, D. Christie Murray, and F. Scudamore, *The Great War of 189–: A Forecast.* (London: William Heinemann, 1893.) This text is also referred to as *The Great War of 1892* in some references.
22 Brassey et. al., *The Naval Annual: 1892*, 539.
23 Ibid, 551.
24 Clarke makes similar observations in *The Great War with Germany, 1890–1914* (Liverpool: Liverpool University Press, 1997), 29.

25  Although illustrated magazines had been in existence since the 1840s, dramatic improvements in both the quality and cost effectiveness of printing graphics engendered a new surge of such publications. It is interesting to note however, that like almost all periodicals of the era, *Black and White* did not have a section for 'Letters to the Editor' nor did it encourage reader commentary of any type. This makes any reader-response analysis of such serialized narratives virtually impossible to conduct a century later.
26  It is also worth noting that in 1901, a 'New Battle of Dorking' would be written, in which Lord Roberts saves the realm with his masterful generalship and military foresight. This underscores how the population of the 'future-warfare community' crossed the increasingly porous boundaries between authors, editors, and government officials. It also illustrates how it often provided its more august allies (such as Roberts) with fictional glories that were almost as widely read as the news reportage of their actual achievements. Lastly, it is instructive that an author could pen a 'New Battle of Dorking' thirty years after the original, secure in the expectation that his new tale's intertextual reference would be clear to most readers. Evidently, Victorian future-war fiction had a very long shelf-life.
27  Colomb et al., *The Great War of 189–*, 1.
28  Editorial, *Black and White*, Volume III, No. 52, January 30, 1892, 144.
29  Colomb et al., *The Great War of 189–*, 305–06.
30  Ibid, 308,
31  Ibid, 172.
32  Ibid, 276.
33  Ibid, 180–81.
34  Ibid, 114.
35  Ibid, 83–85.
36  Ibid, 114.
37  Ibid, 115.
38  Literally, 'war games.'
39  Colomb et al., *The Great War of 189–*, 117.
40  Ibid, 229.
41  Ibid, 254.
42  Ibid, 115.
43  Ibid, 116. This scene anticipates the disciplinary and morale problems of the Somme, where British officers were compelled to 'lead' their troops from the rear rank of the unit, not the front, and to do so with pistols drawn as a disincentive to desertion.
44  Ibid, 185.
45  Ibid, 131. 'Rambleton Seaforth' is not, of course, the name of an actual contributor.
46  Ibid, 274.
47  Ibid, 275.

## Notes to Chapter 2

1  Reginald Pound and Geoffrey Harmsworth, *Northcliffe* (London: Cassell, 1959), 182.

2   William Le Queux, 'How I write my Sensational Novels,' *Pearson's Weekly*, no. 862, January 24 1907, 1.
3   N. St. Barbe Sladen, *The Real Le Queux* (London: Nicholson & Watson, 1939), 181.
4   Ibid, 182.
5   Ibid, 182.
6   Ibid, 190.
7   Ibid.
8   Ibid, 191.
9   Charles Lowe, 'About German Spies,' *Contemporary Review*, January 1910, 97, 42–56.
10  William Le Queux, 'Introduction,' *The Invasion of 1910* (London: Eveleigh Nash, 1906), vi.
11  The identity of these experts is revealed in St. Barbe Sladen's biography of Le Queux: they did not originally disclose their identities.
12  Le Queux, 'Introduction' to *The Invasion*, vii.
13  Roberts wrote: 'The catastrophe that may happen if we remain in our present state of unpreparedness is vividly and forcibly illustrated in Mr. Le Queux's new book, which I recommend to the perusal of everyone who has the welfare of the British Empire at heart.'
14  'Bobs' was the contemporary nickname for Earl Roberts.
15  Bernard Falk, *Bouquets for Fleet Street* (London: Hutchinson, 1951), 65.
16  St. Barbe Sladen, *The Real Le Queux*, 192.
17  Ibid.
18  Ibid, 195.
19  *The Annual Register*, 1906, 136. I. F. Clarke gives a fine overview of the nervous last-ditch efforts to discourage and disparage Britain's Teutophobic journalists and serial-writers in *The Great War with Germany, 1890–1914*, with particularly relevant details recounted on pp. 255–56.
20  Le Queux. *The Invasion*, 24.
21  Assessments of Le Queux's naval depictions are further complicated by the vague frontispiece credit that announces, 'Naval Chapters by H. W. Wilson.' Unless Wilson (one of Le Queux's 'technical advisors') had a prose style that was identical to Le Queux's, it seems improbable that Wilson was the actual wordsmith on these sections. However, that leaves a reader in considerable doubt regarding the degree and details of Wilson's contributions. Did he furnish some prose, or only information? If prose, how much and at what points? If information, was it on tactics, weapons, and/or ship statistics, and was it complete, partial, or sparse? No evidence remains with which to answer these questions.
22  Le Queux, *The Invasion*, 179.
23  Ibid, 306.
24  Ibid, 341.
25  Ibid, 115.
26  Ibid, 165.
27  Ibid.
28  Ibid.

29 Ibid, 402.
30 Ibid, 186–201.
31 The latter is the notorious gangster 'tommy-gun' which, according to one macabre punster, 'made the Twenties Roar.'
32 Le Queux also seems indirectly to appreciate the now common military axiom that 'amateurs study tactics; professionals study logistics.' The victories of the Germans are largely due to the excellence of their engineering units and their foresight regarding the local acquisition of adequate auxiliary transport, harbor and wharf facilities, and comestibles (the latter allows their invasion transports to dedicate maximum cargo space and weight to ammunition and nonreplenishable stocks).
33 Le Queux, *The Invasion*, 225.
34 Ibid, 229. This 'head cover' reference is another indication of how keenly aware Le Queux became of the growing importance of air-burst artillery attacks.
35 Ibid, 317.
36 Ibid, 336–37.
37 Ibid, 45.
38 Ibid, 168.
39 Ibid, 214.
40 Ibid, 360.
41 Ibid, 221.
42 Maurice Hankey, *THE WAR*, August 1914, to 31st May, 1915 (Secret Committee for Imperial Defense), 15–16. Available in the Public Records Office at Kew, Surrey, UK
43 Ibid.
44 Ibid.
45 For instance, Wells spoke of many of his future-war stories as being intentionally structured as 'parables.'
46 Le Queux, *The Invasion*, 360.
47 Ibid, 288.
48 Ibid, 334.
49 Ibid, 476.
50 Ibid.
51 Ibid, 449.
52 Ibid, 58.
53 Ibid, 482.
54 Ibid, 82.
55 Since these reporters are plying their trade by telegraph and telephone, they are, technically speaking, 'tele'-journalists—harbingers of Britain's almost-completed evolution into the world's first superpower state.
56 Le Queux, *The Invasion*, 19.
57 Ibid, 72.
58 Ibid, 342.
59 Ibid, 363.
60 Ibid, 176.
61 The German invaders destroy or significantly damage the Houses of

Parliament, Westminster Abbey (including, significantly, the Coronation Chair), and the British Museum and Library, the loss of the latter echoing the loss of the Great Library at Alexandria.
62 Le Queux, *The Invasion*, 347.
63 Ibid, 356.
64 Ibid.
65 Ibid, 280.
66 Ibid, 453.
67 Ibid, 497.
68 Ibid, 498.
69 Japan, due to its naval expansion, was another, albeit less frequent, hypothetical adversary of the Empire.
70 Karl Bleibtrau, *Die 'Offensiv-Invasion' gegen England* (Berlin: Schall & Rentel, 1907), 9.
71 Interestingly, this text also features Lord Roberts as a recurring character. Once again, Roberts has his greatness reproven (and restressed) through entirely fictional deeds—a nice advertisement with distinct political implications.
72 Louis Tracy, *The Final War* (New York: G.P. Putnam, 1896), 463.
73 This is asserted in numerous selections from N. St. Barbe Sladen's biography.

## Notes to Chapter 3

1 H. G. Wells, 'The Land Ironclads' (1903), in *The Complete Short Stories of H. G. Wells* (London: Ernest Benn Limited, 1966), 115–38.
2 Ibid, 115.
3 Jan Bloch (Ivan Bliokh), *Modern Weapons and Modern War, being an abridgment of 'The war of the future in its technical, economic and political relations,' with a prefatory conversation with the author by W. T. Stead*, trans. from the Russian (London: G. Richards, 1900). This intertextual reference also illustrates how, in a superpower state, the discursive domains of futurism (Bloch) and future-war fiction (Wells) are so linked and interpenetrated that they might be more accurately perceived as two halves of a larger, composite body of discourse. This invocation of a non-fictional futurist tract is not uncommon in Wells; he does it again in *The War in the Air* (1907) and in many other works.
4 Wells would later try other ways to break the stalemate—and end the horrors—of trench warfare. A recently discovered example is his successful design for what he named a 'mobile telpherage system.' This was a cargo rope system, powered by a gasoline engine, that delivered ammunition to the front lines by remote operation. This dramatically reduced the horrible casualties inflicted upon troops who manually moved these loads over the muddy, broken, incessantly shelled moonscape that was the immediate rear area. Wells gave the proposal and design to Churchill over lunch, but was told that the army had rejected the device. In fact, it was put through a set of tests in 1917, after which it was put into immediate, and highly secret, operation. Conservative estimates indicate that the device saved thousands of lives: it took 15 men and about 1 pint of gasoline to move the same amount of ammunition that had formerly required 1,500 to 2,000 men with backpacks. Wells

was never informed of the development, employment, or success of the device. However, this episode is yet another example of the extraordinary overlap and exchange between the discursive domain of military agenda-setters and authors of future-war fiction. (Reported in *Locus*, Vol. 36, no. 5 (#424), May 1996, 9, 68).

5  There has been some question raised in the scholarship surrounding 'The Land Ironclads' as to whether Wells actually intended his vehicles to be perceived as treaded or not. Most of this confusion stems from the author's atypically awkward and unclear description of the caterpillar tread mechanism itself: '[I]t had lifted its skirt and displayed along the length of it—*feet!* They were thick, stumpy feet, between knobs and buttons in shape—flat, broad things, reminding one of the feet of elephants or the legs of caterpillars; and then, as the skirt rose higher, the war correspondent . . . saw that these feet hung . . .on the rims of wheels . . .' (Wells, 'The Land Ironclads', 125–26). Admittedly, it is rather difficult to tell from this description what, exactly, Wells had in mind. However, the very next line—a sudden expostulation by the war correspondent upon seeing the propulsion method—makes Wells' intentions irrefutably clear. Recalling an earlier encounter with this type of mechanism, the war correspondent exclaims, 'Mr Diplock . . . called them Pedrails . . . Fancy meeting them here!' (ibid, 126). This reference is decisive: the Diplock Pedrail Company was one of Britain's first two manufacturers of caterpillar treads, according to 'The History of the Ministry of Munitions; Volume XII; The Supply of Munitions, Part III: Tanks' (1920, Crown Copyright Reserved (Confidential)), 2.
6  Wells, 'The Land Ironclads,' 124–25.
7  Ibid, 131.
8  It should be pointed out that Churchill often had a keen interest in new weapons technologies and was an outspoken, energetic, and persistent advocate for many of them over the course of his political career.
9  The Royal Commission on Awards to Inventors, Minutes of the Hearings of 7 October and 21 October, 1919, 6, Public Records Office, Kew, Surrey, UK
10 Notably, J. P. Harris, *Men, Ideas, and Tanks* (Manchester: Manchester University Press, 1995) proposes that Swinton inflated his claims and was not, in fact, the primary conceptual motivator behind the tank. I agree with Harris' conclusion, but my reasons are entirely different.
11 The emphasis is Swinton's.
12 E. D. Swinton, *Eyewitness* (London: Hodder and Stoughton Limited, 1932).
13 E. D. Swinton, *Over my shoulder* (Oxford: G. Ronald, 1951).
14 There is no evidence in these, or any other of Swinton's pre-war 'scribblings,' that he had any previsions of armored fighting vehicles.
15 Swinton and a colleague hit upon the name 'tank' because they were trying to find an intelligence-neutral, 'non-committal word to take the place of "landship",' one that was also 'likely to catch on and be remembered' (Swinton, *Eyewitness*, 186–87).
16 E. D. Swinton, Letter to the Secretary of the Royal Commission on Awards to Inventors. September 26, 1919, 1, Public Records Office, Kew, Surrey, UK.
17 Interested readers should consult Swinton, *Eyewitness*; 'The Proceedings of

Royal Commission on Awards to Inventors, 1919'; and 'The History of the Ministry of Munitions; Volume XII; The Supply of Munitions, Part III: Tanks'.

18  'The History of the Ministry of Munitions; Volume XII; The Supply of Munitions, Part III: Tanks,' 3.

19  Lieutenant-General Baron von Ardenne in the *Berliner Tageblatt*, cited by E. D. Swinton in 'The Tanks' (pamphlet, reprinted and adapted from *The Strand Magazine*) (London: S.N. & S.I, 1918).

20  'The Tank as a Tactical Factor,' *Die Wien neue Freie Presse*, August 8, [1918?] (cited in *Weekly Tank Notes 2*), Public Records Office, Kew, Surrey, UK.

21  'A Statement from the Supreme Command of the German Army to the Party Leaders in the Reichstag, October 2, 1918,' in *Official Records of the Events leading up to the Armistice, 1918 (Amtliche Urkunden zur Vorgeschichte des Waffenstillstandes, 1918)* (Berlin, 1924), 29.

22  Swinton, 'The Tanks,' 13–14. This 'military officer' is never specifically identified, and although some facts would allow it to be T. G. Tulloch, it is more probable that it is Charles E. Vickers (about whom more later). Indeed, the mere fact that Swinton fails to identify the 'military officer' by name is a politically significant, and even suspicious, omission.

23  Clarke. *The Tale of the Next Great War, 1871–1914*, 382.

24  Charles E. Vickers, 'The Trenches' (1907), in Clarke (ed.), *The Tale of the Next Great War, 1871–1914*, 243.

25  Ibid, 250.

26  Ibid, 243.

27  E. D. Swinton, 'Memoirs' (obituary column), *The Royal Engineer's Journal*, vol VII, Jan–June 1908, 392–94.

28  E. D. Swinton, Letter to Mr Blackwood. October, 1906, Blackwood Archives, The National Library of Scotland. Edinburgh.

29  E. D. Swinton, Letter to Mr Blackwood. December 29, 1906, Blackwood Archives. In using the word 'neither,' Swinton indicates that the following pronoun 'us' (and all uses of 'we') refers to himself and only *one* other collaborator.

30  E. D. Swinton, Letter to Mr Blackwood. March 11, 1907, Blackwood Archives.

31  E. D. Swinton, 'The Joint in the Harness,' *Blackwood's Magazine*, Jan 1907, Vol. 181, No. 1095, 6.

32  Swinton—or should that be Swann-ton?—was, in fact, a Major then.

33  Vickers, 'The Trenches,' 243.

34  E. D. Swinton, Letter to Mr Blackwood, March 28, 1907, Blackwood Archives.

35  Swinton refers to Vickers as his 'pal' in several of his letters to Blackwood (Blackwood Archives).

36  Charles E. Vickers, Letter to Mr Blackwood, October 10, 1907, Blackwood Archives.

37  E. D. Swinton, Letter to Mr Blackwood, December 12, 1907, Blackwood Archives.

38  E. D. Swinton, Letter to Mr Blackwood, January 8, 1908, Blackwood Archives.

39  E. D. Swinton, Letter to Mr Blackwood, February 9, 1908, Blackwood Archives.

40  Emily Vickers, Letter to Mr Blackwood, March 9, 1909, Blackwood Archives.

41 According to Captain Tulloch, a Holt-modeled tractor was also on display at the Agricultural Hall in London from 1906–1908. It is difficult to imagine that Swinton would have been unaware of this.
42 Arthur Conan Doyle, 'Danger!' (1914), in Clarke (ed.), *The Tale of the Next Great War, 1871–1914*, 294.
43 Between January and July of 1942, a mere 14 German U-boats sunk 450 allied ships. This equals slightly more than one ship per U-boat per week.
44 Appendix to 'Danger!', *Strand Magazine*, July 1914, 20–22. Cited by I. F. Clarke in *Voices Prophesying War*, 91.
45 This is the same Hankey who helped Swinton promote his idea of the tank within both the War Office and the Admiralty.
46 Maurice Hankey, Appendation (for Kitchener?) to a 'Private and Confidential' letter sent from the Committee of Imperial Defence, 11 June, 1915, pg. 3, Public Records Office, Kew, Surrey, UK. It is interesting to note that Hankey —ever a realist and adherent of *realpolitik*—shared Conan Doyle's assumption that neither international treaties nor traditional chivalry would prevent the submarine from being used to its full, destructive, potential. In the same letter, he conjectures that 'If . . . we devote ourselves seriously to developing the antidote to the submarine, we shall probably find means of dealing with it. But . . . it is difficult to see how or why . . . any international body will protect us more effectively than we can protect ourselves against the German submarines. . . . The crux of the question is this—can any reliance whatsoever be placed on an international body? It is submitted that the answer must be in the negative' (ibid, 3).
47 Maurice Hankey, *THE WAR* (August 1914 to 31 May, 1915). For the Secret Committee for Imperial Defence, and the Secretary for the State of War (Kitchener), London, 24 June 1915, pg. 6, Public Records Office, Kew, Surrey, UK.
48 H. G. Wells, *The War in the Air* (published along with *The History of Mr Polly*) (London: Odhams Press Limited, n.d.), 293–96.
49 E. D. Swinton, Letter to Mr Blackwood, May 10, 1906, Blackwood Archives. Swinton's use of 'Q.F.' indicates that he is speaking of 'quick-firing,' or what would now be called 'repeating,' or possibly 'semiautomatic,' guns.
50 E. D. Swinton, Letter to Mr Blackwood, May 28, 1906, Blackwood Archives.
51 This article exists only as a clipping in the Blackwood Archives, included in a letter from Swinton to Blackwood on October 26, 1906. The clipping has been so cropped that neither the identity of the paper nor the date is included.
52 An excellent review of the early history of the air arm of the British military —including its susceptibility to the influence of future-war fictions—is presented by Michael Paris in *Winged Warfare: The literature and theory of aerial warfare in Britain, 1859–1917* (Manchester: Manchester University Press, 1992), 66–73.
53 It is also worth noting that there is no record of an engineer actually designing or officially proposing such a device as this 'Kite.' Indeed, the first interest and actual development of aircraft for military purposes in Britain occurred in the Admiralty, a completely separate (and often, rival) branch of the military.
54 Lord Northcliffe, *Daily Mail*, 6 November 1906.

55  H. G. Wells, 'Of a cross-channel passage,' *Daily Mail*, 27 July 1909.
56  E. D. Swinton, Letter to Mr Blackwood, September 23, 1906, Blackwood Archives. This is yet another voice in the already growing chorus of speculative authors and sympathetic middle-echelon experts (e.g. Wells, Hankey, Conan Doyle) who, unlike their more tradition-bound superiors, anticipate bombing and the recourse to the philosophy of 'total war'—the operational military hallmark of the superpower state.
57  These various details strongly imply that the unidentified enemy power is Germany.
58  Swinton, 'The Joint in the Harness,' 16.
59  The tactical value of such (often unmanned) aircraft has dramatically increased in the last two decades, as the emphasis on portable, stealthy, precision-capable aircraft has grown along with an increased reliance on covert operations and commando infiltrations.
60  Swinton, 'The Joint in the Harness.'
61  Ibid.
62  Ibid, 15.
63  This story is 'The Green Curve,' which is a survival yarn that has profound thematic similarities to Thomas Godwin's classic 'hard' science fiction story, 'The Cold Equations.'
64  E. D. Swinton, Letter to Mr Blackwood, December 29, 1906, Blackwood Archives.
65  H. G. Wells, *The Contemporary Novel* (London: n.p., 1914), 163.
66  Orwell asserts Wells' influence in 'Wells, Hitler and the world state' (in *Collected Essays*, 1961).
67  Paris, *Winged Warfare*, 16.
68  H. G. Wells, 'Preface,' *The War in the Air*, 167.
69  Ibid, 255.
70  Ibid, 278. Wells' overt marginalization of colonized—and, by his implication, routinely brutalized—peoples provides an instructive insight into Wells' very inconstant approach to the question of developing or Third World populations. In the same novel, Wells depicts the Chinese as ultimately faring best in the 'war in the air' and often lambasts the West (and England in particular) for 'expressing contempt for the Subject Races' (Wells, *War in the Air*, 222). However, Wells frequently lapses into marginalization of such peoples, making any assessment of his attitudes on race and colonialism extremely problematical.
71  Ibid, 220.
72  Ibid, 223.
73  Ibid. 223–24.
74  Pound and Harmsworth, *Northcliffe*, 434.
75  Wells, *War in the Air*, 265.
76  Ibid, 265. Wells' prediction that warmaking would evolve into a highly specialized skill, exercised by an ever-decreasing number of trained 'specialists' is another remarkable insight into the observable trends of military operations in the twentieth century, particularly in its closing years and in those states which are themselves, or are hegemonically linked to, superpowers.

# NOTES

77   Ibid, 299.
78   Thomas Scortia, 'Science Fiction as the Imaginary Experiment,' in *Science Fiction, Today and Tomorrow*, ed. Reginald Bretnor (New York: Harper and Row, 1974), 142.
79   Wells, *War in the Air*, 225.
80   Paris, *Winged Warfare*, 25.
81   E. D. Swinton, 'An Eddy of War,' *Blackwood's Magazine*, November 1909, Vol. 186, No 1124, 461.
82   E. D. Swinton, Letter to Mr Blackwood, January 29, 1909, Blackwood Archives. 'An Englishman's Home' is a play by Gerald du Maurier.
83   Evidence of this claim will be presented in Chapter 9.
84   Wells, *The War in the Air*, 300–01.
85   Ibid, 347.

## Notes to Chapter 4

1   H. G. Wells, Preface, *The War in the Air* (1908) (London: n.p., 1940).
2   H. Bruce Franklin, *War Stars: The Superweapon and the American Imagination* (New York: Oxford University Press, 1988), 131.
3   Leo Szilard, *Leo Szilard: His Version of the Facts (Selected Recollections and Correspondence)*, ed. Spencer Weart and Gertrud Weiss Szilard (Cambridge, MA: The MIT Press, 1978), 18.
4   This nuclear substance, Carolinum, with a half-life of 17 days, anticipates the 'enriched' nuclear materials that are actually used for warheads (plutonium). H. G. Wells, *The World Set Free* (1914) (London: Corgi Books, n.d.), 72.
5   Ibid, 30.
6   A painstakingly detailed account of these events is provided by H. Bruce Franklin in *War Stars*.
7   Wells, *The World Set Free*, 138.
8   Ibid, 139.
9   Ibid, 95.
10  Ibid, 95–96.
11  Ibid, 9.
12  Ibid, 190–91.
13  Ibid, 191.
14  Ibid, 73.
15  Ibid, 178.
16  Ibid, 176.
17  Ibid, 173.
18  Ibid, 155.
19  It is possible that Wells intended to represent this as a 'weakness' in the structure of his post-war Utopia; in the last pages of the narrative, Karenin warns that—in order for the next phase of social evolution to occur—even detachment from sexual and romantic preoccupation will have to be achieved.
20  Wells, *The World Set Free*, 57.
21  Ibid, 108.
22  Egbert is the former British monarch. His retention of the title is purely honorific.

23 Wells, *The World Set Free*, 121.
24 H. G. Wells, *The War of the Worlds* (1898), reprinted in *The Time Machine and The War of the Worlds: A Critical Edition*, ed. Frank D. McConnell (New York: Oxford University Press, 1977), 224–25.
25 Ibid, 202.
26 Ibid, 181.
27 Ibid, 184.
28 Ibid, 205.
29 Ibid, 224.
30 Ibid, 264.
31 Ibid, 268.
32 Ibid, 151.
33 Ibid, 125.
34 H. G. Wells, cited by Frank D. McConnell in a 'Frontispiece footnote' in *The Time Machine and The War of the Worlds, a Critical Edition*, 119.
35 Wells, *The War of the Worlds*, 272.
36 Ibid, 274.
37 Ibid, 276.
38 Ibid, 276.
39 Ibid, 277.
40 Ibid, 246.
41 Ibid, 247.
42 Ibid, 169.
43 H. G. Wells, 'The Land Ironclads' (1903), *The Complete Short Stories of H. G. Wells* (London: Ernest Benn Limited, 1966), 137.
44 Stuart Cloete, *Yesterday is Dead* (New York: Smith & Durrell, 1940), 134.
45 Review of *The War of the Worlds* by H. G. Wells, *The Critic*, 29, April 23, 1898, 282.
46 Review of *The War of the Worlds* by H. G. Wells, *The Nation*, 66.1719, June 9, 1898, 447.
47 Sydney Brooks, Review of *The War of the Worlds* by H. G. Wells, *Harper's Weekly: A Journal of Civilization*, 42, April 2, 1898, 321.
48 Clement Shorter, Review of *The War of the Worlds* by H. G. Wells, *The Bookman* (New York), 7, May 1898, 246–47.
49 Franklin. *War Stars*, 68.
50 H. G. Wells, *Anticipations* (London: n.p., 1902), 212.
51 Clarke, *Voices Prophesying War*, 88.

## Notes to Chapter 5

1 John Ulrich Giesy, *All for His Country* (1914) (New York: Macaulay, 1915). This early twentieth-century text, and others which reveal America's growing interest in, and appetite for, global dominion, are exhaustively and insightfully examined in H. Bruce Franklin's *War Stars*.
2 For instance, publisher George Putnam, in the Introduction to J. Bernard Walker's *America Fallen* (1915), explicitly invokes Chesney's 'The Battle of Dorking' as the rhetorical inspiration and model for this cautionary tale of war with Germany.

3   Wells' fiction was not an isolated example, but representative of a whole trend in British popular literature that capitalized on a rapidly growing interest in new technological marvels and their use in war-oriented scenarios. Examples of this fiction include George Griffith's many novels—such as *The Angel of the Revolution* (1893) and *The Great Weather Syndicate* (1906)—and those of D. W. Horner—*By Aeroplane to the Sun* (1911) and *Their Winged Destiny* (1912).

4   A more complete overview of the Soviet experience with science fiction can be found in my article 'At the Gates of Absolutism: Science Fiction and Lysenkoism in the Soviet Union,' *The Journal of Social and Evolutionary Systems*, No. 19 (1), 1–16.

5   For interested readers, I recommend Peter S. Fisher's *Fantasy and Politics: Visions of the Future in the Weimar Republic.* (Madison, WI: University of Wisconsin Press, 1991). Fisher's consideration of post-World War I German future-war fantasies and their relationship to the development and technophilic aspects of the Nazi regime is exhaustive, insightful, and provides an excellent illustration of the literary and political processes and predilections characteristic of superpower states.

6   Project Paperclip was the codename for the OSS's collective activities to locate and appropriate—if possible, with the benefit of advance contact and agreement—the top scientific minds of the Third Reich before the advancing Soviet armies reached them. Wernher von Braun—the charismatic German uncle of the American space program—is only the most celebrated of the many scientists who were removed from Germany in the last weeks of the war, along with hundreds of items of technological interest, including examples of the V-1 and V-2 rockets, various jets, rocket planes, tanks, communications systems, sensors, heavy water experimentation gear, and other advanced equipment. It is also worth noting that the Russians had a similar (but ultimately less successful) operation underway to 'acquire the cooperation' and products of the Nazi 'wonder weapon' infrastructure. This race for the technological spoils of the defeated Reich is one of the most compelling indications of how powerfully technology and science determines the strategic activities of true superpower states.

7   Both of these incidents are described and explained in Chapter 4.

8   The commonplace rebuttal to this perspective—the unconquerability of Russia—qualifies and limits but does not invalidate the assertion that America's contribution to World War II was crucial. Without massive injections of lend-lease matériel from the US, the Soviet Union might have collapsed, or have been forced to sue for peace. Without a two-front war, the Nazis would have had the time and resources to better consolidate their hold on their European conquests, making them more expensive for the Western Allies to roll back and defeat. Considering how close the Allies believed the Nazis to be to succeeding with their 'heavy water' atomic weapons research, such a delay was not acceptable.

9   Howard P. Segal, *Technological Utopianism in American Culture* (Chicago. University of Chicago Press, 1985), 1.

10  George Steiner, *Real Presences* (Chicago: University of Chicago Press, 1989), 32.

11  H. Bruce Franklin traces the roots of this new literature in *War Stars* with a convincing assessment of the intimate connections between America's most

famous inventors (Fulton, Edison, and others) and the development of new, even 'super,' weapons.

12   Thomas Edison, interviewed in *The New York Times*, October 16, 1915, 4.
13   Franklin, *War Stars*, 42.
14   In *The Creation of Tomorrow* (New York: Columbia University Press, 1977, 120–25), Paul A. Carter explores the many 'hard sf' stories which not only identified Hitler's Third Reich as America's most dangerous potential adversary, but anticipated its predilection for weapons that broke the accustomed boundaries of technology and destructiveness.
15   It is significant that the name of the Rand Corporation is actually a truncated and compressed version of 'Research and Development.'
16   John McHale, *The Future of the Future* (New York: George Braziller, Inc., 1969), 254.
17   Chris Hables Gray. '"There Will Be War!": Future War Fantasies and Militaristic Science Fiction in the 1980s,' *Science Fiction Studies*, Volume 21, 1994, 318.
18   Scortia, 'Science Fiction as the Imaginary Experiment'. Scortia also asserts the near-interchangeability of the practices that dominate both the writing of hard science fiction and the generation of strategic scenarios: 'Science fiction's function as a framework for the imaginary experiment has surprisingly been formalized in such government support "think tanks" as the Institute for Defense Analysis and Dr. Herman Kahn's Hudson Institute. This latter institute has for years been engaged in writing scenarios projecting a series of alternate futures, depending on possible development in the social and political forces now at work. This of course, is the purist exercise in the science fiction *gedankenexperimenten*' (ibid, 141).
19   Caspar Weinberger and Peter Schweizer, *The Next War* (Washington, DC: Regnery, 1996).
20   Harold Coyle's *Team Yankee*—possibly the most narrowly focused of all Cold War military technothrillers—was specifically written as a 'zoomed in,' tactical view of Hackett's *The Third World War* scenario, according to Coyle's 'Foreword.'
21   Raymond Williams, *Television: Technology and Cultural Form* (New York: Schocken Books, 1975), 150–51.
22   Frank W. Elwell, *The Evolution of the Future* (New York: Praeger Publishers, 1991), 23.
23   Kris Neville, 'Cold War' (1949), in *The Astounding Science Fiction Anthology*, ed. John W. Campbell Jr. (New York: Berkley Publishing, 1964), 175.
24   Gray makes a similar observation in '"There Will Be War!"'.
25   These and other confirmed accounts of science fiction authors participating directly in domains of official, often military, discourse are recorded in Frederick Lerner's *Modern Science Fiction and the American Literary Community* (Metuchen, NJ: The Scarecrow Press, 1985).
26   L. Sprague de Camp, Pilgrim Award Acceptance Speech, 1998: 'Something Personal for the Science Fiction Research Association,' *SFRA Review*, No. 234, July 1998, 3.
27   Lerner, *Modern Science Fiction*, 148.
28   Clarke, *Voices Prophesying War*, 40.
29   George Steiner, *Language and Silence* (New York: Atheneum, 1967), 19.

## Notes to Chapter 6

1 Spencer Weart, *Nuclear Fear: A History of Images* (Cambridge, MA: Harvard University Press, 1988), 97.
2 Ibid, 383.
3 Whitley Strieber and James W. Kunetka, *Warday and the journey onward* (New York: Holt, Rinehart, and Winston, 1984).
4 Weart, *Nuclear Fear*, 81. Weart gives no source for the statements attributed to the members of the Paris team.
5 The Campbell–Cartmill story is recounted in greater and authoritative detail in 'The *Astounding* Investigation,' *Analog*, September 1984, 125–37.
6 Wylie's misadventure with military intelligence is detailed in Sam Moskowitz's *Explorers of the Infinite* (Cleveland, OH: Meridian Books, 1963), 292–93.
7 United States Government, documents of Cabinet meeting, 11 December 1956, Box 15, Ann Whitman Cabinet Series, The Dwight D. Eisenhower Library, Abilene, Kansas. H. Bruce Franklin refers to these documents in *War Stars*.
8 James M. Welsh, 'The Modern Apocalypse: *The War Game*,' *Journal of Popular Film and Television*, 1983, Volume 11, Part 1, 27.
9 Ibid, 32.
10 Weart adduces other direct political effects in *Nuclear Fear*, including a connection between the 'popular book and movie, *Seven Days in May*,' and 'Goldwater's electoral defeat' (ibid, 278). He also connects the downturn in Wallace's presidential bid with nuclear czar Curtis Le May's appointment as his running mate (278). Weart's arguments and evidence are convincing, but not as conclusive or elegant as the simple proof of censorship itself.
11 Weart, *Nuclear Fear*, 250.
12 Ronald Reagan, *An American Life* (New York: Simon & Schuster, 1990), 585.
13 Films and novels were not the only fictional venues through which American society conversed with itself over the anxieties and instrumentalities of a possible atomic conflict. In the immediate post-World War II years, American papers and periodicals were arguably the most important facilitators of this process. Prominent examples include 'World Aflame: The Russian–American War of 1950' (Engel and Piller, 1947) and Collier's 'Preview of the War We Do Not Want: Principal Events of World War III,' (1951); shorter, less prestigious narratives were legion.
14 The number of factors which contribute to this do not warrant extensive consideration here, but in addition to the prevailing weather conditions, there are these additional factors: whether the blast was ground-burst or air-burst; the yield of the warhead; if the warhead fell as part of a cluster or alone; terrain features of the impact zone.
15 Pat Frank, *Alas, Babylon* (New York: Bantam, 1969), 311.
16 Ibid, 309.
17 In *Nuclear Fear*, Weart cites *Alas, Babylon* as 'probably the best-selling book about a world after the bombs,' pointing out that it 'remained in print for decades' (222).
18 Walter M. Miller, Jr., *A Canticle for Liebowitz* (Philadelphia: Lippincott, 1959). Another powerful and enduring presence in both popular literature and nuclear discourse, Miller's *Canticle* sold more than a million copies over twenty

years and was translated into five languages. It is still in print today and is no stranger to high school and college English syllabi.
19 Eugene Burdick and Harvey Wheeler, 'Preface,' *Fail-Safe* (New York: McGraw-Hill, 1962), 7.
20 Ibid, 8.
21 Ibid, 44.
22 Richard Halloran, 'Computer Error Falsely Indicates A Soviet Attack,' *The New York Times*, June 6, 1980.
23 'Missile Alerts Traced to 46¢ Item,' *The New York Times*, June 18, 1980. H. Bruce Franklin also cites this incident in *War Stars*, and is quick to point out (as were Pentagon spokespersons) that it was the 'human element' in the defense control apparatus that was vital to revealing the alert as a false alarm: 'Fortunately, there were still human beings involved in this decision making too. They had time to notice the inexplicable—to human comprehension—fact that the Soviet 'missiles' were all coming in pairs. . . . a forty-six cent chip had shorted out, causing the transmission of a series of 2s that simulated paired incoming missiles' (208). However, it is also important to note that these anomalous signatures were completely unconfirmed by any of the other elements in the massive array of early warning sensors. A precautionary cross-check was evidently the first response of the experts: 'Within three minutes, however, officers studying data coming directly from sensors, before they reached the computer, ascertained that satellites, radar, and other warning devices had not reported flying missiles' (Halloran, 'Computer Error'). In addition to the lack of independent confirmation from any other element in the multi-tiered detection system that included 'ground-based radar near the Arctic Circle, infrared satellites able to detect missile exhaust, and a new radar on the Massachusetts coast able to pick up Soviet submarine-launched rockets' (Richard Burt, 'False Nuclear Alarms Spur Urgent Effort to Find Flaws,' *The New York Times*, June 13, 1980), there was other data suggesting that the apparent assault was actually a malfunction. These would include absolute lack of thermal launch signature either from silos or the ocean; no change in the Soviet military air traffic pattern; no pre-launch venting from Soviet ICBMs (many of which, in 1980, still needed to be fueled immediately prior to launch with extremely exothermic liquids); and of course, a political climate which contra-indicated such action. Indeed, the greatest danger might have been from Soviet perceptions of the US precautionary readiness preparations: 'Assistant Secretary of Defense Thomas B. Ross . . . declined to discuss the wider implications of the false alarm. Specifically, he refused to comment on the suggestion that an alert could set off a series of escalating responses in the United States and the Soviet Union that would build momentum into a confrontation' (Halloran, 'Computer Error')
24 Neville, 'Cold War'.
25 Strieber and Kunetka's scenario closely resembles the outcome of a 1987 M.I.T. computer simulation of a 'limited' nuclear war, according to Michael Dorris and Louise Erdrich in 'The Days After Tomorrow: Novelists at Armageddon,' in *The Nightmare Considered*, ed. N. Anisfield (Bowling Green, OH: Bowling Green State University Popular Press, 1991), 53.

## Notes to Chapter 7

1. *Threads*, a 1984 BBC TV film directed by Mick Jackson, may be the most devastating and horrifying of all the cinematic renderings of the nuclear nightmare. Its visual power and its effective synthesis of various rhetorical modes result in a singularly compelling—and arresting—anti-nuclear statement.
2. H.G. Wells, *The World Set Free* (1914) (London: Corgi Books, n.d).
3. *The Day After* is a 1983, ABC-produced made-for-TV movie, directed by Nicholas Meyer.
4. Patrick Mannix, *The Rhetoric of Antinuclear Fiction: Persuasive Strategies in Novels and Films* (Lewisburg: Bucknell University Press, 1992), 82–83.
5. Ibid, 137.
6. Ibid, 138.
7. Susan Sontag, 'The Imagination of Disaster,' in *Against Interpretation* (New York: Dell, 1966).
8. Vivian Sobchack, 'The Violent Dance: A Personal Memoir of Death in the Movies,' *Journal of Popular Film*, 3.1 (Winter 1974), 2–14.
9. Wells, *The War of the Worlds* (1898).
10. Pat Frank, *Alas, Babylon*; Walter M. Miller, *A Canticle for Leibowitz*; Whitley Streiber and James Kunetka, *Warday*. *Testament* is a film based on Carol Amen's 'The Last Testament' (1980).
11. Larry Niven and Jerry Pournelle, *Footfall* (New York: Ballantine Books, 1983).
12. Michael Crichton, *The Andromeda Strain* (1969) (New York: Dell Publishing, 1981).
13. Eugene Burdick and Harvey Wheeler, *Fail-Safe* (New York: McGraw Hill, 1962).
14. I am neither claiming nor implying that it can be conclusively proven that Operation Olympic could have been made unnecessary through other methods. Many lengthy and compelling arguments have been adduced which suggest that the US decision to employ the atomic bomb was not motivated by military concerns, so much as it was intended as a political statement to the post-war world and also, as a chillingly utilitarian field test of an untried weapon. However, the Japanese propensity for suicide attacks did give military planners reasonable pause when considering any campaign to land upon and pacify the Japanese home islands, despite the utter ruination that had already been rained upon them. The strategic situation was further complicated by the Russian eagerness to enter the war with Japan at the eleventh hour, and to participate in both the conquest and occupation of the home islands, possibly with the intent of converting Japan into a Soviet satellite state.
15. Jacqueline Smetak, 'Sex and Death in Nuclear Holocaust Literature of the 1950's,' in *The Nightmare Considered: Critical Essays on Nuclear War Literature*, ed. Nancy Anisfield (Bowling Green, OH: Bowling Green State University Popular Press, 1991), 21.
16. Helen Caldicott, *Missile Envy* (Bantam. New York, 1985), 319.
17. Burdick and Wheeler, *Fail-Safe*, 123–24.
18. Robert Heinlein, 'Blowups Happen,' *Astounding Science Fiction*, 26 no. 1, Sept. 1940, 51–85.
19. John Campbell, Editorial, *Astounding Science Fiction*, 26 no. 1, 5–6.

20  Weart, *Nuclear Fear*, 82. There were other stories at that time which dealt with the same issue. One famous example is Lester Del Rey's 'Nerves' *(Astounding Science Fiction*, No. 30, September 1942).
21  Weart, *Nuclear Fear*, 151.
22  Ibid, 251–52.
23  These, and several following anecdotes, were first unveiled in H. Bruce Franklin's ground-breaking investigations into Truman's probable susceptibility to future-war fiction and poetry, extensively detailed in *War Stars*. The two stanzas that reputedly inspired Truman's vision are: '[I] Heard the heavens fill with shouting, and there rained a ghastly dew / From the nations' airy navies grappling in the central blue; . . . Till the war-drum throbbed no longer, and the battle-flags were furled / In the Parliament of man, the Federation of the world.'
24  Roy Norton, *The Vanishing Fleets* (New York: D. Appleton, 1908), 237, 244.
25  In *War Stars*, H. Bruce Franklin offers further, compelling evidence that suggests that Truman was indeed exposed, and receptive, to the concepts in this narrative.
26  Robert Heinlein, 'Solution Unsatisfactory' (1941), reprinted in *Expanded Universe* (New York: Ace Books, 1980), 100.
27  *War Stars*, 142. Franklin provides a detailed overview of the themes and influences associated with the narrative, and several of his researches and conclusions on 'Solution Unsatisfactory' have influenced my own approach to the narrative. I gratefully acknowledge his trailblazing and masterful scholarship on this short story.
28  Heinlein, 'Solution Unsatisfactory,' 111.
29  Ibid, 111–12.
30  Ibid, 139.
31  Robert A. Heinlein, *Grumbles from the Grave*, ed. Virginia Heinlein (New York: Del Rey Books, 1990), 43.
32  Robert Heinlein, 'Foreword' to 'The Last Days of The United States,' in *Expanded Universe* (New York: Ace Books, 1980), 147.
33  Weart, *Nuclear Fear*, 83.
34  Sontag, 'The Imagination of Disaster,' 218.
35  This line (in slightly different form) is also found in Wells' text, and it is one of the few lines that Pal actually retained from the novel. It is also one of Wells' very few references to God.
36  Robert Jay Lifton and Richard Falk, *Indefensible Weapons: The Political and Psychological Case Against Nuclearism* (New York: Basic Books, 1982), 3.
37  Weart, *Nuclear Fear*, 107.
38  Ibid, 135, 265–67.
39  Ibid, 265.
40  Jane Caputi, 'Psychic Numbing, Radical Futurelessness, and Sexual Violence in Nuclear Film,' in Anisfield (ed.), *The Nightmare Considered*, 58
41  George Orwell, *1984* (1946) (New York: Signet, 1964).
42  Russell Hoban, *Riddley Walker* (London: Macmillan, 1982), 96–97.
43  Strieber and Kunetka, *Warday*.
44  Paul Auster, *In the Country of Last Things* (New York: Viking, 1987), 89.

45 Strictly speaking, this genre had its inception in the Australian film *Mad Max*. However, its success, sequels, and imitators were encouraged and enabled by the response of audiences in America, not Australia.

46 In his consideration of post-apocalypse films, 'Surviving Armageddon: Beyond the Imagination of Disaster' (*Science Fiction Studies*, Vol. 20, 1993), Mick Broderick points out that 'the punk villain of *World Gone Wild* (1988) reads the "Wit and Wisdom of Charles Manson" to his followers' while another film's eponymous *Texas Gladiators* 'violate nuns and crucify a priest' (ibid, 377).

## Notes to Chapter 8

1 Philip A. Pecorino, 'Philosophy and Science Fiction,' in *The Intersection of Science Fiction and Philosophy*, ed. Robert Myers (Westport, CT: Greenwood Press, 1983), 5.

2 'Mach' is a speed rating which is equal to the speed of sound at sea level; therefore 'Mach 10' is ten times the speed of sound.

3 The definition of 'common' knowledge is—obviously—similarly problematic.

4 To this day, the top speed of the SR-71 remains highly classified, with official sources only admitting that it stands in excess of 2500 miles per hour.

5 Dean McLaughlin, 'Hawk Among the Sparrows,' *War and Peace: Possible Futures from 'Analog,'* Anthology #6, summer 1983 (New York: Davis Publishing Inc.), 133–72.

6 Ibid, 138.

7 There is considerable discrepancy among various, reasonably authoritative sources as to the technical and operational specifications of the SR-71. There are several reasons for this (all of which further illustrate the difficulties attached to determining the temporal and informational ambiguities associated with technological speculations). These include different degrees of declassification that prevailed when different texts were being written; varying degrees of authorial care, research and extrapolation; and terminological imprecision and/or inconstancy ('Blackbird' is often used as a catch-all label for the SR-71 reconaissance plane, the interceptor variant known as the YF-12, and the A-12 prototype versions, all of which differ in certain particulars, and which were further distinguished by being produced in a variety of models). The sources consulted for this work include: Enzo Angelucci and Peter Bowers, *The American Fighter* (New York: Orion Books, 1987); Paul F. Crickmore, *Lockheed SR-71: The Secret Missions Exposed* (London: Osprey Publishing, 1993); Paul F. Crickmore, *SR-71 Blackbird* (London: Osprey Publishing, 1987); Rene J. Francillon, *Lockheed Aircraft Since 1913* (Naval Institute Press, 1987); Peter Garrison, 'Desert Blackbirds,' *Flying*, October 1994, 96–99; Art Hanley, 'Why The Blackbird Went Away,' *Airpower*, Vol. 27, No. 4, July 1997 (online copy); C.L. Johnson, 'Some Development Aspects of the YF-12A Interceptor Aircraft,' *Journal of Aircraft*, Vol. 7, No. 4, July–Aug. 1970, 355–59; Jay Miller, *Lockheed SR-71 (A-12/YF-12/D-21), Aerofax Minigraph 1* (Aerofax, Inc., 1985); Ben R Rich, 'F-12 Series Aircraft Aerodynamic and

Thermodynamic Design in Retrospect,' *Journal of Aircraft*, Vol. 11, No. 7, July 1974, 401–06; R. R. Ropelewski, 'SR-71 Impressive in High Speed Regime,' *Aviation Week*, May 18, 1981; Anthony M. Thorborough and Peter E. Davies, *Lockheed Blackbirds* (Osceola, WI: Motorbooks International, 1988).

8   McLaughlin, 'Hawk Among the Sparrows,' 140.
9   Ibid, 143.
10  Ibid, 151.
11  Ibid.
12  Daniel Graham Jr., *The Gatekeepers* (New York: Baen Books, 1995).
13  Jerry Shelton, 'Eyewitness Report,' *Astounding Science Fiction*, No. 36, October 1945.
14  Denis Gabor, *Inventing the Future* (New York: Alfred A. Knopf, 1963), 207–08.
15  John McHale, *The Future of the Future* (New York: George Braziller, 1969), 242.
16  Frederick I. Ordway, III and Randy Lieberman (eds), 'Introduction,' *Blueprint for Space: Science Fiction to Science Fact* (Washington, DC: Smithsonian Institute Press, 1992), 10.
17  Ibid.
18  See Frank H. Winter's 'Planning for Spaceflight: 1880s to 1930s,' in Ordway and Lieberman (eds), *Blueprint for Space* for more details on Tsiolkovskiy's motivations and subsequent work in the field of space science and technology.
19  Konstantin Tsiolkovskiy, 'The Exploration of Space with Reactive Devices,' *Nauchnoe Obozrenie (Scientific Review)*, May 1903.
20  A. A. Blagonravov articulates Tsiolkovskiy's seminal contributions to Soviet space flight and engineering in his 'Introduction' to *K.E. Tsiolkovsky: Selected Works* (Moscow: Mir Publishers, 1968), where he avers that 'The works of Tsiolkovsky contain in embryo nearly all the scientific-technical attainments of the Soviet Union in the exploration of space. With amazing accuracy he determined the path, stage by stage, of the development of engineering facilities for the solution of this problem. It is quite natural therefore that with each new development in this field we recall Tsiolkovsky as the scientist who foresaw in one way or another the outcome of these events' (7).
21  Konstantin Tsiolkovskiy, 'Investigation of World Spaces by Reactive Vehicles,' *Vestnik Vozdukhoplavaniya (Herald of Aeronautics)*, 1911, No. 19, 16–17.
22  Konstantin Tsiolkovskiy, *Beyond the Planet Earth* (1896) (New York: Pergamon Press, 1960). An extended consideration of this text is provided in my article 'At the Gates of Absolutism: Literature and Lysenkoism in the Soviet Union,' *The Journal of Social and Evolutionary Systems*, Vol. 19, No. 1, spring 1996.
23  Goddard's professed ignorance of Tsiolkovskiy's work may sound improbable to those of the Internet generation, but is almost unquestionably true. At the turn of the twentieth century, most Russian publications, including those in which Tsiolkovskiy's relevant works appeared, were not translated into English, and Goddard spoke no Russian. Furthermore, not until some years after the emergence of the Soviet regime was Tsiolkovskiy's work brought to light, and the author/engineer hailed as a genius. Another example of how independent researchers were converging on the physical secrets of rocketry is afforded by the career of inventor and space technology theorist Robert Esnault-Pelterie of France. Esnault-Pelterie was working at roughly the same

time as Goddard, evolving roughly the same theories, and they too worked in mutual ignorance. These apparent coincidences illustrate that the idea of spaceflight was rapidly gathering momentum as an impending 'mind-step.'
24 'A Strain on Credulity,' *New York Times*, January 13, 1920, 12.
25 Forest Ray Moulton, *Consider the Heavens* (Garden City, NY: Doubleday, Doran & Co., 1935).
26 Ley, like von Braun, was one the *wunderkinder* who were spirited away from the Third Reich as part of Project Paperclip, and were to become the energetic German uncles who mentored the American space program into eventual maturity.
27 Willy Ley's account is reported in Paul A. Carter's *The Creation of Tomorrow* (New York: Columbia University Press, 1977), 33.
28 Hermann Oberth, *Die Rakete zu den Planetenraumen (The Rocket into Planetary Space)* (Munich: R. Oldenbourg, 1923).
29 Hermann Oberth, *Wege zur Raumshiffahrt von Hermann Oberth, mit 4 Tafeln und 159 Abbildungen (Ways to Spaceflight)* (Munich and Berlin: R. Oldenbourg, 1929).
30 In addition, in 'The Spaceship as Icon: Designs from Verne to the Early 1950s' (in Ordway and Lieberman (eds), *Blueprint for Space*), Ron Miller asserts that von Braun was '[i]nfluenced in his youth by the space travel science fiction of Jules Verne, Kurd Lasswitz, and others . . .' (166).
31 Arthur C. Clarke, *How the World Was One: Beyond the Global Village* (New York: Bantam, 1992), 162–63.
32 Joe Haldeman, 'Confessions of a Space Junkie,' in *Viet Nam and Other Alien Worlds* (Framingham, MA: NESFA Press, 1994), 166.
33 Thomas Disch, 'The Road to Heaven: Science Fiction and the Militarization of Space,' *The Nation*, May 10, 1986, No. 242, 652.
34 Ordway and Lieberman (eds), *Blueprint for Space*, 127.
35 Constance Penley, *NASA/Trek* (New York: Verso, 1997).
36 McHale, *The Future of the Future*, 192–93.
37 'Introduction,' in Ordway and Lieberman (eds), *Blueprint for Space*, 12.
38 John M. Logsdon, 'The Challenge of Space: Linking Aspirations and Political Will,' in Ordway and Lieberman (eds), *Blueprint for Space*, 147.
39 Ordway and Lieberman (eds), *Blueprint for Space*, 135.
40 Ibid, 142.
41 Ibid, 145–46.
42 'Introduction,' in Ordway and Lieberman (eds), *Blueprint for Space*, 12.
43 Clarke, *How the World Was One*, 152.
44 Oberth, *Rocket into Planetary Space*, translated and cited in Clarke's *How the World Was One*, 164–65.
45 Clarke, *How the World Was One*, 182.
46 Ibid, 254–55.
47 Ibid, 255.
48 Ibid, 242.
49 Carl W. Spohr, 'The Final War,' *Wonder Stories* 3, April 1932, 1282. It is noteworthy that this story—possibly the first clear prevision of a technological defense net akin to that which was the objective of SDI—ends not with the preservation of peace, but absolute destruction of the biosphere. This echoes Wells' assertions that it is unavoidable that, as science and technology mature,

the forces and speed with which an aggressor can destroy are consistently increasing and further outstripping whatever advances there might be in defense. This has been a consistent theme in most of the visions of SDI advanced by future-war authors, even those who supported the development of the project.

50  When read in the context of the rest of his article, Asimov clearly uses the word 'fantastic' to mean something that is 'unreal' or 'fanciful.'
51  Clarke, *How the World Was One*, 253.
52  See Edward Reiss, *The Strategic Defense Initiative* (Cambridge: Cambridge University Press, 1992) for a discussion of the various contending conceptions and representations of SDI, particularly its proponents' disagreements regarding the degree of protection it could reasonably offer (45 and 52–54).
53  The Reagan Administration's eventual accommodation with, and fondness for, the 'Star Wars' label is recounted by Sanford Lakoff and Herbert F. York in *A Shield in Space? Technology Politics, and the Strategic Defense Initiative* (Berkeley and Los Angeles: University of California Press, 1989), 29–30.
54  Jerry Pournelle and Stefan T. Possony, 'Preface,' *The Strategy of Technology* (Cambridge, MA: University Press of Cambridge, 1970), xxxii.
55  H G Wells, *Anticipations* (London: n.p., 1902), 212.
56  Pournelle and Possony, *The Strategy of Technology*, 18n.
57  William J. Broad, *Star Warriors* (New York: Simon and Schuster, 1985), 119–20.
58  Ibid, 131.
59  Gordon R. Dickson, *The Tactics of Mistake* (1971) (New York: Tor Books, 1998).
60  Robert A. Heinlein, *The Moon is a Harsh Mistress* (New York: Berkeley, 1968).
61  Robert A. Heinlein, *Starship Troopers*. (1959) (New York: Berkeley, 1968).
62  Jerry Pournelle and Dean Ing, *Mutual Assured Survival* (New York: Baen, 1984), back cover.
63  Ben Bova's ideas were also considered in the course of the project, it seems, but he either did not attend the sessions or elected not to participate officially.
64  Pournelle and Ing, *Mutual Assured Survival*, 20.
65  Tom Clancy, *The Cardinal of the Kremlin* (New York: Putnam's, 1988).
66  William E. Ramsey, review of *The Cardinal of the Kremlin*, *Proceedings of the Naval Institute*; October 1988, Vol. 114, No. 10, 181.
67  Ibid.
68  'Interview: William E. Ramsey, Vice Admiral, US Navy,' *Proceedings of the Naval Institute*, October 1988, Vol. 114, No. 10, 145.
69  By 2002, the BMDO had evolved yet again, this time into the MDA (Missile Defense Agency).
70  As of November 25, 2002, the BMDO's latest declassified project updates were available online at http://www.acq.osd.mil/bmdo/
71  'Army Shoots Down Artillery Shell with Laser' (Reuters), *New York Times*, November 5, 2002.
72  David Niven and Jerry Pournelle, *Footfall* (New York: Del Rey, 1985), 239.
73  Ibid, 269.
74  Other fictional author/real author parallels seem to exist in the group of writers described in *Footfall*, but these are not pertinent here.
75  Alvin Toffler, *The Third Wave* (1979) (New York: Bantam Books, 1982), 291.

76  Larry Niven and Jerry Pournelle, *Lucifer's Hammer* (1977) (New York: Ballantine, 1983).
77  William J. Broad, 'For Killer Asteroids, Respect at Last,' *New York Times*, Tuesday, May 14, 1996, C1, C7.
78  Malcolm W. Browne, 'Asteroid is Expected to Make a Pass Close to Earth in 2028,' *New York Times*, Thursday, March 12, 1998, A1, A20. Subsequent remeasurement of the asteroid's vector is largely, but not conclusively, indicative of a 'miss' by a distance of 50,000–400,000 miles. This number will probably undergo further change as additional observations are made.
79  In *Lucifer's Hammer*, Earth is unable to do anything to stop the collision of the approaching comet; it is a tale of the devastation of the impact, the grim aftermath, and subsequent struggle to preserve civilization.
80  *Air Force 2025* (White paper collection: Air Force University Press, 1996), Vol. 3, Ch. 16, 41–42. Available either through Defense Technical Information Center (ATTN: DTIC-BRR), 8725 John J. Kingman Road, Suite 0944, Ft. Belvior, VA 22060–6218, or online at http://www.au.af.mil/au/2025/

## Notes to Chapter 9

1  Alan Nourse, *Science Fiction, Today and Tomorrow*, ed. Reginald Bretnor (New York: Harper and Row, 1974), 131.
2  Clarke, *Voices Prophesying War*, 196.
3  Heinlein's date is not accurate, if—as seems to be the case—he is referring to the publication date of Wells' *The World Set Free* (1913).
4  Robert A. Heinlein, letter to Lurton Blassingame, September 24, 1949, reprinted in *Grumbles from the Grave*, ed. Virginia Heinlein (New York: Ballantine, 1989), 174. Not only does Heinlein shrewdly assess the advantages a science fiction writer enjoys in comparison to a specialized futurist, but he also indicates that he is self-consciously operating within the distinct and long-established discursive tradition of 'synthesizing prophets,' whose authorial motivations have often included overt attempts to influence the societies in which they lived (e.g. Wells).
5  According to Heinlein, his *raison d'être* for actually writing science fiction was not to present a reader with a conclusive prediction or prophesy. Rather, his primary purpose was to explore possibilities through 'extrapolation and/or speculation,' and therefore his purpose 'may have nothing to do with the probability that these storied events may happen' (*Expanded Universe* (New York: Ace Books, 1980, 309)).
6  Chris Hables Gray, '"There Will Be War!": Future-war Fantasies and Militaristic Science Fiction in the 1980s,' *Science Fiction Studies*, No. 63, Vol. 21, Part 3, November 1994, 316.
7  In his article, Gray provides considerable additional evidence supporting Heinlein's claim.
8  Full information regarding Heinlein's specific involvement and contributions never became available since, as his widow later reported (according to Gray, '"There Will Be War!,"' 319), 'she wasn't familiar with most of his work because of secrecy rules, which they kept their whole lives.'

9 Heinlein recounts in a letter to Lurton Blassingame on August 21, 1952, that one day's typical set of visitors included 'the chairman of the British Interplanetary Society . . . [a] physicist from Johns Hopkins . . . an air force intelligence officer . . . [and the air force's] . . . head of the Flying Saucer project' (Heinlein, *Grumbles from the Grave*, 161). This same year, Heinlein was a guest on Edward R. Murrow's CBS program, 'This I Believe.'
10 See Heinlein's *Expanded Universe*, his wife's compilation *Grumbles from the Grave*, and Franklin's *War Stars*, 141 for further information on these activities, which include an astounding array of distinguished recognitions by the military.
11 Gray, '"There Will Be War!,"' 320.
12 Very little is known about 'Futurist I,' except that its content warranted a much higher level of confidentiality. Gray's attempts to learn more about this conference were fruitless.
13 Joe Haldeman (ed.), 'Introduction,' *Space-Fighters* (New York: Ace Books, 1988), 1.
14 Ibid, 5.
15 This is according to Dean Ing in his Introduction to *Firefight 2000* (New York: Baen Books, 1984), 12.
16 Robert A. Heinlein, *Starship Troopers* (1959) (New York: Berkley, 1968), 11, 83.
17 Ibid, 187.
18 Ibid, 11.
19 Ibid, 13.
20 Ibid, 18.
21 Ibid, 195–96.
22 Ibid, 81–82.
23 Jim Garamone, 'Army tests land warrior for 21st century soldiers,' *Army Link, Army News Service*, Sept. 14, 1998, http://www.dtic.mil/armylink/news/Sep1998/a19980914lanwar.html
24 Heinlein, *Starship Troopers*, 13–14.
25 Ibid, 17.
26 Ibid, 80.
27 Ibid, 16–17.
28 Ibid, 19–20.
29 Ibid, 80.
30 DARPA, United States Government, 'Exoskeletons for Human Performance Augmentation' (N.d.; accessed July 12, 2000) http://www.darpa.mil/dso/solicitations/00/Baa00-34/cbd.htm
31 Robert A. Heinlein, letter to Lurton Blassingame, November 7, 1949, reprinted in *Grumbles from the Grave*, 172–73.
32 At that time, McDonnell-Douglas was one of the largest US defense contractors, the world's third largest aerospace company, and particularly well known for its pioneering work in new weapons technologies.
33 I have elected to include only the comments from the individual whose overall responses were the *least* corroborative in order to present a maximally critical respondent. Furthermore, this individual had no prior relationship with the interviewer, had no previous indication of the nature of the questions, and had

no idea regarding which ideas or answers would support or problematize any given researches or hypotheses. The questions were structured to be as 'value-neutral' as possible in their semantics, and were a mix of positive and negative inquiries. 'False' inquiry topics were seeded into the interview, so as to deny the interviewee a sense of the 'essential thrust' of the interview.

34  Attempts have been made to minimize all editing in these transcript excerpts, although some has been necessary due to concerns of length, comprehensibility, and context.
35  Jerry McClellan, personal interview, March 7, 1996. Mr. McClellan is referring here to Tom Clancy's numerous near-future-war technothrillers.
36  Isaac Asimov is best known for science fiction stories focusing on robotics, computers, and artificial intelligence. McClellan's interest in, and admiration of, Asimov was so intense that he was able to recite that author's 'Three Laws of Robotics,' which have actually had considerable influence within the field of artificial intelligence research and development.
37  Other comments by the interviewee implied that peer interest in technothrillers such as Clancy's was even higher. It is also worth noting that the '25–30%' of similarly interested science fiction readers were known to McClellan because they overtly expressed this interest. Any readers who are less open about their interest would constitute an additional, unaccounted percentage.
38  George and Meredith Friedman, *The Future of War: Power, Technology and American World Dominance in the 21st Century* (New York: Random House/Crown, 1996), 378–79.
39  Jay W. Kelley, 'Brilliant Warriors,' *Air Force 2025*, Vol. 1, Ch. 8, 8.
40  Robert Smullen, 'We Can Make Starship Troopers,' *Proceedings of the Naval Institute*; Vol. 121, No. 11, October 1996, 39, 41.
41  Alan Brown, letter to the Editor, *SFWA Forum* (official newsletter), December 1996, No. 152.
42  Specific URLs are not provided due to considerations of length and the volatility (and therefore limited bibliographic value) of online references. Interested parties may contact me for further information. The search results screened out any 'fan' sites or any webpages that referred not to Heinlein's book, but to the laughable and misleading film of the same name.
43  In a further example of how numerous and intimate the interpenetrations are between the various domains of discourse under investigation—technothriller, far-future science fiction, and the military—it is worth noting that one of the reviewers whose jacket-blurb praise is most lavish—and prominently featured—on the covers of Pournelle's and Niven's *Footfall* (discussed in Chapter 8) is Tom Clancy. This not only indicates the degree of mutual admiration and interest that exists between the practitioners of these two related but distinct subgenres, but is also evidence of a substantial overlap in terms of their audiences. Obviously, the marketing staff who were responsible for promoting *Footfall* (which sold quite well) had solid reasons to expect that readers who might be interested in war-oriented 'hard' science fiction would be familiar with Clancy's work, and would also consider his opinion both credible and valuable. This is not the only incident that suggests Clancy's sustained personal

interest in, and familiarity with, far-future war fiction: he, along with Jerry Pournelle, was included among the many guest speakers at the ceremony in which Heinlein was posthumously awarded NASA's Distinguished Public Service Medal. To the sizable audience at that affair, 'Clancy told how Robert's work had taught him to write' (*Grumbles from the Grave*, 308).

44  James William Gibson, *Warrior Dreams: Paramilitary Culture in Post-Vietnam America* (New York: Hill and Wang, 1994), cited in Gray, '"There Will Be War!,"' 322.
45  Gray, ibid, 320.
46  S. M. Stirling, 'Necessity,' in *War World: The Burning Eye*, ed. John Carr and Jerry Pournelle (New York: Baen Books, 1988).
47  Ibid, 227.
48  Ibid, 233.
49  US Army Materiel Command, 'Objective Individual Combat Weapon (OICW): "No Place To Hide,"' *Science and Technology News*, Vol. 4, No. 1, Spring 1999, 2. Accessed online at <http://www2.brtrc.com/amc/scitech/library/Spring99/SPRING99.htm>
50  Ibid, 234–35.
51  Ibid, 235–36.
52  Gerry J. Gilmore, 'Land Warrior: Soldier of the Future,' *Army Link, Army News Service*, Feb. 27, 1997, <http://www.dtic.mil/armylink/news/Feb1997/a19970227landwar1.html>
53  US Army Materiel Command, 'Ballistic Protection for Individual Protection,' *Science and Technology News*, Vol. 4, No. 1, Spring 1999, 4. Accessed online at <http://www2.brtrc.com/amc/scitech/library/Spring99/SPRING99.htm>
54  Stirling, 'Necessity', 254–55.
55  Ibid, 255.
56  Nikola Tesla, 'The Problem of Increasing Human Energy,' *The Century Magazine*, June 1900, 183.
57  Ibid, 183–84.
58  Keith Laumer, *Bolo* (New York: Ace Books, 1986), 2, 4.
59  Ibid, 124.
60  Ibid, 140–41.
61  Ibid, 124.
62  Ibid, 5.
63  Reginald Bretnor, 'Science Fiction and the Semantics of Conflict,' in *Fights of Fancy: Armed Conflict in Science Fiction and Fantasy*, ed. George Slusser and Eric S. Rabkin (Athens, GA: University of Georgia Press, 1993), 26.
64  Reginald Bretnor, 'Specialization in Warfare,' *There Will be War, Vol. 7, Call to Battle* (New York: Baen, 1988), 258.
65  Gray, '"There Will Be War!,"' 327.
66  'Boeing unmanned combat aircraft to be developed,' *Boeing News*, Vol. 58, No. 15, April 16, 1999, 12.
67  US Government, Office of Assistant Secretary of Defense (Public Affairs), 'Darpa And Army Select Contractors For Future Combat Systems Programs,' News Release No. 236-00, May 9, 2000. Accessed online at <http://www.darpa.mil/fcs/news/news_release.htm>

## Notes to Chapter 10

1 Ernest Hemingway, *A Farewell To Arms* (1929) (New York: Scribner's, 1969), 54.
2 Harold Coyle, *Team Yankee* (New York: Berkley, 1988), 159–60. Coyle's *Team Yankee* is particularly interesting because of its overt intertextuality: according to Coyle's Foreword, it is a microcosmic view of one isolated action within Hackett's macroscopic *The Third World War*. However, just as was the case with Colomb's *The Great War of 189–*, Hackett's concerns were tied to a finite—and relatively brief—moment in history, one that is now buried beneath the ruins of the Berlin Wall and the rusting hulls of derelict Soviet tanks, ships, and planes. In contrast, because *Team Yankee* focused on the technology and personal *experience* of Hackett's imaginary war, rather than the international politics that caused it, Coyle's tale retains a considerable measure of both its personal and social meaning and pertinence. It is more lastingly *political* in that it invites the reader to vicariously experience a contemporary episode of that most inherently—and pervasively—political act: warmaking.
3 Tom Clancy, *Red Storm Rising* (New York: Berkley, 1987), 408.
4 James William Gibson, *Warrior Dreams: Paramilitary Culture in Post-Vietnam America* (New York: Hill and Wang, 1994).
5 A particularly pertinent example of this would be the human feedback target acquisition and tracking system employed in the AH-64 Apache attack helicopter. The aircraft's 'chin turret' is actually 'slaved' to the helmet motions of the gunner; turning one's head to the right or left, up or down, automatically swivels the turret's weaponry in that direction.
6 This category of responsible future-war depictions is almost exclusively comprised of *text* narratives.
7 Bretnor, 'Science Fiction and the Semantics of Conflict.'
8 The use of 'dominant' and 'emergent' in this sentence is informed by, and in reference to, Raymond Williams' theories on the progressive phases of hegemonic culture, particularly as articulated in his works *Marxism and Literature* (London: Verso, 1980), 112–14, 125–26, and *Problems in Materialism and Culture* (London: Verso, 1980), 45.
9 Wells, *Anticipations*.
10 Dawn Alford, 'The Creeping Terror,' *The Express* (Manchester, UK), Sunday, October 6, 1996, 15. Since this article was published, various tiny 'robot mines' have been refined to the point where they can be produced for general use. Only widespread international outcry against such devices has impeded large-scale (or, perhaps more accurately, overt) adoption of these truly 'infernal machines.'
11 Actually, the net effect of all this individually enhancing technology would be to attract the concentrated firepower of one's adversaries, who would probably lie in ambush rather than risking an open engagement.
12 Heinlein, *Starship Troopers*, 27.
13 Joe Haldeman, *The Forever War* (1974) (New York: Ballantine, 1976), 8. It is interesting to note that, at another point in the text, Haldeman's protagonist explains a social phenomenon by referring to Alvin Toffler's *Future Shock*, which had only been published a few years earlier than *The Forever War* (87).

This is further evidence of the extraordinary overlap between future-war and futurist discourses. More important, their mutual and unhesitating willingness to attest to this kind of intertextual reference suggests that the authors in both fields assume that their readers will have knowledge of—and interest in—both discursive domains.

14. Heinlein, *Starship Troopers*, 6.
15. Haldeman, *Forever War*, 25. Haldeman is referring to the number of 'man-hours' it takes to produce the equipment used by each soldier.
16. Heinlein, *Starship Troopers*, 13.
17. Haldeman, *Forever War*, 60–61.
18. Ibid, 57–58.
19. Heinlein, *Starship Troopers*, 14.
20. Poul Anderson, *Kings Who Die. 8th Annual Edition: The Year's Best S-F*, ed. Judith Merrill (New York: Dell, 1964), 134.
21. Both *Starship Troopers* and *The Forever War* received the Hugo Award—the most popular science fiction novel of the year, as voted by readers. This would seem to indicate that, at the time, these texts were considered (at least) reasonably pertinent and innovative by a fairly sizable audience.

## Note to the Afterword

1. John Gardner, *On Moral Fiction* (New York: Harper Colophon, 1978), 4.

# Selected Bibliography

*Airforce 2025* (White paper collection: Air Force University Press, 1996). Available either through Defense Technical Information Center (ATTN: DTIC-BRR), 8725 John J. Kingman Road, Suite 0944, Ft. Belvior, VA 22060–6218, or online at http://www.au.af.mil/au/2025/

Anderson, Poul, *Kings Who Die. 8th Annual Edition: The Year's Best S-F*, ed. Judith Merrill (New York: Dell, 1964)

Arnold-Forster, Hugh Oakley, 'In a Conning Tower' (1888), in *The Tale of the Next Great War, 1871–1914: Fictions of Future Warfare and of Battles Still-to-come*, ed. I. F. Clarke (Liverpool: Liverpool University Press, 1995)

Auster, Paul, *In the Country of Last Things* (New York: Viking, 1987)

Blagonravov, A. A., *K.E. Tsiolkovsky: Selected Works* (Moscow: Mir Publishers, 1968)

Bretnor, Reginald, 'Science Fiction and the Semantics of Conflict,' in *Fights of Fancy: Armed Conflict in Science Fiction and Fantasy*, ed. George Slusser and Eric S. Rabkin (Athens, GA: University of Georgia Press, 1993), 26

Bretnor, Reginald, 'Specialization in Warfare,' in *There Will be War, Vol. 7, Call to Battle* (New York: Baen, 1988), 258

Broad, William J., *Star Warriors* (New York: Simon and Schuster, 1985)

Brown, Alan, Letter to the Editor, *SFWA Forum* (official newsletter), December 1996, No. 152

Burdick, Eugene and Harvey Wheeler, *Fail-Safe* (New York: McGraw–Hill, 1962)

Caldicott, Helen, *Missile Envy* (Bantam: New York, 1985)

Caputi, Jane, 'Psychic Numbing, Radical Futurelessness, and Sexual Violence in Nuclear Film,' in *The Nightmare Considered*, ed. N. Anisfield (Bowling Green, OH: Bowling Green State University Popular Press, 1991)

Clancy, Tom, *Red Storm Rising* (New York: Berkeley, 1987)

Clancy, Tom, *The Cardinal of the Kremlin* (New York: Putnam's, 1988)

Clarke, Arthur C., *How the World Was One: Beyond the Global Village* (New York: Bantam, 1992)

Clarke, I. F. (ed.), *The Great War with Germany, 1890–1914* (Liverpool: Liverpool University Press, 1997)

Clarke, I. F., *The Tale of the Next Great War, 1871–1914* (Liverpool: Liverpool University Press, 1995)

Clarke, I. F., *Voices Prophesying War: Future Wars, 1763–3749* (Second Edition. New York: Oxford University Press, 1992)

Colomb (P. H.), J. F. Maurice, F. N. Maude, Archibald Forbes, Charles Lowe, D. Christie Murray, and F. Scudamore, *The Great War of 189–: A Forecast*. (London: William Heinemann, 1893). This text is also referred to as *The Great War of 1892* in some references

Coyle, Harold, *Team Yankee* (New York: Berkeley, 1988)

Crichton, Michael, *The Andromeda Strain* (1969) (New York: Dell Publishing, 1981)

de Camp, L. Sprague, Pilgrim Award Acceptance Speech, 1998: 'Something Personal for the Science Fiction Research Association,' *SFRA Review*, No. 234 (July 1998), 2–3

Dickson, Gordon R., *The Tactics of Mistake* (1971) (New York: Tor Books, 1998)

Disch, Thomas, 'The Road to Heaven: Science Fiction and the Militarization of Space,' *The Nation*, May 10, 1986, No. 242, 650–56

Doyle, Arthur Conan, 'Danger!' (1914), in *The Tale of the Next Great War, 1871–1914*, ed. I. F. Clarke (Liverpool: Liverpool University Press, 1995), 294

Elwell, Frank W., *The Evolution of the Future* (New York: Praeger Publishers, 1991)

Fisher, Peter S., *Fantasy and Politics: Visions of the Future in the Weimar Republic* (Madison, WI: University of Wisconsin Press, 1991)

Frank, Pat, *Alas, Babylon* (New York: Bantam, 1969)

Franklin, H. Bruce, *War Stars: The Superweapon and the American Imagination* (New York: Oxford University Press, 1988)

Friedman, George and Meredith, *The Future of War: Power, Technology and American World Dominance in the 21$^{st}$ Century* (New York: Random House/Crown, 1996)

Gabor, Denis, *Inventing the Future* (New York: Alfred A. Knopf, 1963)

Gibson, James William, *Warrior Dreams: Paramilitary Culture in Post-Vietnam America* (New York: Hill and Wang, 1994)

Graham, Daniel, Jr., *The Gatekeepers* (New York: Baen Books, 1995)

Gray, Chris Hables, '"There Will Be War!": Future War Fantasies and Militaristic Science Fiction in the 1980s,' *Science Fiction Studies*, Volume 21, 1994, 315–36

Haldeman, Joe, 'Confessions of a Space Junkie,' *Viet Nam and Other Alien Worlds* (Framingham, MA: NESFA Press, 1994)

Haldeman, Joe, 'Introduction,' *Space-Fighters* (New York: Ace Books, 1988)

Haldeman, Joe, *The Forever War* (New York: Ballantine, 1980)

Halloran, Richard, 'Computer Error Falsely Indicates A Soviet Attack,' *The New York Times*, June 6, 1980

Hankey, Maurice, THE WAR (August 1914 to 31 May, 1915). For the Secret Committee for Imperial Defense, and the Secretary for the State of War (Kitchener) London, 24 June 1915, Public Records Office, Kew, Surrey, UK

Heinlein, Robert A., *Expanded Universe* (New York: Ace Books, 1980)

Heinlein, Robert A., *Grumbles from the Grave*, ed. Virginia Heinlein (New York: Del Rey Books, 1990)

Heinlein, Robert A., *Starship Troopers* (1959) (New York: Berkeley, 1968)

Heinlein, Robert A., *The Moon is a Harsh Mistress* (New York: Berkeley, 1968)

Heinlein, Robert A., 'Foreword' to 'The Last Days of The United States,' *Expanded Universe* (New York: Ace Books, 1980)

Heinlein, Robert A., 'Solution Unsatisfactory' (1941), reprinted in *Expanded Universe* (New York: Ace Books, 1980)

Heinlein, Robert A., 'Blowups Happen,' *Astounding Science Fiction*, 26 No. 1, Sept. 1940, 51–85

Hemingway, Ernest, *A Farewell To Arms* (1929) (New York: Scribner's, 1969)

Hoban, Russell, *Riddley Walker* (London: Macmillan, 1982)

Ing, Dean, Introduction to *Firefight 2000* (New York: Baen Books, 1984)

# SELECTED BIBLIOGRAPHY 289

Lakoff, Sanford and Herbert F. York, in *A Shield in Space? Technology Politics, and the Strategic Defense Initiative* (Berkeley and Los Angeles: University of California Press, 1989).

Laumer, Keith, *Bolo* (New York: Ace Books, 1986)

Le Queux, William, 'How I write my Sensational Novels,' *Pearson's Weekly*, No. 862, January 24 1907

Le Queux, William, *The Invasion of 1910* (London: Eveleigh Nash, 1906)

Lerner, Frederick, *Modern Science Fiction and the American Literary Community* (Metuchen, NJ: The Scarecrow Press, 1985)

Lifton, Robert Jay and Richard Falk, *Indefensible Weapons: The Political and Psychological Case Against Nuclearism* (New York: Basic Books, 1982)

Logsdon, John M., 'The Challenge of Space: Linking Aspirations and Political Will,' in *Blueprint for Space*. ed. Frederick I. Ordway (III) and Randy Lieberman (Washington, DC: Smithsonian Institute Press, 1992)

Mannix, Patrick, *The Rhetoric of Antinuclear Fiction: Persuasive Strategies in Novels and Films* (Lewisburg, PA: Bucknell University Press, 1992)

McHale, John, *The Future of the Future* (New York: George Braziller, Inc., 1969)

McLaughlin, Dean, 'Hawk Among the Sparrows,' *War and Peace: Possible Futures from 'Analog,'* Anthology #6, summer 1983, (New York: Davis Publishing Inc.), 133–72

Miller, Walter M., Jr., *A Canticle for Liebowitz* (Philadelphia: Lippincott, 1959)

Neville, Kris, 'Cold War' (1949), in *The Astounding Science Fiction Anthology*, ed. John W. Campbell Jr. (New York: Berkeley Publishing, 1964), 167–78

Niven, David and Jerry Pournelle, *Footfall* (New York: Del Rey, 1985)

Niven, Larry and Jerry Pournelle, *Lucifer's Hammer.* 1977 (New York: Ballantine, 1983)

Nourse, Alan, *Science Fiction, Today and Tomorrow*, ed. Reginald Bretnor (New York: Harper and Row, 1974)

Oberth, Hermann, *Die Rakete zu den Planetenraumen* (*The Rocket into Planetary Space*) (Munich: R. Oldenbourg, 1923)

Oberth, Hermann, *Wege zur Raumshiffahrt von Hermann Oberth, mit 4 Tafeln und 159 Abbildungen* (*Ways to Spaceflight*) (Munich and Berlin: R. Oldenbourg, 1929)

Ordway, Frederick I. (III) and Randy Lieberman, eds, *Blueprint for Space: Science Fiction to Science Fact* (Washington, DC: Smithsonian Institute Press, 1992)

Paris, Michael, *Winged Warfare: The literature and theory of aerial warfare in Britain, 1859–1917* (Manchester: Manchester University Press, 1992)

Pecorino, Philip A., 'Philosophy and Science Fiction,' *The Intersection of Science Fiction and Philosophy*, ed. Robert Myers (Westport, CT: Greenwood Press, 1983)

Penley, Constance, *NASA/Trek* (New York: Verso, 1997)

Pournelle, Jerry and Dean Ing, *Mutual Assured Survival* (New York: Baen, 1984)

Pournelle, Jerry and Stefan T. Possony, *The Strategy of Technology* (Cambridge, MA: University Press of Cambridge, 1970)

Ramsey, William E., Review of *The Cardinal of the Kremlin, Proceedings of the Naval Institute*, October 1988, Vol. 114, No. 10, 181

Reagan, Ronald, *An American Life* (New York: Simon & Schuster, 1990)

Royal Commission on Awards to Inventors, Minutes of the Hearings of 7 October and 21 October, 1919, Public Records Office, Kew, Surrey, UK

Scortia, Thomas N., 'Science Fiction as the Imaginary Experiment,' in *Science Fiction, Today and Tomorrow*, ed. Reginald Bretnor (New York: Harper and Row, 1974)

Segal, Howard P., *Technological Utopianism in American Culture* (Chicago: The University of Chicago Press, 1985)

Shelton, Jerry, 'Eyewitness Report,' *Astounding Science Fiction*, No. 36, October 1945

Smetak, Jacqueline, 'Sex and Death in Nuclear Holocaust Literature of the 1950s,' in *The Nightmare Considered: Critical Essays on Nuclear War Literature*, ed. Nancy Anisfield (Bowling Green, OH: Bowling Green State University Popular Press, 1991), 15–26

Smullen, Robert, 'We Can Make Starship Troopers,' *Proceedings of the Naval Institute*, October 1996, Vol. 121, No. 11, 39–41

Sobchack, Vivian, 'The Violent Dance: A Personal Memoir of Death in the Movies,' *Journal of Popular Film*, 3.1 (Winter 1974), 2–14

Sontag, Susan, 'The Imagination of Disaster,' *Against Interpretation* (New York: Dell, 1966)

Spohr, Carl W., 'The Final War,' *Wonder Stories 3*, April 1932, 1267–286

St Barbe Sladen, N., *The Real Le Queux* (London: Nicholson & Watson, 1939)

Stirling, S. M., 'Necessity,' *War World: The Burning Eye*, ed. John Carr and Jerry Pournelle (New York: Baen Books, 1988)

Strieber, Whitley and James W. Kunetka, *Warday and the journey onward* (New York: Holt, Rinehart, and Winston, 1984)

Suvin, Darko, *Metamorphoses of Science Fiction* (New Haven, CT: Yale University Press, 1979)

Swinton, E. D., 'An Eddy of War,' *Blackwood's Magazine*, November 1909, Vol. 186, No 1124

Swinton, E. D., *Eyewitness* (London: Hodder and Stoughton Limited, 1932)

Swinton, E. D., *Over my shoulder* (Oxford: G. Ronald, 1951)

Swinton, E. D., 'The Joint in the Harness,' *Blackwood's Magazine*, Jan 1907, No. 1095, Vol. 181, 1–20

Swinton, E. D., 'The Tanks' (pamphlet, reprinted and adapted from *The Strand Magazine*)(London: S.N. & S.I, 1918)

Swinton, E. D., Letter to the Secretary of the Royal Commission on Awards to Inventors, September 26, 1919, Public Records Office, Kew, Surrey, UK

Tesla, Nikola, 'The Problem of Increasing Human Energy,' *The Century Magazine*, June 1900, 183

Tsiolkovskiy, Konstantin, *Beyond the Planet Earth* (1896) (New York: Pergamon Press, 1960)

Tsiolkovskiy, Konstantin, 'Investigation of World Spaces by Reactive Vehicles,' *Vestnik Vozdukhoplavaniya (Herald of Aeronautics)*, 1911, No. 19, 16–17

Tsiolkovskiy, Konstantin, 'The Exploration of Space with Reactive Devices,' *Nauchnoe Obozrenie (Scientific Review)*, May 1903

Vickers, Charles E., 'The Trenches' (1907), in *The Tale of the Next Great War, 1871–1914*, ed. I. F. Clarke (Liverpool: Liverpool University Press, 1995)

Weart, Spencer, *Nuclear Fear: A History of Images* (Cambridge, MA: Harvard University Press, 1988)

Wells, H G., *Anticipations* (London: n.p., 1902)

Wells, H. G., *The War in the Air* (published along with *The History of Mr Polly*) (London: Odhams Press Limited, n.d.)
Wells, H. G., *The War of the Worlds* (1898), reprinted in *The Time Machine and The War of the Worlds: A Critical Edition*, ed. Frank D. McConnell (New York: Oxford University Press, 1977)
Wells, H. G., 'The Land Ironclads' (1903), *The Complete Short Stories of H. G. Wells* (London: Ernest Benn Limited, 1966), 115–38
Wells, H. G., *The World Set Free* (1914) (London: Corgi Books, n.d)

# Index

Note: page numbers in *italics* refer to illustrations.

7.92 millimeter Mauser bolt-action rifle 39
*1984* (1984) 150, 167
*1984* (Orwell) 130
activism, anti-nuclear 134–5
Admiralty (British) 92
Advanced Tactical Fighter (ATF) project 219
*Air Force 2025* (white paper) 207, 213, 223
Air Force Academy 207, 213
Air Force Airborne Laser (ABL) System 201
air war 62, 76–90, 91
   detachment from the responsibility of 84
   in the First World War 46, 51
   indecisive nature of 87
   social effects of 82, 83, 86–7
   SR-71 Blackbird reconnaissance jet 175, 176, 177–8, 180, 219
air-bursting artillery shells 41–2
*Alas, Babylon* (Frank) 130, 139–40, 151
Aldrin, Buzz 198
Alexander the Great 257
Alhoff, Fred 159
alien invasions 99–101, 102, 103–10, 162–4, 201–2
*Aliens* 244
*All for His Country* (Giesy) 112
   'Peacemaker' aircraft 112
*All Quiet on the Western Front* (Remarque) 239, 240
all-weather targeting scopes 64
Alldredge, Rich 236
Alvarez, Luis 204
Alvarez theory 203–4
Alvarez, Walter 204
American Century 153

American dream 203
American psyche 165, 170–1
American Rocket Society 187
amphibious assaults 43
*Analog Science Fiction* magazine 175, 177
Anderson, Poul 7, 113, 124, 251–2
*Andromeda Nebula* (Yefremov) 189
*Andromeda Strain* (Crichton) 153, 170
Anglo-German Friendship Committee 38
'Aniara' (Martinson) 130
*Answers* 12, 14
anti-aircraft defenses 87
anti-colonialism 102
anti-tank weapons 69
*Anticipations* (Wells) 216
*Ape and Essence* (Huxley) 130
apocalypse
   atomic 94–5, 113–14, 130, 145, 168, 169
   biochemical 170–1
   by alien invasion 101, 108, 164, 165
   by meteor 206
   Wells' warnings of 89–90, 94–5, 101, 108
   *see also* Armageddon
Apollo 11 moon landings 186
Apollo Command Module 185
Ardenne, Lieutenant-General Baron von 66
Argyll, Duke of 37
*Armageddon: 2419 AD* (Nowlan) 125
Armageddon
   atomic 129, 135, 136, 137–9, 142, 157, 163, 169
   US 147
   *see also* apocalypse
*Armageddon* (1998) 206

# INDEX

armor, cyborg 215, 216–18, 229, 230, 231, 245, 247, 248
armored fighting vehicles
 of the First World War 45–6
 *see also* tanks
arms-control agreements 193
Armstrong, Neil 173, 182
Army Joint Services Small Arms program 213
Arnold, Matthew 18
Arnold-Forster, Hugh 12, 16–17, 18, 19, 32, 34, 125, 136
artificial intelligence (AI) 233–5
artillery
 air-bursting 41–2
 increased potency of 23, 24–6, *24–5*
 Le Queux on 41–3
asexual reproduction 105, 106
Asimov, Isaac 124, 132, 186, 194, 219–20
*Associated Sunday Magazine* 159
*Assured Survival* (Bova) 195
*Asteroid* (TV mini-series) 205, 206
asteroids, killer 203–7
 anti-asteroid weapons 205
 films 206
*Astounding Science Fiction* (magazine) 132–3, 156, 180
atom, splitting of 132
atomic aftermath
 British portrayals of 150–1, 152, 167
 psychological effects of 165–6, 167
 survival narratives 138, 139–40, 152
 US depictions of 149, 151–2, 167, 169–70
atomic weapons/war 91–8, 146–71, 211
 anticipatory apologetics for the use of 162–3
 atomic annihilation in British nuclear fiction 146–7, 149–50
 atomic annihilation in US nuclear fiction 146–9, 150
 'bomb as tool' concept 152–3
 censorship of 132–4
 chain-reaction theory 92
 dehumanizing effects of 98, 153–4, 155, 156, 165, 167, 169

 emotional detachment/degeneration of 156–8
 ever-present threat of 171, 172
 full strike conflicts 152
 human effects of 147
 influence of future-war fiction on 132
 inhuman effects of 156
 limited exchange conflicts 144–5, 152
 link to space exploration 173–4
 literary anticipations of 129, 130
 and machine errors 141–3
 and madness 156–7
 and megalomania 155–6
 and the missile gap 193
 monopoly held by US 158–61
 perversity/pornography of 154–6
 political influence of future-war fiction regarding 132–6, 158–62, 171–2
 preemptive strikes 90, 93, 94
 prohibitive effects of future-war fiction regarding 134–6
 psychological effects of 129, 165–7
 race for 117–18
 and satellite technology 193, 194–5
 sneak-attacks 137
 space-based 143
 US 97, 112, 117, 118, 132–4, 158–61, 162–3
 in US future-war fiction 113–14, 121–2, 123, 128–45, 146–9, 150
 use-it-or-lose-it scenarios 138, 144
 Wells on 91, 92–8, 108, 113, 128, 129, 132, 152, 158, 163, 211
Atwood, Margaret 170
Auster, Paul 169
authors, cast as characters 131–2
automatic weapons 243, 244, 245–6, 247–9
 *see also* machine guns
automation
 military 17, 209, 214, 227, 232–9, 236–7, 245–9, 251–4
 US obsession with 120–1
AV-8B Harrier jump jet 178

B-1 bomber 212
B-2 Stealth bombers 188–9, *188*
B-29 Superfortress 112
Baen, Jim 198
Balfour, Arthur James Balfour, 1st Earl 65
Balkans 46, 52
Ballistic Missile Defense Organization 200–1, 203, 207
Balmer 203
barbed wire 26–7
Baruch Proposal 158, 159
'Battle of Dorking, The' (Chesney) 8–11, 89, 125
battle groups 43
battlefield chivalry 53–4, 58
battlefield intelligence 28
Bear, Greg 198
*Bedsitting Room, The* (1969) 130, 147, 150
*Beggars in Spain* (Kress) 170
Bell Telephone Labs 124
Belloc, Hilaire 14, 88
Benford, Gregory 198
Beresford, Charles 35, 79
*Beyond the Planet Earth* (Tsiolkovskiy) 183
biochemical weapons 171
biomechanical feedback 215
*Black and White* (weekly publication) 13, 14, 20–2, 29, 31
Blackwood 72, 77–8, 80, 89
Blackwood, John 9, 10
Blackwood, William 10
*Blackwood's Magazine* 8–10, 65, 70, 72, 78, 79
*Blade Runner* (1982) 106, 171
Blagonravov, A. A. 183
Blassingame, Lurton 218
Bleibtrau, Karl 59
Bleriot, Louis 79
Blitz 150
*blitzkrieg* (lightning war) 44, 46
Bloch, Jan 63
'Blowups Happen' (Heinlein) 156–7
*Blue Book* (magazine) 133
Boeing Aerospace Corporation 195, 236

Boer War 27, 46, 52, 71
'Bolo' series (Laumer) 197, 234–5, 237
bomb-sploitation movies 130, 134, 149
bombs 42–3, 80
 *see also* atomic weapons/war
Bond, Larry 226
Boodle's 37
Bova, Ben 143, 193, 195
Bradbury, Ray 186
Brassey, Lord 19, 37, 38
Braun, Wernher von 185, 187, 190, 191
*Brave New World* (Huxley) 97
*Brazil* (1985) 171
Bretnor, Reginald 119, 171, 235, 238, 246
Brilliant Pebbles project 191, 201–2
Britain 3, 4–6
 Anglo-US parallels 59–61
 atomic aftermath portrayals 150–1, 152, 167
 atomic annihilation in nuclear fiction 146–7, 149–50
 atomic censorship 134
 attempts to create own future 61
 decline of 116
 invasion hysteria 8–11, 14, 32–61
 'Island Fortress' myth 79, 85, 150–1
 psychological effects of atomic weapons/war on 165
 threat of military aircraft to 79
 *see also* Edwardian speculative fiction; Victorian speculative fiction
British army 39, 78
British Broadcasting Corporation (BBC) 134
British Expeditionary Force (BEF) 49, 50, 65
Broad, William J. 196–7, 198, 204–5, 222
Brooks, Sydney 109
Brown, Alan 225
Browne, Malcolm W. 205
Browning automatic rifle 46
Bull, John 21

# INDEX

Bullard, Robert Lee 159
*Bulletin of Atomic Scientists, The* 128
Bülow, General Von 14
Burdick, Eugene 140–2, 153, 155–6
Burgoyne, Alan Hughes 11
Bush, George W. 200
Bush, Vannevar 128
Butler, William Francis 11

CAD-CAM/3-D graphics computers 214
Caesar, Julius 257
Caldicott, Helen 155
camouflage 229
Campaign for Nuclear Disarmament (CND) 134
Campbell, John W. 132–3, 156, 160, 180
Campbell-Bannerman, Henry 37
'Can We Go To Mars' (Randolph) 184
*Canticle for Leibowitz, A* (Miller) 130, 151, 168
Caputi, Jane 167
*Cardinal of the Kremlin, The* (Clancy) 130, 199–200
Cartmill, Cleve 132–3
casualty figures 43
catharsis, US depiction of atomic annihilation as 149
cause-and-effect relationship, between science fiction and military technology 222
cavalry 48, 49, 50
CBS 186
censorship
  future-war fiction's by-passing of 180
  US, of atomic subject matter 132–4
chain of command 54–5
chameleon suit 230, 231
chemical warfare 100
Chesney, George Tomkyns 8, 9, 10–11, 89, 125
Childers, Erskine 14
chivalry, battlefield 53–4, 58
Churchill, Winston 38, 45, 64–5

Citizen's Advisory Panel on National Space Policy 197, 198
civilians, loss of the inviolability of 74–5
Clancy, Tom 12, 201, 219, 220, 226–7, 243
  anticipatory ability of 199
  *The Cardinal of the Kremlin* 130, 199–200
  *The Hunt For Red October* 130
  *Patriot Games* 227
  *Red Storm Rising* 120, 130, 227, 239, 241–2
  *The Sum of All Fears* 130
  technological accuracy of 199–200
Clarke, Arthur C. 124, 128, 186
  and the geosynchronous satellite 191–2, 193
  on the Strategic Defense Initiative 194, 195
Clarke, I. F. 9–10, 11, 12, 15, 16, 43, 67, 110, 125, 210
Cloete, Stuart 108
Clowes, William Laird 11, 19
CNN 210
Cold War 146, 258
'Cold War' (Neville) 121–3, 143, 193
*Colliers* articles 189, 190
Colomb, P. H. 13, 14, 19, 21, 22, 23, 24, 26, 27, 28, 29–30, 31, 32, 34, 61, 114
colonization 101–4
combat narratives
  contemporary future-war fiction 239–55
  traditional future-war fiction 239–40
  world of warfare as no longer human 242
  *see also* cyborgs
comets, killer 203–7
comfort-seeking behavior 103–4
Commager, Henry Steele 186
command-and-control, centralization of 17
Committee for Imperial Defence (CID) 75

communications
  cyborg 214–15, 230
  in the First World War 51
  Le Queux on 40–1, 54–5
  multiplexing with secure and encrypted channel redundancy 214–15
  real-time two-way with rear area/staff analysis 215
  and satellites 191–4
  telegraph 28
  wireless 40–1
communism 116
computers 227
  science fiction's prediction of the widespread use of 208–9
  for soldiers 209–10, 214, 215–16, 229, 230, 231, 232, 245–6
  US obsession with 120–1
Conan Doyle, Arthur 21, 74, 75, 76, 171
Congress (US) 203
Connaught, Duke of 14
consumerism 191
cowboys 170
  *see also* Westerns
Coyle, Harold 120, 226, 239, 240–1, 242, 243, 246
Crane, Stephen 239–40
Crichton, Michael 106, 153, 170
*Critic, The* 108
Cronkite, Walter 186
Crowe, Eyre 88
cruise missiles 233
cultural change, effects of new war technology on 238
cultural identity, eradication of 102–3
cultural tradition, future-war fiction as a challenge to 252–3, 255
cyborgs 106–7
  cyborg warrior heroes 243–6, 248, 252–4
  soldiers 197, 207, 214–18, 223–5, 227–32, 239, 249–50, 251
  weaponry of 243, 244, 245, 246
  Wells' 106

*Daily Mail* (newspaper) 12, 32, 33, 35, 36–7
*Daily Mirror* (newspaper) 73
Dalmas, John 226
'Danger!' (Conan Doyle) 74, 75, 76
*Day After, The* (1983) 130, 134, 135, 147–9
  depiction of atomic aftermath 149
  depiction of atomic annihilation 148–9
  sense of dread 148
  setting 148, 151
DC-X 'Delta Clipper' orbital interface vehicle 179
de Camp, L. Sprague 124, 132
de Havilland, Geoffrey de 88
de Horsey, Algernon 75
de la Ferté, Joubert 88
de Maurier, Guy 14
'Deadline' (Cartmill) 132–3
death instinct 154, 156, 170
*Deep Impact* (1998) 206
Defense Advanced Research and Planning Agency (DARPA) 216, 217–18, 236–7
dehumanization 58, 254
  of air war 83–4, 87
  of atomic weapons/war 98, 153–4, 155, 156, 165, 167, 169
  of automated combat 251–2
  of colonization 101, 102, 103–5
  as a consequence of further evolution 105–6
  of contemporary combat narratives 241, 246, 250–2
  of the enemy/opponents 60, 250–1
  through information technology 121
  of machine gun victims 246
  of the masses 153–4
  of mechanized humanity 106–7
  of post-nuclear apocalypse 140
  of super-advanced weaponry 100–1
  of total war 75, 100
deliverance, through space technology 203, 206
'Delta Clipper' SSTO reusable space vehicle 179

democracy
    effects of nuclear weapons on 122, 123
    failure during technowar 86–7
Derby, Earl of 37
Desert Storm 209
Devonshire Club 37
Dick, Philip K. 106
Dickson, Gordon 197
Digital Equipment Corp. (DEC) 208
Dilke, Charles 22–3
dirigibles 81
Disch, Thomas 187
discourse, domains of 125
discursive exchange *see* trickle-down model of discursive exchange; trickle-up model of discursive exchange
Disney 189, 190, 191
*Do Androids Dream of Electric Sheep?* (Dick) 106
domains of discourse 125
dominant narratives, patriarchal 246–7, 252
Domvile, Compton 75
*Down to A Sunless Sea* (Graham) 130
*Dr Strangelove* (1964) 130, 134, 154–5, 158
Drake, David 226
Drake, Edwin L. 62
Duell, Charles H. 91
Dunne, John 88
dystopia 121

'Eddy of War, An' (Swinton and Vickers) 70, 72, 89
Edison, Thomas 117, 196, 232–4
'Edison's Conquest of Mars' (Serviss) 109–10
education *see* public education
Edward VII, King of England 38, 73
Edwardian speculative fiction 3, 4, 15, 32–61
    British invasion hysteria 32–61
    H. G. Wells 91–111
    near-future war fiction 62–90
Einstein, Albert 92

Eisenhower, Dwight D. 76, 134, 190
Elwell, Frank 121
emotional detachment/degeneration, and atomic weapons/war 156–8
Enfield .303 bolt-action rifle 39
*Enterprise* (*Star Trek* space craft) 188–9, *188*
epidemic hysteria 170–1
errors, machine, in nuclear technology 141–3
Esher 79
eternal readiness, war as a state of 55
*Evening Mail* (Portsmouth newspaper) 32–3
exoatmospheric kill vehicles 201
exoskeletons 215, 216–18
'Exploration of Space with Reactive Devices, The' (Tsiolkovskiy) 182–3
extrapolation 126, 218
    and information leaks 226–7
    regarding killer asteroids 206

F-18 fighter aircraft 219
fact
    fiction's influence on 125–7
    *see also* political influence of future-war fiction; present, future-war fiction's portrayal of; public education, by future-war fiction; science fact
*Fail-Safe* (Burdick and Wheeler) 130, 140–2, 143, 153, 155, 158
Falk, Bernard 36
Falk, Richard 165–6
far-future narratives 113, 213–18, 222, 223–6
    combat narratives 239–55
    cyborg soldiers 214–18, 223–5, 227–32, 239, 249–50, 251
    value of 210–11
*Farewell to Arms, A* (Hemingway) 240
Ferdinand, Archduke 22
Fermi, Enrico 160
Field, Cyril 36
Fife, Duke of 37
*Figaro* 14

*Filmer* (Wells) 81
films
    of alien invasion 152, 163, 164–5
    of atomic war 130, 133–6, 147–51, 153
    of killer asteroids 206
    of space exploration 189, 190
*Final War, The* (Spohr) 194
*Final War, The* (Tracy) 59–60
financially successful future-war fiction 12, 13
    key components of 14
First World War 15, 23–4, 44–6, 107, 117
    anti-tank weapons 69
    artillery 41
    battlefield chivalry 54
    casualty figures 43
    chain of command vs. personal initiative 54–5
    conclusions of 116
    fiction's prediction of the cause of 22
    grinding down enemies' economy/resource base as strategic goal of 46
    military technologies of 45–6, 49–50, 51–2, 62–3
    motorized units 45, 49–50
    outmoded strategists of 51–2, 54–5
    submarines 74, 75–6
    tanks 62–3, 65–6, 69
    trench warfare 44, 45, 46, 47–8
*Fiskadoro* 130
Fitzgerald, Penrose 75
*Five* 130
Flanders 51
flanking movements 27–8
*Flottenverein* Navy League 34
Foch, Ferdinand 45, 76
*Footfall* (Pournelle and Niven) 152–3, 201–3
'For Killer Asteroids, Respect at Last' (Broad) 204–5
*Forever War, The* (Haldeman) 113, 249, 250–1
Fort Bliss, Texas 185
Foucault, Michel 4, 125

France 46
Francis, William 32
Frank, Pat 138, 139–40, 151
*Frankenstein* (Mary Shelley) 106, 157
Franklin, H. Bruce 91, 110, 115, 117, 158, 160
Free Rockets Over Ground (FROGs) 100
*Friday Review of Defense Literature of the Pentagon* 227
Friedman, George 223
Friedman, Meredith 223
friendly fire 52
frontier mentality 151
    definition 151
    post-nuclear 139–40, 151–2, 169–70
'Future Combat Systems' (FCSs) 237, 237
*Future of the Future, The* (McHale) 189
*Future Shock* (Toffler) 186
futurelessness 167
*Futurist* conferences 4, 213
futurology, rise of 118–20

Gabor, Denis 181
games theory 118, 119, 257
Gardner, John 256
*Gatekeepers, The* (Graham) 179
Gates, Bill 208
*gedankenexperimenten* (thought experiments) 2, 120, 162, 185
Gehrels, Tom 204
gender bias
    male, in future-war fiction 6, 7
    *see also* patriarchy
General Electric 124
Genghis (anti-personnel mine) 247
geographical isolation, end of 79, 85, 150–1
geosynchronous satellites 191–4
German army 39
German espionage scares 34–5, 38, 60
German fifth column (secret army) 38
Germany
    air power 88
    dehumanization of the opponents of 60

First World War weaponry 46
fleet construction 33–4
invasion of the Soviet Union 44, 46, 48
recognizes US technological power 86
relations with Britain sour following 1900 34, 38
rocket technology 184–5
use of submarines 74, 75–6
*see also* Nazi Germany; Third Reich
Gernsback, Hugo 124
Gibson, James William 227, 242
Giesy, John Ulrich 112
Gilliam, Terry 171
Gladstone, W. E. 9, 10
global positioning system (GPS) 192, 209, 214, 215
Global Protection Against Limited Strikes (GPALS) program 200
Goddard, Robert 173, 183-4, 187
gospels 1
government, global 85, 96–8
Graham, Daniel, Jr. 179
Graham, Daniel O. 195
Gray, Chris Hables 119, 211, 227, 235
*Great Naval War in 1887, The* 32, 56
*Great War of 189–: A Forecast, The* 13, 19–20, 21–31, 35, 58–9, 114
  accuracies of 23–9
  attention to detail 20
  disclaimer 29–30
  inaccuracies of 23–4, 29, 30–1
  lackluster conclusion 30–1
*Great War of 1892* 20–1
'Great War in England in 1897, The' (Le Queux) 14
Griggs, Ted 204
Guderian, Heinz 46
Gulf War 209–10, 239
guns
  magazine rifles 23, 26, 27
  submachine guns 46
  tank 64
  *see also* machine guns

habituation, to violence 83
Hackett, General Sir John 120

Hagelstein, Peter 196–7
Haldane, Lord 79, 86
Haldeman, Joe 7, 113, 186–7, 194, 213, 249, 250–1, 254–5
Hale, William Bayard 86, 115
*Hamburg und Bremen in Gefahr* (1906) 38
*Hammer's Slammers* (Drake) 226
*Handmaid's Tale, The* (Atwood) 170
Hankey, Maurice 49–50, 66, 75–6
hard science fiction 2–4
  definition 2
  Heinlein on 136, 211
  importance of to superpowers 123
  popularity in the Soviet Union 114
  as self-fulfilling prophecy 219–20
  US 3–4
Hardinge, Viscount 37
Harmsworth, Alfred (later Lord Northcliffe) 12, 13, 14, 20
  *see also* Northcliffe, Lord
*Harper's Weekly* 109
Hart, Basil Liddell 67
Hart, Harry *see* Frank, Pat
'Hawk Among the Sparrows' (McLaughlin) 175–8
  *Pika-Don* 176–8
Hawkins, Gerald 182
head's-up display (HUD) 214, 215, 229
Heinlein, Robert A. 113, 132, 202, 254–5
  on atomic weapons/war 156–7, 159–62
  'Blowups Happen' 156–7
  on the Citizen's Advisory Panel on National Space Policy 198
  influence on military ethos 223–5
  'The Man Who Sold the Moon' 186
  military involvement 124–5, 212
  and the military think tanks 212
  *The Moon is a Harsh Mistress* 197
  on the nature of hard science fiction 136, 211
  professional respect of 212
  'Solution Unsatisfactory' 159–62
  *Starship Troopers* 113, 197, 213–18, 222, 223–6, *224*, 249–50, 251

Heinlein, Robert A. (*cont.*)
   on the Strategic Defense Initiative 195
Heinlein, Virginia 161, 202
Hemingway, Ernest 240
Henderson, William Hannam 75
Henry, Frederic 240
Henry, O. 161
Herbert, Frank 124
heroes 170
   cyborg warrior heroes 243–7, 248, 252–4
   position in contemporary combat narratives 242, 249–50
   of technofantasies 243–7, 248
   of technothrillers 242
   traditional 246, 252–3
*High Frontier, The* (Graham) 195
*High Road, The* (Bova) 195
high-rate-of-fire weapons 51, 52
   *see also* automatic weapons; machine guns; submachine guns
Hiroshima 112, 129–30, 133, 153, 173
   survivors 165–6
   Wells' prediction of 91
Hitler, Adolf 60, 92, 117, 118, 183, 184
Hoban, Russell 168
Hollywood
   and the cyborg warrior hero 243–7, 252–3
   and personal combat technology 243–7, 248
   use of automatic weapons in 243, 244, 245, 246, 248–9
Holt tractor 73
Hornsby-Ackroyd Caterpillar Tractor 67, 73
'Horses, The' (Muir) 130
'How I Write my Sensational Novels' (Le Queux) 34
Hudson Institute 118
Hughes Aircraft 124
human costs of war 232–3, 238
*Hunt For Red October, The* (Clancy) 130
Huxley, Aldous 97
Hyde, Rod 197, 198

hypersonic aircraft 175–8
   *see also* SR-71 Blackbird reconnaissance jet

IBM 208
Ibsen, Henrik 21
*Ice Station Zebra* (Maclean) 130
ideas, new, origins of 62, 77
'In a Conning Tower' (Arnold-Forster) 12, 16–18, 19, 125, 136
*In the Country of Last Things* (Auster) 169
incendiary bombs 80
India 200
individual
   impact of air war on 86–7
   soldier as 46, 51, 54, 216, 225
   and the state 255
infection hysteria 170–1
infernal machines 3, 7
   definition 1–2
information control 180
information leaks, extrapolation as 226–7
information technology 120–1
Ing, Dean 195, 198, 213
inspiration-through-fiction 88
intelligence, battlefield 28
International Geophysical Year 1957-1958 190
internet 225–6
*Invasion of 1910, The* (Le Queux) 14, 20, 32–60, 62, 114, 240
   appreciation of 37–8
   background to the writing of 34–5, 60
   battles of 44, 47, 48
   conclusions 57
   first appearance 36–7
   German responses to 38
   military accuracy of 41–3, 48–9, 50
   military inaccuracy of 39–41, 43
   political influence of 37, 38, 39
   and the promotion of warfare with Germany 38
   research of 36
   ridicule of 35

as successful anticipation of the Second World War 51
invasion hysteria, British 8–11, 14, 32–61
invention, future as 181
*Invisible Ray, The* 157
Iran 200
Iraq 210
'Island Fortress' myth 79, 85
inversion 150–1
Italy 44, 46

James Bond series 130
James, Henry 21
Jameson, Sir Leander Starr 4
Japan 118
Japanophobia 112, 159
Jesus Christ 1
jet-aircraft 176, 178
Joffre, Joseph Jacques Césaire 23, 45
*Johnny Got his Gun* (Trumbo) 239
Johnson, Lyndon B. 193
'Joint in the Harness, The' (Swinton) 71, 77, 78, 79–80
Joint Service Small Arms Program 228
Joynson-Hicks, William 88

Kahn, Herman 118
Kaiser Wilhelm 34, 86, 115
Kelley, Jay W. 223
Kelvin, Lord 76
*Kings Who Die* (Anderson) 113, 251–2
Kitchener, Lord 49–50, 65, 76
'Kite, The' (Swinton) 77–8
kites, navigable 77–8
Kramer, Stanley 133–4
Kress, Nancy 170
Krupp (weapon manufacturer) 34
Kubrick, Stanley 154
Kuhn, Thomas 4, 92, 218
Kunetka, James 131–2, 144–5, 151, 170

Laird Clowes, William 32–3
'Land Ironclads, The' (Wells) 63, 64, 66, 67, 68, 69, 107
Land Warrior program 215–16, *230*, 231
Lang, Fritz 106

language
and self-annihilation 168
stunting of following nuclear war 167–9
lasers
space-based for boostphase intercept of ICBMs 201
Wells' anticipation of 99
X-ray 196–7
Lasswitz, Kurd 191
*Last Man, The* (Mary Shelley) 171
Laumer, Keith 197, 234, 235, 237
lay–expert discourses, future-war fiction as bridge between 125–7, 145
*see also* public education, by future-war fiction; trickle-down model of discursive exchange
Le Carré, John 130
Le May, Curtis 118, 157
Le Queux, William 12, 13, 14, 20, 21, 31–48, 50–8, 60, 61, 62, 114, 199, 240
applauded for *The Invasion* 37–8
on artillery 41
on battlefield chivalry 53–4, 58
on the behavioral/psychological make-up of the individual soldier 54
on chain of command vs. personal initiative 54–5
on the death of morality 58
denounced as scaremonger 37
on German espionage 34–5, 60
on habituation to the horrors of war 57–8
lack of expertise in military matters/technology 39–41, 43
military accuracy of 41–3, 48–9, 50, 51
military inaccuracy of 39–41, 43
political influence of 37, 38
predicts loss of English culture 56–7
on psychological warfare 55
on the psychology of the battlefield 52–8
researches *The Invasion* 36

302    INDEX

Le Queux, William (*cont.*)
  rhetorical strategy of 41
  strategic reasoning of 43–5, 46–8, 50, 51
  successful anticipation of the Second World War 51
  translation of technology into vicarious narrative experience 42
  underestimation of casualty figures 43
  use of emotional appeal 55–6
  xenophobia of 57
Leary, Timothy 186–7
Leonardo da Vinci 63
Lerner, Frederick 125
*Level Seven* 130
Levertov, Denise 130
Ley, Willy 184
*Liberty Magazine* 159
Lieberman, Randy 182, 190
life instinct 154, 156
Lifton, Robert Jay 165–6
*Lightning in the Night* (Alhoff) 159, 160
Livermore Laboratories 196–7, 222
Livock, G. E. 88
Lloyd George, David Lloyd George, 1st Earl 65
Lockwood, Colonel (later Lord Lambourne) 35
Logsdon, John M. 190
London, Jack 171
lone genius narrative 117
Louis of Batternberg, Prince (later Marquis of Milford Haven) 35
Lowe, Charles 13, 27–8, 35
Lowell, Robert 115, 130
*Lucifer's Hammer* (Niven and Pournelle) 204, 206
Ludendorff, Erich von 23

M-16A2 assault rifle 228
McClellan, Jerry 219–22, 227
McDonnell Douglas Corporation 179, 219
McHale, John 118–19, 181, 186, 189
Macherey, Pierre 163
machine errors, in nuclear technology 141–3

machine guns 243, 246
  belt-fed 29
  and cavalry 50
  Le Queux's prediction regarding 49
  and tank development 65–6
machine-machine war 232–8
McLaughlin, Dean 175–8
Maclean, Alistair 130
McLuhan, Marshall 6, 209
*Mad Max* 130, 169
madness, and atomic weapons/war 156–7
magazine rifles 23, 26, 27
*Man in the Moon* ('Tomorrowland' space film) 191
*Man in Space* (1955) 189–90, 191
'Man Who Sold the Moon, The' (Heinlein) 186
man-as-inferior animal 100–1, 102, 103–5
man-as-insect 100, 103
Manhattan project 92, 129, 158, 160
Mannix, Patrick 147–8, 149
Mark (apostle) 1
Marne 47, 51
*Mars and Beyond* ('Tomorrowland' space film) 191
Marshall Plan 112
Martin, Rudolf 88
Martinson, Harry 130
martyrdom 164
Massachusetts Institute of Technology (MIT) 247
masses 153–4
Matson, Major 36
Matthew (apostle) 1
meaning, stunting of following nuclear war 167–8
media culture, pervasive nature of US 121
megalomania 155–6
Menzies, William Cameron 128
merchant shipping 74, 75
*Meteor* (1979) 2, 204, 206
*Metropolis* (Lang) 106
Meyer, Nicholas 147–9
Middle East 44

military-industrial complex 219, 222
  and cyborgs 227
  influence of science fiction authors
    on 222–3
  political underpinnings of the
    evolution of 117
  precursors of 110
  rise of 76, 117
*Millennium* (Bova) 143–4, 193
Miller, Walter J. 140, 151, 168
Milner, Viscount 37
mines, anti-personnel 247
*Missile Envy* (Caldicott) 155
missiles, personal self-guided 214
*Mit deutschen Waffen uber Paris nach
  London* (1906) 38
Mobile Tactical High Energy Laser
  (MTHEL) 201
mobility tactics, battlefield 46, 47, 48,
  49–50, 216–17
  evolution of 43–4
*Modern Weapons and Modern Warfare*
  (Bloch) 63
Moltke, Helmuth von 23, 36
*Moon is a Harsh Mistress, The* (Heinlein)
  197
Moon landings 173, 182
morality
  death of 58
  political 122–3
*Mote in God's Eye, The* (Pournelle and
  Niven) 197
motorized units
  of the First World War 45–6,
    49–50
  Le Queux's use of 48–9
  *see also* tanks
Moulton, Forest Ray 184
Muir, Edwin 130
Munro, H. H. 14
Murray, D. Christie 13
*Murray's Magazine* 12, 17 18
muskets 39
Mutual Assured Destruction (MAD)
  144, 153, 171, 195–6
*Mutual Assured Survival* (Pournelle and
  Ing) 195, 197–9, 202

Nagasaki 129–30
napalm 80
Napoleon Bonaparte 1, 2, 257
NASA 187, 206
*NASA/Trek* (Penley) 187
*Nation, The* 108–9
National Aeronautics and Space
  Administration 204
national technical means of
  verification (NTMs) 193
*Naval Annual: 1892* 32
Naval Bibliography 32
Naval Consulting Board 117
naval technology
  Le Queux's inaccuracies regarding 40
  Victorian predictions regarding 17,
    18, 19
  *see also* submarines
Nazi Germany 52
  and atomic weapons 92, 117, 118,
    133
  and future-war fiction/science
    fiction 114–15
  perceives US as true rival 115
  reaches for superpower status
    110–11
  and rocket technology 180, 184
  and space technology 184
  use of 'The Battle of Dorking' 10
  *see also* Third Reich
NBC 205
near-future war fiction 12
  Edwardian 62–90
  very near-future technothrillers
    226–7
'Necessity' (Stirling) 227–32, 247
  DZ-7 Light Assault Rifle 228–9,
    231–2
nerve agents, non-persistent 100
Neville, Kris 121–3, 193
new journalism, fictional 13–14, 21,
  25–9, 30–1
*New York Times* (newspaper) 86, 173,
  174, 184, 204, 205, 206
*Newsweek* (magazine) 135
*Next War, The* (Weinberger and
  Schweizer) 119–20

night vision 214, 215
Niven, Larry 152–3, 197, 198, 201–3, 204
No-Man's Land 45
Noordung, Hermann *see* Potocnik, H.
NORAD 55
North Korea 200
North Vietnam 87
Northcliffe, Lord 32, 65
  assessment of his readership 33
  on the German threat 33
  introduced to Lord Roberts 35
  on military aircraft 79
  newspaper empire of 32–3
  political ambitions 32, 33
  political influence 38
  and *The Invasion* 36, 37, 39
  *see also* Harmsworth, Alfred
Northrop Grumman 187–8
Northumberland, Duke of 37
Norton, Ray 159
Nourse, Alan 208–9
Nowlan, Philip 125
nuclear frontier ethos 139–40, 151–2, 169–70
nuclear weapons/war *see* atomic weapons/war

Oberth, Hermann 184–5, 191, 192
Objective Infantry Combat Weapon (OICW) 228–9, *229*, *230*
official secrecy, future-war fiction treads on the toes of 174, 176
Olson, Ken 208
*On the Beach* (film) 130, 133–4, 135
*On the Beach* (Shute) 130, 138, 144
*On Moral Fiction* (Gardner) 256
Opel-Darracq armoured cars 48, 62
Operation Olympic 153
*Opinione* 14
Oppenheimer, J. Robert 129, 158, 160
orbital technology
  defense satellites 191, 193–5, 197–201
  sensors 137
  weapons 143, 144
Ordway, Fred 182, 189–90

Orwell, George 81
Other
  opponents as 100, 105, 106
  opposition to Anglo-US alliance as 60, 61
*Outbreak* (1995) 171
outcome predictions 118
OV-7, MV-/V-22 Osprey 178–9
Owen, Wilfred 56

Pal, George 152, 163, 164–5
*Paradise Crater, The* (Wylie) 133
Paris, Michael 82, 88
patriarchy 7, 170, 246–7, 252
*Patriot Games* (Clancy) 227
Patton, George S. 46
Pecorino, Philip A. 174–5
Pendray, G. Edwards 187
Penley, Constance 187
Pentagon 55, 90, 112, 124, 125, 190, 193, 198, 235
personal head's-up display 214, 215, 229
personal initiative 54–5
personal self-guided missiles 214
perversity, of atomic weapons/war 154–6
petrol bombs 42–3
Philadelphia Naval Yard projects 212
Philippine Insurrection 46
pincer movements 27–8, 48
Pioneer 10 spacecraft 203
plagues 170–1
Pohl, Frederick 124, 213
*Poison Belt, The* (Conan Doyle) 171
*Poisoned Bullet, The* (Le Queux) 14
Polaris nuclear missiles 139
political future-war narratives 8–11
political influence of future-war fiction
  nuclear fiction 158–62, 171–2
  space fiction narratives 197–9
  and tanks 64, 65, 67
  *The Invasion of 1910* 37, 38, 39
  in the United States 112–13, 114, 119–20, 158–62, 171–2
  in the Victorian/Edwardian eras 16, 64, 65, 67, 88–9

political moral dilemmas 122–3
political process and fiction, merging of 10–11, 18
political shock narratives *see Invasion of 1910, The*
*Popular Mechanics* (magazine) 208
*Popular Science* (magazine) 232
pornography, of atomic weapons/war 154–6
possible histories 8
Possony, Stefan T. 195
postcolonialism 102–4
Potocnik, H. (Hermann Noordung) 192
Pournelle, Jerry 124, 152–3, 195–9, 201–3, 204
power, and knowledge 95
Pratt & Whitney J58 turbo-ramjets 177
Predator RPV 235
predictive failure, future-war fiction's aspiration to 123
preeminence of technology 254
present, future-war fiction's portrayal of 174–8, 179
Prinçip, Gavrilo 22
*Privateers* (Bova) 195
'Problem of Increasing Human Energy, The' (Tesla) 233
*Proceedings of the US Naval Institute* 200, 223–5, 232
Program Spacewatch 204
Project Paperclip 115, 185
propaganda 88
propeller driven tilt-rotor aircraft 178–9
prophets, science fiction authors as 211, 218
prophylaxis, US depiction of atomic annihilation as 149, 152–3
proximity fuses 41
Prussian armies 8, 10
pseudo-realities 218–19
psyche
  American 165, 170–1
  nuclear 165–6
psychology
  battlefield 52–8
  effects of atomic weapons/war on 165–7
public education, by future-war fiction 11, 12, 107–8, 180–1
  regarding atomic weapons/war 114, 136–8, 140–1, 145
  regarding space travel 186
*Puppet Masters, The* (1994) 171

Quayle, Dan 227

racism 59–60
radiation sickness 93, 159–60
*Rakete zu den Planetenraumen, Die* (Oberth) 185, 192
rams 18, 19
Ramsey, William E. 199–200
RAND corporation 118
Randolph, James R. 184
rangefinders 214
reaction principle 182, 183, 184
Reagan, Ronald 135, 143, 193, 195, 198
realism 20
*realpolitik* 122
*Red Badge of Courage, The* (Crane) 239–40
*Red Storm Rising* (Clancy) 120, 130, 227, 239, 241–2
Reform Club 37
*Regiment, The* (Dalmas) 226
religious imagery 164–5
Remarque, Erich Maria 239, 240
remote piloted vehicles (RPVs) 233, 235
remote-controlled vehicles 99
reproduction, asexual 105, 106
resistance 104–5
responsibility
  avoidance in contemporary combat narratives 241
  detachment from in air war 84
  in nuclear confrontation 157–8
Rickover, Admiral 157
*Riddley Walker* (Hoban) 130, 168–9
'Road to Heaven: Science Fiction and the Militarization of Space, The' (Disch) 187

## INDEX

Roberts, Lord 14, 20, 34–5, 36, 37–8, 88, 199
Robida, Albert 63
*Robocop* series 243, 244–5
*Rock, The* (1996) 171
rocket technology development 180–1, 184–6
  application to warfare 184, 185
  liquid-fueled 139, 183, 187
  reaction principle 182, 183, 184
  solid-fueled 139
Rockwell International 195
Rommel, Erwin 46
Roosevelt, Franklin D. 92
Rosebery, Earl of 37
*Round the Moon* (Verne) 182
Royal Commission on Awards to Inventors 69
Royal Engineers 73
Royal Navy 40
Royal Review 1908, Aldershot 73
rumors of war 1, 2–3, 7
Russia 46
  *see also* Soviet Union
Russo-Japanese war 1904 40

Said, Edward W. 4
St. Barbe Sladen, N. 34, 37–8
Saki (H. H. Munro) 14
Santos-Dumont, Alberto 79, 88
Sarin 100
Sarnoff, David 62
satellites
  battlefield 214, 229
  geosynchronous 191–4
  orbital defence 191, 193–5, 197–201
Saussure, Ferdinand de 218
Savage Club 37
Sawyer, Robert 170–1
scenario analysis, predictive 118, 119
Schoemacher-Levy comet 204
Schweizer, Peter 119–20
Sci-Fi channel 204
science fact, unwitting portrayal as science fiction 174–8, 179
scientific advancement, destructive consequences of 95–6

*Scientific American* 184
Scoles, A. B. 124–5, 212
Scortia, Thomas 87, 119
Scott, Ridley 171
Scudamore, F. 13
Search for Extra-Terrestrial Intelligence (SETI) 203
*Secolo* 14
Second World War 257
  artillery 41
  *blitzkrieg* strategy 44
  *Invasion of 1910* as successful anticipation of 51
  mobile strategies of 46, 47
  submarines 74
Segal, Howard P. 115
self
  fictional used as mirror of a changed world 131, 132
  fractured 156
self-annihilation, and language/knowledge 168
self-fulfilling prophecies, of science fiction authors 181, 211, 218–26
sensationalism 147–8
sentience, machine 233–5
September 11th tragedy 235
Serviss, Garrett P. 109–10
*Seven Days in May* 130
Shelley, Mary 106, 171
Shelton, Jerry 180–1
'Short History of the Bolo Fighting Machines, A' (Laumer) 235
Shorter, Clement 109
'Shunting Puzzle, The' (Vickers) 73
Shute, Neville 133, 138, 139, 140, 143, 144
silo psychosis 145, 164, 167
  antidote for 203
Situation Room 55
small arms development 213, 228–9, 229, 230, 231–2
  *see also specific weapons*
small team action 216, 225
Smetak, Jacqueline 154
*Smiley's People* (Le Carré) 130
*Smithsonian* magazine 184

smokeless powder/propellant 26, 27
Smullen, Robert 223–5
Snail, The (fictional armored vehicle) 67–8, 69, 73
sniping 27
Sobchack, Vivian 149
social influence
　of air war 82, 83, 86–7
　of fictional narratives 4
　of nuclear war films 135–6
soldiers
　behavioral/psychological make-up of 54
　contemporary/traditional comparisons 257
　cyborg 197, 207, 214–18, 223–5, 227–32, 239, 249–50, 251
　firepower 46, 51
　increasing expense of 249
　individual 46, 51, 54, 216, 225
　'robot' 157
　see also combat narratives
'Solution Unsatisfactory' (Heinlein) 159–62
Somme 23, 44, 48, 51
Sontag, Susan 149, 162–3, 170
Soviet Union
　and Afghanistan 52
　and atomic weapons 117
　and chemical warfare 100
　German invasion of 44, 46, 48
　and hard science fiction 114
　influence of science fiction on the development of space technology in 189
　and orbital defence satellites 195
　as superpower 110
　see also Russia
space technology 173–4, 179, 180–206
　becomes mainstream 185–6
　deliverance/transcendence through 203, 206
　films 189, 190
　and Robert Goddard 183–4
　influence of science fiction on the development of 174, 181–2, 183, 185, 186–95, 196–200, 201–3
　influence of science fiction on specific examples of 191–5, 196–200, 201–3
　initial scorning of 184
　killer asteroids 203–7
　and Konstantin Tsiolkovskiy 182–3
　V-2 rockets as harbinger of 180–1
space-based atomic weapons 143
spaceman as deus-ex-machina 143–4
speculative fiction 126, 219
　about killer asteroids 206
　dilemmas of 174–6, 177–8, 179–80
　wider range of 210
Spivak, Gayatri 4
Spock, Benjamin 166
Spohr, Carl W. 194
spy scares 61
　German espionage 34–5, 38, 60
SR-71 Blackbird reconnaissance jet 175, 176, 177–8, 180, 219
Stalin, Josef 26, 117
*Star Trek* (TV series) 187–9
　*Enterprise* 188–9, *188*
star vehicles (films) 248
'Star Wars' defense system 143, 144, 193–5, 201, 203
　see also Strategic Defense Initiative
*Starship Troopers* (Heinlein) 113, 197, 213–18, 222, 223–6, *224*, 249–50, 251
state, and the individual 255
Steiner, George 4, 115–16, 127, 133, 167
Sterling, Yates 159
Stevenson, Robert Louis 21
Stirling, S. M. 227–32, 247
*Strand Magazine* 75, 102
Strategic Air Command 157
Strategic Defense Initiative (SDI) 136, 143, 144, 193–5, 196, 197–200, 201, 203, 207, 222
　budget 194
*Strategy of Technology, The* (Pournelle and Possony) 195–6
street fighting 52
Strieber, Whitley 131–2, 144–5, 151, 169, 170

submachine guns 46
submarines 62, 74–6
  nuclear 138, 139, 157
*Sum of All Fears, The* (Clancy) 130
superpowers 3, 5, 6–7, 85, 253–4
  dependence on information technology 120–1
  importance of hard science fiction war stories to 123
  and information control 180
  propaganda processes of 100
  race for the status of 110–11
  US as 111, 112, 115, 120, 153, 162
  and the US-Britain link 61
  Wells on 97–8
surgical strikes 99
survival narratives 89–90
  post-alien invasion 104–5
  post-nuclear conflict 138, 139–40, 152
Suvin, Darko 2
Swinton, Ernest D. 65–7, 69
  on the ability of fiction to influence the public 81
  co-writes with R. E. Vickers 70–2
  contacts of 70, 89
  on military aircraft 77–81
  Ole-Luk-Oie pseudonym of 65, 77–8, 79
  on tanks 65–7, 69, 73–4
  oversees Vicker's posthumous affairs 72–3
Szilard, Leo 91–3, 132, 158

*Tactics of Mistake, The* (Dickson) 197
tanks 51, 62–9
  anti-tank defenses 69
  Churchill on 64–5
  Ernest D. Swinton on 65–7, 69, 73–4
  first (Mother) 66, 67
  First World War 62–3, 65–6, 69
  guns 64
  strategic purpose of 64
  Vickers on 67–9
  Wells' vision of 63–5, 66–8, 69
*Team Yankee* (Coyle) 120, 239, 240–1, 246

technofantasies 243–7, 252
  heroes of 243–7, 248
technological future-war narratives 11–12, 18–19
technological obsoleteness 18, 19
technological rivalry 85–6
technophilia 109–10
  Nazi Germany 114–15
  US 113, 114, 115–16, 127, 207
technothrillers 226–7, 242, 243, 248, 254
  heroes of 242
  origins of 12
technowar
  demands of 86
  explosion of 109
  *see also* automation, military; cyborgs
telegraph 28
television, satellite 192
Teller, Edward 158, 166, 195
Tennyson, Alfred 158
*Terminal Experiment, The* (Sawyer) 170–1
*Terminal Man, The* (Crichton) 106
*Terminator* 106, 130, 243, 244, 245
*Terminator 2: Judgment Day* (1991) 106, 130, 147, 243, 244, 245
*Terror in the Year Zero* 130
terrorism
  Le Queux's prediction of 52–3, 58
  nuclear 94
Tesla, Nikola 233–4, 235, 244
*Testament* (1983) 130, 151
Teutophobia 33–4, 38, 39, 60
*Things to Come* (1936) 128
*Things to Come* (Wells) 81
think-tanks, US military, use of science fiction authors in 4, 113, 118, 124–5, 212–13
Third Reich 110–11, 114–15, 117
*Third World War, The* (Hackett) 120
Thompson submachine gun 46
*Threads* (1984) 130, 135, 147, 150, 169
tilt-rotor aircraft 178–9
*Times, The* (newspaper) 32
Todorov (Tertz) 4
Toffler, Alvin 136, 186, 203, 209

# INDEX

Tolstoy, Leo 239
'Tomorrowland' space films 191
*Total Recall* 244
total war 74–5, 100
Tracy, Louis 59–60
transcendence, through space technology 203, 207
trench brooms 46
trench warfare 44, 45, 46, 47–8
  and tanks 64, 68
'Trenches, The' (Vickers) 67–9, 71, 72, 73, 77
trenching machines 68
trickle-down model of discursive exchange 160, 220–1, 226–32, 254–5
  and nuclear technologies 145
  and space technology 174, 189–90
  *see also* public education, by future-war fiction
trickle-up model of discursive exchange 213, 219–26, 227–31, 232, 254–5
  and nuclear technologies 145
  and space technology 174
  *see also* political influence of future-war fiction
Trinity test 129
Truman, Harry S. 158, 159
Trumbo, Dalton 56, 239
Tsiolkovskiy, Konstantin Edouardovich 173, 182–3
Tulloch, T. G. 66
Tupper, Charles 22, 23
Turkey 46
Tweedmouth, Lord 37
*Twelve Monkeys* (1994) 171

Ukraine 52
ultralight autogiros 80
*United Service Magazine* 31
United States 3–6
  aircraft of 82
  anticipatory apologetic for atomic weapon usage 162–3
  atomic aftermath depictions 149, 151–2, 167, 169–70
  atomic annihilation in nuclear fiction 146–9, 150
  atomic monopoly of 158–61
  atomic weapons/war 97, 112, 117, 118, 128–45, 132–4, 146–72, 158–61, 162–3
  attempts to create own future 61
  British discursive transfer to 3, 4, 5–6
  cast as ally in early British future-war fiction 59–60
  cast as enemy in early British future-war fiction 59
  censorship of atomic future-war fiction 132–3
  Cold War psychology 146
  First World War weaponry 46
  hard science fiction of 3–4
  hegemony 112
  influence of nuclear fiction on the politics of 158–62, 171–2
  influence of science fiction on the development of space technology in 187–91, 192, 193, 194–201, 203
  and killer asteroids 203–7
  military-industrial complex of 110
  parallels with Britain 59–61
  perceived by Germany as true rival 96, 115
  politics and future-war fiction in 112–27
  post-World War II reality 118
  psychological effects of atomic weapons/war in 165
  science fact unwittingly portrayed as science fiction in 175–8
  self-brainwashing of 60–1
  superpower status 111, 112, 115, 120, 153, 162
  technological supremacy of 196
  technophilia of 113, 114, 115–16, 127, 207
  utopian visions of 115–16, 203
  vastness of 151, 170
  and Vietnam 52
  Wells' influence on 108–9

Unmanned Air Vehicles (UAVs) 201, 233
Unmanned Combat Air Vehicles (UCAVs) 236, *236*
'Unparalleled Invasion, The' (London) 171
US air force 4
US Army 215–16, 231
US Congress 203
use-it-or-lose-it scenarios 138, 144
utilitarianism 113
utopia, American/technological visions of 115–16, 203

V-rockets 186, 187
V-2 rockets 180–1, 183, 184
*Vanishing Fleets, The* (Norton) 159, 160
Verdun 24–5, *24–5*
Verne, Jules 75, 88, 108, 132, 182, 183, 184, 211
vertical take-off and landing (VTOL) 176, 178–9
very near-future technothrillers 226–7
Vickers, Captain R. E. 67–74, 77
  co-writes with Swinton 70–2
  contacts of 89
  death 72–3
  on The Snail (fictional armored vehicle) 67–8, 69
  writing ability 69–70
Vickers, Emily 72–3
Victorian speculative fiction 3, 4, 5, 8–31, 58–9
  in official political discourse 15
  invasion anxieties 32
  political influence 16
  strategic accuracy 21–2
  strategic inaccuracy 15, 16, 23
  technological accuracy 15–17, 23–9
  technological inaccuracy 18, 23–4, 29, 30–1
Vietnam 52, 87
violence, habituation to 83
von Clausewitz, Karl 203, 257

*Wall Street Journal* 227
*War in the Air, The* (Wells) 77, 81, 82–7, 88, 89–90, 91, 115

*War Game, The* (1965) 130, 134, 147
War Office 70, 71, 73
*War and Peace* (Tolstoy) 239
war reportage, *faux* 13–14, 21, 25–9, 30–1
*War of the Worlds, The* (1953) 152, 163, 164–5
  religious imagery 164–5
  search for an ultimate refuge/protective power 165
*War of the Worlds, The* (Wells) 99–101, 102–9, 110, 150, 163–4, 183, 184
  far-reaching nature of 210
  human resistance in 104–5
  man-as-inferior animal analogy 100–1, 102, 103–5
  Martian characteristics 105–6
  as mirror to human nature 104
  political predictions of 102–3
  US response to 108–9
*Warday* (Kunetka and Strieber) 130, 131–2, 144–5, 151, 169, 170
Watkins, James 200
Watkins, Peter 134
Watson, Thomas 208
Waugh, Evelyn 14
weapons control, centralized 97
Weart, Spencer 129, 132, 134, 156, 157, 161, 166
*Wege zur Raumshiffahrt* (Ways to Spaceflight) (Oberth) 185
Wehrmacht 44, 48
Weimar Republic 114–15
Weinberger, Caspar 119–20, 227
Welles, Orson 108
Wells, Frank 102
Wells, H. G. 8, 91–111, 112, 115, 196, 197, 247
  on the ability of fiction to influence the public 81–2
  on aircraft/air war 77, 79, 81, 82–90, 91
  on an initial knockout blow 90
  *Anticipations* 216
  on the apocalyptic end of Western civilization 89–90, 94–5, 101, 108

on atomic weapons/war 91, 92–8,
    108, 113, 128, 129, 132, 152, 158,
    163, 211
beyond nuclear weaponry 98–109,
    110
on colonization 101–4
education of the public through
    fiction 107–8
expert opinion of 88
failure to anticipate air war 87
*Filmer* 81
on human survival 89–90
influence on Robert Goddard 183,
    184
influence of 81
and the military-industrial complex
    110
political predictions of 102–3
social contacts of 88
on submarines 74
on tanks 63–5, 66–8, 69
'The Land Ironclads' 63, 64, 66, 67,
    68, 69, 107
*The War in the Air* 77, 81, 82–7, 88,
    89–90, 91, 115
*The War of the Worlds* 99–101, 102–9,
    110, 150, 163–4, 183, 184, 210
*The World Set Free* 81, 90, 91–8, 108,
    132, 147, 150, 158
*Things to Come* 81
US popularity 114
on world government 96–7
Welsh, James M. 134
Wemyss, Earl of 37
Western Europe 118
Western Front 15, 22, 46, 50, 117
    as anomaly 47
    Bloch's prediction of 63
    as symbol of the First World War 45
Western Union 62
Westerns 169–70, 245
Westmoreland, General 87
Wheeler, Harvey 140–2, 153, 155–6

*When Worlds Collide* (1951) 203
*When Worlds Collide* (Wylie and
    Balmer) 203
Whipple, Fred L. 187
White, George 37
White Sands N.M. test range 201
Who, The 167
Williams, Raymond 4, 121, 209
Willson, Beckles 33
Wilson, H. W. 36
*Winged Warfare* (Paris) 82, 88
wireless communications 40–1
*Wireless World* 191
Wodehouse, Sir P. G. 14
Wolseley, Lord 14
*Wonder Stories* 187
Wood, Lowell 198
world government 85, 96–8
*World Set Free, The* (Wells) 81, 90,
    91–8, 108, 132, 147, 150, 158
    apocalyptic end of Western
        civilization in 94–5, 108
    endgame of nuclear war 94
    ground zero depictions of 93
    influence on atomic research 132
    world government of 96–8
*World, the Flesh and the Devil, The* 130
Wright brothers 182
Wylie, Philip 133, 203

*X-Files, The* (TV series) 122
xenophobia 57, 60
XM214 rotary machine gun 245

Yeats, W. B. 90
Yefremov 189
yellow journalism 79
Ypres 51

Zeppelins 81, 84
Zola, Emile 21
*Zweckrational* (technocratic thinking)
    121